THE KINGS AND QUEENS OF ENGLAND

IAN CROFTON

THE KINGS AND QUEENS OF ENGLAND

Quercus

Quercus Publishing Plc
21 Bloomsbury Square
London
WC1A 2NS

First published in 2006
This edition published in 2008

A catalogue record of this book is available from the British Library

Cloth case edition:
ISBN 13: 978 1 84724 628 8

Paperback edition:
ISBN 13: 978 1 906719 03 6

Printed and bound in China

10 9 8 7 6 5 4 3 2 1
Picture acknowledgements:
AKG Images: pp. 10, 17, 29a, 35, 43, 44, 49, 51, 53, 54, 57, 59, 65, 67, 69, 71, 81, 87, 89, 91, 95, 97, 106, 108, 112, 114, 127,129, 130, 133, 134, 140, 148, 153, 155, 156, 159, 163, 164, 167, 169, 179, 180, 186, 192, 193, 196, 198, 200, 204, 206, 215
Alamy Image Library: pp. 30, 93, 146, 208
Art Archive: pp. 13, 63, 92, 128, 195
Bridgeman: pp. 75, 84, 105, 211, 212
British Library: pp. 15, 33, 47, 61, 73, 79, 99
British Museum: p. 29b
Corbis: pp. 11, 37, 41, 119, 124, 138, 189, 207, 216, 217, 218, 220, 223, 224, 227, 228, 229, 236, 241, 242
The Fitzwilliam Museum: p. 21
Getty Images: pp. 170, 225, 231, 233, 238
Heritage Image Partnership: pp. 64, 142
The National Archives: p. 46
The National Portrait Gallery: pp. 9a, 103, 107, 111, 117, 121, 122, 144, 173, 175, 184, 187
TopFoto: pp. 9b, 39, 82, 85, 101, 168
V&A Images/Victoria & Albert Museum: pp. 31, 160

The publishers would like to thank the following:
The Trustees of the National Library of Scotland for the image from the King James Bible on p. 157
Henry Bedingfeld, York Herald, of the Royal College of Arms for providing the coats of arms from 1337 to the present.

Note on the coats of arms: all heraldic symbols featured before 1337 are attributed coats of arms, designed retrospectively by heralds in the Middle Ages.

For Sally, Claire and Archie

CONTENTS

THE ANGLO-SAXONS AND NORSE KINGS

871–899	Alfred the Great	8
899–924	Edward the Elder	14
924–939	Athelstan	16
939–946	Edmund I	18
946–955	Edred	19
955–959	Eadwig	20
959–975	Edgar	21
975–978	Edward the Martyr	23
978–1016	Æthelred the Unready	24
1013–1014	Sweyn Forkbeard	26
1016	Edmund II Ironside	27
1016–1035	Cnut	28
1035–1042	Harold Harefoot & Harthacnut	32
1042–1066	Edward the Confessor	34
1066	Harold II Godwineson	38

THE NORMANS

1066–1087	William I the Conqueror	40
1087–1100	William II Rufus	48
1100–1135	Henry I	52
1135–1154	Stephen	56
1141	Matilda	60
1154–1189	Henry II	62
1189–1199	Richard I Lionheart	68
1199–1216	John	72

THE PLANTAGENETS

1216–1272	Henry III	76
1272–1307	Edward I	80
1307–1327	Edward II	86
1327–1377	Edward III	90
1377–1399	Richard II	94
1399–1413	Henry IV	98
1413–1422	Henry V	102
1422–1461, 1470–1471	Henry VI	107
1461–1470, 1471–1483	Edward IV	111
1483	Edward V	115
1483–1485	Richard III	116

THE TUDORS

1485–1509	Henry VII	120
1509–1547	Henry VIII	126
1547–1553	Edward VI	134
1553	Jane	137
1553–1558	Mary I	139
1558–1603	Elizabeth I	143

THE STUARTS

1603–1625	James I	152
1625–1649	Charles I	158
1649–1660	Interregnum	164
1660–1685	Charles II	168
1685–1689	James II	174
1689–1702	William III and Mary II	178
1702–1714	Anne	183

THE HOUSE OF HANOVER

1714–1727	George I	186
1727–1760	George II	191
1760–1820	George III	197
1820–1830	George IV	203
1830–1837	William IV	209
1837–1901	Victoria	214

THE HOUSE OF SAXE-COBURG-GOTHA

1901–1910	Edward VII	222

THE HOUSE OF WINDSOR

1910–1936	George V	226
1936	Edward VIII	232
1936–1952	George VI	235
1952–present	Elizabeth II	238

APPENDIX: DYNASTIC FAMILY TREES 244

INDEX 249

ALFRED THE GREAT

871-899

Alfred – more properly Ælfred – is the only English king ever to have been designated 'the Great'. He earned this epithet by his stalwart resistance to the Danes, by his wise government and law-making, and because of his revival of learning in England. Even though he never ruled the whole of the country, he was the first king of Wessex to call himself 'King of England', and all the English not under Danish rule came to recognize him as their sovereign lord.

Alfred probably never expected to become king, as he had three elder brothers (a fourth had died before his father). Alfred was perhaps the most promising of the four boys, if the following story is to be believed (as recounted by his flattering biographer Asser, writing towards the end of his reign):

> One day, when his mother was showing him and his brothers a book of English poetry, she said 'I shall give this book to whichever one of you can learn it the fastest.' Spurred on by these words and attracted by the beauty of the initial letter in the book, Alfred immediately took the book from her hand, went to his teacher and learnt it, took it back to his mother and recited it.

Biography

In fact it was not until much later in his life that Alfred actually learnt to read and write.

In 853, at the age of only four, Alfred was sent to Rome, and again in 855, possibly on pilgrimage with his father Æthelwulf. During these journeys he spent some time at the court of Charles the Bald, king of the West Franks, and it seems from this that Alfred acquired some knowledge and admiration for Charles's grandfather, Charlemagne.

BORN 849, in Wantage

FATHER Æthelwulf of Wessex

MOTHER Osburh

MARRIED Ealhswith, in 867. She was descended from the royal house of Mercia.

CHILDREN five or six, including Edward the Elder and Ethelfleda, future queen of Mercia

SUCCEEDED April 871, on the death of his older brother

DIED 26 October 899

BURIED Hyde Abbey

THE DANISH THREAT

Alfred's father died in 858, and was succeeded in rapid succession by his eldest son Æthelbald, then by the next son, Æthelbert, and in 866 by the third, Æthelred. It was under Æthelred that Alfred began to learn the arts of war, in the long-running battle against the Danes.

Since the last years of the previous century England had been subject to raids by the Vikings – a catch-all phrase for the Scandinavian raiders or Norsemen, most of whom, as far as England was concerned, came from Denmark. Eventually the Viking raiders, arriving in ever larger numbers, turned to conquest and settlement. In the mid-860s a Danish 'Great Army' under Ivar the Boneless landed in eastern England

and occupied Northumbria (then comprising all of eastern England north of the Humber). Then the Danes began to cast their eyes on Mercia (an Anglo-Saxon kingdom roughly occupying the area of the Midlands) and on Wessex itself, which extended across much of southern England.

In 867, the year of Alfred's marriage to Ealhswith, a princess of Mercian descent, he and his brother led an expedition to resist Danish incursions into Mercia. The Danes refused to give battle, and were eventually bought off by the Mercians. But the sortie took the pressure off Æthelred's own kingdom – for a while. The Danes went on to penetrate East Anglia, killing its king. Then at the end of 870 they turned their attentions towards the south-west – to Wessex.

The majestic statue of Alfred the Great in Winchester, former capital of Wessex and original site of Alfred's burial. The work of the sculptor Hamo Thornycroft (1850–1925), it was unveiled during the millenary celebrations of Alfred's death. Soldier, strategist, scholar, patron of the arts and legal and bureaucratic reformer, Alfred is the only English king to have been awarded the epithet 'the Great'.

THE FIGHT FOR SURVIVAL

The year 871 was known as 'the Year of Battles'. It began with the Battle of Reading, the first in which Alfred appears to have taken part as a commander. The Danes under Halfdan, Ivar's brother, had taken the town and now the Saxons sought to take it back. But as they charged against the Viking fortifications, the defenders burst out 'like wolves' and put the attackers to flight. Although the Saxons achieved a victory four days later at Ashdown, this was followed by a series of further defeats, at Basing, Meretun and Wilton.

A 9th-century silver penny bearing the face of Alfred the Great.

In mid-April 871, before the last of these battles, Alfred's brother Æthelred had died, and Alfred had become king. Although Æthelred had left two young sons, the succession

❝ So completely had learning decayed in England that there were very few men on this side of the Humber who could apprehend their services in English or even translate a letter from Latin into English ...❞ ALFRED, WRITING C. 890, DESCRIBES THE STATE OF LEARNING IN ENGLAND WHEN HE SUCCEEDED TO THE THRONE IN 871.

Timeline

849
Birth of Alfred

853
Visits Rome, where, according to legend, he is anointed by the Pope

855
Second visit to Rome

858
Death of Alfred's father Æthelwulf

860
Winchester sacked by the Danes

867
Marries Ealhswith

868
Accompanies his brother Æthelred in a campaign against the Danes in Mercia

870
Danish victory at Englefield

871
(4 January) Defeated by the Danes at Reading

(8 January) With his brother, defeats the Danes at Ashdown

(22 January) Defeated at Basing

(March) Defeated at Meretun

(April) Succeeds to the throne of Wessex after the death of his brother

(May) Defeated at Wilton

878
Victories over the Danes at Cynwit and Ethandun (May)

An initial letter 'e' containing an image of King Alfred the Great, from a 14th-century illuminated manuscript.

in those days often passed to the most competent relative – and by this time Alfred was an experienced military leader. After the defeat at Wilton in May, a peace was agreed, and for five years the Danes turned their attentions to other parts of England.

RENEWED ATTACKS

But the Danes were not done with Wessex. In the late 870s under Guthrum, and again in the 890s under Haesten, the Danes launched onslaughts on Alfred's kingdom, penetrating from Kent in the south-east to the Welsh borders in the north-west, attacking by both land and sea.

But as he grew older and wiser, Alfred adopted different, more cautious tactics for dealing with the invaders. He would besiege their fortified positions and starve them out, or shadow their armies with guerrilla forces and prevent them from living off the land. He reorganized the *fyrd*, the militia of each shire, dividing it into two groups working in shifts, so that cultivation of land would not be entirely neglected while the men were at war. He also fortified and permanently garrisoned key positions (old Roman towns, new settlements, old and new forts), to protect the population and their goods, saving them from Viking plunder.

> This is the peace which King Alfred and King Guthrum ... have agreed on ... First concerning our boundaries: up the Thames, and then up the Lea, and along the Lea to its source, then in a straight line to Bedford, then up the Ouse to the Watling Street. TREATY OF 889, DESCRIBING THE BORDER BETWEEN ALFRED'S AREA OF ENGLAND AND THE DANELAW.

Most famously, Alfred built a fleet of warships, and is thus traditionally regarded as the 'Father of the English Navy' (and, by extension, 'Father of the American Navy' – the first ship to serve the Americans during their war of independence was named the USS *Alfred*). The *Anglo-Saxon Chronicle* describes Alfred's warships as 'almost twice as long' as those of the Danes, with 60 or more oars. Quite how successful they were in battle is somewhat open to doubt, although in a naval engagement in the Solent in 896 they scored a victory over a Danish fleet.

The result of these changes was that Alfred defeated the Danes at Cynwit and Ethandun in 878, forcing their leader Guthrum to convert to Christianity (Alfred was godfather at his christening). In another campaign in the mid-880s Alfred took London (886), and scored further victories at Farnham, Benfleet and Buttington in 893. In this latter year Alfred's diplomacy with the Welsh paid off, as they sent troops to aid him in his fight against the Norsemen. It was after the capture of London that all the English not under Danish rule (and perhaps also the Welsh) submitted to Alfred. By 896 the Danish threat to Alfred's kingdom had

Alfred and the cakes

The most famous tale told about Alfred is probably apocryphal (it first appears in a 12th-century life of St Neot), although it is always possible that there is a grain of truth in it. It tells how Alfred – probably during the period of guerrilla war in the 870s when he had his base of operations on the Isle of Athelney in the marshlands of the Somerset Levels – took shelter, incognito, in the cottage of a swineherd. The swineherd's wife had put on some bread (cakes in later versions) to bake by the fire, by which the king sat, deep in thought. The wife busied herself with her domestic chores, until she smelt burning. Rushing to the fire she found her bread on fire, and flew in a rage at the man who had just sat by as the food was ruined. 'You wretch,' she shouted, 'you're only too fond of 'them when they're nicely done; why can't you turn them when you see them burning?'

884
Defeats the Danes at Rochester

886
Captures London

887
Learns to read

892
Begins his series of translations of Latin texts

893
Victories over the Danes at Farnham, Benfleet and Buttington

896
Naval victory in the Solent

899
Death of Alfred

dwindled away – although they still held fast to their vast territories in eastern England. And it is possible that Alfred may have bought peace by paying tribute money – the so-called Danegeld.

GOVERNMENT AND ADMINISTRATION

Alfred's innovations concerning the organization of the *fyrds* – the shire militias – has already been touched on, as has his fortification of key locations. These strongholds, known as *burhs* (the Old English word is the origin of our word 'borough'), were positioned no more than 20 miles from each other, and their defence had to be paid for by the inhabitants. Some had street plans, from which it seems that Alfred intended them to be permanent market towns and commercial centres, rather than just strongholds in time of war.

Alfred also promulgated his own code of laws, incorporating statutes from both Mercia and Kent, presumably to encourage acceptance of his claim to dominion over all the English. He reinforced his kingly authority by introducing a new law on treason and an oath of allegiance. His own introduction to the law code links his laws with the Ten Commandments, suggesting he wanted people to think of him as a lawgiver with divinely sanctioned authority.

CULTURE AND LEARNING

The long years of raiding by the Danes had had a disastrous effect on learning. Even many of the English clergy were ignorant of Latin, the universal language of the Church, and Alfred recalled that when he ascended to the throne he knew of no man south of the Thames who could translate a letter from Latin. Alfred longed for learning, and later in his reign he established a court school, as Charlemagne had done at Aix-la-Chapelle, and imported scholars from Europe and Wales; among the latter was Asser, who was to write his biography (albeit a hagiographical one). Alfred also encouraged art and architecture, and, although the enthusiasm for monasticism was not to arrive in England for two centuries or more, he was responsible for foundations at Athelney and Shaftesbury.

I desired to live worthily as long as I lived, and to leave after my life, to the men who should come after, my memory in good works. KING ALFRED, ANNOTATION TO HIS TRANSLATION OF *THE CONSOLATION OF PHILOSOPHY* BY BOETHIUS.

> ❝ We must bring it to pass, if we have the peace, that all the youth now in England, born of free men who have the means that they can apply to it, may be devoted to learning until such time as they can read well what is written in England. ❞ KING ALFRED, LETTER TO HIS BISHOPS, C. 890.

Alfred set himself the task of translating (and sometimes annotating with his own comments) a series of texts from Latin into Old English, including Pope Gregory's *Pastoral Care*, St Augustine of Hippo's *Soliloquies* and Boethius' *Consolation of Philosophy*. Various other works and translations originally attributed to him (such as Bede's *History*) are now thought to be by others, but were carried out at his bidding. One of Alfred's most lasting legacies was his patronage of the *Anglo-Saxon Chronicle*, the compilation of which began during his reign, and continued until 1155, providing one of the most important sources for the history of England in the early Middle Ages. Alfred's own purpose may have been somewhat different. The early parts of the *Chronicle*, written in the mid-890s, emphasize Alfred and his predecessors as the champions of Christianity against Norse paganism, and celebrate Alfred as the ruler of a peaceful and prosperous Wessex, destined to rule a peaceful and prosperous England.

Alfred's mystery illness

Asser, Alfred's biographer, left this tantalizing glimpse into the human being behind the legend:

> *From his twentieth to his forty-fifth year (in which he now is) he has been troubled incessantly by the severe visitation of an unknown disease; never an hour passes but he suffers from it, or is nearly desperate from fear of it.*

Apparently the worst visitation occurred on the day of his wedding, so one may perhaps infer a psychosomatic element in the affliction, as well as a degree of hypochondria – although all the other evidence of Alfred's life points to a man of great sanity and sagacity.

The Alfred Jewel, discovered near North Petherton, Somerset, in 1693. Dating from the late 9th century, it is inscribed with 'AELFRED MEC HEHT GEWYRCAN', which translates from the Old English as 'Alfred ordered me made'. There has been much speculation about the purpose of the ornament, but most recently it has been suggested that it was used as an 'aestel' or pointer, used to follow the text in a gospel book.

EDWARD THE ELDER

899-924

Alfred's son Edward – or Eadweard – succeeded his father as king of Wessex in 899, and proceeded to carry on Alfred's work in fighting the Danes and extending the dominion of Wessex over England. He took possession of East Anglia and Mercia, and his overlordship was at various times recognized – although perhaps only notionally – by the Northumbrians, the Welsh, the Scots and the Britons of Strathclyde.

Biography

BORN c. 875

FATHER Alfred the Great

MOTHER Ealhswith

MARRIED (1) Ecgwynn, (2) Ælffæd, (3) Eadgifu

CHILDREN about 18, including the future kings Athelstan, Edmund and Edred

SUCCEEDED 26 October 899

DIED 17 July 924

BURIED Winchester Cathedral

Compared to his father, Edward is a shadowy figure, even though he was a great soldier, whose military achievements probably outshone those of Alfred.

ESTABLISHING A DYNASTY

Edward married for the first time in 893, and around two years later his wife Ecgwynn gave birth to his successor, Athelstan. When he became king in 899, Edward discarded Ecgwynn for a more lofty match, marrying Ælffæd, daughter of the ealdorman (ruler) of Wiltshire. It says something for England's growing importance in the world that the two daughters of this match married, respectively, Charles the Simple, king of the West Franks, and Otto I, the Holy Roman Emperor. There was also a son, Ethelweard, who according to one account became king for 16 days following his father's death, before dying himself (possibly assassinated on the orders of his half-brother Athelstan). In 919 Edward wed for the third time, marrying Eadgifu, daughter of the ealdorman of Kent. Their two sons, Edmund and Edred became kings of England in their turn.

EXTENDING THE POWER OF WESSEX

Soon after he succeeded to the throne, Edward had to face a revolt from his cousin Æthelwold, the son of Alfred's elder brother. Æthelwold drew support from the Danes of Northumbria and East Anglia, but his attempt to seize the throne ended with his death in battle at The Holme in Cambridgeshire, probably in 903.

With Æthelwold out of the way, Edward turned his attention to the reconquest of the Danish-held territories of eastern England. He was aided in this by the fact that his sister Æthelfleda was married to Æthelred, the ealdorman of Mercia, and Edward and the Mercians cooperated in taking back the Midlands and the southeast for the Christian English. After the death of Æthelfleda, 'the Lady of the

Mercians', in 918, Edward ruled Mercia directly – despite a short-lived local revolt in favour of Æthelfleda's daughter Ælfwynn.

Edward consolidated his gains by extending his father's system of *burhs* – fortified settlements – into the newly conquered territories, providing Wessex with stronger defences. Among the *burhs* created or restored by Edward were those at Bedford, Buckingham, Hertford and Towcester, while in the north Æthelfleda had fortified places such as Runcorn, Stafford and Warwick.

By the end of his reign Edward had established the dominance of his dynasty in all of England south of the Humber. But Viking power remained more or less unchallenged in the north, with the Irish–Norse establishing a kingdom at York, and making inroads into Cumbria and Lancashire.

c. 875
Birth of Edward

893
Marries Ecgwynn

899
(26 October) Succeeds his father, Alfred the Great, as king

Marries Ælffæd

903
Revolt of Edward's cousin Æthelwold ends with the latter's death in battle

910
Edward defeats an invading Danish army at Tettenhall, Staffordshire

918
Following the death of his sister Æthelfleda, 'the Lady of the Mercians', Edward becomes ruler of Mercia

Edward defeats the Danes at Tempsford, Bedfordshire

919
Marries Eadgifu

924
(17 July) Death of Edward

Four Anglo-Saxon kings depicted on a folio from the 13th-century Abbreviatio Chronicorum Angliae, *by Matthew Paris. Clockwise from top left: Edmund the Martyr, Edward the Elder, Athelstan and Alfred.*

ATHELSTAN
924-939

Athelstan – the eldest son of the eldest son of Alfred the Great – was the first king to rule over all of England, apart from Cumbria. A great soldier and 'lord of warriors', he annihilated a joint Norse–Scottish–Irish invasion force at Brunanburh, so securing his kingdom.

Athelstan was also an effective ruler, arranging dynastic matches for his sisters, and at home securing the peace, drawing up codes of law and establishing national assemblies of nobles and churchmen from all over the country. He thus helped to shape the future political life of 10th-century England.

TOWARDS UNIFICATION

Athelstan was brought up in Mercia by his aunt Æthelfleda, the Lady of the Mercians, and this probably helped to secure the loyalty of the Mercians to Athelstan's dynasty, the house of Wessex. After Æthelfleda died in 918 his father Edward ruled Mercia directly, and on Edward's own death in 924, Athelstan was proclaimed king of Mercia, being crowned king of Wessex the following year.

In 926 he arranged the wedding of one of his sisters to Sihtric, ruler of the Viking kingdom of York. When Sihtric died a year later, Athelstan seized not only York but the whole of Northumbria – a vast territory extending from the Humber to the Tweed. Constantine II, king of Scots, submitted to Athelstan at Bamburgh, the ancient stronghold of the Northumbrian kings. At Hereford, the Welsh princes had already made their own submissions.

THE BATTLE OF BRUNANBURH

Athelstan's expansionist moves made many enemies. His military incursion in 934 as far north as Edinburgh alienated the Scots, while Olaf Guthfrithsson, son of the ousted Irish–Norse ruler of York, planned his revenge from his base in Dublin.

Eventually Olaf assembled a coalition of Irish Vikings, Scots and Strathclyde Britons, and in 937 launched an invasion of England. They met the English army at a place called Brunanburh, somewhere in Mercia.

The fighting lasted all day, and losses on both sides were heavy, but the English came out victorious. The coalition lost many of its great men, five kings and seven earls among them, including Owain of Strathclyde and the son of Constantine II of Scotland. It was a mighty victory, and was celebrated as such in a splendid narrative poem by an unknown hand, incorporated in the *Anglo-Saxon Chronicle*.

Biography

BORN 895

FATHER Edward the Elder

MOTHER Ecgwynn

MARRIED died a bachelor

SUCCEEDED 2 August 924

STYLE *Rex totius Britanniae* ('King of all Britain')

DIED 22 October 939, at Gloucester

BURIED Malmesbury Abbey

An image from the Athelstan Psalter, a devotional work depicting Christ in glory surrounded by the hierarchies of saints. Written in continental Europe during the 9th century, and brought to England in the late 9th or early 10th century, the manuscript is believed to have belonged to King Athelstan.

Timeline

c. 895
Birth of Athelstan

924
(2 August) Proclaimed king of Mercia

925
Crowned king of Wessex

927
Takes control of Northumbria

934
Invades Scotland

937
Defeats a coalition of Vikings, Scots and Strathclyde Britons at Brunanburh

939
(22 October) Death of Athelstan

ATHELSTAN AND EUROPE

As the threat from the pagan Northmen receded, Athelstan positioned himself as one of the princes of Christendom, establishing bonds with his fellow Christian princes in Europe. One of his sisters married Otto the Great, who became Holy Roman Emperor; another married Hugh the Great, duke of the Franks; and two became (in succession) the wives of Conrad, duke of Burgundy. European royalty also came to Athelstan's court: Louis IV of France took refuge there, while Haakon of Norway was raised in England as Athelstan's foster-son.

Athelstan, something of a connoisseur, exchanged precious gifts with rulers all over Europe. Among the presents from Duke Hugh – sent with the emissaries seeking the hand of the king's sister – were two of Athelstan's most treasured possessions: the sword of the Emperor Constantine, and the lance of Charlemagne, weapons belonging to two of the great champions of Christendom. There is little doubt that Athelstan saw himself as one of these champions, for was he not, in his own words, 'King of the English, elevated by the right hand of the Almighty, which is Christ, to the Throne of the Whole Kingdom of Britain'? By the time of his death, with substantial parts of Britain under his suzerainty and purged of the pagans, this claim was only a partial exaggeration.

> He offered indeed most ample gifts, which might instantly satisfy the cupidity of the most avaricious: perfumes, jewellery … a vase of onyx, carved with such subtle engraver's art that the cornfields seemed really to wave, the vines really to bud, the forms of the men really to move, and so clear and polished that it reflected like a mirror the faces of the onlookers … WILLIAM OF MALMESBURY, WRITING IN THE 12TH CENTURY, DESCRIBES SOME GIFTS SENT TO ATHELSTAN BY HUGH, DUKE OF THE FRANKS.

EDMUND I
939-946

Edmund – known as the Deed-Doer – succeeded his half-brother Athelstan on the latter's death. As a young warrior, he had participated in Athelstan's victory at Brunanburh, but soon after his accession he had to face renewed military threats.

Timeline

- **921**
  Birth of Edmund
- **939**
  (27 October) Succeeds to the throne
- **942**
  Reconquers the Midlands
- **944**
  Reconquers Northumbria
- **945**
  Conquers Strathclyde
- **946**
  (26 May) Death of Edmund

The first of these came from Olaf Guthfrithsson, king of Dublin, who had been comprehensively defeated at Brunanburh. Olaf was still determined to recover the kingdom of York, from which his father had been ousted by Athelstan in 927. After Athelstan's death Olaf reoccupied Northumbria and pushed southward into the Midlands. Arbitration by the archbishops awarded Northumbria to Olaf.

SAXON RECOVERY

The year after Olaf died in 941, Edmund reconquered the area of the Five Boroughs (Derby, Leicester, Lincoln, Nottingham and Stamford) in the Midlands. It seems that the Christianized Anglo-Danish population were more than happy to get rid of their Irish–Norse rulers. Edmund's victory was celebrated in a poem in the *Anglo-Saxon Chronicle*:

Long had the Danes under the Norsemen,
Been subjected by force to heathen bondage,
Until finally liberated by the valour of Edward's son,
King Edmund, protector of warriors.

In 944 Edmund took back York and Northumbria, and the following year he conquered Strathclyde (then an independent kingdom covering all of south-west Scotland), although in a treaty he ceded it to Malcolm I, king of Scots.

After he had narrowly escaped death while hunting near the Cheddar Gorge, Edmund installed St Dunstan as Abbot of Glastonbury, and supported Dunstan's revival of monasticism in England. Edmund might have gone on to greater achievements had he not been murdered by an outlaw called Leofa in Pucklechurch, Gloucestershire.

Biography

BORN 921 in Wessex

FATHER Edward the Elder

MOTHER Eadgifu

MARRIED (1) Elgiva or Ælfgifu, (2) Æthelfleda

CHILDREN included Eadwig and Edgar, both future kings of England

SUCCEEDED 27 October 939

DIED 26 May 946

BURIED Glastonbury Abbey

EDRED
946-955

King Edred – or Eadred – was the third of Edward the Elder's sons to succeed to the throne. Although his reign saw further victories over the Vikings, Edred was a sick man, and died young, fearing the return of paganism.

Timeline

✦ **923**
Birth of Edred

✦ **946**
(26 May) Succeeded to the throne

✦ **954**
Death of Erik Bloodaxe

✦ **955**
(23 November) Death of Edred

Edred was strongly religious, and left large sums in his will to help the poor and to relieve suffering – and also to strengthen the country's defences against Viking raids. His chief minister was St Dunstan, Abbot of Glastonbury, with whom he worked to establish a sound administration.

THE DEFEAT OF ERIK BLOODAXE

For much of Edred's reign the Viking kingdom of York remained independent, first under Olaf Sihtricsson, then under Erik Bloodaxe, king of Norway, a ruthless man who had had four of his younger brothers killed. Erik had the support of Wulfstan, Archbishop of York, who wanted to keep Northumbria free from the rule of the house of Wessex.

Biography

BORN 923, in Wessex

FATHER Edward the Elder

MOTHER Eadgifu

MARRIED remained a bachelor

SUCCEEDED 26 May 946

DIED 23 November 955, at Frome, Somerset

BURIED Winchester Cathedral

When Erik defeated an English force at Castleford in 948, Edred threatened to lay waste the land, until Erik's subjects deposed him. Erik came back to power in 954, but when Edred captured Wulfstan, Erik's political support collapsed and he fled westward with his followers, over the Pennines to where his longships awaited him at Carlisle. But he never reached the west coast. At Stainmore, the highest point in the old Roman road across the Pennines (now followed by the A66), he was ambushed and killed – by tradition at the Rey Cross, which still stands.

It was only after Erik's death that Edred ruled over a unified England. But within a year the sickly Edred was dead, at the age of 32. In the 12th century, William of Malmesbury recorded that his death was 'accompanied with the utmost grief of men and joy of angels'. He was succeeded by his nephew Eadwig.

EADWIG
955-959

Eadwig or Edwy, known as 'All-Fair', succeeded his uncle Edred to the throne at about the age of 15, and was dead before he was out of his teens. Nevertheless, his short reign was not without incident.

Timeline

- **941**
  Birth of Eadwig
- **955**
  (23 November) Succeeds to the throne
- **957**
  His brother Edgar becomes king of Mercia and Northumbria
- **958**
  Marriage to Ælfgifu annulled
- **959**
  (1 October) Death of Eadwig

Biography

BORN c. 941

FATHER Edmund I

MOTHER Elgiva

MARRIED Ælfgifu

SUCCEEDED 23 November 955

DIED 1 October 959

BURIED Winchester Cathedral

One story about Eadwig that may or may not be apocryphal concerns the day of his coronation. It is said that he left the feast following the ceremony to dally with a young woman (or two young women) who may or may not have been of easy virtue, and one of whom may have been his future wife Ælfgifu (or Elgiva, or Ethelgive). St Dunstan, who had been his uncle's chief minister, was outraged, made the youthful king cast her off, and hauled him back to the feast. Realizing that he had perhaps overstepped the mark, Dunstan withdrew to his abbey, whither he was pursued by the angry king, who forced Dunstan into exile in Flanders. Dunstan did not return to England until after Eadwig's death.

Eadwig went on to marry Ælfgifu, but the marriage was subsequently annulled on the grounds of consanguinity. As Ælfgifu was only distantly related to Eadwig – they were third cousins once removed – the real reasons for the annulment may have been personal antipathy or political expediency.

THE KINGDOM DIVIDED

In 957 Eadwig's younger brother Edgar was declared king of the Mercians and Northumbrians. This seems to have followed a revolt of the northern nobles against Eadwig's misgovernment, but it is possible that the division of the kingdom was planned, with Edgar acknowledging Eadwig's overlordship. In any case, within two years Eadwig was dead, and Edgar succeeded to a reunited kingdom.

EDGAR
959-975

In contrast to the uncertainties of the reign of his elder brother Eadwig, Edgar's reign was marked by peace and stability. There was a growth in royal power, while culture and education flourished under the monastic revival spearheaded by St Dunstan, Edgar's chief adviser. Edgar himself became known as 'the Peaceful'.

Edgar was already ruler of Mercia and Northumbria by the time he succeeded Eadwig, the latter having given up all his territory north of the Thames in 957. On Edgar's accession to the throne of Wessex in 959, England came under the rule of a single king once more.

In an effort to further bring unity to his kingdom, Edgar recognized local laws and traditions in the areas of England settled by the Danes. He did this from a position of strength, not in a spirit of appeasement. He also exerted his control over the minting of coins, and initiated a reform of the coinage, recalling old coins to be reminted.

EDGAR AND THE CHURCH
Soon after his accession, Edgar recalled Dunstan from Flanders, whither he had been exiled by Eadwig. The king made Dunstan Bishop of Worcester, then Bishop of London, and finally Archbishop of Canterbury. Edgar received strong

Biography

BORN	*c.* 942
FATHER	Edmund I
MOTHER	Elgiva
MARRIED	(1) Æthelfleda, (2) Ælfthryth
CHILDREN	Edward, his son by his first wife, became king, as did Æthelred, his son by his second wife
SUCCEEDED	1 October 959
DIED	8 July 975, at Winchester
BURIED	Glastonbury Abbey

A coin of the period showing the head of King Edgar.

There was great rejoicing come to all on that blessed day, which children of men name and call Pentecost Day. There was gathered, as I have heard, a pile of priests, a great multitude of monks, of learned men. By then had passed, reckoned by number, ten hundred years, from the time of birth of the illustrious King, Shepherd of Lights … THE *ANGLO-SAXON CHRONICLE*, DESCRIBING EDGAR'S CORONATION, LINKS THE ENGLISH MONARCH TO THE KING OF KINGS.

◆ **c. 942**
Birth of Edgar

957
Becomes king of Mercia and
Northumbria

◆ **959**
Becomes king of Wessex

◆ **961**
Fathers a child by his mistress,
a nun

◆ **973**
(11 May) Coronation ceremony
in Bath

Six kings of Britain do homage
to Edgar

◆ **975**
(8 July) Death of Edgar

support from Dunstan, and also from Oswald, Archbishop of York, and Æthelwold, Bishop of Worcester, and in turn the king supported these three in their restoration of the Benedictine Rule in English monasticism.

The treatise *Regularis Concordia*, probably penned by Æthelwold, recounts how the monasteries were freed from control by local lords and placed under the patronage of the king, who is depicted as God's securer of good order on earth, and a man of great piety and vision:

> Lest the spark of faith, which was beginning gradually to brighten,
> should be extinguished by sloth and idleness, he [Edgar] began
> carefully and earnestly to consider by what holy and deserving works
> it could be made to burn with the brilliance and ardour of perfection.

Although the descriptions of Edgar left by Æthelwold and the other churchmen are excessive in their flattery, it is unlikely that these authors would be quite so complimentary to the king if he had not, to some extent, deserved it.

THE CORONATION OF A CHRISTIAN KING

Despite these encomiums, Edgar was far from saintly in his personal life. He had a mistress, Wulfthryth, a nun, and by her had a daughter in 961. According to one story, it was because of this that Edgar was not actually crowned until 973, the delay signalling Dunstan's disapproval.

Whatever the truth of this tale, the coronation that eventually took place in Bath was a magnificent affair, and provided the model for all subsequent coronation ceremonies.

One of the most enduring images from Edgar's reign comes from the same year, 973, shortly after his coronation. Six kings – from Wales, Scotland and Strathclyde – came to Chester to do homage to Edgar, promising to serve him by sea and by land. According to the story, these kings then rowed Edgar in his royal barge on the River Dee. This may well be a later fabrication, but there is a symbolic truth in the image of Edgar as an imperial king.

The Wolf Tax

As a sign of his submission, the Welsh king Hywel (according to William of Malmesbury, writing in the 12th century) agreed to pay to Edgar a yearly tribute of 300 wolves. He only managed to perform this for three years, after which he declared that he could find no more wolves to give to the king.

EDWARD THE MARTYR

975-978

Edward – or Eadward – was the son of King Edgar by his first wife Æthelfleda. He was only just in his teens when his father died suddenly. A dispute about the succession followed between Edward's supporters and those of Æthelred, Edgar's son by his second wife, Ælfthryth.

Æthelred's faction included many nobles and members of the royal household, who were alarmed at Edward's instability – the boy was prone to violence and rages. But in the end Edward emerged as the favoured candidate.

A VIOLENT END

It was a short reign, in which the only significant development was a check on the amount of land coming under monastic ownership. What makes Edward's reign memorable, however, was the nature of its end.

In 978 (or possibly 979), visiting his stepmother Ælfthryth and stepbrother Æthelred at Corfe in Dorset, Edgar was fatally stabbed by one of his stepbrother's retainers. Later chroniclers laid the blame firmly on Ælfthryth herself. William of Malmesbury, for example, writing in the 12th century, says that Ælfthryth

> … allured him to her with female blandishment and made him lean forward, and after saluting him while he was eagerly drinking from the cup which had been presented, the dagger of an attendant pierced him through.

EDWARD THE SAINT

No one was ever convicted of the assassination, and Edward was buried at Wareham, 'without any kingly honours', according to the *Anglo-Saxon Chronicle*. A year or so later his body was reburied at the abbey at Shaftesbury. No doubt encouraged by the nuns, in whose interests it would have been to make Shaftesbury a pilgrimage destination, reports began to circulate about miracles associated with Edward's body and burial place. By 1001 a charter of Edward's successor, Æthelred, was referring to Edward as a saint and martyr, and his cult soon spread across England. His feast day is 18 March, and today some of his relics are still held at the Eastern Orthodox church at Brookwood in Surrey.

Biography

BORN c. 962

FATHER Edgar

MOTHER Æthelfleda

MARRIED remained unmarried

SUCCEEDED 8 July 975

DIED 18 March 978

BURIED Shaftesbury

Timeline

962
Birth of Edward

975
(8 July) Succeeded to the throne

978
(18 March) Murdered

1001
Declared a saint and martyr

Æthelred the Unready

978-1016

Æthelred's epithet – 'the Unready' – has often been misunderstood. The Old English word *unræd* is better translated as 'lacking good counsel', and thus a play on Æthelred's own name, a compound of *æthel* and *ræd*, meaning 'noble counsel'. Certainly Æthelred, who came to the throne when only about ten years old, did not always benefit from the best advice.

A story – doubtless concocted by Æthelred's enemies – tells how Æthelred, as an infant, defecated in the baptismal font. Dunstan, the Archbishop of Canterbury presiding over the ceremony, declared that this portent predicted the overthrow of the English monarchy should Æthelred ever become king.

Domestic discontent

Æthelred began his reign in the shadow of his brother's murder, which had been carried out by Æthelred's own retainers. A cult grew up around the dead King Edward, which may have been encouraged by discontented nobles, and in 1001 Æthelred was obliged to declare Edward a saint and martyr. Rumblings of dissent and threatened revolt continued intermittently throughout Æthelred's reign.

Æthelred, not the wisest of kings, was also unlucky – in the manner he had come to the throne, in his choice of advisers, in his lack of martial prowess. But his worst piece of bad luck was the return in strength of the Vikings.

The onslaught from the north

The motives of the Viking raiders were plunder and profit. When in the summer of 991 Olaf Tryggvason, the future king of Norway, led his 90 ships up the Blackwater estuary in Essex, he made an offer he thought the English could not refuse:

> Better for you all that you should buy off this onslaught of spears with tribute money, than that we should join battle so grievously.

The English army was commanded by the fiercely loyal ealdorman of Essex, Byrhtnoth, who spurned the offer. The resulting fight was celebrated in the anonymous contemporary poem, *The Battle of Maldon*.

The fighting was fierce, the English resistance stiff, but in the end Byrhtnoth was felled by an axe blow and his head cut off. Some of his followers fought to the death, while the rest fled the field. The defeat was a huge blow to English morale.

Biography

BORN C. 968

FATHER Edgar

MOTHER Ælfthryth

MARRIED (1) Ælflaed, (2) Ælgifu, (3) Emma of Normandy

CHILDREN at least six sons, including Edmund Ironside, Edward the Confessor (both future kings) and Alfred the Atheling

SUCCEEDED 18 March 978

DIED 23 April 1016, in London

BURIED St Paul's, London

PAYING THE DANEGELD

The rights and wrongs of the policy that Æthelred now adopted have been much debated. Within two years of the defeat at Maldon, Æthelred acceded to Olaf's demands, and handed over £10,000, the first of many tribute payments to the Norsemen made by Æthelred and his successors – a total of £236,000 in Æthelred's reign alone. These payments were later referred to as Danegeld.

Some say that as England was so weak militarily, but rich financially, it was the only possible strategy to prevent the country being laid to waste. The country's military weakness was demonstrated by a string of Danish victories in the first decade of the 11th century, and the inadequacies of its commanders exemplified by Ealdorman Ælfric who, in 1003, preferred to feign illness rather than take charge of an army. Even Alfred the Great, a capable general, had resorted to tribute payments from time to time. Others say that by offering money, Æthelred only encouraged more Viking armies to sail across the North Sea to try their hand at extorting the Danegeld from the English.

Timeline

◆ **c. 968**
Birth of Æthelred

◆ **978**
(18 March) Becomes king

◆ **991**
(10/11 August) Battle of Maldon

◆ **1002**
Massacre of Danes in England

◆ **1013**
Sweyn Forkbeard forces Æthelred into exile

◆ **1014**
Æthelred returns fromexile

◆ **1016**
(23 April) Death of Æthelred

SWEYN'S CAMPAIGN OF CONQUEST

On St Brice's Day 1002 Æthelred – presumably in a misguided effort to restore national dignity – ordered the massacre of all Danes in England. Among the slain was the sister of Sweyn Forkbeard, king of Denmark. Although Sweyn continued to demand and receive Danegeld, his motive for attacking England shifted from profit to revenge by conquest. In 1013 Sweyn himself landed in England, and gained the submission of much of the country. Æthelred fled to Normandy, where his wife Emma's brother was duke, and where Emma's great-nephew was to become duke in his turn – and king of England as William I.

Early in 1014 Sweyn suddenly died. His young son, Cnut, returned to Scandinavia, and the English nobles invited Æthelred to return, if he promised to redress their grievances and rule more justly. Æthelred's resumption of the crown was thus the result of the first constitutional agreement in English history.

❛ Then the wolves of the slaughter, careless of water, came wading westward through shimmering rivers, bearing shields landward ... There Byrhtnoth awaited, stood fast against anger – his warriors round him – bade them with their shields build the firm hedge of battle, strong against foemen ... ❜ ANON., *THE BATTLE OF MALDON, C. 1000.*

SWEYN FORKBEARD

1013-1014

Although Sweyn reigned as king of England for only six weeks, his impact on the country was greater than this might suggest. Sweyn's Viking armies had been attacking England for decades, and his heirs were to reign for another quarter of a century.

Biography

BORN *c.* 960, in Denmark

FATHER Harold Bluetooth

MOTHER Gunhild

MARRIED Gunhilde

CHILDREN several, including Harold, who succeeded to the throne of Denmark, and Cnut, a future king of England

SUCCEEDED 25 December 1013

DIED 3 February 1014

BURIED Roskilde Cathedral, on the Danish island of Zealand

Timeline

- ✦ *c.* 960
  Birth of Forkbeard

- ✦ 985
  Succeeds to Danish throne

- ✦ 994
  First expedition against England

- ✦ 1000–1012
  Sweyn's armies raid England

- ✦ 1013
  Sweyn invades and takes the throne

- ✦ 1014
  (3 February) Death of Forkbeard

Sweyn was the son of King Harold I of Denmark, known as Bluetooth. His own nickname, 'Forkbeard', refers to the points of his long, drooping moustache; he probably did not have a full beard. Early in his career Sweyn led a pagan reaction against the Christianization of his homeland, but later in life he was content to pay lip-service to the Church.

ALLIANCE WITH NORWAY

Sweyn became king of Denmark in 985, and in 994 joined with the Norwegian Olaf Tryggvason in a raid on England. It seems that some of the English nobility would have welcomed Sweyn as their king, so disgruntled were they with the rule of King Æthelred the Unready. However, the Viking army withdrew after accepting a payment of £16,000 from the English. Olaf converted to Christianity, and made an oath never to return to England in arms. After Olaf's death in battle in 999 or 1000, Sweyn turned Norway into a vassal state. Thereafter he commanded both Danish and Norwegian forces in his attacks on England.

THE DANISH CONQUEST

In 1002 Sweyn's brother-in-law, Pallig, raided the south coast of England, despite having accepted gifts from Æthelred. It is probable that it was this action that provoked Æthelred into one of the unwisest decisions of his career, the order to kill all the Danes of England. It is unlikely that the massacre that ensued on St Brice's Day achieved quite this degree of slaughter, but Pallig's wife Gunnhild – Sweyn's sister – was among the dead.

Revenge is a dish that is best served cold, according to the old proverb. Sweyn bided his time, sending raiding expeditions against England throughout the first decade of the 11th century, scoring victories and extracting tribute. Then in 1013 he appeared in person, at the head of a vast fleet. Æthelred fled to Normandy, and the whole of England accepted Sweyn as their king. But within six weeks the new king was dead.

EDMUND II IRONSIDE

1016

Æthelred the Unready's son Edmund was a more capable military leader than his father, hence his nickname 'Ironside'. But he faced a formidable and ruthless opponent: Cnut, son of Sweyn Forkbeard, the Danish king who had seized the English throne from Æthelred in 1013.

The sudden death of Sweyn Forkbeard in early 1014 had thrown England into turmoil. There were three possible candidates for the throne: Sweyn's son Cnut; Edmund Ironside, then in his mid-twenties; and Æthelred, the old king himself.

The young Cnut, at this stage inexperienced as a military commander, returned to Denmark. Somewhat reluctantly, the English nobles invited Æthelred to return from exile, while Edmund, at odds with his father, set up his own power base in the north of England.

THE DANES RETURN

Cnut returned in force in 1015, landing at Poole Harbour on the south coast, and rapidly taking possession of Wessex. While Edmund carried out a scorched-earth policy in the West Midlands, Cnut outflanked him to seize Northumbria. The Danes then sailed down the east coast, heading for the Thames. Edmund rapidly joined his father in London, where Æthelred died on 23 April 1016. Edmund was at once acclaimed as king by the citizens of London and by those nobles who had taken refuge there.

But Edmund's accession did not go unchallenged. A few days later in Southampton a more representative gathering of nobles and churchmen selected Cnut to be their king. Fighting continued through the summer, Edmund scoring several victories, before being decisively beaten at Assandune in Essex on 18 October.

It shows something for Edmund's popular support that Cnut agreed to divide the kingdom, leaving Edmund to reign in Wessex while all the land north of the Thames came under Danish rule. It is unlikely that the peace would have lasted long, had not Edmund died on 30 November.

Biography

BORN C. 989

FATHER Æthelred the Unready

MOTHER Ælgifu

MARRIED Edith

CHILDREN after his death Edmund's children went into exile in Hungary. One of his grandchildren, Edgar the Atheling, was briefly acclaimed as king in 1066, after the death of Harold

SUCCEEDED 23 APRIL 1016

DIED 30 November 1016

BURIED Glastonbury Abbey

Timeline

989
Birth of Ironside

1015
Effectively in revolt against his father

1016
(23 April) Succeeds to the throne

(18 October) Defeated by Cnut at Assandune

(30 November) Death of Edmund

CNUT
1016-1035

Cnut – or Canute – was, in his time, the most powerful monarch in western Europe after the Holy Roman Emperor. England was just one of his several realms: in contemporary records he was known as 'King of Englishmen, Danes, Norwegians, and part of the Swedes', and his command of the trade routes through the North Sea, the English Channel and the entrance to the Baltic made him a power to reckon with.

Cnut began his military career campaigning with his father Sweyn Forkbeard, who seized the throne of England at the end of 1013. When Sweyn died in early 1014 Cnut seems to have lacked the confidence to vie for the English throne, and returned to his native Denmark – but not before he had left a token of what could be in store for the English, when, before his departure, he put ashore his father's hostages, horribly mutilated.

THE ASSAULT ON ENGLAND

Cnut returned the following year at the head of a great army, and proceeded to seize large parts of the country. As a contemporary Scandinavian poet recalled:

Still you pressed on, blunting swords upon weapons; they could not defend their strongholds when you attacked …

After the death in April 1016 of King Æthelred, who had been restored after the death of Sweyn, the English in London declared Æthelred's son Edmund Ironside king – but the majority of the English nobility and ecclesiastical establishment opted for Cnut.

Through the summer of 1016 Edmund and Cnut slogged it out, until Edmund was decisively defeated at Assandune in October. At a parley on an island in the River Severn, Cnut and Edmund agreed to divide the country between them; but Edmund's death in November left the throne of all England vacant.

CNUT'S SEIZURE OF POWER

Mounting the empty throne, Cnut promptly had Edmund's brother Eadwig put to death, along with four leading English nobles – including Eadric, who had played such a treacherous role at Assandune on Cnut's behalf.

Edmund's two children were dispatched to Hungary,

Biography

BORN 994 or 995, in Denmark

FATHER Sweyn Forkbeard

MOTHER Gunhilde

MARRIED (1) Ælfgifu of Northampton, (2) Emma of Normandy

CHILDREN included Harold Harefoot (Cnut's successor) and Sweyn by Ælfgifu, and Harthacnut (Harold Harefoot's successor as king of England) by Emma

SUCCEEDED 30 November 1016

DIED 12 November 1035

BURIED Winchester Cathedral

An initial letter 'h' containing an image of King Cnut, from a 14th-century illuminated manuscript.

beyond the reach of Cnut's assassins, while Æthelred's two children by his second wife, Emma of Normandy, took refuge at the Norman court. Cnut secured himself against threats from that direction by promptly marrying Emma himself – even though he already had a 'temporary wife', Ælfgifu of Northampton.

Having firmly established himself on the English throne by means of what today would be called a decapitation strategy, and protected by his large bodyguard of professional warriors or housecarles, Cnut set about ensuring continuity and stability in his new kingdom.

ADMINISTRATION AND THE CHURCH

Under Æthelred, England's embryonic civil service had enlarged in order to collect the taxes necessary to pay the Danegeld – the tribute money offered to the Vikings in return for peace. The structure of civil administration was undisturbed under Cnut, although taxes were now raised first and foremost to support a standing force, and the Danegeld became the *heregeld* – the 'army tax'. Similarly, the monastic foundations of England continued calmly through the change of regime as centres of spirituality and learning.

Cnut did reward his Danish (and Saxon) followers with English estates, creating some potentially powerful regional earldoms, but there was nothing like the ruthless country-wide land-grab and brutal subordination of the native English that occurred half a century later under William the Conqueror. Scandinavian rule did not bring with it a cultural revolution: 1016 was no Year Zero.

Cnut was a great supporter and protector of the English Church, rightly recognizing its importance in the governance of his new realm. As a

Coins from the reign of King Cnut, the top one bearing an image of his helmeted head.

❝ I have borne in mind the letters and messages from the pope, that I should everywhere exalt God's praise and suppress wrong and establish full security, by that power which it has pleased God to give me. ❞ CNUT'S LETTER TO HIS ARCHBISHOPS AND BISHOPS, 1019 OR 1020.

Timeline

994 or 995
Birth of Cnut

1013
Accompanies his father's expedition against England

1014
Returns to Denmark after his father's death

1015
Cnut returns to England in force

1016
(April) After Edmund Ironside is declared king in London, an assembly in Southampton elects Cnut

(18 October) Cnut defeats Edmund at Assandune

(30 November) Cnut becomes king on Edmund's death

1019
Succeeds to the throne of Denmark

1026
Defeated by Norwegians and Swedes at the Battle of the Holy River

1027
Travels to Rome for the coronation of the emperor

1028
Seizes Norway, driving out King Olaf

1030
Olaf attempts to retake Norway, but is killed

1035
Death of Cnut

King Cnut commanding the sea. According to legend, when a flatterer opined that the king could even command the obedience of the sea, Cnut demonstrated the limits of his royal power by showing he could not order the incoming tide to turn.

young man he relied heavily on clerical advice, and it was Wulfstan, Archbishop of York, who drafted Cnut's great code of laws. This code, mostly based on existing English legal traditions, deals with both the religious duties of clergy and laity, and with secular matters, but throughout there are exhortations towards piety and Christian virtue.

CNUT AND SCANDINAVIA

The peace of England under Cnut's rule was for the most part undisturbed. An exception was the fluid northern frontier with Scotland, where the 'Debatable Lands' (as they were later known) continued to witness various invasions and counter-invasions of the sort that were to characterize cross-border relations for the next 500 years.

But, generally speaking, the stability of his English kingdom allowed Cnut to concentrate on Scandinavian affairs. His confidence in his power in England is shown by the fact that between 1019 and 1028 he led four expeditions to Scandinavia. The first followed the death of the Danish king, Cnut's elder brother Harold. Cnut at once set sail to claim the throne of Denmark, where he installed his brother-in-law Ulf as regent. Subsequently Ulf entered an alliance with Olaf Haroldson of Norway and the king of Sweden against Cnut, and in 1026 they scored a major victory against him at the Holy River.

In 1028 Cnut went on the offensive, seized Norway from Olaf, installed his son Harthacnut as ruler of Denmark, and his 'temporary wife' Ælfgifu and their son Sweyn as rulers of

Norway. The rule of Ælfgifu and Sweyn was bitterly resented, and Anglo-Danish rule of Norway ended with Cnut's death.

A POWER IN EUROPE

In 1027 Cnut became the first English monarch since Alfred to make a pilgrimage to Rome – and even Alfred had only visited the Holy City as a young boy, long before he had succeeded to the throne. As with his Scandinavian expeditions, Cnut's willingness to leave England shows his confidence in his position there.

The journey was both pious and political, for in Rome Cnut was a guest at the coronation of the Holy Roman Emperor, Conrad II, and was received by both pope and emperor in the full panoply of his power, as a Christian prince among Christian princes. While in Rome, Cnut discussed with Conrad their mutual frontier – between Germany and Jutland – and negotiated reductions in tolls and levies on English pilgrims and traders travelling through Europe to Rome. He also secured from the pope various privileges for the English clergy.

On his return to England Cnut addressed a proclamation to all his English subjects, detailing the work he had undertaken on their behalf while absent from his realm. As there was no need for Cnut to curry favour with any man in England, his proclamation suggests how seriously he took his responsibilities as king.

After his death in 1035, as befitted the inheritor of the mantle of Anglo-Saxon kingship, Cnut was laid to rest in Winchester Cathedral. He had travelled a long way from the freebooting, brutal Viking adventurer who had come to ravage England with his semi-pagan father. But quite how far he had in fact travelled is difficult to assess, because his support for the Church meant that contemporary historians, churchmen to a man, were almost certainly selective in what they chose to record about this colossus of the north.

Cnut commands the tide

In the most famous story told about Cnut the king demonstrates to his sycophantic courtiers that there are limits to his temporal power. The tale was thus intended to show his Christian humility. This version of the story is from Geoffrey Gaimar's *History of the English* (c. 1140): 'He was in London on the Thames; the tide was flowing near the church called Westminster ... Cnut held his sceptre in his hand, and he said to the tide, "Return back, flee from me lest I strike thee." The sea did not retire for him, more and more tide rose; the king remained, and struck the water with his sceptre. The river retired not for that, so it reached the king and wetted him.'

The Pusey Horn, a ceremonial drinking vessel from c. 1400. There is a local tradition that the manor of Pusey in Berkshire (now in Oxfordshire) was given to William Pusey by Cnut as a reward for warning of an impending attack. The horn was delivered to William with his letter of tenure (or so the tradition has it), and remained in the Pusey family until it was presented to the Victoria and Albert Museum in 1938. The horn is inscribed with the words 'I kynge knowde [Cnut] gave Wyllyam Pecote [a mistranscription of Pusey] thys horne to holde by thy lande.'

HAROLD HAREFOOT
1035-1042 & HARTHACNUT

The succession following the death of Cnut was disputed by two of his sons: Harold Harefoot, son of Cnut's 'temporary wife' Ælfgifu of Northampton; and Harthacnut, son of his second, legitimate wife, Emma of Normandy. As both the heirs were no more than youths, it is likely that the active agents in the rivalry were their respective mothers.

At first it was agreed that Harold should be king in the north, and in the south regent for his younger half-brother Harthacnut, who was already ruler of Denmark. Harthacnut's mother Emma set up court on his behalf in Wessex. Then in 1037 Harold became sole king of England. By 1040 Harthacnut was planning an invasion to take the throne, but this was forestalled by Harold's death, and for two years Harthacnut was undisputed king of England, until his own death.

Biography

HAROLD HAREFOOT

BORN 1012/1016, in Denmark

FATHER Cnut

MOTHER Ælfgifu of Northampton

MARRIED never married

CHILDREN an illegitimate son, Ælfwine, who became a monk on mainland Europe

SUCCEEDED 1035/1037

DIED 17 March 1040, at Oxford

BURIED St Clement Danes Church, Westminster

HARTHACNUT

BORN 1018, in England

FATHER Cnut

MOTHER Emma of Normandy

MARRIED never married

SUCCEEDED 17 March 1040

DIED 8 June 1042

BURIED Winchester Cathedral

HAROLD TAKES POWER

Harold earned his nickname 'Harefoot' from his fleet-footedness in the chase, but generally speaking he seems to have made little impact as an individual: it was his mother Ælfgifu who was the power behind the throne. It was she, together with Earl Leofric of Mercia and the majority of the English nobility, who supported his claim, while Harthacnut was supported by his mother Emma and, initially, the powerful Earl Godwine of Wessex.

The compromise by which Harold became ruler in the north and regent for the rest was reached in early 1036 at Oxford. Shortly after this, Harold seized the treasury at Winchester and thus effectively took power of the whole realm. Now having the support of Earl Godwine, his position as king was formally recognized in 1037, and Emma fled into exile in Flanders.

HARTHACNUT RETURNS TO ENGLAND

At the time of Cnut's death Harthacnut stayed put in Denmark, concerned that Magnus of Norway was about to invade, and so was unable to travel to England himself to

Harthacnut and his half-brother Edward (later King Edward the Confessor) look on as their mother, Queen Emma of Normandy, receives the Encomium Emmae *(Encomium of Emma) from its author. Commissioned by Emma herself, the* Encomium Emmae *is a highly selective history of the period before, during and after the reign of Cnut, Emma's second husband.*

Timeline

◆ **1012 or 1016**
Birth of Harold

◆ **1018**
Birth of Harthacnut

◆ **1028**
Harthacnut made king of Denmark by his father Cnut

◆ **1035**
Both Harthacnut and Harold claim the throne of England

◆ **1036**
Murder of Æthelred's son Alfred

◆ **1037**
Harold becomes sole king

◆ **1040**
(17 March) Harthacnut succeeds on death of Harold

◆ **1042**
(8 June) Death of Harthacnut

stake his claim. But he resolved his conflict with Magnus, and Harold Harefoot's death in 1040 brought him back to England to take the throne. He immediately set about desecrating Harold's tomb in London, exhuming the body, beheading it and tossing it into a marsh near the Thames.

Harthacnut's conflict with Magnus had ended in around 1039, the two agreeing that if either of them should die without an heir, they would inherit the other's kingdom. Magnus and his successor Harold Hardrada took this to include England as well as Denmark. But Harthacnut had different ideas: in 1041 he invited the murdered Alfred's elder brother Edward – another son of Æthelred the Unready and Emma – to join his household, and seems to have appointed him his successor. The following year Harthacnut drank to excess at the wedding feast of his standard-bearer, suffered a convulsion and died.

 He never did anything worthy of a king while he reigned. 🙴

THE *ANGLO-SAXON CHRONICLE* DELIVERS ITS VERDICT ON HARTHACNUT.

The murder of Alfred the Atheling

Another potential claimant to the throne appeared shortly after Cnut's death. In 1036 Alfred, Emma's younger son by her first marriage, to King Æthelred, returned to England from exile in Normandy. But he was treacherously murdered, the responsibility for this deed being widely attributed to Earl Godwine, as in this account by Geoffrey Gaimar in his *History of the English* (c. 1140):

Earl Godwine took him under his protection, and led him into the town of Guildford, and lodged his soldiers there. But when it was morning the innocent men were led out, and some were sold for money, some were beheaded, some were mutilated, some were scalped shamefully. Then they took Alfred, slung him naked across a horse and brought him to Ely. There they put out his eyes.

The unfortunate young man either died as a result of this mutilation, or was put to death by disembowelling.

EDWARD THE CONFESSOR

1042-1066

Edward was the great-great-great-grandson of Alfred the Great, the last of his line to ascend the throne, and the last but one of England's Anglo-Saxon kings. His byname 'the Confessor' comes from the religious devotion of his later years, which resulted in his canonization in 1161. But Edward's piety, almost certainly exaggerated by his later hagiographers, coexisted with a lifelong love of worldly pursuits, most notably hunting.

OPPOSITE: Edward the Confessor, penultimate Anglo-Saxon king of England, as depicted in a late 12th-century manuscript illumination from the Westminster Abbey Psalter.

Edward's reign was largely dominated by the powerful regional earls who had been put in place by Cnut, although Edward never lost his supreme position to these men. His lack of children led to great uncertainties about the succession, uncertainties that were to be put to the proof of the sword after his death.

FAMILY, UPBRINGING AND SUCCESSION

Edward's father was Æthelred the Unready, and his mother was Emma, sister of Duke Richard II of Normandy and great-aunt of William the Conqueror. After Æthelred's death, Cnut, king of Denmark, had seized the throne and made Emma his second wife, while Edward and his brother Alfred went into exile. They were brought up in Normandy, without any expectation of succeeding to the English throne. At the Norman court Edward acquired a taste for the cosmopolitan culture of mainland Europe, and his preference for Norman-French advisers was later to put him at odds with the Anglo-Danish nobility in England.

In 1036, during the uncertain period following Cnut's death when his sons Harold Harefoot and Harthacnut disputed the throne, Edward and Alfred returned to England, where Alfred was treacherously and brutally murdered. Edward escaped back to Normandy, but after Harold's death he returned at the invitation of Harthacnut in 1041. Harthacnut died childless on 8 June 1042, and the nobles and churchmen of England acclaimed Edward as king. He was crowned in Winchester Cathedral the following April.

EDWARD AND EARL GODWINE

On ascending the throne Edward had to come to an accommodation with one of the most powerful men in England after himself – Earl Godwine of Wessex, the man who was generally held responsible for his brother Alfred's murder. Two other great men also had to be taken into consideration by the king: Leofric, earl of Mercia, and

Biography

BORN c. 1005, in Islip, Oxfordshire

FATHER Æthelred the Unready

MOTHER Emma of Normandy

MARRIED Eadgyth (Edith), daughter of Earl Godwine of Wessex

CHILDREN none

SUCCEEDED 8 June 1042

DIED 4/5 January 1066

BURIED Westminster Abbey

The death of Earl Godwine

At Easter 1053, Godwine – who had long been suspected of responsibility for the murder of the king's brother Alfred the Atheling – swore an oath that he was innocent of the crime. Having thus sworn, so the story goes, he then choked to death on a communion wafer.

Siward, earl of Northumbria. They too were suspicious of Edward's pro-Norman leanings.

For his part, Godwine sought to secure his position by offering Edward the hand of his daughter Eadgyth (Edith). The two married in 1045, but Godwine's hopes of his heirs succeeding to the throne diminished year by year, as Edith remained childless. Whether this was due to fertility problems, mutual antipathy or (as Edward's later hagiographers claimed) a vow of celibacy on Edward's part, is not clear. It is even possible that Edward deliberately avoided siring an heir with Eadgyth in order to bar the Godwine family from the succession, in favour of his cousin, William of Normandy.

In 1051 relations between the king and his father-in-law came to a head when Earl Godwine opposed Edward's appointment of a Norman as Archbishop of Canterbury. With the backing of the northern earls, Leofric and Siward, Edward forced Godwine and his family into exile, and Eadgyth was confined to a nunnery. The following year Godwine returned in arms and secured the restoration of his title and of his daughter as queen, and the

He was a very proper figure of a man – of outstanding height, and distinguished by his milky white hair and beard, full face and rosy cheeks, thin white hands, and long translucent fingers; in all the rest of his body he was an unblemished royal person. ANON., *VITA EDWARDI REGIS* (C. 1067).

dismissal of the archbishop and some of the king's Norman advisers. But with Godwine's death in 1053 Edward once more had the upper hand.

MANOEUVRING FOR THE SUCCESSION

Godwine had five sons, all of whom became earls. The most important of these were Tostig, who in 1055 succeeded Siward as earl of Northumbria, and Harold, who succeeded his father as earl of Wessex. Harold became one of the most important men in the kingdom, successfully guarding the Welsh border, but he never threatened Edward's supremacy.

Apparently confident in his position once more – and perhaps to keep the Godwines on their toes – Edward now sent for his nephew Edward Atheling (also known as Edward the Exile), the son of his half-brother Edmund Ironside, who as an infant had been sent to Hungary when Cnut had seized the throne some 40 years earlier. Presumably, by this gesture, Edward was identifying his namesake as a possible heir, although Edward Atheling died (somewhat mysteriously) before the two could meet.

By the time of Edward's death, there were four claimants to the throne: Edward the Exile's young son Edgar Atheling, who was the closest male relation; William of Normandy, who claimed that King Edward had promised him the succession; Harold, who claimed that on his deathbed Edward had bestowed the crown on him; and Harold Hardrada, king of Norway, who based his claim on the agreement made by his father and Harthacnut in 1038 or 1039, that if either died without issue, the other would take over their kingdom.

THE CULT OF THE CONFESSOR

England during Edward's reign appears to have been relatively stable and prosperous – as attested by Edward's great project in his later years, the building of Westminster Abbey. Construction began *c.* 1050, on the site of an older monastery, and the new church, in the Romanesque or Norman style with which Edward was familiar, was dedicated on 28 December 1065, as the king lay dying, too sick to attend. Today, nothing of this Norman structure remains above ground.

Apart from this great work, there does not appear to be much evidence of exceptional sanctity on Edward's part. But Edward, as the son of a Saxon king and the daughter of a duke of Normandy, symbolized the union of the two realms, so it was

Timeline

c. 1005
Birth of Edward

1016
Sent into exile in Normandy

1042
(8 June) Succeeds to the throne

1043
(3 April) Crowned in Winchester Cathedral

1045
Marries Eadgyth (Edith), daughter of Earl Godwine

1051
Earl Godwine goes into exile

1052
Return of Earl Godwine

1053
(Easter) Death of Earl Godwine

1065
(28 December) Dedication of Westminster Abbey

1066
(4/5 January) Death of Edward

1161
Achieves sainthood

The burial of Edward the Confessor in 1066, from a 13th-century manuscript illumination. During the reign of Henry II in the following century a cult of Edward the Confessor was promoted, and Edward was canonized by Pope Alexander III in 1161. 'Confessor' was a title accorded to those saints who died a natural death, as opposed to 'martyr', which was accorded to those saints who were put to death for their devotion to Christ.

politically useful for his successors to emphasize his holiness – just as it was useful for Henry I, son of William the Conqueror, to marry the granddaughter of Edward Atheling.

Accounts of miracles associated with Edward the Confessor began to appear shortly after his death, and in 1102 his body was examined and was said to be untouched by decay. But it was not until 1161, after a number of failed attempts, that Edward was canonized by Pope Alexander III. A century later, in 1269, Edward was reburied in a magnificent new shrine in Westminster Abbey, and for much of the Middle Ages he was regarded as England's national saint, until supplanted by St George.

> Since these who have climbed to the highest offices in the kingdom of England, the earls, bishops and abbots, and all those in holy orders, are not what they seem to be, but on the contrary, are servants of the devil … and the devils shall come through all this land with fire and sword and havoc of war. ANON., *VITA EDWARDI REGIS* (C. 1067).

HAROLD II GODWINESON

1066

Harold Godwineson, earl of Wessex, had no blood-based claim to the throne of England. However, on his deathbed Edward the Confessor, his childless brother-in-law, supposedly designated him his heir – perhaps believing that he was the only man to whom the English would give their loyalty.

Biography

BORN C. 1022

FATHER Godwine, earl of Wessex

MOTHER Gytha Thorkelsdættir

MARRIED Ealdgyth

SUCCEEDED 4/5 January 1066

DIED 14 October 1066

BURIED possibly Waltham Abbey

Harold was the son of Godwine, earl of Wessex, and became, as his father had been before him, the most important man in England after the king. When he himself became king he had to face invasions by the two other major claimants to the throne, Harold Hardrada of Norway and William of Normandy.

EARLY CAREER

Harold had not always been so favoured by King Edward. In 1051 he had been forced into exile, along with his brothers and father. But after his father's death Harold came back into favour, inherited Godwine's title as earl of Wessex and secured earldoms for his brothers Tostig, Gyrth and Leofwine.

Harold helped to secure Edward's frontiers by leading expeditions into Wales in 1062–3. He also served as a diplomat on Edward's behalf, arranging the return to England in 1057 of Edward's ill-fated nephew Edward Atheling. The most contentious episode in Harold's career concerns a visit he appears to have made to Normandy in 1064 or 1065. According to contemporary Norman chroniclers, Harold had come to confirm Edward's earlier promise that Duke William should be his successor.

According to William of Poitiers, writing in the 1070s:

In a council assembled at Bonneville-sur-Touques, Harold took an oath of fealty to William in a religious ceremony; and, according to the testimony of truthful and distinguished men of high repute who were present, Harold, in the final stages of his oath, of his own free will made these distinct promises: that he would be William's proxy in the court of his lord, King Edward, as long as the king lived; that after Edward's death he would use all his influence and resources to secure the English throne for William …

It appears that William had rescued Harold from the clutches of a neighbouring magnate, on whose shores Harold had been shipwrecked, and that Harold had then been pressurized or tricked into making this oath. Whatever the truth of the matter, William claimed that when Harold assumed the throne on Edward's death he had perjured himself, so providing William with the necessary moral window-dressing for his brutal and ruthless conquest.

A famous image from the Bayeux Tapestry, a long, embroidered cloth dating from the late 11th century and depicting scenes before, during and after the Battle of Hastings in 1066. This scene suggests that Harold was killed when he was hit in the eye by a Norman arrow. However, it is more likely that he was cut down in the thick of battle, still in command of his men, his personal standard of the Fighting Man, embroidered by his mother Gytha, flying proudly above him.

TROUBLE IN THE NORTH

When Harold assumed the throne in January 1066, he had already made one important enemy: his brother Tostig. The rupture had taken place late in the previous year, when Harold had failed to help Tostig put down a revolt in his earldom of Northumbria. Tostig then joined up with Harold Hardrada, who, in September 1066, launched an invasion of England, sailing up the Humber and penetrating towards York.

Harold, who had been awaiting an invasion of the south coast from William of Normandy, marched his army north, and defeated the Norwegians at Stamford Bridge, on the River Derwent just east of York. Both Tostig and the Norwegian king were killed. But no sooner had the victory been won than Harold heard that the Normans had crossed the Channel and landed on the Sussex coast. He marched his army back down to London in no more than a week – a speed of around 30 miles per day. He then pressed on south into Sussex, to a place called Senlac Hill, near Hastings, where he – and Anglo-Saxon England – were to meet their ends.

Timeline

c. 1022
Birth of Harold

1051–1052
In exile with his father

1062–1063
Leads campaigns against the Welsh

1064 or 1065
Visits Normandy

1066
(4/5 January) Succeeds to the throne

(25 September) Defeats Tostig and Harold Hardrada at Stamford Bridge

(14 October) Death of Harold at the Battle of Hastings

❝ Far and wide the ground was covered with the flower of the English nobility and youth, soiled by their own blood. The two brothers of the king were found lying beside him. He himself, all dignity lost, was recognized not by his face but by certain indications and was carried to the camp of the duke … ❞ WILLIAM OF POITIERS

DESCRIBES THE FIELD AT HASTINGS AFTER THE BATTLE; FROM *GESTA WILHELMI DUCIS NORMANNORUM ET REGIS ANGLORUM* (C. 1071–4). APPARENTLY ONLY HAROLD'S MISTRESS COULD IDENTIFY HIS BODY.

WILLIAM I THE CONQUEROR

1066-1087

In 1066 William of Normandy, the bastard son of Robert the Devil, installed himself as king of England. His seizure of the throne, although dressed up in legal justifications, was achieved by bloody conquest and sustained by pitiless subjugation. It marked the end of Anglo-Saxon England, and the beginning of an era in which England turned its face to France.

Biography

William claimed that in 1051 his childless cousin Edward the Confessor had nominated him as his successor. But no one in England – noble or commoner – had invited William and his Norman adventurers. The consequences for many of the native English were grim, as William and his warriors set about imposing a rule of iron across the land.

The English long remembered these days as a time of oppression, and right up until the 20th century the phrase 'the Norman Yoke' became a rallying cry of rebels, radicals and democrats, as they sought to resist the power of the crown and the landed aristocracy.

THE EARLY YEARS OF DUKE WILLIAM

William's father, known as Robert the Magnificent or Robert the Devil because of his daring and cruelty, later became the subject of a number of fanciful legends. His mother, Herleva, the daughter of one Fulbert, a tanner, was Robert's long-term partner, although they never formally married – hence William's other byname: William the Bastard. One story tells how Robert first spied Herleva as she did her washing in the stream at the foot of Falaise Castle, another that he fell in love with her at a dance. Her father, although not of noble birth, was probably a prosperous businessman, and later became chamberlain to the duke.

William was only eight years old when his father died in 1035, and his early years as a young duke were not easy. Three noblemen who protected and advised him were murdered before the end of the decade, and in 1047 his cousin Guy of Burgundy, who claimed the dukedom, formed an alliance against him. The French king, Henry I, came to William's aid, and the rebels were defeated near Caen – the young duke's first taste of battle. By 1054, however, Henry I had begun to cast envious eyes over the duchy, and with some of the great magnates of France mounted an invasion.

BORN 1027 or 1028, in Normandy

FATHER Robert the Magnificent, duke of Normandy

MOTHER Herleva

MARRIED Matilda, daughter of the count of Flanders

CHILDREN Robert Curthose, William Rufus, Adela of Blois, Henry. Both William and Henry became kings of England, respectively as William II and Henry I

SUCCEEDED 14 October 1066

CROWNED 25 December 1066

ROYAL HOUSE Normandy

STYLE *Willielmus Rex Anglorum* ('William, King of the English')

DIED 9 September 1087, at the Convent of St Gervais, near Rouen

BURIED St Peter's Church, Caen

This was successfully resisted, as was another in 1057. William went on to expand the boundaries of his dukedom, acquiring the large territory of Maine.

To survive all these assaults on his position required a man of steely qualities. By the 1060s William – a physically and mentally strong man, of unusual size and bulk – was a hardened warrior and a skilled politician, knowing the value to a ruler of instilling fear, in enemies and subjects alike. He was also a cunning diplomat, whose cultivation of the Church was to stand him in good stead.

Falaise Castle, in Normandy, where William the Conqueror was born in 1027 or 1028. The castle was the seat of the dukes of Normandy, and, according to one story, it was at the foot of the castle that William's father, Robert the Magnificent, first laid eyes on his mother, Herleva.

WILLIAM, HIS WIFE, THE POPE AND THE ABBOT

William supported the reform movement initiated by Pope Leo IX in 1049, which sought to ensure that bishoprics were held by dedicated and spiritual churchmen rather than worldly noblemen appointed by the local prince. William's support paid off, when in 1066 the papacy gave its blessing to William's seizure of the English throne by force of arms.

William's relations with the Church were not universally smooth, however. In 1049 the pope forbade his proposed match with Matilda, daughter of Count Baldwin of Flanders, possibly on the grounds of some distant relationship by blood or marriage. But William defied the pope and the wedding went ahead in 1053. This led to a temporary falling-out with his closest adviser, a pious yet politically able Italian monk called Lanfranc of Pavia. But in 1059 the pope relented, the marriage was confirmed, and Lanfranc and William were reconciled. In 1063 William appointed Lanfranc as Abbot of St Etienne in Caen, while after the conquest of England, Lanfranc rose to the position of Archbishop of Canterbury, and helped to impose Norman control over the English Church.

William's marriage to Matilda was by no means a love match, but his insecurity about his own illegitimacy and the difficulties strewn in his path to the altar appear to have formed in William a single-minded and lifelong devotion to his wife. Although he may not have been absolutely faithful, we know of no regular mistresses, and Matilda bore him more than the requisite

Timeline

1027 or 1028
Birth of William

1035
Succeeds to the dukedom of Normandy

1047
Guy of Burgundy attempts to seize Normandy

1049
The pope prohibits William from marrying Matilda of Flanders

1051

According to William, Edward the Confessor promises him the throne of England

1053

William marries Matilda

1054

Henry I of France attempts to seize Normandy

1057

Henry I of France makes another failed attempt to seize Normandy

1059

Pope confirms William's marriage

1064 or 1065

According to the Normans, Harold Godwineson swears an oath of fealty to William

Who were the Normans?

The Normans were originally 'Northmen' or 'Norsemen' – in other words Vikings, the fearsome raiders from Scandinavia who had terrorized western Europe since the later 8th century. In 911 a Viking leader called Rollo, in exchange for a promise of peace, was awarded the area around the mouth of the River Seine by the French king, Charles the Simple. Rollo and his successors settled and flourished in the land now known as Normandy, and before long had adopted the language, culture and customs of the French.

The Normans were one of the most vigorous military peoples of Europe. In addition to the conquest of England in 1066, and later incursions into Wales, Scotland and Ireland, Norman freebooters also captured southern Italy from the Byzantines and Sicily from the Arabs, and, in the Middle East, carved out the principality of Antioch.

number of heirs, two of whom were to become kings of England. It was also a politically useful match: an alliance with Flanders strengthened his position at the time of the invasion in 1066, and the fact that Matilda was a descendant of Alfred the Great helped to legitimize William's claim to the English throne.

THE EVE OF CONQUEST

When after the death of Edward the Confessor in January 1066 Harold Godwineson, earl of Wessex, was acclaimed king in England, the Norman propaganda machine went into overdrive. The Normans claimed that Harold, on a previous visit to Normandy, had sworn an oath of allegiance to William, in which he committed himself to helping William secure the English throne promised him by Edward. Having now accepted the crown himself, Harold was damned as a perjurer.

Writing less than ten years later, the French chronicler William of Poitiers summed up the Norman position vis-à-vis Harold:

This insane Englishman was not a choice of the people, but on that sorrowful day when the best of kings [i.e. Edward the Confessor] was buried and the whole nation mourned his passing, he seized the royal throne with the acclaim of certain iniquitous confederates and thereby perjured himself. He was made king by the unholy consecration of Stigand [Archbishop of Canterbury], who had been deprived of his ministry by the justified fervour of papal anathema.

Thus was Harold's assumption of the throne discounted – on political, legal and theological grounds.

The fact that Harold almost certainly was the 'choice of the people' is shown by his remarkable military campaigns of 1066, which would not have been half so effective without the widespread support of his countrymen. The Battle of Hastings was, after all, like the Battle of Waterloo 750 years later, a 'close-run thing'.

BI hAROLD:SACRAMENTVM:FECIT:✓ hIC h
VVILLELMO DVCI:⁘

A scene from the Bayeux Tapestry showing Harold's oath of allegiance to Duke William. According to French chroniclers, Harold swore not to stand in the way of William's claim to the throne of England. The tapestry was probably commissioned by William's half-brother, Odo of Bayeux, and while it is invaluable as a chronological record, its purpose was also political and propagandist: to highlight that perjury following an oath would lead to retribution being visited on Harold.

THE COMING OF THE NORMANS

On 28 September 1066 William of Normandy, at the head of a fleet of several hundred ships carrying several thousand soldiers, landed on the beach at Pevensey, Sussex, on the south coast of England. There is a story that Duke William stumbled as he came ashore, picking up a handful of sand as he rose: 'Thus do I hold England in my hand,' he is said to have boasted. Among the men striding up the beach with William was his court minstrel, Taillefeu, who juggled with his sword as he went, singing songs of Charlemagne and Roland.

William set up headquarters in a temporary wooden fort on the cliff top at Hastings, further east along the coast, from where he sent out parties to forage, plunder and provoke. He knew it would not be long before news of his arrival reached Harold in the north, where the English king had just put paid to a Norwegian invasion at Stamford Bridge.

After a remarkable forced march of his army southward, Harold arrived in Sussex to face the new invaders. The Battle of Hastings – perhaps the most famous event in English history – was not fought at Hastings itself, but several miles inland, at a place then identified as Senlac Hill, near the present-day town of Battle.

❛ My narrative has frequently had occasion to praise William, but this act which condemned the innocent and guilty alike to die by slow starvation I cannot commend him ... Moreover, I declare that assuredly such brutal slaughter cannot remain unpunished. ❜ ORDERIC VITALIS (C. 1114–41).

THE BATTLE OF HASTINGS

Harold and his army held the high ground, forming a shieldwall against the attackers, flying the great Dragon Banner of Wessex in defiance. All day, wave after wave of Norman cavalry charged up the hill, but failed to break the English formation. William himself is said to have lost three horses in the attacks. Meanwhile, in the English ranks, according to William of Poitiers, 'the only movement was the dropping of the dead; the living stood motionless'.

At one point some of the English broke away to pursue retreating cavalry, and were themselves overwhelmed. Whether this, or William's deployment of his archers with their 'death-bearing clouds of arrows', decided the day, is open to debate, but in the end the shieldwall was breached, and then began the bloody work of sword on flesh, axe on skull.

By the end of a long day, King Harold and the flower of the English army lay dead. Norman losses were also high, and William cautiously awaited reinforcements before moving on London.

SHOCK AND AWE: COERCION, RESISTANCE AND OPPRESSION

When the news of the slaughter reached London, Edgar the Atheling was proclaimed as Harold's successor. Edgar, the great-grandson of Æthelred the Unready, was no more than a stripling youth, and his claim lacked credibility even with the English, and was entirely disregarded by the victor of Hastings. On Christmas Day 1066 William was crowned king in Westminster Abbey. But one victory had not won him a kingdom.

Many of the Norman knights who had fought at Hastings were rewarded with

In this section of the Bayeux Tapestry, William the Conqueror's ships land at Pevensey, as the Norman invasion of England commences.

new estates, which they secured by building castles, initially in wood, and later in stone. From these forbidding strongholds – a novelty in 11th-century England – they controlled their new dominions, enforcing their claim on the land and compelling the subservience of the people, by violence if required.

But resistance continued, and was dealt with mercilessly. In the so-called Harrying of the North in 1069–70, the Normans laid waste to a vast area of north-eastern England. Flocks were killed, crops destroyed, villages burnt and the people put to the sword. Survivors were faced with starvation, and some resorted to cannibalism, 'eating the brains out of shattered skulls', according to one source. In all an estimated 150,000 people died. Even William's contemporaries were shocked.

Despite this, revolts continued into the 1070s, only ending with the defeat of the earls of Northumbria and East Anglia in 1075. William, who had originally intended to rule with the cooperation of the existing English nobility, now relied solely on his Norman barons.

WILLIAM'S LEGACY: CONTINUITY AND CHANGE

The year 1066 is often taken as marking the end of the Dark Ages in England, and the beginning of the Middle Ages – a transition between an England founded by barbaric Germanic invaders – the Anglo-Saxons – and an England of cosmopolitan sophistication, oriented towards the rich and vibrant cultures of France and the Mediterranean. All this is so, but only up to a point.

Historians today largely eschew the term 'Dark Ages', and speak instead of the 'Early Middle Ages'. They point to the survival of the Church after the fall of Rome in the 5th century, and the continued use of Latin as an international language. More specifically, they point out the continuity in the mechanisms of government between the Anglo-Saxon and Norman periods in England. They also highlight the great cultural achievements of the Anglo-Saxons – the illuminated manuscripts, the fine metalwork, the building of magnificent abbeys and churches (although few of these survive intact).

1066
(28 September) William lands in England

(14 October) Battle of Hastings

(25 December) William crowned in London

1068
Revolt in Northumbria

1069–1070
The Harrying of the North

1070
Lanfranc, William's chief adviser, becomes Archbishop of Canterbury in place of the Englishman Stigand

1070–1071
Revolt of Hereward the Wake in the Fens of East Anglia

1074
Revolt in Normandy

1075
Revolt of two English earls, Waltheof of Northumbria and Ralf of East Anglia

1079
William defeated in battle in Normandy by his son Robert Curthose

❝ Duke William instructed the archers not to shoot their arrows directly at the enemy, but rather into the air, so that the arrows might blind the enemy squadron. This caused great losses amongst the English. ❞ HENRY OF HUNTINGDON, *HISTORIA ANGLORUM* (C. 1130).

One man's meat

Symptomatic of the social and economic gulf between Normans and Saxons were the pairs of words used to describe animals and their flesh. The Saxon herdsman tended his lord's cows, sheep and pigs, while his Norman master served at his table beef (from French *boeuf*, 'cow'), mutton (from French *mouton*, 'sheep') and pork (from French *porc*, 'pig').

Anglo-Saxon kings such as Alfred and Athelstan, and even the Viking Cnut, regarded themselves as European monarchs, and parleyed and exchanged gifts with the other princes of Christendom. Edward the Confessor, born of a Saxon father and a Norman mother and brought up in Normandy, had already acquired Norman tastes, and introduced these to England – Westminster Abbey, dedicated in 1065, was built in the international Romanesque or Norman style. So to what extent did 1066 mark the beginning of a cultural revolution in England?

A NEW LANGUAGE

The most significant change was linguistic. Despite a degree of intermarriage with the native English, Norman-French became the language of king, court and nobility. It was also the predominant language of business and secular culture (although Latin remained the language of the Church). It was via the Normans that many words of French origin still in use today entered the English language.

French was still the language of the elite in the later 14th century, and it was remarkable even at that time that Geoffrey

1080
William secures the north of England and invades Scotland

Bayeux Tapestry commissioned by William's half-brother Odo, Bishop of Bayeux

1081
William secures England against the Welsh by establishing Marcher lordships along the border (or 'Marches')

1083
Revolt against William in Maine

1085
Threatened Danish invasion of England

Domesday Book commissioned

1087
(9 September) Death of William

The Domesday Book

In 1085 William commissioned a comprehensive survey of his new realm. It became known as the Domesday Book because it was regarded as the final authority, like God's judgement at the end of the world, against which there is no appeal. William's purpose was to assess how much tax he could extract from each town, village and hamlet. The survey was also intended to establish who owned what, and the lists of landowners, their holdings, livestock, ploughs and the numbers of peasants on their land has proved an invaluable source for historians.

A folio from the Chronique de Normandie, showing the funeral of William I at the Abbaye aux Hommes, in Caen (left), and the crowning of William's successor, William Rufus, by Archbishop Lanfranc (right).

Chaucer – a court poet – chose to write in English, rather than in French.

The French connection of the Norman kings had another important historical consequence. While reorienting England away from the Scandinavian world and towards France, it drew England into centuries of continental warfare, as the kings of England pressed their claims to the throne of France.

DEATH OF A CONQUEROR

By William's last decade his new kingdom was largely peaceful. The king spent most of his time in Normandy, dealing with rumblings of revolt, in which his eldest son Robert Curthose was involved. By the time of William's death, father and son had been reconciled, and the old duke had bestowed Normandy on the former rebel – but not the throne of England, which was to go to his second son, William Rufus.

In August 1087 William suffered a fall from his horse while campaigning to recover territory from the French king. As his horse stumbled William was crushed against the pommel of his saddle, sustaining severe abdominal injuries. The great man – now great in girth as well as deeds – was taken to the Convent of St Gervais, near Rouen, where for several weeks he lay dying. So much more feared was he than loved that at his death only the monks remained to tend his body. The tomb that had been prepared proved too small, and as the monks tried to fit the Conqueror into his final resting place, his bloated cadaver burst, and the church was filled with the stench of his mortality.

WILLIAM II RUFUS

1087-1100

William Rufus was the second son of the Conqueror, and like his father was a man of considerable bulk, although shorter in stature. He had piercing eyes, long blond hair and a stammer, and was known as 'Rufus' because of his ruddy features. The chroniclers paint him as a ruthless, God-hating ruler, tactless and blustering, but at the same time effeminate and decadent, 'a dandy dressed in the height of fashion, however outrageous'.

Biography

BORN c.1056, in Normandy

FATHER William I the Conqueror

MOTHER Matilda of Flanders

MARRIED never married

CHILDREN no record of any

SUCCEEDED 9 September 1087

CROWNED 26 September 1087

ROYAL HOUSE Normandy

STYLE *Dei Gratia Rex Anglorum* ('By the grace of God, King of the English')

DIED 2 August 1100, in the New Forest

BURIED Winchester Cathedral

The chroniclers were by no means objective observers, however. Throughout his reign William displayed a cynicism in regard to religion, and treated the Church with considerable disdain, so it is not surprising that the chroniclers – churchmen to a man – should have given him a bad press.

For many centuries, historians echoed this disapproval, and even damned William (as damnation it was in less enlightened times) with the 'sin' of homosexuality. There is no clear evidence regarding William's sexual preferences, although it is perfectly possible he preferred men. Nor is there evidence that as a ruler he was more than averagely savage for his time – and there is plenty of evidence that he was loyal and generous to his friends.

THE SONS OF THE CONQUEROR

Relations between William the Conqueror's three sons – Robert, William and Henry – were never very harmonious. There is a story that one day the two younger brothers poured the contents of a chamber pot on Robert's head, to his shame and fury, and a fight broke out, until the boys' father separated them. The older William left his eldest son Robert the duchy of Normandy, but seems to have deliberately deprived him of the throne of England. Immediately on his father's death in Rouen, William Rufus crossed the Channel, and within three weeks was crowned by Archbishop Lanfranc, the Conqueror's closest adviser. Henry, the youngest brother, had to be content with 5,000 pounds of silver.

Robert had many supporters among the Norman barons who held lands on both sides of the Channel. They were unhappy with two different overlords, and in 1088 mounted a widespread revolt in favour of Robert. This was crushed, and William went on to campaign against his brother in Normandy. William and Robert were eventually reconciled, and when Robert went off on the First Crusade

THE KINGS AND QUEENS OF ENGLAND

in 1096, he raised the money by mortgaging his duchy to William. William for his part found the 10,000 marks required by imposing a heavy and much-hated tax on his English subjects. The deal with his brother done, William became the effective ruler of Normandy until his death.

WILLIAM AND THE CHURCH

During Archbishop Lanfranc's lifetime William maintained good relations with the English Church, but when Lanfranc died in 1089 he delayed finding a replacement for the see of Canterbury for four years, appropriating the archiepiscopal revenues for himself. It was not until 1093, when William became seriously ill, that he was persuaded to appoint the saintly Anselm, Abbot of Bec in Normandy. Once he recovered, William made it clear that he regretted the appointment – as did Anselm, who described it as yoking together an untameable bull and a feeble old sheep.

William was intent on treating the English Church as his personal fiefdom, extracting from it as much revenue as he could. Anselm upbraided the king, much to William's annoyance, to which Anselm responded, 'I would rather have you angry with me than have God angry with you.' The dispute between them grew, not helped by the king frequently blaspheming in public, and in 1097 Anselm went into exile, and remained there until William's death.

A manuscript illumination depicting William II Rufus, from the Historia Anglorum *of Matthew Paris, dating from 1250/59.*

Timeline

c. 1056
Birth of William II

1087
(9 September) Succeeded

(26 September) Crowned

1088
Revolt in England against William in favour of his brother Robert

1089
Death of Archbishop Lanfranc

1091
William mounts expedition to Normandy

1092
Seizes Cumbria from the Scots

1093
Anselm becomes Archbishop of Canterbury

After Malcolm III's death and defeat at Alnwick, William effectively controls Scotland

❝ He was hated by almost all his people and abhorrent to God. ❞
THE *ANGLO-SAXON CHRONICLE* (C. 1121).

❝ William ... has the ferocity of an unbroken bull. ❞
EADMER, *HISTORIA NOVORUM IN ANGLIA* (C. 1095–1123).

1094
Second expedition to Normandy

1095
Failed revolt in England, led by Robert de Mowbray, earl of Northumbria

1096
William becomes regent of Normandy while his brother goes on Crusade

1097
Suppression of Welsh revolt

Archbishop Anselm goes into exile

1097–1099
William campaigns in France

1100
(2 August) Killed in the New Forest

Death in the forest

The conventional accounts of William's death ascribe it to a hunting accident in the New Forest, one of the many large areas that the Norman kings and lords enclosed for their own private sport. One of the earliest accounts is by William of Malmesbury, writing *c.* 1125:

> After dinner [Rufus] went into the forest with a very small number of attendants. Among these the most intimate with the king was Walter, surnamed Tirel, who had come from France, attracted by the liberality of the king. This man alone remained with him, while the others were widely scattered in the chase. The sun was now setting, and the king drawing his bow let fly an arrow which slightly wounded a stag which passed before him. He ran in pursuit, keeping his gaze fixed rigidly on the quarry, and holding up his hand to shield his eyes from the sun's rays. At this instant, Walter tried to transfix another stag, which by chance came near him while the king's attention was otherwise occupied. And thus it was that unknowingly (oh gracious God!) he pierced the king's breast with a fatal arrow.

The king's body was not found until the next day, and his noble companions all hastened back to their estates, expecting upheavals. William of Malmesbury continues:

> A few of the peasants carried his corpse to the cathedral at Winchester on a horse-drawn wagon, with blood dripping from it the whole way. There in the cathedral crossing, under the tower, he was interred, in the presence of many great men, mourned by few.

The chronicler goes on to describe how the cathedral tower collapsed the following year, but discounts the theory that this was because a sinful king had been buried there; he simply states that the tower had been badly built.

William of Malmesbury's account is backed up by that of Orderic Vitalis, writing *c.* 1135:

> He got up, mounted his horse and sped into the wood. Count Henry [William's brother, shortly to become king as Henry I] and William de Breteuil and other great men were there; they went into the woodland, and the huntsmen were scattered in their various positions. The king and Walter de Poix [i.e. Tirel] established themselves with a few companions in the wood, and waited eagerly for prey, with weapons ready. Suddenly a beast ran between them; the king jumped back from his place, and Walter let an arrow fly. The arrow shaved the hair on the animal's back, sped on and wounded the king standing beyond. He soon fell to the ground, and died – proh dolor! – instantly.

Conspiracy theories

Various other sources from the period report that Walter Tirel denied he was involved in the king's death, or even present at it. This throws some doubt on the two descriptions above, as does the earliest account of William's death, in the *Anglo-Saxon Chronicle* (probably before 1121):

He was killed with an arrow while hunting by one of his people ... He was hated by almost all his people and abhorrent to God. This his end testified, for he died in the midst of his sins without repentance or any atonement for his evil deeds.

The *Anglo-Saxon Chronicle* thus omits any mention of an accident, while emphasizing the king's less than popular status. This has led some to suggest that William was murdered.

The obvious beneficiary was William's younger brother, Henry, who was a member of the hunting expedition and who wasted no time in taking over the kingdom – within three days he was crowned at Westminster Abbey. Another possible beneficiary was the king of France, who was certainly worried by William's expansionist ambitions beyond Normandy.

William's hostility to the Church has even led to wild speculations that he was an adherent of a secret religion of pagan devil-worshippers, and that his death was a ritual murder of the king, as carried out by some ancient Middle Eastern fertility cults (Dr Margaret Murray, *The God of the Witches*, 1931).

But the consensus among modern historians is that William was killed by accident. Even at the time, the 'official' story of William's accidental death was widely believed. Thus, as far as many of his contemporaries were concerned, the stray arrow was the instrument of God's justice on an irreligious, cruel and wicked man.

❝ From a moral standpoint ... probably the worst king that has occupied the throne of England. ❞ A.L. POOLE, *FROM DOMESDAY BOOK TO MAGNA CARTA* (1901).

A manuscript illumination from the Chroniques de St Denis, dating from c. 1335/40, depicting the death in the New Forest of William Rufus. The circumstances of William's death have given rise to a plethora of conspiracy theories. The question cui bono? *('who benefits?') might be said to point the finger at William's brother and successor, Henry I.*

Henry I

1100-1135

Henry was an able if opportunistic politician who kept England secure and largely at peace. The youngest son of William the Conqueror, he seized the throne when his elder brother William Rufus was killed in the New Forest. By his flatterers Henry was nicknamed 'Beauclerc' (because of his love of learning), and 'the Lion of Justice'.

Biography

BORN c. 1068, in Selby, Yorkshire

FATHER William I the Conqueror

MOTHER Matilda of Flanders

MARRIED (1) Matilda (originally Edith), niece of Edgar the Atheling, (2) Adela of Louvain

CHILDREN William, who died on the *White Ship*, and Matilda (who briefly became queen of England), both by his first marriage. Henry also had many illegitimate children

SUCCEEDED 2 August 1100

CROWNED 5 August 1100

ROYAL HOUSE Normandy

STYLE *Dei Gratia Rex Anglorum* ('By the grace of God, King of the English')

DIED 1 December 1135, at Lyons-la-Fôret

BURIED Reading Abbey, which Henry had founded. (Some of his organs – including his brain – remained in Normandy, at Rouen.)

Unlike William Rufus, Henry cultivated generally good relations with the Church, and in return the monastic chroniclers – who so damned his elder brother – credited Henry with both kingly and manly virtues.

THE CHARACTER OF THE KING

The chroniclers did not offer unadulterated flattery, however: Henry of Huntingdon praised the king for wisdom, victory and riches, but condemned him for avarice, cruelty and lust.

Certainly Henry was adept at acquiring and holding on to riches. His lust is attested by the fact that he sired more bastards than any other English monarch – between 20 and 22 – from at least six different mistresses. William of Malmesbury, writing c. 1125, not altogether convincingly explained: 'His intercourse with women was undertaken not for the satisfaction of his lusts, but from his desire for children.'

It is difficult to assess whether Henry was markedly more cruel than any other medieval monarch. At one point he commanded that all the moneyers (coiners) of England be mutilated, without bothering to investigate which ones were actually issuing false coin. But later in his reign he often replaced such punishments with fines, as his avarice got the better of his cruelty. His blinding of two of his granddaughters by his illegitimate daughter Juliana was politically motivated: Henry held them as hostages, and when their father blinded his hostages, Henry retaliated in kind. Such an act may have been brutal, but it was not unusual.

HENRY'S COUP D'ÉTAT

On the death of the Conqueror, Henry's older brothers had succeeded to their father's titles – Robert became duke of

Normandy and William Rufus king of England – but Henry was left nothing but a large sum of money. He used this to buy lands in Normandy and bided his time, while Robert and William struggled with each other for the control of their father's Anglo-Norman realm. In 1096 Robert and William patched up their quarrel: William was to be regent in Normandy while Robert went on the First Crusade, and each made the other his heir.

This last arrangement would have come into effect after William was killed in the New Forest in August 1100, had not Henry moved fast. Robert was due back from crusade in September and, what was more, brought with him a new wife, with the promise of a future heir. As soon as William's body was discovered with an arrow through his lungs, Henry rushed to Winchester, took possession of the royal treasury, and then rode hard for London. There, three days after his brother's death, he was crowned by the Bishop of London in Westminster Abbey.

Henry immediately set about establishing that his reign would be very different from that of his elder brother. He issued a Charter of Liberties, in which he declared his intention to redress the injustices of William's reign. Anselm, the Archbishop of Canterbury exiled by William, was recalled (although later exiled

Timeline

c. 1068
Birth of Henry

1100
(2 August) Henry's brother William Rufus killed while out hunting

(5 August) Henry crowned in London

(11 November) Marries Edith of Scotland, who takes the name Matilda

1101
(July) Robert of Normandy, Henry's older brother, invades England

King Henry ... was excellent, wealthy and easy of access. He was the peace and glory of the earth. ROBERT DE TORIGNY, WRITING C. 1149.

Henry I and the White Ship, as depicted in an early 14th-century book illumination. The White Ship sank in the English Channel off Barfleur on 25 November 1120, on its way from Normandy to England. Among those drowned was Henry I's heir and sole legitimate son, William. The disaster led to a crisis over the succession, and contributed to the domestic chaos under Stephen, Henry's successor.

1103
(27 April) Henry exiles Anselm, Archbishop of Canterbury, after the latter denies Henry the right to appoint bishops

1105
Henry's first invasion of Normandy

1106
Henry invades Normandy again, and defeats Robert at Tinchebrai

1107
Reconciliation between Henry and Anselm

1109–1113
War with Louis VI of France

1116–1119
Second war with Louis VI

1118
Death of Henry's first wife Matilda

again), and the unpopular Ranulf Flambard, William's chief adviser, was thrown into the Tower of London. William and his circle were condemned for their decadence, effeminacy and moral laxity, and the young men at court were obliged to cut their long hair short. Henry placed the administration of England – particularly in the areas of finance and justice – in the capable hands of Roger, Bishop of Salisbury.

THE STRUGGLE WITH ROBERT OF NORMANDY
The year after Henry was crowned, his brother Robert launched an invasion of England, with the support of some of the English barons. No battle was fought, and Henry and Robert came to terms: Henry renounced his claim to Normandy, and both promised to make the other his successor.

But Henry seems to have had no intention of keeping his side of the bargain, and manoeuvred against his brother by buying alliances with Robert's neighbours.

He invaded Normandy in 1105, and again in 1106, this time defeating Robert, whom he kept in prison until his death in 1134. Henry had succeeded in reuniting his father's realms, but this was to involve him in wars in northern France for decades.

MARRIAGES AND HEIRS

Henry's first marriage, in 1100, was to Edith, the daughter of Malcolm III of Scotland and his queen, St Margaret – the sister of Edgar the Atheling, the last Anglo-Saxon claimant to the throne of England. Henry thus linked his line to the ancient house of Wessex, and so sought to add legitimacy to his occupation of the throne of England. For her part, Edith changed her name to Matilda to sound more Norman – although some in court sneered at the marriage, referring to the couple as 'Godric and Godgiva'.

Only two of the couple's children survived infancy. Henry's male heir, William, drowned in the wreck of the *White Ship* in 1120, leaving only a female successor, Matilda. Henry's first wife had died in 1118, and in 1121 Henry took Adela of Louvain as his wife. But she bore him no heirs, and Henry announced that his daughter Matilda would succeed him.

Succession by the closest blood relative had not been firmly established in England, and Henry could have made his nephew Stephen or one of his illegitimate sons his heir. Perhaps Henry insisted the crown pass to his daughter because he had based his own claim to the throne of England on the fact that he alone of his brothers had been born after their father had become king. Whatever the reason, Henry's decision would embroil England in years of civil war.

A SURFEIT OF LAMPREYS

It was while in Normandy that Henry met his end. He had been out hunting one day, and, with a hunter's appetite, set about a dish of lampreys, even though it was a fish his physician had warned him against. Henry at once suffered 'a most destructive humour' and 'a sudden and extreme convulsion'. Shortly afterwards the old king breathed his last. Back in England, his nephew Stephen, with the backing of the barons, seized power. What was to follow became known as 'the Anarchy'.

1120
(25 November) Henry's male heir William dies in the wreck of the *White Ship*

1121
(2 February) Henry marries Adela of Louvain

1122
Henry reasserts English dominion in Cumbria

1123–1124
Third war with Louis VI

1127
Henry makes his barons swear to accept his daughter Matilda as his successor

1133
(March) Birth of Matilda's son, the future Henry II

1135
(1 December) Death of Henry

The wreck of the *White Ship*

On the evening of 25 November 1120 Henry's son William, then aged 17, set sail from Normandy for England in the *White Ship*. He was accompanied by many young nobles, and it seems that both they and the crew had had too much wine. Before even reaching the open sea, the ship hit a rock, and foundered. All were lost. 'No ship,' wrote William of Malmesbury, 'ever brought so much misery to England; none was ever so notorious in the history of the world.' It was said that Henry never smiled again.

STEPHEN
1135-1154

Stephen rested his claim to the throne on the fact that he was a grandson of William the Conqueror. He had previously sworn to support the succession of his cousin Matilda, daughter of Henry I, who had chosen her as his heir. But when Henry died in 1135, Stephen grasped the opportunity to make himself king of England.

Biography

BORN c. 1096, in Blois, France

FATHER Stephen, count of Blois

MOTHER Adela, daughter of William I the Conqueror

MARRIED Matilda, daughter of Eustace II, count of Boulogne

CHILDREN Baudouin (died young), Eustace, William, Marie

SUCCEEDED 1 December 1135

CROWNED 22 December 1135, at Canterbury

ROYAL HOUSE Normandy

STYLE *Dei Gratia Rex Anglorum* ('By the grace of God, King of the English')

DIED 25 October 1154, at Dover

BURIED Faversham Abbey, Kent

During the years of civil war that followed, Stephen showed himself to be a better soldier than a politician. He cut a dashing and courageous figure, and had a personal warmth lacking in his Norman predecessors. But he inspired more affection than either trust or loyalty, and was not up to the great challenges of his era, nor a match for the powerful, brilliant personalities who dominated it.

EARLY LIFE

Stephen was a younger son of the count of Blois, and was born in the valley of the River Loire in France. At the age of about ten he was sent to England, to be raised at the court of his uncle Henry I, who appears to have been genuinely fond of his nephew. Henry made Stephen count of Mortain, giving him the richest lands in Normandy, and awarded him extensive estates in south-east and north-west England, where he founded the great abbey of Furness.

In 1125 Stephen married Matilda, daughter of the count of Boulogne. Stephen's wife – who was to prove to be one of his most formidable allies – was also a granddaughter of St Margaret of Scotland, the sister of Edgar the Atheling, which linked her to the ancient Anglo-Saxon line of succession to the throne of England.

In 1128 Stephen's cousin Matilda – Henry I's nominated successor as ruler of England and Normandy, and the widow of the Emperor Henry V – took as her second husband Geoffrey of Anjou. Stephen and his elder brother, Count Theobald, must have been concerned about the potential threat to Blois from an alliance of Normandy and Anjou, and perhaps it was at this stage that Stephen conceived the idea of making a bid for the throne of England.

THE WINTER PUTSCH

When Henry I died suddenly in December 1135, the Empress Matilda, his heir, was with her husband in Anjou. Stephen, who was in Boulogne, much closer to England, quickly made the short voyage across the Channel, and in London announced that Henry had, on his deathbed, named him as his successor.

Among Stephen's many supporters in England, the most influential were Bishop Roger of Salisbury, Henry's chief minister, and Stephen's younger brother, the fiercely ambitious Henry of Blois, whom Henry I had made Bishop of Winchester. It was Henry of Blois who persuaded the Archbishop of Canterbury to crown Stephen on 22 December.

Stephen of Blois depicted as a falconer, in an early 14th-century manuscript illumination.

At Easter 1136 Stephen held court in Oxford, and all the leading churchmen and barons attended – including Henry's powerful bastard son, Robert of Gloucester – thus acknowledging Stephen's kingship. Stephen was also acclaimed as duke in Normandy, and he had the support of the pope.

RUMBLINGS OF DISCONTENT

Stephen was almost immediately faced with opposition. By the end of 1135 David I of Scotland, uncle of the Empress Matilda, had sent his armies into Cumbria and Northumbria in support of his niece's claim to the English throne. They returned in 1138, although beaten at the Battle of the Standard, in Yorkshire. There were also rebellions against Stephen in the Welsh Marches (borders) and elsewhere, although again Stephen successfully dealt with these. In Normandy there were pressures from Geoffrey of Anjou and Robert of Gloucester, who had come out in support of his half-sister, the Empress.

In 1139 Stephen made the mistake of making enemies of Bishop Roger of Salisbury and his powerful sons, who between them effectively controlled the administration of England. There had been a rumour that they too were about to come out in

Timeline

c. 1096
Birth of Stephen

1106
Sent to England to be raised at the court of Henry I

1125
Marries Matilda of Boulogne

1135
(1 December) Succeeded

(22 December) Crowned

1136

Makes peace with the Scots who had invaded the previous year

1138

(May) Robert, earl of Gloucester, illegitimate son of Henry I, comes out in favour of the claim of his half-sister, the Empress Matilda

(22 August) David I of Scotland, uncle of the Empress Matilda, defeated at the Battle of the Standard

1139

(30 September) The Empress Matilda and Robert of Gloucester land in England

1141

(2 February) Stephen defeated and captured at Lincoln

(August) Stephen's wife, Queen Matilda, lifts the siege of Winchester, forcing the Empress to flee

(1 November) Stephen released from captivity

favour of Matilda. The Empress took advantage of the confusion of loyalties around Stephen, and on 30 September crossed the Channel with Robert of Gloucester, landing on the coast of Sussex. Thus began many years of civil war.

THE KING IN CAPTIVITY

There were two significant battles near the start of the upheavals. In February 1141 Stephen was preparing for an assault on the castle at Lincoln, but was surprised by superior forces in the streets of the city. Surrounded, the king laid about him with a huge double-headed axe, grinding his teeth and foaming at the mouth like a boar (according to one contemporary description). When the axe broke he fought on with his sword, until that too broke. The king was knocked unconscious by a rock and taken prisoner.

With Stephen in captivity, his queen, also Matilda, took command of his interests – for after Lincoln even his brother, Bishop Henry of Winchester, fancying himself as a king-maker, had declared for the Empress (albeit temporarily). 'God has executed his judgement on my brother,' the politic bishop opined, 'in allowing him to fall into the power of the strong.'

In March the Empress Matilda was acclaimed as queen, but she did not reach London until the summer. There her arrogance and demands for money alienated the citizenry, and she was soon driven out without being crowned. Having also fallen out with Bishop Henry, she then moved on Winchester, location of both the bishop's palace and the royal treasury.

When Christ and his saints slept: the Anarchy

The chroniclers recorded the years of civil war as a time when the barons took advantage of the king's weakness to further their own ends and pursue local feuds, resorting to lawlessness, violence, rapine and plunder. Here, for example, is the *Anglo-Saxon Chronicle*:

For every man built himself castles and held them against the king; and they filled the whole land with these castles. They sorely burdened the unhappy people of the country with forced labour on the castles; and when the castles were built they filled them with devils and wicked men. By night and day they seized those whom they believed to have any wealth, whether they were men or women; and in order to get their gold and silver, they put them into prison and

tortured them with unspeakable tortures ... [they] plundered and burnt all the villages, so that you could easily go a day's journey without ever finding a village inhabited or a field cultivated ... Wherever the ground was tilled the earth bore no corn, for the land was ruined by such doings; and men said openly that Christ and his saints slept.

Basing their judgement on passages such as this, the historians of the Victorian era labelled this period 'the Anarchy'. However, more recently doubt has been expressed as to whether such conditions were widespread throughout the period; there is evidence that in many areas good order was generally maintained.

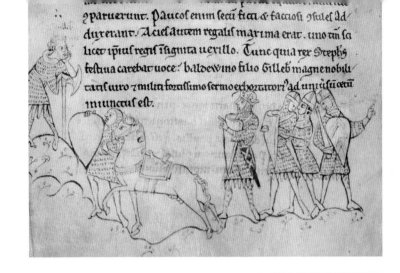

The Battle of Lincoln, 2 February 1141, as depicted in a 12th-century manuscript illumination. The landing in Sussex of Empress Matilda in the late summer of 1139 began a lengthy period of civil war in England. While besieging Lincoln Castle, King Stephen's forces were attacked and routed by a relief force loyal to Matilda and commanded by her half-brother Robert, earl of Gloucester.

But her siege of the city was itself encircled by supporters of Stephen and his queen, and the Empress only just managed to escape. Her half-brother, Robert of Gloucester, was captured. Before long, the two sides came to an agreement, and in November, in exchange for Robert, Stephen was released from imprisonment, so ending the Empress's short spell as *de facto* queen of England.

THE YEARS OF STRUGGLE

This brief truce did not end the Empress's campaign for the throne, however. The conflict continued, albeit less intensively, throughout the 1140s and into the 1150s: even after Matilda returned to the Continent in 1148, her son Henry mounted an expedition to England in 1149, and another one four years later.

Stephen's son Eustace died in August 1153. The English Church had refused to recognize him as Stephen's heir, probably believing his succession would only further destabilize the kingdom. Although Stephen had another son, William, after two decades of warfare the king had lost his taste for the fight.

The Church – in the persons of Stephen's brother, Henry of Winchester, and Archbishop Theobald of Canterbury – brought the two sides together. In November 1153, by the Treaty of Winchester, a peace was agreed, by which Stephen recognized Matilda's son Henry as his heir. Less than a year later Stephen was dead, and Henry II was crowned king of England.

1143
(1 July) Stephen narrowly escapes capture at the Battle of Wilton

1147
(October) Death of Robert of Gloucester

1148
(Spring) The Empress Matilda leaves England

1152
(May) Death of Stephen's wife Matilda

1153
(August) Death of Stephen's heir Eustace

(November) By the Treaty of Winchester, Stephen recognizes the Empress Matilda's son Henry (the future Henry II) as his heir

1154
(25 October) Death of Stephen

❝ It was the king's custom to start many endeavours with vigour, but to bring few to a praiseworthy end. ❞ GERVAISE OF CANTERBURY, WRITING IN THE LATE 12TH CENTURY.

MATILDA
1141

Matilda, or Maud, was the daughter of Henry I, and his nominated heir. But when her father died in 1135 the throne of England was seized by Stephen of Blois, her cousin. Matilda invaded England and succeeded in deposing Stephen – but only for a few months. But she did not give up her claim for many years, until she had secured the succession for her son – the future Henry II.

Matilda was the matriarch of the Plantagenets, the royal house that was to reign in England until the Tudor revolution of 1485. She was a formidable lady, as befits the first female ruler of England. But she was no diplomat, and her haughty manner made her few friends among the English.

MATILDA'S MARRIAGES

From an early age Matilda was a dynastic pawn. When she was only 7 she was engaged to Henry V, the Holy Roman Emperor, whom she married when barely 12. The marriage was childless, and after the Emperor's death in 1125 Matilda returned to England.

In 1127 her father made his barons – including Stephen of Blois – swear to uphold her as his successor to both the kingdom of England and the duchy of Normandy. He then arranged a second marriage for her, to Geoffrey of Anjou, in 1128, when she was 26 and he only 14.

The union of Normandy and Anjou was a formidable one, but the marriage was loveless. For a while the couple were estranged and Matilda returned to her father, but she was reunited with Geoffrey in 1131, and went on to bear him three sons.

THE EMPRESS IN ENGLAND

Matilda (often referred to as the Empress, to distinguish her from Stephen's queen, also called Matilda) landed in England in September 1139, but it was not until February 1141 that her forces scored a decisive victory over Stephen, at Lincoln. With Stephen held captive, the kingdom seemed hers. Having bribed the keeper of the Tower of London with an earldom, she entered the capital early that summer. Here, according to the anonymous author of *Gesta Stephani* ('deeds of King Stephen'):

Biography

BORN February 1102, in London

FATHER Henry I

MOTHER Matilda (Edith) of Scotland

MARRIED (1) Henry V, Holy Roman Emperor, (2) Geoffrey of Anjou

CHILDREN Three sons by her second marriage: Henry (later Henry II), Geoffrey and William

DE FACTO REIGN March–November 1141

ROYAL HOUSE Normandy

STYLE *Imperatrix Henrici Regis filia et Anglorum domina* ('Empress, daughter of King Henry and Mistress of the English')

DIED 10 September 1167, near Rouen, Normandy

BURIED Rouen Cathedral

The origin of the Plantagenets

Geoffrey of Anjou, Matilda's second husband, was nicknamed Plantagenet, from the sprig of broom (*plante genet* in French) that he wore in his hat. Thus Plantagenet became the name of the royal house descended from the union of Geoffrey and Matilda, a dynasty that was to rule England for three centuries. Their more immediate descendants were also known as Angevins ('people from Anjou').

She at once put on an extremely arrogant demeanour instead of the modest gait and bearing proper to the gentle sex, began to walk and speak and do all the things more stiffly and more haughtily than she had been wont.

The anonymous chronicler may just have been a typical male of the time reacting to a woman with power, but Matilda's imposition of a stiff tax on the citizens of London and her refusal to confirm their privileges caused considerable alienation. On 24 June she was expelled from the capital, without having been crowned.

In November 1141, in exchange for Matilda's ally, her half-brother Robert of Gloucester, Stephen was freed and effectively restored to the throne. A year later he was on the verge of capturing Matilda in Oxford, when she made a dramatic escape across the frozen River Thames under cover of darkness, dressed in a white cloak to camouflage her against the winter snow.

After that her power base in England gradually shrunk, and in 1148 she at last abandoned the struggle and returned to Normandy. But she did not retire from politics entirely, acting as adviser to and sometimes as regent for her son, Henry II, ruler of one of the greatest empires in medieval Europe.

Matilda holding a charter, from the Golden Book of St Albans by Thomas Walsingham. Matilda was a benefactor of St Albans Abbey.

1102
(February) Birth of Matilda

1111
Sent to the imperial court in Germany

1114
Marries the Emperor Henry V

1125
Death of Emperor Henry V

1127
Her father, Henry I, names Matilda his heir

1128
Matilda marries Geoffrey, count of Anjou

1133
(5 March) Birth of her first son, Henry

1139
(September) Lands in England to claim throne

1141
(2 February) Stephen defeated and captured at Lincoln

(1 November) Stephen freed, so ending Matilda's usurpation

1148
Matilda returns to Normandy

1167
(10 September) Death of Matilda

HENRY II
1154-1189

Henry II, known as Curtmantle because of the short cloaks he favoured, was not just king of England – he was ruler of a vast empire, extending from the Pyrenees to the River Tweed. Despite hostilities with the French king, his barons and his own sons, he not only restored stability to England after 'the Anarchy' of Stephen's reign, but also successfully extended the reach of royal power into many aspects of life in his kingdom.

Biography

Henry's famous quarrel with Thomas Becket has left an impression that he was a man at the mercy of his temper. But this is just one aspect of his personality, and his rages may have been politically calculated displays. Physically, he was red-haired and freckled, of average height and stocky build, modest in his appetites, and possessed of a restless energy, never sitting unless in a saddle or at table – an advantage for a man who had to travel great distances to govern his scattered empire.

BORN 5 March 1133, at Le Mans

FATHER Count Geoffrey of Anjou

MOTHER Empress Matilda

MARRIED Eleanor of Aquitaine

CHILDREN William (died aged three), Henry ('the Young King', who died before his father), Richard (later King Richard I), Geoffrey (duke of Brittany), Matilda (duchess of Saxony), Leonora, Joan and John (later King John). His illegitimate children included Geoffrey (Archbishop of York) and William de Longespee (earl of Salisbury).

SUCCEEDED 25 October 1153

CROWNED 19 December 1154

ROYAL HOUSE Plantagenet

STYLE *Rex Angliae, Dux Norminiae et Aquitaniae et Comes Andigaviae* ('King of England, Duke of Normandy and Aquitaine and Count of Anjou')

DIED 6 July 1189, at Chinon, near Tours

BURIED Fontevraud Abbey (later reburied in Westminster Abbey)

THE ANGEVIN EMPIRE

Henry, a great-grandson of William the Conqueror, inherited Normandy from his mother, the Empress Matilda, and Anjou from her second husband, his father Geoffrey of Anjou (hence the 'Angevin' Empire). Henry spent some of his boyhood in England, where his mother was pursuing her claim to the throne, and up to the age of 12 received a full-time education. He then returned to France. In 1147 and 1149 he made brief visits to England at the head of expeditions in support of his mother's claim – although these amounted to little more than short-lived adventures.

In 1152 Henry acquired a vast new territory in south-

In a single day, if need be, he can travel the length of four or five day-marches. Thus outsmarting his enemies, he often mocks their plots with his sudden appearance ... In his hands he always has bow, sword, spear and arrow, except when in council or at study. PETER OF BLOIS, WRITING IN 1177.

west France when he married Eleanor, duchess of Aquitaine. Eleanor, who was 9 years his senior, had been married for 15 years to Louis VII of France, but the marriage was childless: 'I have married a monk, not a king,' she complained. The union was annulled on grounds of consanguinity, and within weeks Eleanor married young Henry, who now directly controlled more of France than the French king.

In 1153 Henry led a more serious expedition to England, and in November King Stephen, in a peace agreement brokered by the Church, named Henry as his successor. The following October Stephen died, and on 19 December 1154 Henry was crowned king of England.

A detail from a 12th–13th-century fresco, showing Eleanor of Aquitaine being led into captivity by her husband Henry II following the Great Rebellion of 1173. When Henry II granted his youngest son John certain castles, his three elder sons mounted a rebellion against him, supported by his wife Eleanor. The rebellion ended in 1174 with the capture of the Scottish king William the Lion, an ally of the rebels, though Eleanor remained in prison for the next 15 years.

THE ADMINISTRATION OF ENGLAND

In total, Henry spent some 21 years of his reign – including two 4-year absences – not in England but in France, attending to the Continental parts of his empire. It says something for his capabilities that he managed to rule England so effectively, even when away, through various trusted viceroys.

Henry wasted no time in reasserting his authority over the barons, who had grown powerful and dangerously independent under Stephen. Castles that they had illegally built during the Anarchy were pulled down, and offices and lands belonging to the Crown were recovered.

Most importantly, Henry introduced uniformity to the administration of justice throughout England. Royal courts superseded baronial courts for both civil and criminal trials, the first legal textbook was produced, and trial by jury became the standard following the Assize of Clarendon in 1166, replacing such procedures as trial by combat.

But Henry was careful not to alienate the nobility, and made sure that they played a role in the government of the kingdom. The fact that only a few of the barons took part in the Great Rebellion of 1173–4 is an indication of how successful Henry was.

A charter of Henry II, with a seal used by the king. The seal became the basis of the logo of the Public Record Office.

Henry's faithful servant

Although Henry managed to end the judicial independence of the barons, the independent power of the Church was a more enduring thorn in his side – as it was to many medieval monarchs, who at times found it difficult to accommodate this *imperium in imperio*, or 'kingdom within a kingdom'. The Church – a great landowner – had its own courts and its own laws, and was answerable not to the king but to the pope.

This is the background to Henry's famous quarrel with Thomas Becket, who became Archbishop of Canterbury in 1162. Becket, the son of a merchant, was archdeacon to Archbishop Theobald, who had eased Henry's way onto the throne of England. When Henry became king, he made Becket – still in his thirties – his chancellor, in which role Becket proved himself a loyal and effective servant to the king, even supporting Henry rather than the Church when conflicts of interest arose.

When Theobald died, Henry pressed for Becket to succeed him. Becket at this stage was not even an ordained priest, and the necessary ceremony was hastily conducted the day before he was consecrated as archbishop. Henry might reasonably have expected Becket – who had shown himself to be secularly minded and appreciative of worldly pleasures – to continue as his faithful and trusted minister.

The turbulent priest

For reasons that historians have been unable to fathom, as soon as he became archbishop Becket abandoned his life of conspicuous consumption for one of ostentatious asceticism, wearing rough and lice-infested clothes next to his skin. What was worse, he quarrelled with the king over a whole range of matters that more pragmatic men would have put to one side. But Becket set himself up as the defender of the Church. Henry was furious.

In 1164 Henry, determined to break the archbishop's resistance, instituted proceedings against Becket relating to his time as chancellor. Becket fled into exile in France. Neither the French king nor the pope managed to effect a reconciliation, and Becket did not return until 1170. The final straw came when Becket excommunicated the Archbishop of York, who had performed the crowning of Henry's oldest son, 'the Young King', a ceremony intended by Henry to consolidate the succession.

Timeline

1133
(5 March) Birth of Henry

1147
First expedition against Stephen in England

1149
Second expedition to England

1152
(18 May) Marries Eleanor of Aquitaine

Murder in the Cathedral

Henry was in Normandy when he heard the news. Flying into a rage, he angrily demanded, 'Who will rid me of this turbulent priest?' (or so tradition has us believe). Hearing this, that night four of Henry's knights, seeking to curry favour, secretly sailed for England.

On 29 December 1170 they found Becket in his cathedral at Canterbury, and cut him down. An eyewitness, Edward Grim, who was wounded while attempting to shield the archbishop, described what happened next:

> The third knight inflicted a terrible wound as he lay prostrate, at which blow the sword struck the stone paving, and the crown of the head, which was large, was separated from the rest, so that the blood, whitened by the brains, and the brains, reddened with the blood, stained the floor of the cathedral with the white of the lily and red of the rose, the colours of the Virgin Mother of the Church …

The Church immediately recognized Becket as a martyr, and in just over a year, in February 1173, Becket was declared a saint by Pope Alexander III.

In no time at all the monks of Canterbury were doing good business from the hordes of pilgrims who came to St Thomas's shrine. Canterbury became one of the most popular pilgrimage destinations of medieval Europe, and it was thither that Chaucer's pilgrims were heading when they told each other the *Canterbury Tales.*

Among the first of the pilgrims to the shrine of St Thomas was Henry himself, who protested that he had never intended the death of his one-time friend, but had spoken only in anger. In July 1174 he joined the pilgrims to

The assassination of Archbishop Thomas Becket in Canterbury Cathedral, 29 December 1170, as depicted in a 13th-century manuscript illumination. Becket was assassinated by four of Henry II's knights following the king's alleged demand, 'Who will rid me of this turbulent priest?' The faithful throughout Europe soon began venerating Becket as a martyr, and he was canonized by Pope Alexander III in 1173, just three years after his death.

1153

Third expedition to England results in Treaty of Winchester (November), by which Stephen nominates Henry his heir

(25 October) Succeeds to the English throne

1154

(19 December) Crowned

c. 1155

Adrian IV, the English pope, issues the bull *Laudabiliter*, giving Henry his blessing to invade Ireland

1162

Thomas Becket becomes Archbishop of Canterbury

1164

Becket goes into exile

1166

Assize of Clarendon establishes trial by jury as the norm

Canterbury, walking in bare feet to the shrine. As a public demonstration of his penance, he doffed his shirt and begged the priests thrash his back with birch rods.

THE REVOLTS OF HENRY'S SONS

Henry's later years were dominated by squabbles with and between his sons over the disposal of his vast empire. Henry intended that England, Normandy, Maine and Anjou should go to his eldest son, Henry, known as 'the Young King', who was crowned as the appointed heir in 1170. His next son, Richard, would take over the northern part of Aquitaine, and Geoffrey, his third son, was to be married to the heiress of Brittany. His youngest son, John, was not granted any lands at this stage, hence his nickname 'Lackland'.

When in 1173 Henry granted John – his favourite – certain castles in Anjou, the young Henry was furious. The three elder brothers – supported by their mother Eleanor, from whom Henry had become estranged – mounted a revolt against their father, and were joined by those barons with grievances in both England and France. But the so-called Great Rebellion did not last long, and ended with the capture of the Scottish king (who had allied himself with the rebels) at the Battle of Alnwick in July 1174.

There was another falling out in 1182–3, when the young

The Irish adventure

Henry's efforts to extend his power to other parts of the British Isles beyond England met with mixed success. He made some inroads into Wales, receiving submission from two of the native princes. In 1174 he captured the Scottish king, William the Lion, made him do homage, and installed garrisons in the castles of Edinburgh, Roxburgh and Berwick.

But it was the Anglo-Norman incursion into Ireland that was to have the most far-reaching consequences. Early in his reign Henry had obtained the pope's blessing for the subjugation of the Irish, 'for the restraint of the downward course of vice, the correction of evil customs, the plantation of virtue, and the increase of the Christian religion'. Henry's plans were put on hold, and it was left to one of his barons, acting in a freelance capacity, to lead the way.

In 1166 Dermot MacMurrough, king of Leinster, was

driven from his kingdom, and came to England seeking help in the recovery of his throne. Henry gave permission to his barons to assist Dermot, should they so wish. In 1170 Richard de Clare, earl of Pembroke, nicknamed Strongbow, led a band of adventurers across the Irish Sea, Dermot having promised him the hand of his daughter and his kingdom after his death. Landing at Waterford, the Anglo-Normans seized the leading citizens, broke their limbs and threw them into the sea. They went on to take Dublin, and when Dermot died in 1171, Strongbow succeeded him.

Alarmed at one of his subjects assuming the title of king, Henry sailed to Ireland, and made Strongbow acknowledge him as his overlord. Ireland was thus absorbed into Henry's empire – although in reality English dominion only extended over a relatively small part of the island, known as the Pale.

The tomb of Eleanor of Aquitaine, at Fontevraud Abbey near Chinon, France. Shortly before her death Eleanor took the veil as a nun, and her tomb effigy shows her reading a bible. The abbey also contains the tombs of her husband Henry II, their son Richard I, their daughter Joan, their grandson Raymond VII of Toulouse, and Isabella of Angoulême, wife of their son King John.

1170
Invasion of Ireland by Richard de Clare (Strongbow)

1171
Strongbow acknowledges Henry as his overlord in Ireland

1173
Outbreak of Great Rebellion, led by Henry's sons

1174
(13 July) Great Rebellion ends with the defeat of William the Lion of Scotland at Alnwick

(July) Henry does penance at the shrine of St Thomas Becket

1176
Assize of Northampton makes land ownership dependent on royal law

1182–1183
Henry 'the Young King' rebels

1188–1189
Richard, Henry's oldest surviving son after the Young King's death, allies himself with the French king against his father

1189
(6 July) Death of Henry

Henry and Geoffrey allied themselves against Richard and his father, but this crisis passed when the young Henry died. Richard then became the king's principal heir, but was angered when his father indicated that he wanted Aquitaine to go to John, and even more incensed when, in 1184, he had to resist an invasion by John and Geoffrey.

Manoeuvring continued through the 1180s, with Richard allying himself with the French king – and finally with John – against his father. Two days before his death of a fever, Henry was forced to recognize Richard as his heir, and to do homage for all his French lands to Philip II of France. It was a humiliating end to a brilliant reign, and Henry's last recorded words were bitter: 'Shame,' he whispered, 'shame on a conquered king.'

RICHARD I LIONHEART

1189-1199

It was from his status as a Crusader and warrior king that Richard earned his byname *Coeur de Lion* or Lionheart. Although he was for centuries celebrated as one of the heroes of English history, Richard was in fact a Frenchman – only his great-grandmother Matilda was English – and during his ten-year reign he spent only six months in England.

Biography

There have been considerable debates among historians as to Richard's merits as a king. For many years he was depicted as vainglorious and neglectful of his responsibilities towards England. But more recently historians have veered towards the view that, by going on crusade, Richard was only doing what was expected of a Christian monarch, and that his campaigns in France, like those of his father, were in defence of the heart of the Angevin Empire.

BORN 8 September 1157, at Beaumont Palace, Oxford

FATHER Henry II

MOTHER Eleanor of Aquitaine

MARRIED Berengaria of Navarre

CHILDREN No legitimate offspring

SUCCEEDED 6 July 1189

CROWNED 3 September 1189

ROYAL HOUSE Plantagenet

STYLE *Rex Angliae, Dux Norminiae et Aquitaniae et Comes Andigaviae* ('King of England, Duke of Normandy and Aquitaine and Count of Anjou')

DIED 6 April 1199, at Châlus, in the Limousin

BURIED Fontevraud Abbey

CHARACTER AND EARLY LIFE

Richard was a man of culture (he wrote troubadour poetry in both French and Provençal), but was also capable of fierce outbreaks of temper, and of great cruelty. He was praised at the time for his courage and his chivalry, and his decisiveness led to his contemporary nickname 'Richard Yea and Nay'. Some historians have suggested he was a homosexual, but there is no conclusive evidence: although his marriage was without issue, he fathered at least one illegitimate child. Physically, Richard was tall, blond and blue-eyed, and from an early age he seems to have found his *métier* in soldiering.

After his parents became estranged, Richard was brought up in France by his mother, Eleanor. The 1170s and 1180s saw a series of manoeuvrings and revolts by Richard and his brothers, as they vied for the choicest parts of their father's empire. Richard had to fight hard for his share, and just before his father's death in July 1189 he forced the old king to acknowledge him as heir to an undivided inheritance.

RICHARD TAKES THE CROSS

Quite what motivated Richard to take the cross and go on crusade is unclear, but the capture of Jerusalem by Saladin in October 1187 was the spur. Perhaps Richard wished to make amends for past sins. Chief among these was cruelty, of such an extreme variety that it had pushed his Gascon subjects to rebellion. In addition,

Richard was accused (by the preacher Fulk of Neuilly) of consorting with three ladies of easy virtue, namely *'Superbia, Luxuria et Cupiditas'* (in other words, pride, luxury and greed). To these one might add persistent rumours of sodomy.

Richard waited until he was firmly established on the English throne before embarking on his great adventure. He also sought to secure his French territories by persuading Philip II of France to join him on crusade. This achieved, Richard set about raising money to fund a great army, selling offices, lands and titles to the highest bidder. He even made his chancellor, William Longchamp, reapply for his job, at a cost of £3,000. 'I would have sold London if I could have found a buyer,' he famously remarked.

FOREIGN ADVENTURES

Richard set sail on 12 December 1189. En route for Palestine, he stopped at Sicily, where he forcibly obtained the succession for his nephew Arthur – to the annoyance of the German emperor, who also had designs on the island. Richard then sailed for Cyprus, which he conquered, and where he married Berengaria of Navarre, the territory to the south of Aquitaine. Richard had previously been engaged to Alice, sister of Philip II of France, but he presumably regarded Navarre as a more reliable ally.

Richard landed at Acre, in the Holy Land, on 8 June 1191, and the following month the Crusaders captured the city. In September Richard scored a great victory at Arsuf, and took Joppa. But the capture of Jerusalem evaded him, and the Crusaders became bogged down in squabbles among themselves. A year after Arsuf Richard agreed a three-year truce with Saladin, under which the Crusaders kept control of Acre and a thin strip of coast, and Christian pilgrims had unfettered access to the holy sites.

The coronation of Richard I in Westminster Abbey, as depicted in a 14th-century manuscript illumination. In the background, the Norman town of Gisors is shown in flames, an allusion to Richard's defeat near here of Philip II of France in 1198. Tradition has it that it was at the Battle of Gisors that Richard first used 'Dieu et mon droit' ('God and my right') as his motto, echoing his earlier boast to the Emperor Henry that his rank as king acknowledged no superior but God.

Timeline

1157
(8 September) Birth of Richard

1168
Becomes duke of Aquitaine

1172
Becomes duke of Poitiers

1173–1174
Rebels against his father
Henry II

1182–1183
Resists attacks by his brothers
Henry and Geoffrey

1189
(4 July) Forces Henry II to
recognize him as his heir

(6 July) Succeeds his father
Henry II as king of England,
duke of Normandy and count
of Anjou

(3 September) Crowned as king
of England

(12 December) Embarks from
England on Third Crusade

The massacre of the Jews

An unfortunate accompaniment to the revival of the
crusading spirit was an outbreak of hostility to
those of different faiths – and in England this meant
the small communities of Jews. There was a
pogrom in London, while in York the small Jewish
community took refuge in Clifford's Tower, and there
burnt themselves to death rather than fall into the
hands of the mob.

THE LONG JOURNEY HOME

On his way back from Palestine, Richard was captured by Duke
Leopold of Austria, whom he had insulted in Palestine by tearing
down his banner. Leopold handed Richard over to his overlord,
the German emperor, Henry VI. According to medieval romances,
Richard's faithful minstrel Blondel found his master by singing
his favourite song outside one castle after another, until, outside
the walls of Dürnstein on the Danube, he heard the voice of his
master join in the refrain.

The more prosaic truth is that the emperor let it be known
that a ransom of £100,000 would be acceptable. The money was
raised and Richard was released, landing at Sandwich in Kent on 13
March 1194. He had been away from England for over four years.

JOHN SCHEMES FOR THE THRONE

The uncertainty about Henry II's succession had not been entirely
banished by his death. In exchange for lands in England, Richard
made his brother John promise to stay out of the country for three
years while he was away on crusade. Richard's half-brother
Geoffrey (an illegitimate son of Henry II) had also made such a
promise. Neither kept to their word.

John took advantage of Richard's imprisonment to plot against
his brother with the French king, Philip II, who had returned from
crusade in 1191. John did homage to Philip for Richard's lands in
France (and possibly also for England), and agreed to marry
Philip's sister Alice. As Philip planned to invade England, John
announced that Richard was dead. Few in England believed him,
and the truth emerged when the emperor's ransom demand was received. On
Richard's return John threw himself on his brother's mercy. ' Think no more of it,'
Richard reassured him. 'You are only a child who has
had evil counsellors.'

RICHARD'S LAST YEARS

Richard left England for the last time in May 1194,
having arranged for himself a second coronation
ceremony during his brief, two-month sojourn. The
kingdom was left in the hands of Hubert Walter,
Archbishop of Canterbury. Richard spent his few
remaining years fighting in France to recover the
territories seized in his absence by Philip II.

It was Richard's continuing dalliance with *Cupiditas* (whose company Fulk the preacher had enjoined him to eschew) that was to lead to Richard's death, at the age of 42. Hearing that the viscount of Limoges, one of his more unruly barons, had acquired a hoard of buried treasure, Richard laid siege to the viscount's castle at Châlus. He was shot in the shoulder by a bolt from a crossbow, and the surgeon who pulled out the barbed head made a mess of the procedure. The wound turned gangrenous, and as Richard lay on his deathbed he asked to speak to Bertram de Gourdon, the man who had fired the bolt.

> *'What harm did I ever do thee,' asked the king, 'that thou should'st kill me?'*
>
> *'You killed with your own hand my father and two of my brothers,' replied Bertram, 'and you likewise designed to have killed me. You may take your revenge. I should cheerfully suffer all the torments that can be inflicted were I sure of having delivered the world of a tyrant who filled it with blood and carnage.'*

Richard was impressed by this courageous answer, and ordered that Bertram be given his freedom and a hundred marks. However, after the king's death, the unfortunate agent of his end was flayed alive.

1191
(12 May) Marries Berengaria of Navarre in Cyprus

(8 June) Lands at Acre, in the Holy Land

(July) Fall of Acre to the Crusaders

(7 September) Richard defeats Saladin at Arsuf

1192
(October) Leaves the Holy Land, but is taken prisoner on the way home by Duke Leopold of Austria

1193
(June) Agrees terms for his release

1194
(February) Released from captivity

(13 March) Arrives back in England

(17 April) Crowned for a second time as king of England

(May) Leaves England for the last time

1199
(6 April) Death of Richard

JOHN
1199-1216

Apart from Richard III, King John has had the worst press of any English king. The traditional view of John – which began to emerge towards the end of his own reign – was that he was a cruel, grasping, treacherous and incompetent tyrant, who schemed against his noble brother Richard, imposed oppressive taxes on his subjects, and lost his father's empire in France. The only good to come out of his reign was Magna Carta, the charter of English liberties.

Biography

So goes the legend. Some of this appalling reputation was deserved, but not all of it. John was dealt a tricky hand, and played it with mixed success. Some historians have praised his abilities as an administrator and diplomat, and others have justified his extortions as the only means by which he could fund the defence of his French lands. Had he not lost Normandy and Anjou, posterity might have judged him more sympathetically.

BORN 24 December 1167, at Beaumont Palace, Oxford

FATHER Henry II

MOTHER Eleanor of Aquitaine

MARRIED (1) Isabella of Gloucester, (2) Isabella of Angoulême

CHILDREN Henry (the future Henry III), Richard, Joan (later married to Alexander II of Scotland), Isabella (later married to the Emperor Frederick II), Eleanor, all from his second marriage

SUCCEEDED 6 April 1199

CROWNED 27 May 1199, at Westminster Abbey

ROYAL HOUSE Plantagenet

STYLE *Johannes Rex Angliae et Dominus Hiberniae, Dux Norminiae et Aquitaniae et Comes Andigaviae* ('John, King of England, Lord of Ireland, Duke of Normandy and Aquitaine and Count of Anjou'

DIED 18/19 October 1216, at Newark Castle

BURIED Worcester Cathedral

THE RIVAL BROTHERS

John acquired the nickname 'John Lackland' as an infant, when his father Henry II arranged for the future disposition of his empire. John's three elder brothers – Henry, Richard and Geoffrey – were all promised extensive territories, but at this stage John, Henry's favourite, received nothing.

But towards the end of his reign, Henry stated his intention of presenting his youngest son with Aquitaine. This pushed John's only surviving brother, Richard, into rebellion. Just before his father's death, John changed sides. Perhaps more out of expediency than gratitude, when he succeeded to the throne Richard made his younger brother count of Mortain and granted him valuable estates in England.

Their amity was short-lived, however. When in 1190 John heard that Richard – then away on crusade – had named as his heir his infant nephew, Arthur of Brittany, John broke the oath he had made not to return to England while Richard was out of the country. While in England John conspired to seize the throne, but his plans were scotched by Richard's return in 1194. Five years later, as he lay dying, the surprisingly forgiving Richard named John as his heir.

King John hunting a stag with hounds. John's political incompetence was such that between 1203 and 1206 most of the Plantagenet empire in western and northern France – Normandy, Anjou, Maine and Brittany – was lost to Philip II Augustus of France.

The end of Prince Arthur

The disappearance of Arthur after his capture at Mirabeau in August 1202 led to suspicions that he had been murdered on the orders of King John. The young prince, then aged about 15, was imprisoned first at Falaise Castle, then in the castle at Rouen. In Shakespeare's *King John*, it is Hubert de Burgh, Arthur's jailer, who is held responsible, having taken a heavy hint from the king:

> *Good Hubert, Hubert, Hubert, throw thine eye*
> *On yon young boy: I'll tell thee what, my friend,*
> *He is a very serpent in my way;*
> *And whereso'er this foot of mine doth tread,*
> *He lies before me: dost thou understand me?*
> *Thou art his keeper …*

This is pure surmise. More historically, Hubert does appear to have had some knowledge of Arthur's death: at one point he made a claim (later withdrawn) that Arthur died of shock as he was castrated by John's agents. The *Margam Annals* stated that John, while 'drunk and possessed of the Devil', killed the prince with his own hand. Although this is unlikely, the consensus among historians today is that John, one way or another, was responsible for Arthur's death.

THE LOSS OF THE ANGEVIN EMPIRE

The question of the succession was not so easily settled, however. Some of the barons in France preferred as their overlord young Arthur of Brittany – son of John's elder brother Geoffrey. Considerable manoeuvring now ensued, but in 1200 John acknowledged Philip II of France as his overlord in his French territories, and Arthur in turn acknowledged John as his overlord.

At this stage John's determination to have his own way embroiled him in the internal politics of Aquitaine. His marriage to Isabella of Gloucester having been dissolved, John took as his second wife another Isabella, the heiress of Angoulême, who had previously been betrothed to Hugh de Lusignan. Hugh and his followers were incensed and rebelled against John, their overlord, and appealed to Philip II. As John failed to appear at Philip's court to explain himself, in 1202 Philip declared all John's French lands forfeit, and handed Anjou and Normandy to Arthur. He then proceeded to wage war against his disobedient vassal.

Despite the capture of Arthur in August of that year and his subsequent disappearance, John's position in France became progressively weaker. By 1204 he had lost Normandy and Anjou, earning the nickname 'Softsword' for his perceived military incompetence. His Angevin Empire was in tatters, reduced to a fragment of Aquitaine and a few insignificant islands in the Channel.

1167
(24 December) Born

1177
Awarded the title 'Lord of Ireland'

1185
John visits Ireland, but alienates both natives and English settlers

1189
Joins his brother Richard in rebellion against their father, Henry II

1190
Returns to England in Richard's absence

1193
Allies with Philip II of France against Richard

1194
Richard forgives John

1199
(6 April) John succeeds his brother Richard

(25 April) Installed as duke of Normandy

(27 May) Crowned king of England

1200
(22 May) By Treaty of Le Goulet, does homage to Philip II of France for his French territories

(August) Marries Isabella of Angoulême

1202
(spring) Philip launches a war against John

ATTEMPTED RECOVERY

John devoted the next ten years to planning the recovery of his French possessions. To raise the necessary cash for a military campaign, he rigorously enforced his prerogatives in England and efficiently collected taxes, measures that alienated him from many of his subjects.

John also fell out with the pope over the latter's appointment in 1206 of Stephen Langton as Archbishop of Canterbury, in place of John's nominee. The dispute led to John's excommunication, and for some years John took advantage of the breakdown in relations with Rome to add various ecclesiastical revenues to his war chest. (The downside was the unfavourable coverage he received from the monastic chroniclers, who as a result of this schism depicted the king in the worst possible light.)

But John needed the support of the papacy if he was to recover his French lands, and so, in 1213, he came to an accommodation, accepting Langton as archbishop and surrendering England to the pope, receiving it back as a papal vassal.

With the support not only of the pope, but also of the Holy Roman Emperor and the counts of Boulogne and Flanders, John landed in France in February 1214. But at the Battle of Bouvines in July he was decisively defeated by Philip II. By October he was back in England, with nothing to show his disgruntled people for the heavy burden he had placed on them for so many years.

CIVIL WAR IN ENGLAND

Rebellion broke out among the English barons in May of 1215, and by June John was forced to acknowledge their grievances by putting his seal to Magna Carta. John was just buying time, however, and asked his ally the pope to annul the charter.

Once the pope had complied with John's wish and annulled Magna Carta, civil war broke out once more, and the rebels invited Prince Louis of France (the future Louis VIII) to come to England to take the crown. Louis landed in May 1216 and he and his supporters were soon in control of large parts of the country.

John's death that autumn changed everything. His spirit and his health had been broken by the loss of his treasures while his baggage train attempted to cross, at low tide, the inlet of the North Sea called the Wash. While staying at Newark Castle he

Magna Carta

The 'Great Charter' that John put his seal to at Runnymede on the Thames in June 1215 set limits on the powers of the monarch, laid out the feudal obligations of the barons, confirmed the liberties of the English Church, and granted rights and liberties 'to all freemen of the realm and their heirs for ever'. Two of the most famous of its 63 clauses read (in part):

39. No freeman shall be arrested, or detained in prison, or deprived of his freehold, or outlawed, or exiled, or in any way molested ... except by the lawful judgement of his peers and by the law of the land. 40. To no one will we sell, to no one will we deny or delay, right or justice.

Magna Carta is regarded as the first written constitution in European history – although at the time it was only the better-off who benefited from it.

1203
(December) John returns to England

1204
(March) Philip captures John's fortress at Château Gaillard, and proceeds to take most of his French territories

1206
John falls out with the pope over the appointment of Stephen Langton as Archbishop of Canterbury

1209
John wages a successful campaign in Scotland

1210
Successfully campaigns in Ireland

1211
Successfully campaigns in North Wales

1213
Reconciled with the pope

1214
(February) Lands at La Rochelle, France

(July) Decisively beaten by Philip II at Bouvines

1215
(May) Rebellion in England

(June) John puts his seal to Magna Carta

1216
(May) Prince Louis of France invades England at the request of the barons

(18/19 October) Death of John

became seriously ill after consuming peaches and beer, and died on the night of 18/19 October, probably of dysentery.

None of the rebels could sustain their grievances against John's son Henry, then not yet ten years old. Nor was Prince Louis ever going to be a popular choice as king: in the historically inaccurate but politically astute words of Philip the Bastard that end Shakespeare's *King John,*

> *This England never did, nor never shall,*
> *Lie at the proud foot of a conqueror.*

Henry was crowned king on 28 October, Magna Carta was reissued in November, and, following military reverses the following year, Louis withdrew his claim to the throne of England.

 Foul as it is, Hell itself is defiled by the fouler presence of John.
MATTHEW PARIS (C. 1200–59).

Henry III
1216-1272

The reign of Henry III was one of the longest of any English monarch, but is also one of the least known. Henry had an elevated notion of the absolute rights of a king. But he lacked sound judgement, and this, combined with the arrogance and pig-headedness of his Plantagenet genes, led to a baronial revolt led by Simon de Montfort.

Biography

Both a cultured and a pious man, Henry was a great patron of the arts, his most memorable achievement being the rebuilding of Westminster Abbey. Physically, he was of stocky build, with a narrow forehead and one eyelid that drooped.

SUCCESSION OF A BOY-KING

Henry was the first king since the Norman Conquest to succeed while still a minor. He was only nine years old when his father, King John, died, and the country was in the throes of the First Barons' War. The rebels had invited Prince Louis of France to come to England to take the throne, but with the death of the old tyrant, many of the barons were content to back the new boy-king and his regent, William, Earl Marshal, a veteran warrior described by his contemporaries as 'so fine a knight, so upright, so respected, so wise'.

London being in the hands of the rebels, Henry's coronation took place on 28 October 1216 in the abbey church at Gloucester, the ceremony being conducted by the Bishop of Winchester. It was a simple affair: the crown jewels were elsewhere, as was the Archbishop of Canterbury, Stephen Langton, who was in Rome, appealing against his suspension by the pope for his support of Magna Carta.

SEEING OFF THE FRENCH

Under William the Marshal, England rapidly returned to stability. In November 1216 Magna Carta – whose abrogation by John had precipitated the First Barons' War – was reissued (albeit minus some controversial clauses), so appeasing the rebel barons. Prince Louis was defeated by the Marshal at the 'Tournament of Lincoln' six months later, so called because it was fought in the narrow lanes of the city.

In August 1217, Louis attempted to bring reinforcements across the Channel, but the French fleet, under its piratical

BORN 1 October 1207, at Winchester Castle

FATHER King John

MOTHER Isabella of Angoulême

MARRIED Eleanor of Provence

CHILDREN Edward (later Edward I), Margaret (later married to Alexander III of Scotland), Beatrice (later married to Duke John of Brittany), Edmund Crouchback (i.e. 'cross back', from the cross he was entitled to wear, having participated in the Ninth Crusade), Katherine (died in infancy)

SUCCEEDED 18/19 October 1216

CROWNED 28 October 1216, at Gloucester Abbey

ROYAL HOUSE Plantagenet

STYLE *Rex Angliae, Dominus Hiberniae et Dux Aquitaniae* ('King of England, Lord of Ireland and Duke of Aquitaine')

DIED 16 November 1272, at Westminster

BURIED Westminster Abbey

commander Eustace the Monk (a man said to be in league with the Devil), was decisively defeated off Sandwich, in the first great English naval victory. The battle was notable for its use of chemical weapons: at one point the English hurled pots of powdered quicklime onto the deck of the French flagship, blinding her crew with the burning dust.

By the Treaty of Kingston later that year, Louis withdrew from England, and Henry's position was secured. He was crowned again in 1220, this time with more pomp and ceremony, and the following year Alexander II of Scotland did homage to Henry and married his sister.

THE KING ACHIEVES HIS MAJORITY

William the Marshal died in 1219, and was succeeded as justiciar (chief minister) by Hubert de Burgh, who carried on the business of the kingdom until in 1232 Henry dismissed Hubert and took over himself. Henry aspired towards a model of kingship in which the monarch's power was divinely sanctioned and absolute, untrammelled by the nit-picking constitutionalism embodied in Magna Carta. Perhaps Henry's attitude was in reaction to the humiliations suffered by his father, but if his pride remembered those humiliations, his reason forgot the lessons they taught.

For long periods Henry ruled without any official ministers, and alienated his English subjects by appointing his French relatives to a number of lucrative positions. (Some of these relatives he acquired following his marriage to Eleanor of Provence in 1236.) The contemporary chronicler Matthew Paris recalled:

> At this time the king daily, and not just slowly, lost the affection of his natural subjects. For like his father he openly attracted to his side whatever foreigners he could, and enriched them, introducing aliens and scorning and despoiling Englishmen.

Henry got into further difficulties with his expensive foreign adventures. His top priority was the restoration of those lands in France that had been lost by his father, but his three campaigns in France (1230, 1242 and 1253) met with little success. In 1254 he secured from the pope the kingdom of Sicily for his son Edmund, but needed to raise a huge sum to pay back the pope or face excommunication. Henry's solution was simple: he would screw his English subjects for every last penny.

THE BARONS DEMAND REFORM

With a heavy burden of taxation and no representation, the barons had had enough. They insisted on reform, and this was embodied in the Provisions of Oxford, drawn up by a committee of barons in 1258. The Provisions established rule through a Council of Fifteen, acting with the king, restored the post of justiciar or chief minister, and called for three parliaments a year. 'Parliament' was a new word, derived from the French *parler*, to speak, but at this stage was little more than a grand council of the nobility. Further reforms were contained in the Provisions of Westminster, drawn up

1207
(10 October) Birth of Henry

1216
(18/19 October) Succeeds

(28 October) Crowned at Gloucester Abbey

(12 November) Magna Carta reissued

1217
(24 August) French invasion fleet defeated off Sandwich

1220
(17 May) Second coronation of Henry, at Westminster

1221
King of Scotland does homage to Henry

1224
Louis VII of France seizes Poitou and northern Gascony from Henry

1228
Death of Stephen Langton, Archbishop of Canterbury

1230
Campaigning in France

1232
(29 July) Henry dismisses Hubert de Burgh and assumes the reins of government

1236
(14 January) Marries Eleanor of Provence

1242
Campaigning in France

1253
Campaigning in France

in 1259. Among its clauses, one aimed particularly at Henry's French favourites insisted that all offices of state and the command of all castles be restricted to Englishmen.

Irked by these impertinent limitations on his power, in 1261 Henry persuaded the pope to absolve him of the oaths he had made to uphold them. It was only a matter of time before things would come to a violent head.

Simon de Montfort and the Second Barons' War

Civil war broke out in 1264. At the head of the rebellious barons was Simon de Montfort, earl of Leicester, the husband of Henry's sister Eleanor. De Montfort is a controversial figure, acclaimed by many as a great champion of the oppressed and denigrated by others as a cynical power-broker.

On 14 May 1264 de Montfort and his ally, Gilbert de Clare, earl of Gloucester, led the barons to victory at Lewes, capturing the king, his son Edward and his brother Richard. After the battle, one of de Montfort's supporters declared that 'now law rules the royal dignity, for law is light and rules the world'.

De Montfort was left as virtual ruler of England, although he had no intention of replacing the king, even though, in the words of the chronicler Roger of Wendover, 'the king himself had nothing but the shadow of a name'. In January 1265 de Montfort summoned a parliament that included not just the nobility, but also knights, burgesses from the towns, and representatives of the clergy – a landmark in English constitutional history.

In May Prince Edward escaped from de Montfort's custody, and Gloucester changed sides and joined him. Edward, a far more capable figure than his father both politically and militarily, raised an army, and in August decisively defeated de Montfort's forces at Evesham. De Montfort himself was killed and horribly mutilated.

More frightening than the thunder

In July 1258 Henry was forced to seek refuge from a thunderstorm in the Palace of the Bishop of Durham on the Thames. Here he met the leader of the discontented barons, Simon de Montfort, to whom he said: 'I fear thunder and lightning beyond measure; but, by God's head, I fear you more than all the thunder and lightning in the world.'

But de Montfort's reforms did not die with him. Although Henry's authority was restored, the Statute of Marlborough (1267) reaffirmed Magna Carta and some of the Provisions of Oxford.

HENRY'S LAST YEARS

As stability returned to the kingdom, the old king turned away from politics towards less worldly matters. Edward the Confessor had been canonized in 1261, and in 1269 his remains were reinterred in the new shrine created for him in Henry's greatest project, the magnificent new abbey church at Westminster. Having heard that St Edward dressed in a simple fashion, Henry followed suit, and when he died he was buried in the saint's old tomb.

Although history has judged Henry one of England's least remarkable kings, he was immortalized by Dante in *The Divine Comedy*. The Italian poet pictured Henry in a flower-strewn valley in Purgatory, the destination of all those princes who neglect the well-being of their realms:

> Vedete il re de la semplice vita
> seder là solo, Arrigo d'Inghilterra:
> questi ha ne' rami suoi migliore uscita.
> *Behold the king of the simple life,*
> *Harry of England, sitting there alone:*
> *He through his branches a better issue yields.*

In 1271 Simon de Montfort's sons Guy and Simon avenged their father's death at Evesham by murdering the king's nephew, Prince Henry of Cornwall, while he attended mass at Viterbo, north of Rome. In *The Divine Comedy*, Dante assigned Guy to the seventh circle of hell for this sacrilegious act.

1254
Secures kingdom of Sicily for his son Edmund

1258
Provisions of Oxford

1259
Provisions of Westminster

Henry renounces his claims to Normandy, Maine and Anjou, and does homage to the French king for Gascony

1261
(12 June) Henry abrogates the Provisions of Westminster

1264
(14 May) Henry and his sons defeated and captured by Simon de Montfort at Lewes

1265
(January) De Montfort's parliament

(4 August) De Montfort defeated and killed at Evesham

1266
Henry restored to full power

1267
Statute of Marlborough

Henry III recognizes Llywelyn ap Gruffudd as prince of Wales in return for Llywelyn's submission

1272
(16 November) Death of Henry

EDWARD I

1272-1307

A man of immense vigour, Edward was a complete contrast to his father, the timorous, languid and neglectful Henry III. Above all, Edward was a soldier, 'the best lance in the world' according to a French troubadour, and with it a terror to his neighbours. For the Welsh and the Scots, Edward still represents the archetype of the cruel English oppressor – hence his nickname, 'Hammer of the Scots'.

Biography

BORN 17 June 1239, at Westminster

FATHER Henry III

MOTHER Eleanor of Provence

MARRIED (1) Eleanor of Castile, (2) Marguerite of France

CHILDREN By his first marriage there were at least 14 children, but only the following survived beyond childhood: Eleanor (later married to Alfonso III of Aragon); Joan of Acre; Margaret; Mary (became a nun); Elizabeth of Rhuddlan; Edward of Caernarfon (the future Edward II). By his second marriage: Thomas, earl of Norfolk; Edmund, earl of Kent

SUCCEEDED 20 November 1272

CROWNED 19 August 1274

ROYAL HOUSE Plantagenet

STYLE *Rex Angliae, Dominus Hiberniae et Dux Aquitaniae* ('King of England, Lord of Ireland and Duke of Aquitaine')

DIED 7 July 1307, at Burgh-by-Sands, Cumberland

BURIED Westminster Abbey

Edward's martial predilections were accompanied by an autocratic disposition, and a tendency towards brutality and violence. He was also, paradoxically, an effective diplomat in the cause of peace, being persuasive – and persuadable – in argument and reasonable in judgement. But if thwarted his temper could be fearsome.

In appearance Edward was slender of face and bearded, with a broad brow and regular features, apart from a drooping left eyelid (a characteristic he inherited from his father). He was wiry and athletic, an imposingly tall man for the period (when his grave was opened in 1774 his skeleton measured 6 ft 2 in), hence his other nickname, 'Longshanks'.

PRINCE EDWARD CUTS HIS TEETH

Edward's apprenticeship was a challenging one. During the period of baronial discontent in the late 1250s and early 1260s, his allegiances were uncertain, but when war broke out in 1264 he fought with the royalist army at Lewes against Simon de Montfort's rebels. The royalists were defeated, and Edward was taken hostage, but the following year he escaped and led the royalists to victory at Evesham. It was a grim fight: by the end of the day possibly only one in five of the rebels had escaped the slaughter. Edward went on to pursue a policy of extreme vengeance against the rebels, which may have prolonged their resistance.

Reconciliation was achieved by the end of 1266, and for the next few years Edward began to prove himself as a politician, playing an important part in the affairs of state. By 1270 the situation at home was stable enough for Edward to go on crusade. His aim was to relieve the Crusader stronghold of Acre, then under siege by the Egyptian

King Edward I with priests and courtiers in an illumination from a 12th-century manuscript. Edward I used Parliament to weaken the power of the nobility and the old feudal structures, and initiated a series of reforms. However, the main emphasis of his reign was his effort to unite the whole island of Britain under the English crown, earning him the nickname 'Hammer of the Scots'.

Mamelukes, and in 1272 he helped to negotiate a peace between the two sides. He was in Sicily, on his way home, when he heard that his father had died.

RULING ENGLAND

Edward did not arrive back in England until 1274, two years after his father's death. It says something for his reputation, and the stability he had helped to achieve in the last years of Henry's reign, that there were no conspiracies against him during the four years he was away from home. Indeed, unlike the majority of his Norman and Angevin predecessors, at no point during his reign did he face any armed challenge to his authority in England.

As soon as Edward returned from crusade, he ordered a commission into local administration, intent on weeding out corruption, particularly where it was at his expense. His government was firm but constitutional, and the first Parliament he summoned, in 1275, followed the precedent set by Simon de Montfort in 1265, in that it included elected knights

A devoted wife

When Edward was on crusade, he was wounded with a poisoned dagger in an assassination attempt. According to an Italian monk writing some fifty years later, his wife, Eleanor of Castile, tended him back to health:

With her tongue she licked his open wounds all the day, and sucked out the humour, and thus by her virtue drew out all the poisonous material.

This is almost certainly a fanciful tale, but Edward and Eleanor were devoted to each other, and she bore him at least 14 children. When Eleanor died at Harby in Nottinghamshire in 1290, Edward was heartbroken. He had her body brought back to London for burial in Westminster Abbey, and at each of the places the funeral cortège stopped on the way he erected a cross. The most famous of these 'Eleanor Crosses' was at Charing Cross in London, but today only three survive, at Geddington, Hardingstone and Waltham.

Timeline

1239
(17 June) Birth of Edward

1254
(1 November) Marries Eleanor of Castile

1264
(14 May) Taken captive by Simon de Montfort at the Battle of Lewes

1265
(4 August) Defeats Simon de Montfort at Evesham

1270
Embarks on crusade

1271
(9 May) Arrives at Acre

A prince for the Welsh

and burgesses, as well as peers. Edward used Parliament to weaken the power of the nobility and the old feudal structures. He introduced numerous statutes, both in response to grievances, and in order to consolidate royal authority. This busy law-making earned him the title of 'the English Justinian'.

But with the erosion of the feudal system – whereby the barons gave military service in return for their lands – the king found himself more and more at the mercy of that other branch of government, Parliament. This new dispensation was thrown into sharp relief in 1297, when the barons refused to serve Edward in defence of his lands in Gascony.

It was only via Parliament that Edward could raise sufficient funds, via taxation, for his military campaigns. And Edward needed a very substantial war-chest indeed if he was to carry through his determination that all of the British Isles should acknowledge him as their overlord.

Caernarfon Castle, one of several castles in North Wales built on Edward's orders by the Savoyard master mason, James of St George. Caernarfon was, according to local legend, the birthplace of Constantine, the first Roman emperor to adopt Christianity, and the castle's polygonal towers topped by eagles, together with its bands of different coloured masonry, were deliberately designed in imitation of the walls of Constantinople, Constantine's capital.

THE WELSH QUESTION

For centuries Wales had been divided among a number of local chieftains and princes, often at odds with each other. Occasionally there arose a leader who attracted loyalty across the country, but this loyalty usually evaporated after the death of the prince in question.

Since Norman times the borders (or Marches) with England had been guarded by Marcher lords, often acting independently of the king, serving their own interests, and not always providing an effective deterrent against Welsh raids. From time to time English kings had mounted expeditions into the Welsh interior, but the native guerrilla forces had the advantage of the terrain, disappearing into the mountains and mists rather than risking a pitched battle.

In 1258, during the troubles between Henry III and his barons, Llywelyn ap Gruffudd, prince of Gwynedd, seized the opportunity to declare himself prince of Wales, and he was recognized as such by most of the Welsh chieftains – and, in 1267, by Henry himself. But Henry's successor was a different proposition, and when Llywelyn refused to acknowledge Edward as his overlord Edward determined to stamp his authority on the upstart prince.

THE CONQUEST OF WALES

Edward took his time. First of all he imposed an economic blockade. Then, rather than sending in heavy cavalry (which in earlier expeditions had become quickly bogged down in the trackless wastes) he dispatched lightly armed troops along the north coast from Chester, cutting a path through the forests. At the same time, the Marcher lords advanced from the east and south, and Edward's fleet sailed for Anglesey. Faced with starvation and overwhelming odds, Llywelyn agreed in 1277 to a settlement: although he kept his title, his rule was confined to the far north-west of the country.

The humiliation seems to have stoked the patriotic spirit of the Welsh, and in 1282 a popular rebellion broke out against the English. But this soon fizzled out after Llywelyn was killed in a skirmish. Another revolt in 1294–5 met with a similar fate. Thus Llywelyn became known, posthumously, as 'Llywelyn the Last'.

Edward consolidated his control of the unruly north-west of the country by building his 'Iron Ring' of castles around Snowdonia, at Harlech, Caernarfon, Conwy and Beaumaris, each a day's march from the next. Other new castles were built at strategic points throughout Wales. By the Statute of Rhuddlan (1284) Edward incorporated Wales into England, introduced the shire system and English laws, and appointed his own officials. Although some Welsh customs continued, a ban was placed on the use of the Welsh language in any official proceeding. Thus began 700 years of political and cultural subjugation.

RELATIONS WITH SCOTLAND AND FRANCE

The difficulties of the last two decades of Edward's reign overshadowed the achievements of the 1270s and 1280s. With the death of Queen Eleanor in 1290 and of his able chancellor, Robert Burnell, in 1292, Edward lost his best advisers. He found himself increasingly at loggerheads with both the Church and some of his magnates, and mired in conflicts in Scotland and France, the costs of which effectively bankrupted him.

1272
(22 May) Negotiates peace treaty between Kingdom of Acre and the Mameluke ruler Baybars I

(20 November) Succeeds to the throne

1273
(spring) Stays with Pope Gregory X at Orvieto

1273
(August) Pays homage in Paris to Philip III of France for his French lands

1274
(19 August) Crowned

1275
Holds his first Parliament, which, among other things, passes restrictions on the Jewish community

1277
Forces Llywelyn ap Gruffudd, prince of Wales, to acknowledge him as his overlord

1282
Crushes Welsh revolt

1284
Annexes Wales as part of England

(25 April) Birth of Prince Edward, Edward's heir

1289

Margaret, Maid of Norway, the infant queen of Scotland, is betrothed to Prince Edward

1290

(September) Margaret's death provokes a succession crisis in Scotland

(28 November) Death of Queen Eleanor

Edward expels the Jews from England, having expropriated their wealth

1292

(17 November) Edward recognizes John Balliol as king of Scotland, in return for Balliol's submission

1294

French attack Edward's lands in Gascony

1295

(5 July) The French and the Scots form an alliance against Edward

1296

(27 April) Edward defeats the Scots at Dunbar

1297

Campaigns in France

(11 September) William Wallace leads the Scots to victory at Stirling Bridge

1298

(22 July) Edward defeats Wallace at Falkirk

1299

(8 September) Marries Marguerite, sister of Philip IV of France

A 15th-century depiction of Edward I receiving homage from the Scots. In 1293, Edward summoned John Balliol to pay him homage at Westminster. Edward made it clear that he expected Balliol's military and financial support against France, but Balliol later made a pact with France, and prepared an army to invade England.

Two decades of reasonably good relations with the French crown came to an end in 1294 when the French seized Gascony. A decade of intermittent warfare and diplomacy followed. The English barons refused to fight for their king, and resisted his demands for money. In 1299 Edward married Marguerite, sister of Philip IV of France, and in 1303 Philip restored Edward's Gascon lands.

The conflict in Scotland was more intractable, but was more of Edward's own making. When the Scots king, Alexander III, died in 1286, he left as his heir the infant Margaret, known as the Maid of Norway (she was the child of Alexander's daughter, who died in childbirth, and the Norwegian king, Eric II). For centuries the kings of England had claimed overlordship of Scotland, and occasionally the Scots kings had made submission. Edward now saw an opportunity to resolve the irregularity once and for all by arranging, in 1289, the betrothal of Margaret to his son Edward, then a boy of five. But Edward's dream of a union of the crowns came to nought the following year when Margaret died at sea en route from Norway to Orkney.

THE WAR IN SCOTLAND

Presenting himself as honest broker, Edward informed the Scottish lords, who had recognized his authority in 1291, that he would decide among the various claimants as to who should have the Scottish crown. In 1292 Edward came out in favour of John Balliol, whom he assumed would be a biddable puppet. This turned out not to be the case: when Edward demanded the military and financial support of the Scots against the French, the Scottish nobles took matters into their own hands, making an alliance with France and preparing to resist Edward by force.

Edward responded predictably. He marched north, and massacred the inhabitants of the border town of Berwick. His forces, under the earl of Surrey, went on to defeat the Scottish army at Dunbar (April 1296). Balliol was forced to abdicate, and imprisoned in the Tower of London. Edward put Scotland directly under English rule.

Popular discontent with English rule in Scotland found a champion in William Wallace, a man of relatively modest background. He led a Scottish army to victory at Stirling Bridge in 1297, but the following year he was decisively beaten at Falkirk. He continued the fight, but his support fell away, until by 1304 nearly all the Scottish leaders had submitted to Edward. The following year Wallace was captured, taken to London, and hanged, drawn and quartered.

Not all the Scots bowed to the yoke. In 1306 Robert Bruce, who had been Balliol's chief rival for the throne, had himself crowned king. Shortly afterwards he was defeated at Methven and forced into hiding. But the following year he re-emerged, and gathered widespread support. Edward marched north once more, determined to crush the upstart. But he never reached Scotland, dying at Burgh-by-Sands near Carlisle, just south of the border.

Edward's body was buried in Westminster Abbey, and on his tomb the following words were engraved:

> Hic est Edwardvs Primus Scottorum Malleus
> *Here is Edward I, Hammer of the Scots.*

He may have hammered the Scots, but he failed to crush them. It was left to his son to try again, but English pride was to suffer a fall at Bannockburn.

A statue of William Wallace, hero of the Scottish War of Independence, on Union Terrace, Aberdeen. Wallace won a famous victory over the English at the Battle of Stirling Bridge in 1297. Eight years later, however, he was captured and taken to London, where he was hanged, drawn and quartered. His dismembered limbs were displayed in four different locations in northern England and Scotland: in Newcastle, Berwick, Stirling and Aberdeen.

1301
(7 February) Edward makes his son prince of Wales

1303
(20 May) By the Treaty of Paris, Philip IV of France returns Gascony to Edward

1304
(March) The Scottish Parliament submits to Edward

1306
(19 June) Robert Bruce, having assumed the crown of Scotland, is defeated at Methven

1307
(7 July) Death of Edward

EDWARD II

1307-1327

Being the son of Edward Longshanks, Hammer of the Scots, Edward II had much to live up to. He failed miserably. He was not helped by the terrible state of the royal finances left him by his father, nor by the unfinished war in Scotland. But his disregard for the magnates and preference for self-seeking favourites immersed his realm in years of misgovernment, culminating in his overthrow and death.

Biography

Like his father, Edward was tall and good-looking, but he had none of the old king's martial or political abilities. He preferred athletics and artistic pursuits, and by nature he was untrustworthy and emotionally unstable. His relations with Edward Senior steadily deteriorated, and on one occasion (at least) his father attacked him physically, pulling out chunks of his hair. It was perhaps because he was so dominated by his father that Edward lacked the self-confidence to reject the blandishments of flattering favourites.

BORN 25 April 1284, at Caernarfon Castle

FATHER Edward I

MOTHER Eleanor of Castile

MARRIED Isabella of France

CHILDREN Edward (later Edward III), John of Eltham (later earl of Cornwall), Eleanor of Woodstock, Joanna (who married David II of Scotland)

SUCCEEDED 7 July 1307

CROWNED 25 February 1308

ROYAL HOUSE Plantagenet

STYLE *Rex Angliae, Dominus Hiberniae et Dux Aquitaniae* ('King of England, Lord of Ireland and Duke of Aquitaine')

DIED 20 or 21 January 1327, at Berkeley Castle

BURIED Gloucester Cathedral

PRINCE OF WALES

Edward – known as Edward of Caernarfon, after his place of birth – was the fourth son of Edward I and Eleanor of Castile, but the only one to survive into adulthood. In 1301 his father made him prince of Wales, to show the Welsh, whose land he had annexed, that their rulers would henceforth be English. Prince Edward accompanied his father on some of his Scottish campaigns, but showed no aptitude for the life of a soldier, being too frivolous and fond of luxury.

His father blamed his son's faults on the young Edward's favourite (and possibly his lover), a Gascon knight called Piers Gaveston. Matters came to head when Edward begged the earldom of Cornwall (normally a royal title) for his friend. According to the chronicler William of Guiseborough, Edward Senior responded with the following furious words:

> *You baseborn whoreson, do you want to give away lands now, you who never gained any?*

The king sent Gaveston into exile, but as soon as the young Edward succeeded to the throne, in July 1307, he abandoned his father's Scottish campaign and recalled Gaveston to

England, making him earl of Cornwall and giving him his niece's hand in marriage.

EARLY YEARS AS KING

Before he was crowned, Edward left Gaveston as his regent while he sailed across the Channel to marry Isabella, daughter of Philip IV of France. If Edward did have a sexual interest in men (and there is no absolute evidence), it was not to the exclusion of heterosexual activity: he had four children by his marriage to Isabella, and at least one illegitimate child.

The barons had learnt to mistrust Edward's father, and adapted the coronation oath in such a way that Edward was obliged to accept limitations to his authority. Edward does not appear to have taken his oath that seriously, and his indulgence of Gaveston led the barons to demand his exile in 1308. The following year the king recalled his favourite.

Another crisis arose in 1311, when the barons elected a committee known as the Ordainers. This group issued a manifesto of governmental reform known as the Ordinances, which sought to overhaul the royal finances and the administration of justice. They also put constraints on the king's actions: for example, he was not to leave the country or wage war without the approval of the barons in Parliament. Finally, the Ordainers called for the exile of Gaveston, charging the foreign favourite with a great list of crimes, including giving the king bad counsel and leading him into evil ways, expropriating royal treasure and royal powers, and estranging the king's heart from his people. Proud and greedy Gaveston may have been, but the barons were clearly jealous, and used Gaveston as a scapegoat for the king's own misrule.

When the king reneged on his promises, the baronial opposition, led by Edward's cousin Thomas, earl of Lancaster, rose in revolt. Gaveston, who had returned from exile, was seized and put to death.

HUMILIATION IN SCOTLAND

While Edward was taken up with attempting to protect his favourite, the Scottish king, Robert the Bruce, was steadily freeing his country from English domination.

Edward II, seated on a bench and holding a sceptre in his left hand, surrenders his crown to his son Edward III, in a manuscript illumination from the early 14th-century Anglo-Norman chronicle of Peter Langtoft. Edward II came to the throne as an energetic 23-year-old, amidst great optimism that he would continue his father's martial legacy. But his reign ended in disaster, with his imprisonment and subsequent murder at Berkeley Castle.

c. 1284
(25 April) Birth of Edward

1301
Declared prince of Wales

1307
(7 July) Succeeds to the throne, and recalls his favourite, Piers Gaveston, from exile, whither he had been sent by Edward's father

1308
(25 January) Marries Isabella of France

(25 February) Crowned

(18 May) Gaveston exiled following pressure from barons

1309
Edward recalls Gaveston

1311
Barons draw up the Ordinances, which restrict the king's power and send Gaveston into exile again

1312
Gaveston returns from exile and is executed

1314
(24 June) Edward's army defeated by the Scots at Bannockburn

1319
(c. 20 September) A Scots army defeats the English at Myton-on-Swale, Yorkshire

1321
(19 August) Barons demand the exile of Edward's new favourites, the Despensers

After seeing off his Scottish rivals, he launched raids into England, offering a truce in return for cash. Once he had built up his war chest he turned his attention to ridding key Scottish castles of their English garrisons. By the spring of 1313, only the castle at Stirling remained in English hands. The Scots settled down for a long siege, and, after a parley, the English governor agreed to surrender the key if an English army had not appeared within sight of the castle by Midsummer Day 1314.

Edward, having hitherto demonstrated little vigour in his policy towards Scotland, now raised a massive army and marched north. On 23 June the English force arrived at Bannockburn, just south of Stirling. By the end of the following day, after a hard-fought battle against superior numbers (perhaps 6,000 against 10,000) the Scots emerged victorious. Some 200 English knights and an unknown number of infantry lay dead, and over 500 nobles were held for ransom.

THE RISE OF THE DESPENSERS

Edward scurried back south, his credibility as a king in tatters. Thomas of Lancaster took effective charge of the kingdom, but he proved no more competent than the king, and earned the enmity of a faction of the barons, led by Aymer de Valence. With the baronial opposition split, Edward recovered some authority, and chose Hugh le Despenser, earl of Winchester, as his chief adviser, and Despenser's son, also called Hugh, as his new favourite.

The king heaped privileges and estates on the Despensers, predictably arousing the jealousy of the barons, who, meeting in Parliament in 1321, decreed that father and son be sent into exile. Civil war broke out, with the earls of Lancaster and Hereford leading the rebels. They were defeated at Boroughbridge in 1322. Hereford was killed in battle, and Lancaster captured and executed.

With the support of the king, the Despensers, now back from exile, ruled England for the next five years. With the baronial opposition eliminated, the Ordinances of 1311 were revoked, restoring the power of the king. Over the next four years the rule of the Despensers and their small clique was marked by corruption, extortion and terror.

THE OVERTHROW OF EDWARD

Edward's queen, Isabella, disliked the favours he bestowed on his new favourites. She returned to France with her son, and there took as her lover Roger Mortimer, one of Edward's baronial opponents in the civil war. They mounted an invasion in 1326, and captured and killed the Despensers. Edward was also taken prisoner. In January 1327 Parliament declared that Edward:

> ... has as good as lost the lands of Gascony and Scotland through bad counsel and bad custody, and how likewise through bad counsel he had caused to be slain a great part of the noble blood of the land, to the dishonour and loss of himself, his realm and the whole people, and had done many other astonishing things. Therefore it was agreed by absolutely all the aforesaid that he ought no longer to reign but that his eldest son ... should reign and wear the crown in his stead.

Thus Edward was deposed, and his son, then aged 14, was acclaimed as Edward III.

The deposition was something of a nicety, as by the end of the month Edward II, held prisoner at Berkeley Castle, was dead. He was almost certainly murdered, but probably not 'with a hot spit put through the secret place posterial', as Ranulf Higden and later chroniclers would have us believe – presumably deeming it a suitable end for one suspected of homosexuality. The king's death was announced eight months later, on 21 September 1327.

1322
(16 March) Rebel barons defeated by royalists at Boroughbridge, leaving the Despensers unchallenged

(c. 12 October) Scots under Robert the Bruce defeat the English at Byland, Yorkshire

Repeal of the Ordinances of 1311

1326
Queen Isabella and Roger Mortimer invade England, kill the Despensers and capture Edward

1327
(20 or 21 January) Edward murdered at Berkeley Castle

EDWARD III

1327-1377

Edward III is traditionally viewed as the archetype of the chivalrous English monarch. At home he participated in tournaments, recreated Arthur's Round Table and founded the Order of the Garter, while in the field he led his country to great victories over the French. But by instigating the Hundred Years' War, Edward condemned vast areas of France – whose crown he claimed – to over a century of plunder, carnage and famine.

Biography

dward inherited the martial enthusiasms of his grandfather, Edward I, but with the rough edges polished off. He also inherited a dose of his grandfather's ruthlessness, and has been charged with opportunism, vanity and dissipation. None of these qualities was regarded at the time as ill-becoming a king. Edward had the affection and loyalty of his subjects – and achieved a degree of political stability in England unknown for some time.

BORN 13 November 1312, at Windsor Castle

FATHER Edward II

MOTHER Isabella of France

MARRIED Philippa of Hainault

CHILDREN Thirteen in all, including: Edward, the Black Prince (father of Edward III's heir, Richard II); Lionel, duke of Clarence; John of Gaunt, duke of Lancaster; Edmund, duke of York; Thomas of Woodstock

SUCCEEDED 20 January 1327

CROWNED 1 February 1327

ROYAL HOUSE Plantagenet

STYLE *Dei Gratia, Rex Angliae et Franciae, et Dominus Hiberniae* ('By the grace of God, King of England and France, and Lord of Ireland')

DIED 21 June 1377, at Sheen Palace

BURIED Westminster Abbey

EDWARD'S MINORITY

Prince Edward – known as Edward of Windsor because of his place of birth – was only 14 years old when his father was deposed and murdered. In a matter of days the young prince was crowned King Edward III, but it was the instigators of Edward II's overthrow, his wife Isabella (known disparagingly as the She-Wolf of France), and her lover Roger Mortimer, who took over the reins of government.

Their rule proved no less incompetent, unscrupulous and self-serving than that of the hated Despensers under Edward II. A particularly unpopular action was the signing of the Treaty of Northampton in 1328, whereby the English crown recognized Scotland as an independent, sovereign nation. This was no more than a recognition of the political reality following the Scottish victory at Bannockburn in 1314, but in England 'the Shameful Peace' was regarded as a national humiliation.

Among those who felt the sting most keenly was the young king himself. As Isabella and Mortimer steadily alienated one magnate after another, in October 1330 Edward – then not quite 18 – judged the time right to stage a coup d'état. While the dowager queen and her lover slept in the castle at Nottingham, a small band of the king's men circum-

Edward III does homage to Philip VI of France in a late 14th-century illumination. The Norman kings of England and their Plantagenet successors owned huge territories in France, but by the 1330s only Gascony in the southwest was still retained by the English king.

vented their armed guard and came to their rooms via one of the castle's subterranean passages. Mortimer was seized, taken to London and tried for a number of crimes, including the murder of Edward II at Berkeley Castle. He was hanged on 29 November, while Isabella was kept under house arrest for the rest of her life.

INTERVENTION IN SCOTLAND

When Robert the Bruce, the victor of Bannockburn, died in 1329, he was succeeded by his five-year-old son, David II. The succession was by no means universally greeted in Scotland, and a group of 'the Disinherited', who had lost estates during the Wars of Independence, rallied in exile around Edward Balliol, son of John Balliol, Edward I's puppet king in Scotland.

Just as his grandfather had backed a Balliol, so did Edward III, seeing him as a means of reversing 'the Shameful Peace'. In 1333 Edward intervened directly, scoring a great victory over the Scots at Halidon Hill. Balliol was installed as king of Scotland, for which he paid homage to the English king.

This was by no means the end of the matter. Civil war continued in Scotland, and in 1341 David II returned from exile. By 1346 he had established his position sufficiently to invade England, but was defeated at Neville's Cross, near Durham, and taken captive. But by this time Edward III's attention had long

❝Honi soit qui mal y pense.❞ 'EVIL BE TO HIM WHO EVIL THINKS' – THE MOTTO OF ENGLAND'S OLDEST ORDER OF KNIGHTHOOD, THE ORDER OF THE GARTER, FOUNDED BY EDWARD IN 1348..

Timeline

◆ **1312**
(13 November) Birth of Edward

◆ **1327**
(20 January) Succeeds

(1 February) Crowned

◆ **1328**
(24 January) Marries Philippa of Hainault

(17 March) Treaty of Northampton recognizes Scottish independence

◆ **1330**
(October) Edward takes power from his mother and her lover

◆ **1333**
(8 June) Isle of Man seized from the Scots

(19 July) Edward defeats the Scots at Halidon Hill

◆ **1337**
Outbreak of Hundred Years' War

◆ **1338**
French raid on Portsmouth

◆ **1340**
(25 January) Edward formally declares himself king of France

(24 June) The English defeat a French invasion fleet at the Battle of Sluys, off the Flemish coast

The Battle of Crécy, 26 August 1346, as depicted in an illumination from Jean Froissart's Chronicles. *Edward III's rout of the French owed much to the firepower of the massed English longbowmen, which overcame the traditional invincibility of the French heavy cavalry.*

1342
(31 March) Scots recapture Roxburgh and expel the English from Scotland

1346
(26 August) Edward defeats the French at Crécy

(17 October) Scots defeated at Neville's Cross, ending their invasion of England

1347
(4 August) English capture Calais

1348
(July–August) Black Death arrives in England

Edward founds Order of the Garter

1351
Statute of Labourers tries to put a freeze on labourers' wages, following manpower shortage caused by the Black Death

1355
Black Prince ravages France

1356
(20 January) Edward invades Scotland, and Edward Balliol repudiates his claim to the Scottish throne in favour of the English king

(19 September) Black Prince defeats French at Poitiers

1360
(8 May) Treaty of Brétigny ushers in lull in Hundred Years' War

1369
Resumption of Hundred Years' War

been diverted by his campaign to take the throne of France – a far greater prize than the rain-drenched moorlands of the north.

CLAIMANT TO THE THRONE OF FRANCE

Edward III's mother, Isabella, was the sister of King Philip IV of France. When in 1328 Charles IV of France died without a direct male heir, Edward had a strong claim to the French throne, although the crown passed to Charles's nephew, who became Philip VI. Quite how seriously Edward himself took his claim is difficult to assess, but it provided a legitimization of various other reasons for waging war in France.

Since the time of Henry II the kings of England had also been dukes of Aquitaine, a vast area of south-west France for which they did homage to the French king. But on many occasions Edward's predecessors had had to fight to protect their French lands from incursions by the French crown. A further thorn in the side of English kings was the 'Auld Alliance' between France and Scotland, forged during the reign of Edward I, which meant that England often found itself fighting a war on two fronts. There was also an economic imperative: the cloth-weavers of Flanders, one of the great manufacturing centres of western Europe, were subjects of

The Black Death

It was during Edward's reign that England was struck by the Black Death, an outbreak of plague in both its bubonic and pneumonic forms. The epidemic arrived in 1348, and there were further outbreaks in the 1360s and 1370s, leading to the deaths of between one-third and one-half of the population, and causing social and economic dislocation.

the French crown, but their livelihood depended on imports of English wool. Therefore it would be better for business if the king of England could also be the king of France.

Perhaps above all, for Edward and his young followers, brought up on the romances of chivalry, war in France was the path to glory – and also the path to fertile lands and untold wealth.

The first forty years of the war

Hostilities began in 1337, Edward forming alliances with the towns and nobles of the Low Countries and campaigning in Flanders. This strategy proved costly for Edward, and the heavy tax burden that resulted was very unpopular in England. Yet Edward managed to weather the domestic storm, and his fortunes in France began to turn when some of the nobles in Brittany and Normandy came over to his side.

Edward's overwhelming victory at Crécy in 1346 demonstrated the effectiveness of the English longbowman against the armoured, mounted knight. The success was repeated at Poitiers ten years later, when the English army was under the command of Edward's son, the Black Prince (so called from the colour of his armour). Negotiations culminated in the Treaty of Brétigny (1360), by which Edward renounced his claim to the French throne in return for full sovereignty over one-third of France.

Nine years later Edward renewed his claim to the throne, and hostilities broke out again, but by the time of Edward's death the English had achieved no more breakthroughs, and Edward had been obliged to agree to a truce.

Edward's last years

Edward's reign witnessed a growth in the power of the House of Commons, as the king increasingly depended on Parliament to raise taxes to fund his wars. Parliament in turn increasingly flexed its muscles. After the death of Queen Philippa in 1369, Edward became more and more under the influence of his corrupt mistress, Alice Perrers, while the rival factions of Edward's powerful sons, the Black Prince and John of Gaunt, jockeyed for position. In 1376 Parliament felt strong enough to impeach some of John of Gaunt's supporters, including Alice Perrers herself, and told the king he must match his ambitions to his means.

By this stage Edward had declined into senility, and the following year he died peacefully in bed, probably of a stroke. He had lived too long to sustain his reputation as the perfect knight and ideal king, and by the time of his death it was all too clear to his subjects that he had failed to realize even a fraction of his vaulting ambitions.

1370
(19 September) Black Prince sacks Limoges

1372
French retake Poitou and Brittany from the English; Edward thwarted by the weather from taking an army to France

1373
John of Gaunt, Edward's third son, campaigns in France, but achieves nothing

1376
'Good Parliament' criticizes Edward and John of Gaunt

(8 June) Death of the Black Prince, Edward's eldest son. John of Gaunt regains power

1377
(21 June) Death of Edward

A gilt bronze effigy on the tomb of Edward, the Black Prince in Canterbury Cathedral. Edward was not known as 'the Black Prince' during his lifetime (the name was not used until the 16th century), but was referred to as Edward of Woodstock, after his birthplace in Oxfordshire.

RICHARD II
1377-1399

The failures of Richard's reign are well known to us – albeit in distorted fashion – from Shakespeare's play. Richard was a weak character, and his heightened view of the powers and privileges of kingship was unmatched by political astuteness. His own arrogance and the frivolity of his followers alienated the powerful magnates and culminated in his downfall and death. In the longer term, the weaknesses of his rule ushered in a century of discord and strife in England.

Biography

Contemporaries describe Richard as of average height and build, with yellowish hair. His face was round and somewhat feminine, and he suffered from a stammer. Although a poor prince, Richard was a fine patron, supporting such important literary figures as the poets Chaucer and Gower, and the chronicler Jean Froissart. Richard was also responsible for the introduction of the handkerchief, and the use of spoons at courtly banquets.

BORN 6 January 1367, at Bordeaux, France

FATHER Edward, the Black Prince, eldest son of Edward III

MOTHER Joan (known as the Fair Maid of Kent)

MARRIED (1) Anne of Bohemia, (2) Isabelle, daughter of Charles VI of France

CHILDREN no issue by either marriage

SUCCEEDED 21 June 1377

CROWNED 16 July 1377

ABDICATED 30 September 1399

ROYAL HOUSE Plantagenet

STYLE *Dei Gratia, Rex Angliae et Franciae, et Dominus Hiberniae* ('By the grace of God, King of England and France, and Lord of Ireland')

DIED 14 February 1400, at Pontefract Castle, Yorkshire

BURIED Westminster Abbey

RICHARD'S MINORITY

Richard's father was Edward, the Black Prince, the eldest son of Edward III, who died the year before the old king passed away. Richard himself was only nine years old when he succeeded to the throne. Government was in the hands of his uncle, John of Gaunt, duke of Lancaster, who by the end of Edward III's reign had recovered power, after the admonishments of the 'Good Parliament'.

Richard's first great test came when he was 14, with the Peasants' Revolt of 1381. The peasants were protesting against the poll tax, and the various measures the ruling classes had taken to counter the rise in wages resulting from the manpower shortages caused by the Black Death. In particular the peasants demanded the end of serfdom and a moderation of rents. In a remarkable show of courage for a boy of his age, Richard himself met the rebels, recognized their loyalty to him personally, and promised to answer their grievances. Once they dispersed he promptly went back on his promises, and the rebel leaders were hunted down and killed.

Richard's success with the rebels may have given him an inflated idea of his unique royal powers, if not his responsi-

An illumination (c. 1460/80) from Jean Froissart's Chronicles, *depicting the encounter between the young Richard II and the rebels at Smithfield in London on 15 June 1381, a meeting that ended the Peasants' Revolt. The rebel leader Wat Tyler is struck by Sir William Walworth, lord mayor of London (left), while Richard II subsequently talks to and mollifies the rebels (right).*

bilities. He began to build up his own political clique, including his frivolous favourite, Robert de Vere, earl of Oxford. He also made powerful political enemies, such as the duke of Gloucester and the earls of Arundel and Warwick – who, with their associates, became known as the Lords Appellant. Matters came to a head in 1386 when Parliament impeached Richard's chancellor, Michael de la Pole, and set up a commission to supervise the actions of the young king. Richard was almost deposed by the Lords Appellant in 1387, and the following year the so-called 'Merciless Parliament' purged Richard's friends from government, and had some of them executed.

THE KING ASSERTS HIS POWER

In May 1389 Richard announced that he had achieved his majority and would assume personal power. The crises of 1386–8 had occurred in the absence of John of Gaunt in Spain, and with his return in late 1389 a measure of stability returned to English politics – but only for a while. Richard was biding his time, waiting for the right moment to avenge his humiliations at the hands of his enemies. At the

Capricious in his manners, prodigal in his gifts, extravagantly splendid in his entertainments and dress. MONK OF EVESHAM, *HISTORY OF THE LIFE AND REIGN OF RICHARD II* (15TH CENTURY).

Timeline

1367
(6 January) Birth of Richard

1376
(8 June) Death of Richard's father, Edward, the Black Prince

1377
(21 June) Richard succeeds on the death of his grandfather, Edward III

(16 July) Crowned

1381
(June) Helps to end the Peasants' Revolt

1382
(20 January) Marries Anne of Bohemia

1386
Parliament impeaches Richard's chancellor, Michael de la Pole, who goes into exile

1387
(20 December) Richard's favourite, Robert de Vere, defeated by rival barons at Radcot Bridge, and goes into exile

1388
'Merciless Parliament' purges Richard's circle

1389
(May) Richard assumes personal power

1394
Death of Anne of Bohemia

same time, opposition grew against the king's policies of peace in France and subjugation in Ireland.

Richard's moment came in 1397. Charges were brought against the king's chief enemies: Arundel was found guilty of treason and executed; Warwick was sent into exile; and Gloucester thrown in prison, where he was murdered. The following year, a quarrel between the two remaining Lords Appellant, the duke of Norfolk and Henry Bolingbroke, son of John of Gaunt, gave Richard the excuse to send both into exile, and to seize the latter's vast estates in Lancashire when 'Old Gaunt' died in February 1399.

'SAD STORIES OF THE DEATH OF KINGS'

It was surely unwise for Richard at this point to go on campaign in Ireland. Bolingbroke took his chance, and, with French aid, launched an invasion of England, where many nobles, alienated by Richard's high-handed rule, rallied round him. When Richard returned from Ireland he found himself without support and without the means to resist. He was taken prisoner in North Wales, and, when brought to London, was pelted with refuse by the mob.

On 30 September Richard signed an abdication document, read aloud to Parliament by the Archbishop of York:

> I Richard by the grace of God king of England and of France and lord of Ireland … resign all my kingly majesty, dignity and crown … And with deed and word I leave off and resign them and go from them for evermore, for I know, acknowledge and deem myself to be, and have been, insufficient, unable and unprofitable, and for my deserts not unworthily to be put down.

A fortnight later, on 13 October, Bolingbroke was crowned king as Henry IV.

Richard was imprisoned in Pontefract Castle in Yorkshire. Within four months he was dead. Some believe he was murdered,

> My God! A wonderful land is this, and a fickle; which has exiled, slain, destroyed, or ruined so many kings, rulers and great men, and is ever tainted and toileth with strife and variance and envy. THE WORDS OF RICHARD II ON 21 SEPTEMBER 1399, WHILE HELD PRISONER IN THE TOWER OF LONDON, AS RECORDED BY THE CONTEMPORARY CHRONICLER ADAM OF USK.

THE KINGS AND QUEENS OF ENGLAND

An illumination from Jean Froissart's Chronicles *showing Richard II being imprisoned in the Tower in August 1399. Returning from campaigning in Ireland, Richard found that a tide of discontent had swept England during his absence. He was captured at Flint in North Wales, brought to London and forced to abdicate. By February of the following year Richard was dead (probably murdered), and Henry Bolingbroke was king of England.*

1396
Richard signs a 28-year truce with France

(4 November) Richard marries Isabelle of Valois, who outlives him by ten years

1397
(September) Richard purges his chief enemies, the duke of Gloucester and the earls of Arundel and Warwick

1398
Richard exiles the duke of Norfolk and Henry Bolingbroke

1399
(March) Richard confiscates the lands Bolingbroke has inherited from his father as duke of Lancaster

(May) Richard embarks for Ireland

(June) Bolingbroke lands in Yorkshire

(30 September) Richard forced to abdicate

1400
(14 February) Death of Richard

others that he starved himself – or was deliberately starved – to death. As his death occurred shortly after the outbreak of a rebellion by his former courtiers, foul play seems likely. His corpse was put on show in London, then buried in the church at Kings Langley. In 1413 Bolingbroke's son, Henry V, had Richard reburied with much ceremony in Westminster Abbey.

HENRY IV
1399-1413

Henry Bolingbroke – so called from his place of birth – had by no means the best claim on the throne of England when he overthrew his cousin Richard II in 1399. Richard himself was the son of Edward III's eldest son, while Henry was the son of Edward's third surviving son, John of Gaunt. Technically, the throne should have gone to the seven-year-old Edmund Mortimer, the direct descendant of Edward III's second son, Lionel of Antwerp. But there is no doubt that Henry, a consummate politician, was a better man for the job.

Biography

BORN April 1366, at Bolingbroke Castle, Lincolnshire

FATHER John of Gaunt, duke of Lancaster, third surviving son of Edward III

MOTHER Blanche of Lancaster, great-great-granddaughter of Henry III

MARRIED (1) Mary de Bohun, (2) Joanna of Navarre, widow of John, duke of Brittany

CHILDREN By his first marriage: Henry (the future Henry V); John, duke of Bedford; Thomas, duke of Clarence; Humphrey, duke of Gloucester; plus two daughters, one of whom, Philippa, married Eric, king of Denmark, Norway and Sweden. No issue by his second marriage

SUCCEEDED 30 September 1399

CROWNED 13 October 1399

ROYAL HOUSE Lancaster

STYLE *Dei Gratia, Rex Angliae et Franciae, et Dominus Hiberniae* ('By the grace of God, King of England and France, and Lord of Ireland')

DIED 20 March 1413, at Westminster

BURIED Canterbury Cathedral

In contrast to Richard's autocratic approach, Henry knew how to compromise, and was an effective manager of men. He was admired not only for his political abilities, but also for his qualities as a chivalric knight – in his prime he was a champion jouster, and demonstrated his piety by going on crusade in Eastern Europe.

EARLY CAREER

Henry was almost of an age with his cousin Richard, and as boys they were companions. In Richard's early years the government was in the hands of Henry's father, John of Gaunt, but after he left for Spain in 1386, Henry joined the ranks of Richard's opponents, the Lords Appellant. After John of Gaunt's return, Richard appears to have forgiven Henry, making him duke of Hereford. For his part, Henry kept out of Richard's way, embarking on crusades against the pagans of Lithuania (1390) and Prussia (1392), and making a pilgrimage to Jerusalem (1393).

Richard dealt less leniently with the other rebellious barons, some of whom were executed and others exiled. It shows something for the atmosphere of fear in Richard's court that a relatively harmless remark of Henry in 1398 regarding Richard's rule could lead to such momentous consequences. Henry's words – addressed to Thomas Mowbray, duke of Norfolk (once his fellow Lord Appellant) – were recorded by the chronicler Jean Froissart:

Henry Bolingbroke (the future King Henry IV) enters London with his followers, in an illumination from Jean Froissart's Chronicles.

Holy Mary, dear cousin, what is our cousin the king up to? Will he drive all the nobles out of England? There will soon be nobody left. He shows quite clearly that he does not want to advance the fortunes of the kingdom.

Norfolk promptly accused Henry, in the king's hearing, of treason, giving rise to a great quarrel between the two noblemen. The issue was to be resolved by trial by combat, but at the last moment, with the two men mounted and ready to charge each other, the king stopped the duel and instead sent both men into exile.

That might have been the end of the matter if, on the death of John of Gaunt in early 1399, Richard had not confiscated all the vast estates Henry was to inherit from his father as duke of Lancaster. In June, with Richard away on campaign in Ireland, Henry returned to England. He may at this stage have been merely intent on recovering his inheritance, but at some point the extent of popular support he received in England must have persuaded him to seize the throne. The king was taken captive on his return to England, and Henry was crowned within a fortnight of Richard's forced abdication. His coronation was the first since the Norman Conquest in which the king made his address in English, rather than French.

A DECADE OF REBELLIONS

'Uneasy lies the head that wears a crown,' as Shakespeare has his Henry say, and certainly, although Henry had much support in England, he also had plenty of enemies. A conspiracy among Richard's followers came to light in January 1400, and it may have been this that led to Richard's death, in all likelihood ordered by Henry.

A few months later Owen Glendower (properly Owain Glyndwr), a wealthy landowner in Denbighshire in north-east

Timeline

1366
(April) Birth of Henry

1380 or 1381
Marries Mary de Bohun

1387
Joins Lords Appellant in opposition to Richard II

1390
Crusading in Lithuania

1392
Crusading in Prussia

1393
Makes pilgrimage to Jerusalem

1394
(4 June) Mary de Bohun dies giving birth to Philippa

1398
Exiled by Richard II

1399
(March) Richard confiscates Henry's estates

(June) Henry lands in Yorkshire

(30 September) Succeeds to throne following abdication of Richard II

1400
(February) Richard II dies in captivity, possibly killed on Henry's orders

(September) Outbreak of Owen Glendower's rebellion in Wales

1402
(22 June) Glendower defeats the English at Pilleth, in Powys

(14 September) Scots invasion defeated at Homildon Hill, Northumberland

1403
(7 February) Henry marries Joanna of Navarre

(21 July) Defeats Glendower and Sir Henry Percy (Hotspur) at Shrewsbury

1405
Defeat of rebellion by Henry Percy, earl of Northumberland, and his allies

Wales who claimed descent from the ancient Welsh princes, rallied his countrymen around him in a rebellion against English rule – 'the best for love of liberty, the basest for desire of booty and spoil' (John Hayward, *Life and Reign of Henry IV*, 1599). On 16 September 1400 Glendower was proclaimed prince of Wales, and by 1405 had liberated the entire country, despite Henry leading a succession of campaigns against him.

Glendower had wooed powerful allies. In 1401 he arranged the marriage of his daughter to young Edmund Mortimer, earl of March, who had been Richard II's heir apparent until Henry's coup; and in 1403 Henry Percy, earl of Northumberland, turned against Henry and declared in favour of Edmund's claim to the throne. The Scots and the French also gave some aid to the Welsh rebels, the former suffering defeat at Homildon Hill in Northumberland in 1402, and the latter sending a force to Wales in 1405–6.

Glendower suffered a setback in 1403 when he was defeated at Shrewsbury together with Archibald, earl of Douglas, and Percy's son, Sir Henry Percy (known as Harry Hotspur), the latter being killed. It was said that Henry wept over Hotspur's corpse, but nevertheless displayed it to public view in Salisbury. Two years later Glendower, Mortimer and Northumberland made an agreement to divide England between themselves. Northumberland was joined in rebellion by Henry's old adversary, Thomas Mowbray, duke of Norfolk, and Richard Scrope, Archbishop of York. Mowbray and Scrope were lured to a meeting, seized and summarily executed, but Percy escaped to Scotland. He returned at the head of another rebel force in 1408, only to die at Bramham Moor in Yorkshire. His head was subsequently put on display on London Bridge. By this time Glendower's rebellion had pretty much fizzled out, and in 1410 Glendower himself disappeared.

THE LATER YEARS

The fact that he had usurped the throne on the basis of a tenuous claim, and that he needed to raise money to resist a succession of rebellions, meant that in the period 1401–6 Henry was obliged to make concessions to Parliament in matters such as royal expenditure and appointments – but he did so in a spirit of pragmatism, and managed to maintain a good deal of royal power.

But in 1406, just as Henry could start to feel secure on the throne, his health

broke. He suffered from a chronic skin condition that his contemporaries diagnosed as leprosy, but which may have been syphilis. He also suffered a number of acute attacks, which may have been strokes. A power struggle broke out between two factions at court, one led by Henry's son, the future Henry V, who had played an important part in military operations against the rebels, notably at Shrewsbury. Relations between father and son in the king's last years were strained, with Prince Henry attempting to take power from his father, but without total success. Shakespeare dramatizes the struggle in the scene where the prince takes the crown from beside his father's bed.

The chronicler Raphael Holinshed reported a prediction that Henry would die in Jerusalem, which the king took to mean that he would die on crusade. As it happened, his death took place in the Jerusalem Chamber at Westminster, a coincidence poignantly evoked by Shakespeare:

> It hath been prophesied to me many years,
> I should not die but in Jerusalem;
> Which vainly I suppos'd the Holy Land.
> But bear me to that chamber; there I'll lie;
> In that Jerusalem shall Harry die.
> Henry IV, Part Two *(1597), IV.v.*

1408
(19 February) Percy killed at Bramham Moor, Yorkshire

1410
Prince Henry takes effective power

1411
Henry reasserts his authority, before declining into complete incapacity

1413
(20 March) Death of Henry

HENRY V
1413-1422

Henry V has long been the hero of English patriots of the more bellicose sort, raised on the rousing speeches put into his mouth by William Shakespeare. Henry's campaign of conquest in France – which Shakespeare so stirringly evokes – had popular support at home, and contributed to the emergence of an English national identity. Starting with Henry, the kings of England began to identify themselves as culturally English rather than French.

Biography

H enry himself was not a warm man, being somewhat severe in both politics and religion, and with a tendency towards ruthlessness. But he inspired loyalty, and his strong sense of justice, his martial valour and his qualities as a leader of men earned him great respect, even from his French enemies.

YOUNG PRINCE HAL

In his two Henry IV plays, Shakespeare calls the young Henry 'Prince Hal', and depicts him as a likeable but irresponsible hellraiser. But as soon as his father dies, Henry casts off the fripperies and friendships of youth, and sternly takes on the mantle of kingly responsibility. Although such a sudden change seems unlikely, the contemporary chronicler Thomas Elmham records that Henry 'was in his youth a diligent follower of idle practices, much given to instruments of music, and fired with the torches of Venus herself'. As this passage suggests, Henry was also a cultured man and well educated: he was the first English monarch to read and write fluently in English, rather than French.

Henry's youth was by no means unremittingly dissolute, nor spent solely in idle pastimes. After 1400 much of his time was taken up campaigning against Owen Glendower's Welsh rebels, and in 1403 he took command of the war. He fought at the Battle of Shrewsbury in that year, and was seriously wounded by an arrow in the face. However, he did not personally kill Harry Hotspur, as Shakespeare has us believe.

As the health of his father, Henry IV, declined, Prince Henry became more and more involved in politics. Two factions emerged at court: on the one side was the ailing king and Thomas Arundel, Archbishop of Canterbury, and on the other Prince Henry and Henry

BORN 16 September 1387, at Monmouth

FATHER Henry IV

MOTHER Mary de Bohun

MARRIED Catherine of Valois, youngest daughter of Charles VI of France

CHILDREN Henry (later Henry VI)

SUCCEEDED 21 March 1413

CROWNED 9 April 1413

ROYAL HOUSE Lancaster

STYLE *Rex Angliae, Haeres, et Regens Franciae, et Dominus Hiberniae* ('King of England, Heir and Regent of the Kingdom of France, and Lord of Ireland')

DIED 31 August 1422, at the Bois de Vincennes

BURIED Westminster Abbey

THE KINGS AND QUEENS OF ENGLAND

Henry and the original Falstaff

Shakespeare's character Falstaff – Prince Hal's fat, witty, wine-soaked companion, whom he casts off when he becomes king ('I know thee not, old man. / Fall to thy prayers') – was based on an actual friend of the historical prince, Sir John Oldcastle. Oldcastle was a Lollard, one of a heretical, reforming sect, and when Henry became king, he reluctantly agreed to a charge of heresy being brought against his old companion. Oldcastle was duly convicted, but escaped from the Tower of London, and became involved in plots against the king. He was eventually captured and executed in 1417.

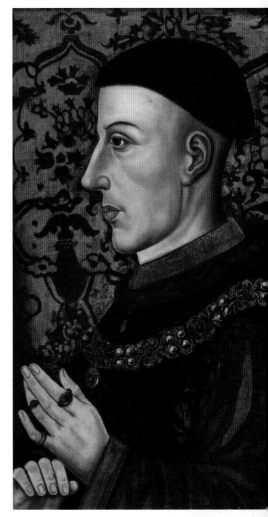

England's warrior-king Henry V, portrayed by an unknown late 16th- or early 17th-century artist. Battlefield victories and strategic European alliances so strengthened Henry's negotiating hand that, by the terms of the Treaty of Troyes (1420), he was made heir to the French throne and regent of France.

and Thomas Beaufort, the natural sons of Henry's grandfather, John of Gaunt. It may have been during this period that exaggerated accounts of the prince's wild behaviour began to be circulated by his political enemies – although the earliest record of his supposed quarrel with the chief justice dates to no earlier than 1531. Prince Henry and the Beauforts came to power in 1410, when they secured the dismissal of Arundel from the chancellorship; they were in turn ousted from power by the king's party in 1411. But in just over a year the old king was dead.

UNITING THE NATION

When Henry ascended the throne, England had been divided against itself for a third of a century. Richard II had been at odds with the great magnates and with Parliament, and Henry IV had faced a series of armed rebellions, partly as a consequence of his usurpation. Henry determined to reunite his kingdom. Thomas Walsingham, the chronicler-monk of St Albans, greeted the advent of the new king by quoting from the Song of Solomon: 'For lo, the winter is past, the rain is over and gone.'

One of Henry's first acts as king was to move the body of Richard II – who in all likelihood had been murdered on the orders of his father – from its humble grave in Kings Langley to Westminster Abbey, the traditional, honoured place of burial of the kings of England. Henry also treated the young Edmund Mortimer, earl of March – who had been Richard's heir apparent – as one of his own family. In 1415 Mortimer repaid Henry's trust by disclosing to him the plot of the earl of Cambridge and Lord Scrope to place Edmund on the throne. Prior to this, in

1387
(16 September) Birth of Henry

1398
His father, Henry Bolingbroke, is exiled by Richard II, who takes the young Henry under his wing

1399
(15 October) After his father usurps the throne, Henry is made earl of Chester, duke of Cornwall and prince of Wales, and shortly afterwards duke of Aquitaine and duke of Lancaster

1403
Takes command of the war against Owen Glendower's Welsh rebels

(21 July) Fights at the Battle of Shrewsbury

1408
Begins to take part in politics

1410
Takes effective power from his father, Henry IV

1411
Henry IV reasserts his authority

1413
(21 March) Henry succeeds to the throne on his father's death

(9 April) Crowned

1414
(9 January) Suppresses Lollard revolt

The affair of the tennis balls

In the spring of 1414 Henry was still in negotiation with the French. But his diplomatic overtures were met with contempt by the French Dauphin (the son and heir of Charles VI). What happened was recorded shortly after Henry's death by John Strecche, in his *Chronicle of the Life of Henry V*:

For these Frenchmen, puffed up with pride and lacking in foresight, hurling mocking words at the ambassadors of the king of England, said foolishly to them that as Henry was but a young man, they would send him little tennis balls to play with ... When the king heard these words he said to those standing by him: 'If God wills, and if my life shall be prolonged with health, in a few months I shall play with such balls in the Frenchmen's courtyards that they will lose the game eventually, and for their game win but grief.'

January 1414, Henry had had to suppress a revolt by the Lollards, a sect of proto-Protestant reformers.

Whether Henry also embarked on his French wars as a means of uniting his people behind a patriotic cause – and as a distraction from domestic discontent – is open to question. But the French wars certainly had this effect.

HENRY'S FRENCH ADVENTURES

Henry's stated *casus belli* was the fulfilment of the 1360 treaty his great-grandfather, Edward III, had agreed with the French, by which the latter had ceded Aquitaine, Poitou and other territories in full sovereignty. Henry also laid claim to other territories held by his Angevin ancestors, namely Normandy, Touraine and Maine. While his ambassadors continued to negotiate, Henry prepared for war.

Henry was a sound military planner, and he had worked out a strategy – as opposed to the ad hoc operations of his predecessors. First of all the political situation in France gave him an opening: the French king, Charles VI, was half the time quite mad, while the dukes of Burgundy and Orleans struggled to fill the power vacuum left by the king's incapacity. Henry then ensured that he had sufficient resources to mount a long campaign, successfully raising large loans and persuading a sympathetic Parliament to grant new taxes. The confidence that he inspired is attested by the large numbers of English nobles and knights who crossed to France with their king.

Henry's strategy was to isolate France diplomatically, secure naval supremacy in the Channel and then to capture the main towns and castles across northern France, from which he could dominate the surrounding countryside. His plan was for long-term occupation, with the installation of English garrisons, and then of tax collectors to raise money for further conquests.

His first year of campaigning, 1415, saw the capture of Harfleur and the great victory at Agincourt. This brought him tremendous prestige, and an alliance with the Emperor Sigismund, who separated France from its Genoese naval allies; the Battle of the Seine in 1416 confirmed English naval supremacy. Campaigning continued, and in 1419 the English captured Rouen. The same year John the Fearless, duke of Burgundy, was murdered

A contemporary illumination depicting the Battle of Agincourt, 25 October 1415. The skills of the English archers enabled Henry V's exhausted army of 9,000 men to overcome a French force of 20,000.

1415
(July) Foils plot against him by the earl of Cambridge and Lord Scrope

(13 August) Invades France

(September) Captures French port of Harfleur

(25 October) Defeats superior French force at Agincourt

1416
(August) French fleet defeated at Battle of the Seine

Emperor Sigismund visits England, and Henry and he help to end the Great Schism, by which there had been two popes, one in Rome and one in Avignon

1419
(January) Captures Rouen

(10 September) Murder of duke of Burgundy brings Burgundy into alliance with England

1420
(21 May) By the Treaty of Troyes, Charles VI of France names Henry as his regent and heir

(2 June) Henry marries Catherine of Valois, daughter of Charles VI of France

1422
(31 August) Death of Henry

by henchmen of the Dauphin (Charles VI's son), pushing the duke's son and successor, Philip the Good, into alliance with the English. In 1420 the French were forced to agree to the Treaty of Troyes, by which Charles VI recognized Henry as his regent and heir, and gave him the hand of his daughter, Catherine of Valois, in marriage.

Henry's campaigns in France were not yet over, but the years of hard fighting had taken their toll, and his health broke during the siege of Meaux in 1422. He died of 'camp fever' (probably dysentery) at Bois de Vincennes, so ending his dream of being crowned king of France, and of his dearest wish – to go on crusade to the Holy Land to rebuild the walls of Jerusalem.

Olivier's Henry V

Sir Laurence Olivier's film of Shakespeare's *Henry V*, in which he starred in the title role as well as directing, was released in 1944, at the height of the Second World War. Olivier had been released from the Royal Navy to make the film, which was regarded as a powerful wartime morale booster. Who, after all, could not be roused to patriotic action by Henry's speech to his men before Agincourt, fought on St Crispin's Day?

This story shall the good man teach his son;
And Crispin Crispian shall ne'er go by,
From this day to the ending of the world,
But we in it shall be remembered –
We few, we happy few, we band of brothers;
For he today that sheds his blood with me
Shall be my brother; be he ne'er so vile,
This day shall gentle his condition;
And gentlemen in England now a-bed
Shall think themselves accurs'd they were not
     here,
And hold their manhoods cheap whiles any
     speaks
That fought with us upon Saint Crispin's day.

In reality, the battle – fought in rain and mud – was not all gallantry and glory. Many of Henry's famed longbowmen, who caused such devastation to the French knights, were suffering from dysentery, and were obliged to fight naked from the waist down. During the course of the day, Henry ordered that all his French prisoners be slaughtered, afraid that they would turn on their captors. The following day, his soldiers roamed the battlefield, cutting the throat of any wounded man they found alive.

Laurence Olivier in a scene from Henry V.

HENRY VI
1422-1461, 1470-1471

A good man, quite unfit for kingship – that is how posterity has judged Henry VI. Unlike his father, he was no leader of men, and held war in abhorrence. Anxious for peace with France, he lost England's French empire for ever. Politically inept and unable – or unwilling – to assert his authority, he allowed himself to be dominated by powerful factions, a state of affairs that led directly to the long period of civil strife known as the Wars of the Roses.

If he had not been king, Henry might have been more admired by his contemporaries. He was devoutly religious, well educated and kind, and founded two great institutes of learning: Eton College, and King's College, Cambridge. Polydore Vergil, the Tudor historian (and thus biased in favour of the House of Lancaster), wrote of Henry that 'his face was handsome, and continually shone with that goodness of heart with which he was abundantly endowed'. Vergil describes Henry as tall in stature, with a slender body, 'to which his limbs were all in correct proportion'.

A LONG MINORITY

Henry was not yet one year old when he came to the throne – the youngest monarch in English history. Within a few weeks, on the death of Charles VI, he also became king of France (following the terms of the Treaty of Troyes wrested by his father, Henry V, from the French). In England a regency council was established, dominated by Henry's uncles Humphrey, duke of Gloucester, and John, duke of Bedford, and his half-uncle, Cardinal Henry Beaufort.

Henry VI portrayed by an unknown artist (c. 1540).

Biography

BORN	6 December 1421, at Windsor Castle
FATHER	Henry V
MOTHER	Catherine of Valois
MARRIED	Margaret, daughter of the duke of Anjou and niece of the French queen
CHILDREN	Edward, prince of Wales (killed 4 May 1471)
SUCCEEDED	31 August 1422
CROWNED	6 November 1429
DEPOSED	4 March 1461
REINSTATED	31 October 1470
DEPOSED	11 April 1471
ROYAL HOUSE	Lancaster
STYLE	*Dei Gratia Rex Angliae et Franciae et Dominus Hiberniae* ('By the grace of God, King of England and France, and Lord of Ireland')
DIED	Stabbed to death 21/22 May 1471, at the Tower of London
BURIED	Windsor Castle

A view of the interior of King's College Chapel, Cambridge (built between 1446 and 1515) showing the fan vaulting characteristic of the Perpendicular style of late English Gothic architecture. Founded by Henry VI in 1441, King's College was specifically intended to take students from Eton College, also founded by Henry (in 1440) as a charity school to provide free education to 70 poor students.

A prudish monarch

Henry's religiosity manifested itself in a number of ways, such as an obsession with religious observance. He also seems to have been a prude. A memoir by a contemporary, John Blacman, tells the story of how, one Christmas, when 'a certain great lord brought before him a dance or show of young ladies with bared bosoms', the king became angry, averted his eyes, and stormed out of the room. Henry also seems to have been persuaded by his confessor to abstain from sexual intercourse with his wife, the beautiful Margaret of Anjou, as much as possible. This may account for the fact that it took them eight years after the wedding to produce an heir. Inevitably there were (politically motivated) rumours that the young Prince Edward was not Henry's child.

The regency was reasonably successful in defending Henry's inheritance in England, and in 1429 the eight-year-old boy – apparently something of a handful – was crowned in Westminster Abbey. That year saw a revival in French fortunes in the Hundred Years' War, partly inspired by Joan of Arc, and on 18 June the son of Charles VI was crowned king of France in Rheims as Charles VII, with Joan by his side. However, three years later the English position in France was still strong enough for Henry to be crowned king of France in the cathedral of Notre Dame in Paris.

HENRY COMES OF AGE

By 1437 the young king was deemed old enough to take control – although in fact he continued to be dominated by a succession of royal relatives, who vied for power with each other. His uncle, Humphrey, duke of Gloucester, was outmanoeuvred in 1447, and his half-uncle Cardinal Beaufort died the same year. William de la Pole, duke of Suffolk, then became the most powerful man in the kingdom, until he too fell in 1450, following losses in France. Then Edmund Beaufort, duke of Somerset (like Henry a descendant of John of Gaunt), and Richard, duke of York (great-grandson of Edmund Mortimer, heir apparent of Richard II) jockeyed for position.

Henry had no taste for war, and he paid little attention to the worsening of the English position in France. In 1440, when he had the opportunity to campaign in Normandy, he sent Richard of York in his place, while he concentrated his attention on the foundation of Eton College. In 1445 Henry sought peace with France by asking for the hand of Margaret of Anjou, niece of Charles VII. Charles agreed, on condition that the English hand over Maine and Anjou. This condition was initially kept secret, and when it became public knowledge the pro-war party were incensed. Henry and his supporters (dominated by Suffolk) responded by charging the pro-war leader, Humphrey of Gloucester, with treason. He died in captivity.

Despite the truce with France, England continued to suffer territorial losses, and by 1450 had lost all of Normandy and Aquitaine, leaving only Calais in English hands. Discontent at home manifested itself in a short-lived popular rebellion in the south-east led by Jack Cade, who was a sympathizer of Richard of York. Two years later, York himself returned to England from Ireland (whither he had been banished), raised an army and demanded the removal of Somerset and the restoration of good government. But Somerset, with the support of Queen Margaret, survived, and York was isolated again.

A SICK, INCAPABLE KING

In August 1453 Henry suffered a complete mental collapse – possibly catatonic schizophrenia – and, until he partially recovered at Christmas 1454, was speechless and completely unaware of everything around him, even the birth of his son, Edward. York became regent during Henry's incapacity and put Somerset in the Tower of London, but his hope of taking the throne was thwarted by the birth of Edward, and by Henry's partial recovery.

In 1455 Somerset, with the support of Queen Margaret, returned to power, York was once again excluded from government, and civil war broke out. This was the beginning of the Wars of the Roses, so dubbed by Sir Walter Scott in the 19th century because the emblem of Henry's house, Lancaster, was the red rose, and that of York the white rose.

THE WARS OF THE ROSES BEGIN

Somerset was killed at the Battle of St Albans in May 1455, and for some years York was again in the ascendancy. But York had many enemies, Queen Margaret not the least of them, and fighting broke out again in 1459. York captured the king – now no more than a puppet – at the Battle of Northampton the following year, and secured the succession for himself, rather than Henry's son Edward. He did indeed have a better claim to the throne, being descended from Lionel, duke of Clarence, the second son of Edward III, whereas Henry was descended from the third son, John of Gaunt, and only held the throne as a

Timeline

1421
(6 December) Birth of Henry

1422
(31 August) Succeeds to the throne of England

(21 October) Succeeds to throne of France

1429
(6 November) Crowned king of England

1432
(16 December) Crowned king of France in Paris

1437
Assumes power

1440
Founds Eton College

1445
(23 April) Marries Margaret of Anjou

1447
Founds King's College, Cambridge

1450
After great territorial losses, the only English possession left in France is Calais

1452
Henry's forces and those of Richard of York confront each other near London

1453
(August) Henry suffers a complete mental breakdown

(13 October) Birth of Henry's son Edward

1454
(Christmas) Henry makes a partial recovery

1455
(22 May) Lancastrians defeated at First Battle of St Albans

1459
(12 October) Yorkists defeated at Ludford Bridge

1460
(10 July) Lancastrians defeated and Henry captured at Battle of Northampton

1461
(c. 3 February) Lancastrians defeated at Mortimer's Cross

(17 February) Yorkists defeated at Second Battle of St Albans

(4 March) Henry deposed as York's son Edward is declared king in London

(29 March) Lancastrians routed at Towton

1464
(July) Henry captured by Yorkists near Clitheroe

1470
(31 October) Restored to the throne

1471
(11 April) Deposed for a second time

(14 April) Lancastrians defeated at Barnet

(4 May) Prince Edward killed and Queen Margaret captured at Battle of Tewkesbury

(21/22 May) Henry murdered

consequence of his grandfather Henry IV's usurpation of Richard II, himself the son of Edward III's eldest son Edward, the Black Prince.

York's triumph was short-lived, however: he was killed at the Battle of Wakefield in December 1460, and the Lancastrians recovered the king at the Second Battle of St Albans two months later. But York's heir – an effective general – declared himself king as Edward IV in March, and went on to rout the Lancastrians at Towton. Henry was eventually captured and confined to the Tower of London.

RESTORATION AND DEATH
York and his son Edward had been supported by Richard Neville, earl of Warwick, one of the richest and most powerful magnates in England, who earned the nickname 'the Kingmaker'. Warwick eventually fell out with Edward, and restored Henry as king in October 1470.

Henry was no more than a cipher, and his second reign lasted for only a few months. Warwick was killed at the Battle of Barnet in April 1471, and Edward IV slaughtered the remaining Lancastrians – including Henry's son and heir, Edward – at Tewkesbury in May. It had not been in the Yorkist interest to dispose of Henry, as this would have left the Lancastrians with a much more formidable head, Prince Edward having the strength of personality and martial bent of his mother. But with Prince Edward dead, the reason to keep Henry alive was removed. He died in the Tower of London, almost certainly killed on King Edward's orders. The Milanese ambassador curtly noted that Edward had 'chosen to crush the seed'.

After Henry's death, something of a cult emerged around his supposed saintliness. Because such a cult could become a focus of opposition to the House of York, both Edward IV and Richard III attempted to suppress it. Following the overthrow of the Yorkists, the Tudor king Henry VII tried to persuade the pope to canonize the murdered king, as part of his cynical programme of rewriting history. Fortunately perhaps for England's dignity, the pope declined to number her most inept king – whose unsuitability for his role plunged the country into decades of bloody strife – among the saints and martyrs of the Holy Roman Church.

EDWARD IV

1461-1470, 1471-1483

Edward was propelled onto the throne by circumstances. That is not to say he was not a man in charge of his own destiny, for Edward was intelligent, ruthless, and the best general of the Wars of the Roses. But he might never have worn the crown had Henry VI not been such a weak monarch, and had his ambitious father not revived a long-dormant claim to the throne of England going back several generations.

Born in Rouen, Normandy, Edward grew to be a handsome youth – hence his sobriquet 'the Rose of Rouen'. He was also a man of impressive stature (his skeleton measured 6 ft 3 in when examined in the 18th century) and great physical appetites, with a particular fondness for food, drink and women. His over-indulgence resulted in a certain portliness in later life, and may have contributed to his early death, at the age of 40.

The Croyland chronicler, writing in the reign of Henry VII (and thus not unbiased), described Edward as 'a gross man addicted to conviviality, vanity, drunkenness, extravagance and passion'. Shakespeare, also writing from the Tudor perspective, pictures him 'lolling on a lewd love-bed dallying with a brace of courtesans'. But Edward had virtues as well as vices: contemporaries attested to his great geniality, and commented on his ability to put people at their ease.

EDWARD COMES TO THE THRONE

Edward's father, Richard, duke of York, was a great-great-great

Edward IV portrayed by an unknown late 16th-century artist.

Biography

BORN 28 April 1442, at Rouen

FATHER Richard, duke of York

MOTHER Cecily Neville, daughter of the earl of Westmorland

MARRIED Elizabeth Woodville

CHILDREN Elizabeth (later queen consort to Henry VII), Mary, Cecily, Edward (briefly king as Edward V), Margaret, Richard (duke of York; presumed to have died with his brother Edward), Anne, George (died in infancy), Catherine, Bridget. Also several children by a number of mistresses

SUCCEEDED 4 March 1461

CROWNED 28 June 1461

DEPOSED 31 October 1470

RESTORED 11 April 1471

ROYAL HOUSE York

STYLE *Dei Gratia Rex Angliae et Franciae et Dominus Hiberniae* ('By the grace of God, King of England and France, and Lord of Ireland')

DIED 9 April 1483, at Westminster

BURIED Windsor Castle

grandson of Edward III, via Edward's second son, Lionel, duke of Clarence. Henry VI, who had come to the throne as an infant in 1422, had a somewhat weaker claim, being descended from Edward III's third son, John of Gaunt, duke of Lancaster. York might not have pressed his claim had he not been denied the position on the royal council that his status warranted, and had not Henry allowed a succession of ministers to rule so ineptly in his name.

After five years of civil war, in July 1460 York captured the king at the Battle of Northampton and secured the succession for himself, rather than for Henry's son, Prince Edward. But York's ambition was ended with his defeat by the Lancastrians at Wakefield at the end of December. York was taken prisoner and executed, and his severed head displayed on the walls of the city of York, wearing a paper crown.

The Yorkist cause was maintained by York's ally, Richard Neville, earl of Warwick, who took York's son, Edward – who then bore the title earl of March – under his wing. At the age of 18 Edward was already showing himself a capable commander, leading a Yorkist army to victory at Mortimer's Cross in February 1461. In March Warwick 'the Kingmaker' and Edward entered London, where Warwick asked the citizens who should be king. According to the *Great Chronicle of London*:

> *It was demanded of the said people whether the said Henry were worthy to reign as king any longer or no. Whereupon the people cried hugely and said, 'Nay! Nay!' And after it was asked of them whether they would have the earl of March for their king, and they cried with one voice, 'Yea! Yea!'*

Chiefly remembered as a vigorous military leader, Edward IV was also an avid book collector. Here he is depicted receiving a volume of the Chronicle of England *from its author, in a contemporary French book illumination.*

THE STRUGGLE WITH WARWICK

Over the next three years Warwick managed the king's affairs, but in 1464 Edward began to display his independence by secretly marrying Elizabeth Woodville, a young widow. This was contrary to the wishes of Warwick, who had wanted Edward to make a dynastic match with a French princess. Although Edward was notably promiscuous, it seems he was very much in love with Elizabeth. The marriage also gave Edward the opportunity to build up his own faction in opposition to Warwick, and he duly ennobled many members of Elizabeth's family. From now on Edward began to conduct his own foreign policy, engineering an alliance with Burgundy (his sister married Duke Charles the Bold) in defiance of Warwick's wish for an alliance with Burgundy's old enemy, France.

Eventually, in 1469, Warwick turned against the man who refused to be his pawn. With the aid of Edward's unreliable younger brother, George, duke of Clarence – 'false, fleeting, perjured Clarence', as Shakespeare calls him

The Battle of Towton

Initially Edward and Warwick worked well together, annihilating the Lancastrian opposition at the Battle of Towton three weeks after Edward had been acclaimed as king. Towton, fought in Yorkshire on 29 March 1461, was one of the bloodiest battles ever fought on English soil. Even the victors were shocked by the carnage. Warwick's brother George Neville estimated the death toll at 28,000 – almost certainly an exaggeration. But for a distance of six miles, the snow-covered ground was stained red with the blood of the fallen.

– Warwick raised an army and defeated Edward's forces at Edgecote Hill, and subsequently captured the king himself. But by now Edward had a secure power base, and Warwick and Clarence were obliged to free the king and flee to France. There they forged an alliance with Henry VI's wife, Margaret of Anjou, and, in September 1470, with the backing of the French king, invaded England. Taken by surprise, Edward fled abroad and sought refuge with his Burgundian allies.

Warwick, finding Henry VI to be a much more amenable puppet, restored him to the throne. But Warwick had underestimated his opponent. In March 1471, with support from Burgundy, Edward and his brother Richard, duke of Gloucester, landed on the coast of Yorkshire and gathered support as they made their way south. Initially, Edward – like Henry Bolingbroke a century before – deemed it politic to restrict his demands to the restoration of his dukedom. But by April he was in London, and the endlessly naive Henry was in his power. Edward's sister Margaret described their meeting thus:

> My lord and brother offered him his hand, but King Henry came and embraced him, saying, 'My cousin, you are very welcome, I know that my life will be in no danger in your hands,' and my lord and brother replied that he should have no worries and should be of good cheer.

This account betrays something of Edward's deceptive charm. For six weeks later Edward – having defeated and killed the would-be kingmaker Warwick at Barnet, and defeated and killed Henry's son Edward at Tewkesbury – ordered that Henry, held captive in the Tower of London, be put to death.

EDWARD'S SECOND REIGN

The last twelve years of Edward's reign saw England return to stability and prosperity. He united the kingdom behind him in

Timeline

1442
(28 April) Birth of Edward

1460
(10 July) Edward's father Richard, duke of York, captures Henry VI at the Battle of Northampton and secures the succession for himself and his heirs

(31 December) York executed after his defeat at Wakefield

1461
(c. 3 February) Edward leads Yorkists to victory at Mortimer's Cross

(17 February) Yorkists defeated at Second Battle of St Albans

(4 March) Edward declared king in London

(29 March) Edward and his ally the earl of Warwick rout the Lancastrians at Towton

1464
(1 May) Edward marries Elizabeth Woodville

1468
(3 July) Edward's sister Margaret marries Charles the Bold, duke of Burgundy, so sealing an Anglo-Burgundian alliance against France

1469
Warwick and Edward's brother the duke of Clarence rebel against Edward

1470
(31 October) Henry is restored following Warwick and Clarence's invasion and Edward's flight to the Low Countries

1471
(March) Edward returns to England

(11 April) Edward restored to the throne

(14 April) Defeats Lancastrians at Barnet, and Warwick is killed. On the same day a second Lancastrian army lands in Dorset, led by Henry's son and wife, Prince Edward and Queen Margaret

(4 May) Edward defeats Prince Edward and Queen Margaret at Tewkesbury; Prince Edward killed

(21/22 May) Henry VI murdered in captivity, probably on Edward's orders

1475
Edward leads expedition against France

1478
(18 February) Edward's brother Clarence 'privately executed' at the Tower of London, following his conviction for treason

1480
War with Scotland

1483
(9 April) Death of Edward

The Battle of Mortimer's Cross, fought near Wigmore, Herefordshire, 2 February 1461. A Yorkist army under Edward, son of Richard, duke of York, routed a Lancastrian force under the earls of Pembroke and Wiltshire. The following month Edward and his ally Richard Neville, earl of Warwick ('the Kingmaker'), entered London, where Edward was proclaimed king as Edward IV.

an expedition to France in 1475, funded by a generous-minded Parliament, and agreed to be bought off by the French for a down payment of 75,000 gold crowns and an annual stipend of 50,000 gold crowns. Edward encouraged international trade, and thrived on the resulting increase in customs revenues, and from his own mercantile enterprises. Various reforms of the royal finances yielded further increases in revenues.

The only skeleton at the feast was Edward's untrustworthy brother George, duke of Clarence, whom Edward had forgiven for his earlier betrayal. There was a story current at the time that Edward had been warned by a soothsayer that he would be succeeded by someone whose name began with the letter G. In 1477 Edward accused his brother George of plotting against him, and the following year had him put to death – by drowning in a butt of malmsey wine, according to the traditional account.

Apart from this hiatus, Edward's second reign was peaceable, and Edward could afford to turn his interests to the arts, collecting books and illuminated manuscripts. But his life came to a premature end after he contracted pneumonia. Before he died, he named his brother Gloucester as protector, to oversee the succession of his young son. But it was not to be: the man whose name began with G declared Edward's son a bastard, and seized the throne as Richard III.

EDWARD V

1483

Had Edward IV lived a little longer, and his son Edward V succeeded as a vigorous youth rather than as a callow boy, England might have found stability under a Yorkist, rather than a Tudor, dynasty.

B ut Edward was only 12 years old when his father died, and the young prince was left to the tender mercies of his ambitious uncle, Richard, duke of Gloucester.

A TWO-MONTH REIGN

Edward was only an infant when, in 1473, he was sent off to Ludlow as notional head of the Council of Wales and the Marches, and was there raised by his mother's brother, Lord Rivers. When news arrived of his father's death, Edward set out for London, accompanied by Rivers. The party was intercepted on its way by the duke of Gloucester, whom Edward IV had appointed as protector to his young heir. Gloucester accused Rivers and others in the Woodville faction of usurping his role of protector, and took the young king into his care.

In May Gloucester lodged the young king in the Tower of London, where, in June, Edward was joined by his younger brother Richard. Gloucester then produced 'evidence' that Edward IV had secretly been married to Lady Eleanor Butler before unlawfully marrying Elizabeth Woodville, so making the princes in the Tower illegitimate. On 26 June Parliament proclaimed Gloucester king as Richard III.

THE FATE OF THE PRINCES

No more was heard of Edward and Richard. It is almost certain that they were murdered, most probably on Richard III's orders.

In 1674 two incomplete skeletons were uncovered at the Tower, and on the orders of Charles II they were buried in Westminster Abbey. In 1933 the remains were examined, but the experts could only say that they were of approximately the right age, and that one skeleton was larger than the other.

Biography

BORN 2 November 1470

FATHER Edward IV

MOTHER Elizabeth Woodville

MARRIED never married

CHILDREN no issue

SUCCEEDED 9 April 1483

CROWNED never crowned

ROYAL HOUSE York

STYLE *Dei Gratia Rex Angliae et Franciae et Dominus Hiberniae* ('By the grace of God, King of England and France, and Lord of Ireland')

DIED August 1483

BURIED unknown (possibly in Westminster Abbey)

Timeline

- **1470**
  (2 November) Birth of Edward
- **1471**
  Created prince of Wales
- **1483**
  (9 April) Succeeds

  (26 June) Declared illegitimate and deposed

  (August) Death of Edward

RICHARD III
1483-1485

Richard III is the ultimate stage villain of English history, thanks to his portrayal in Shakespeare's plays, themselves based on Tudor propaganda. Shakespeare's Richard – a combination of the Vice character in the medieval morality plays and the unscrupulous archetype inspired by the politics of contemporary Italy – boasts that 'I can smile, and murder whiles I smile ... Change shapes with Proteus for advantages, / And set the murtherous Machiavel to school.'

Biography

Although there is no doubt that Richard was both ambitious and ruthless, he was not the deformed and unmitigated monster of the Tudor chroniclers. He was small in stature and slight in strength, but despite this his physical courage was undoubted – as the manner of his death bears witness. But virtually all other historical judgements on Richard are subject to controversy.

BORN 2 October 1452, at Fotheringhay Castle

FATHER Richard, duke of York

MOTHER Cecily Neville, daughter of the earl of Westmorland

MARRIED Anne Neville

CHILDREN Edward (died 1484)

SUCCEEDED 26 June 1483

CROWNED 6 July 1483

ROYAL HOUSE York

STYLE *Dei Gratia Rex Angliae et Franciae et Dominus Hiberniae* ('By the grace of God, King of England and France, and Lord of Ireland')

DIED 22 August 1485, at the Battle of Bosworth Field

BURIED Greyfriars Abbey, Leicestershire (although his remains may have been dug up and thrown away during the Dissolution of the Monasteries)

BIRTH AND BOYHOOD

Richard was the youngest son of Richard Plantagenet, duke of York, and Cecily Neville. It is unlikely that his birth was attended by the portents described by Shakespeare's Henry VI, or that he was the malevolent freak of nature that put such fear into the soon-to-be-murdered king:

> The owl shriek'd at thy birth – an evil sign;
> The night-crow cried, aboding luckless time;
> Dogs howl'd, and hideous tempest shook down trees;
> The raven rook'd her on the chimney's top,
> And chattering pies in dismal discords sung.
> Thy mother felt more than a mother's pain,
> And yet brought forth less than a mother's hope,
> To wit, an indigested and deformed lump,
> Not like the fruit of such a goodly tree.
> Teeth hadst thou in thy head when thou wast born,
> To signify thou camest to bite the world ...
> Henry VI, Part Three *(1592), V.vi.*

Richard's supposed deformities – a withered arm, a hunchback and a limp (not to mention being born with a full set of teeth) – were probably inventions of Sir Thomas More in his pro-Tudor biographical hatchet job, written during the reign of Henry VIII.

After the death of their father, Richard of York, in 1460 at the hands of his Lancastrian enemies, the young Richard and his elder brothers Edward and George were taken under the wing of their father's powerful ally, Richard Neville, earl of Warwick, known as 'the Kingmaker'. While Warwick fought to depose the feeble Henry VI and place Edward on the throne in his stead, Richard, who was still a boy, was raised at Warwick's seat in Yorkshire, Middleham Castle. When Edward became king in 1461, Richard was made duke of Gloucester.

YOUTH AND MARRIAGE

Richard proved a loyal ally to Edward, going into exile with him in 1470 when he was deposed by Warwick. Returning the following year, Richard helped Edward to victory over Warwick at Barnet, and then, at Tewkesbury, to another victory over Warwick's son-in-law, Prince Edward (only son of Henry VI). Both Warwick and Prince Edward were killed; the charge that the latter was murdered by Richard is probably unfounded, but it is less improbable that Richard was involved in the subsequent murder in the Tower of London of King Henry himself.

King Richard III portrayed by an unknown late 16th-century artist.

Timeline

1452
(2 October) Birth of Richard

1461
Made duke of Gloucester

1470–1471
In exile with his brother Edward IV

1471
(14 April) Commands the Yorkist vanguard at the Battle of Barnet

(4 May) Commands the Yorkist vanguard at the Battle of Tewkesbury

1472
(12 July) Marries Anne Neville

1473
Birth of Richard's son Edward

1480
Takes command of operations against the Scots

1482
Captures Berwick-upon-Tweed

In the spirit of the realpolitik of the age, in 1472 Richard married Warwick's daughter and Prince Edward's widow, Anne Neville, who brought with her the extensive Neville estates in the north of England. They only had one son, who died before Richard. Anne died in March 1485, probably of tuberculosis, but given Richard's posthumous reputation, it was rumoured – without foundation – that he had poisoned her. Whether his tears, witnessed at her funeral, were genuine is impossible to say.

Through the second part of Edward IV's reign Richard continued as his brother's loyal ally and was rewarded with more lands in northern England. He led the English armies against the Scots from 1480, and in 1482 captured Berwick-upon-Tweed. He was said – again probably without foundation – to have had a hand in the

(April) The dying Edward IV names Richard as protector of his heir, the young Edward V

(June) Richard exterminates the Woodville faction surrounding Edward IV's widow Elizabeth: Lord Hastings, Lord Rivers (Elizabeth's brother), Richard Grey and Thomas Vaughan are all executed

(26 June) Parliament declares Edward V illegitimate and Richard as the rightful king

(6 July) Richard crowned

(October) Richard's former ally, the duke of Buckingham, rebels and is subsequently captured and executed

1484

(9 April) Death of Richard's son and heir, Prince Edward

Richard unsuccessfully attempts to persuade the duke of Brittany to surrender the exiled Henry Tudor, earl of Richmond

1485

(16 March) Death of Queen Anne

(7 August) Richmond lands his invasion force at Milford Haven

(22 August) Richard killed at the Battle of Bosworth Field

> The Cat, the Rat and Lovell our dog
> Rule all England under a hog.

WILLIAM COLLINGBOURNE, A PLOTTER AGAINST RICHARD, COINED THIS COUPLET CRITICAL OF RICHARD AND HIS SUPPORTERS. THE 'CAT' WAS SIR WILLIAM CATESBY, THE 'RAT' SIR RICHARD RATCLIFFE, AND THE 'DOG' LORD LOVELL (WHOSE CREST WAS A DOG); THE 'HOG' WAS RICHARD HIMSELF, HIS CREST BEING A WILD BOAR.

fall of his elder brother George, duke of Clarence, who had proved much less loyal to Edward and whom Edward had had executed for treason.

RICHARD'S COUP D'ÉTAT

Edward IV's premature death, aged 40, in April 1483 presented Richard with a problem. As Edward lay dying, Richard had gained the king's agreement that he should be protector for Edward's 12-year-old heir, who succeeded as Edward V. But Richard did not have a monopoly of power in England, for Edward IV had raised his wife's extensive family, the Woodvilles, to a position of great importance, and it is likely that Richard feared that if the young king fell into their hands, Richard's position, and even his life, could be in danger.

Whether what Richard did next was a panicked reaction to the momentum of events or the result of a long-pondered plan has been endlessly debated. He seized Edward V and his younger brother and placed them in the Tower of London, arrested and executed the leaders of the Woodville faction, and in June persuaded Parliament to declare the young princes bastards, thus making Richard his brother's rightful heir. His coronation followed in July.

DECLINE AND FALL

The disappearance and supposed death of the princes in the Tower – presumed by most of his contemporaries to have been put to death on Richard's orders – did little for the king's popularity. The contemporary *Great Chronicle of London* commented: 'Had he … suffered the little children to have prospered according to his allegiance and fealty, he would have been honourably lauded over all, whereas now his fame is darkened.'

By September 1483 rebellion had broken out in southern England in the name of Henry Tudor, earl of Richmond, the Lancastrian claimant to the throne, and the following month the rebels were joined by Richard's erstwhile ally, Henry Stafford, duke of Buckingham.

The rebellion was easily suppressed, and Buckingham executed (inspiring Shakespeare's immortal line, 'Off with his head!'). But more and more of Richard's subjects became disaffected, and the opposition rallied round Richmond, who was in exile in Brittany. Richard's ever-present fear of a French-backed invasion was justified on 7 August 1485 when Richmond landed at Milford Haven in south-west Wales, with a group of English followers and 3,000 French mercenaries.

The ruins of Middleham Castle, northern seat of the Neville family, in the dales of North Yorkshire. The future Richard III was brought up here.

THE FINAL BATTLE

Richmond gathered more and more support as he marched east into England, and the two armies met at Bosworth Field in Leicestershire on 22 August. At first neither side could gain the advantage, but when Richard, mounted on his favourite horse White Surrey, spotted Richmond in the distance with only a small force of men, he led a cavalry charge to intercept him. Soon Richard found himself stranded in a bog, cut off from his main force and outnumbered three-to-one. He refused to flee, fought valiantly, and was in the end cut down by a Welsh halberd. The crown of England was subsequently found hanging in a hawthorn tree.

Richard's body, 'despoiled to the skin', according to the *Great Chronicle*, and 'besprung with mire and filth', was trussed up like a hog and paraded through the streets of Leicester, before being buried at Greyfriars Abbey. So ended the life of the last of the House of York – and the last of the line of Plantagenet kings who had ruled England for 400 years, since the time of Henry II.

HENRY VII
1485-1509

The Tudor period marks in the minds of many the emergence of an English national identity. It witnessed the creation and triumph of the Anglican Church, the successful repulsion of foreign invaders, and the flowering of English literature, culminating in the glories of Shakespeare. Yet Henry VII, the founder of the Tudor dynasty, is to most a somewhat shadowy figure; a cold, cautious, austere man who paid assiduous attention to sound administration and the filling of the royal coffers.

Biography

This is only part of the truth. Henry was also a fine soldier, as his victory at Bosworth attests, and a consummate politician who restored peace and stability to England. Henry was more than a dry and spiritless calculator, he was a man of vigour who liked to enjoy himself as much as any other prince – not only in the chase and other athletic activities, but also in such courtly pastimes as music, dancing and cards. Polydore Vergil, an Italian chronicler who knew Henry in his later years, describes him as of above average height, slender, but well built and strong. Despite bad teeth, a sallow complexion and thin hair, Vergil found him 'remarkably attractive', and his face cheerful, especially when speaking.

BORN 28 January 1457, at Pembroke Castle

FATHER Edmund Tudor

MOTHER Margaret Beaufort

MARRIED Elizabeth of York, daughter of Edward IV

CHILDREN Arthur, prince of Wales; Margaret (married James IV of Scotland); Henry (the future Henry VIII); Mary (briefly married to Louis XII of France); Edmund, duke of Somerset; Katherine. Only Margaret, Henry and Mary outlived their father

SUCCEEDED 22 August 1485

CROWNED 30 October 1485

ROYAL HOUSE Tudor

STYLE *Dei Gratia Rex Angliae et Franciae et Dominus Hiberniae* ('By the grace of God, King of England and France, and Lord of Ireland')

DIED 21 April 1509, at Richmond Palace

BURIED Westminster Abbey

THE TUDOR CLAIM

Through his mother, Margaret Beaufort, Henry Tudor was descended from John of Gaunt by his third wife, Catherine Swynford, and thus was the great-great-great-grandson of John of Gaunt's father, Edward III. John of Gaunt's children by Catherine Swynford were born before they married, however, and were only legitimized later; they and their heirs were excluded from the succession by Parliament under Henry IV.

Henry's father, Edmund Tudor, earl of Richmond, was the son of Henry V's widow, Catherine de Valois, by her second (secret and possibly unconsecrated) marriage, to Owen Tudor, a Welsh squire who had entered her service, and who was descended from the Welsh prince Rhys ap Gruffydd (1132–97). Owen's opportune match made Edmund Tudor half-brother to Henry VI. Henry Tudor's claim to the throne of England was thus on the face of it fairly flimsy – but circumstances conspired to change all that.

Towards the throne of England

Henry's youth was dominated by the period of civil strife known as the Wars of the Roses, when the House of York (whose emblem was the white rose) and the House of Lancaster (who wore the red rose) battled it out as to which dynasty should rule England. Apart from Henry's father Edmund, who died before Henry was born, Henry's family was in the thick of it. His grandfather Owen led the defeated Lancastrians at Mortimer's Cross in 1461, and was captured and beheaded, bemoaning the fact that the head that had once lain in Queen Catherine's lap should now lie in the executioner's basket. Henry's uncle, Jasper Tudor, earl of Pembroke, maintained the Lancastrian resistance to Edward IV for the next ten years, but was forced to flee with his young nephew to Brittany after the Lancastrian defeat at Tewkesbury in May 1471. With the death of Prince Edward at Tewkesbury and the murder shortly afterwards of his father Henry VI, the 14-year-old Henry Tudor became the leading Lancastrian claimant to the throne.

King Henry VII clutching the red rose of Lancaster, by an unknown contemporary artist.

That might have been that had not the House of York set about destroying itself. In 1478 Edward IV had his brother, the duke of Clarence, executed for treason, and in 1483, on Edward's death, his other brother, the duke of Gloucester, declared Edward's sons illegitimate and took the throne for himself as Richard III. The subsequent disappearance and presumed murder of the young princes turned many of Richard's subjects against him, and opposition rallied around the exiled Henry Tudor (although it is not absolutely impossible that it was Henry himself who was responsible for the deaths of the princes). By now Henry was the leading claimant to the throne, if one regarded Richard as an illegal usurper and Clarence's son Edward, earl of Warwick, disbarred on account of his father's treason. Henry reinforced his claim by promising to marry Elizabeth of York, daughter of Edward IV – a union that would unite the Houses of Lancaster and York, and which brought dissident Yorkists to Henry's side.

> ❛ He was not devoid of scholarship. In government he was shrewd and prudent, so that no one dared to get the better of him through deceit or guile ... But all these virtues were obscured latterly only by avarice ... ❜ POLYDORE VERGIL, *ANGLICAE HISTORIAE LIBRI XXVI* (1534).

Timeline

c. 1457
(28 January) Birth of Henry

1471
Flees with his uncle Jasper Tudor to Brittany following the Lancastrian defeat at Tewkesbury

1484
Henry leaves Brittany for France, to escape Richard III's attempt to persuade the duke of Brittany to hand him over

1485
(7 August) Henry lands his invasion force at Milford Haven

(22 August) Defeats and kills Richard III at Bosworth Field and becomes king

(30 October) Crowned

1486
(18 January) Marries Elizabeth of York

(27 March) Pope Innocent VIII issues a bull recognizing Henry's title to the throne of England

(April) Henry crushes a rebellion by Lord Lovell

1487
(24 May) The Yorkist impersonator and puppet Lambert Simnel is crowned as King Edward VI in Dublin

(16 June) Simnel and his allies defeated at Stoke

Elizabeth of York, wife of Henry VII, by an unknown artist (c.1500). Henry's marriage to the eldest child of Edward IV unified the warring houses of York and Lancaster, strengthened his claim to the throne, and ensured that his own children would be of royal blood.

If Henry's claim was becoming more and more just, what would seal it would be God's judgement on the field of battle. Henry's first attempt on the throne in the autumn of 1483 met with failure when his ally, the duke of Buckingham, was captured and beheaded, and Henry's own invasion fleet was scattered by storms. During the following year, Richard III attempted to bribe the duke of Brittany into giving up his guest, but Henry moved to France and there secured the backing of the French king for another invasion. This time Henry was successful. He landed at Milford Haven, in south-west Wales, and, drawing on the loyalty of many Welshmen to the Tudors, gathered new troops to his cause as he marched eastward into England. There, on 22 August 1485 at Bosworth Field in Leicestershire, he defeated and killed Richard. God had given his judgement, and Henry was crowned two months later. He married Elizabeth the following January.

A SUCCESSION OF REBELLIONS

Henry took as his badge the Lancastrian red rose superimposed upon the white rose of the House of York. But neither his marriage nor this symbolic gesture put paid to discontent among those Yorkists who had found themselves on the wrong side in 1485. They had fallen victim to Henry's trick of backdating his reign to the day before Bosworth, thus making all those who had fought against him traitors, subject to the forfeit of their lands. The dispossessed were very much a minority, as most of the nobility had hedged their bets and kept aloof from the Bosworth campaign. But England had seen a succession of kings usurped and killed, so winning one battle did not mean – as far as the dispossessed were concerned – that the war was won.

The first revolt, headed by Lord Lovell, one of Richard III's ministers, broke out in April 1486, but came to nothing. A more serious threat came from John de la Pole, earl of Lincoln, whose mother Elizabeth was the sister of Edward IV and Richard III, and who may have been Richard's designated heir. With the backing of his aunt, Margaret, dowager duchess of Burgundy, Lincoln came out in revolt in 1487, around the figurehead of a youthful impersonator, Lambert Simnel, whom his supporters declared to be the Yorkist claimant, the young Edward, earl of Warwick. The revolt was crushed at the Battle of Stoke.

In 1491 another impersonator appeared. This was Perkin Warbeck, the good-looking son of a minor official in Flanders, who was trained by Margaret of Burgundy to play her nephew Richard, the younger of the Princes in the Tower, presumed murdered in 1483. Warbeck made a number of attempts to gather support in Ireland and England, and received the backing (at various times) of Charles VIII of France, the Emperor Maximilian and James IV of Scotland, whose

The boy who would be king

Lambert Simnel, the figurehead in the 1487 revolt against Henry VII, was the son of an Oxford joiner (or possibly a baker). A young priest called Richard Symonds saw in him a resemblance to the late Edward IV, and when in 1486 a rumour circulated that Edward's two sons, the deposed Edward V and his younger brother Richard, had not been murdered but still lived, he determined to pass off his protégé – then around ten years old – as one of the so-called Princes in the Tower.

The following year another rumour circulated, this time that Edward, earl of Warwick, the young Yorkist claimant, was dead, and Symonds seized the opportunity to groom Simnel to impersonate the earl. The boy was taken to Ireland, a Yorkist stronghold, and declared by the Irish Parliament to be the rightful king. On 24 May 1487 he was crowned in Dublin as King Edward VI. Henry attempted to defuse the plot by parading the real earl of Warwick through the streets of London, but to no avail.

Present in Dublin at Simnel's coronation was the real figure behind the revolt, John de la Pole, earl of Lincoln, a

nephew of Edward IV. The following month Lincoln and Simnel, accompanied by 2,000 German mercenaries and an army of 'beggarly, naked and almost unarmed Irishmen', landed in England. On 16 June they were routed by royal forces at Stoke, in Nottinghamshire. Lincoln was killed and Symonds thrown into prison for the rest of his life, but Simnel met a more merciful fate. In his 1622 biography of Henry, Francis Bacon explained the king's motives:

The king would not take his life, both out of magnanimity (taking him but as an image of wax that others had tempered and moulded), and likewise out of wisdom; thinking that if he suffered death he would be forgotten too soon; but being kept alive he would be a continual spectacle, and a kind of remedy against the like enchantments of people in time to come.

So, instead of putting him to death, Henry put the boy who would be king to work in the royal kitchens.

1491

Another Yorkist impersonator, Perkin Warbeck, lands in Ireland, but returns to Europe having failed to gain support

1492

(3 November) After a brief invasion of France, Henry agrees a peace treaty with Charles VIII, by which the latter expels Perkin Warbeck, recognizes the right of the Tudors to the throne of England, and grants Henry a pension

1495

(3 July) Warbeck lands in England with a small force, but soon retreats to Ireland and then to Scotland

1496

Henry makes a peace treaty and free-trade agreement with the Emperor Maximilian

(5 March) Henry commissions the Italian navigator Giovanni Cabot (John Cabot) to make discoveries in the New World; Cabot subsequently reaches Cape Breton Island, Canada

(September) Short-lived Scottish invasion of England in support of Warbeck

1496

(17 June) Dispersal of Cornish rebels at Blackheath, near London. The Cornishmen had objected to the taxes Henry had raised to resist the Scots

(September) Warbeck lands in Cornwall, but is later captured and imprisoned

cousin he married and who mounted expeditions against England in Warbeck's favour. The pretender's last throw of the dice was in 1497, when he landed in Cornwall and made his way towards London. But he gathered little support, and was captured and imprisoned in the Tower of London. In 1499 he and the Yorkist claimant, Edward, earl of Warwick, attempted to escape the Tower. They failed, and both men were executed for treason.

THE ACHIEVEMENT OF STABILITY AND WEALTH

With the death of the last two Yorkist claimants, Henry's position on the throne was that much more secure. He had isolated Warbeck from his erstwhile foreign allies by skilful diplomacy, securing peace with France (1492), the emperor (1496) and Scotland (1499), and went on to marry his daughter Margaret to the Scottish king, James IV (1503). Henry also made a marriage

The so-called Henry VII Chapel in Westminster Abbey. Built in the Perpendicular style in 1503 and dedicated to the Virgin Mary, the Chapel lies at the far eastern end of the Abbey.

alliance with the new rising power in Europe, Spain, by which in 1501 his eldest son Arthur married Catherine of Aragon. (Arthur died the following year, and Henry then arranged that Catherine should marry his surviving son, the future Henry VIII.)

Henry's approach to governance at home has been characterized as 'the new monarchy', marking a break with the medieval past. But more recently historians have concluded that changes under Henry were more a matter of degree than of kind. It was perhaps the rigour with which Henry implemented his policies that was so remarkable – and in no area of policy was he more rigorous than in the raising of money for the Crown. Henry relied more on his servants than aristocratic allies, and employed ruthlessly efficient men such as John Morton (possibly his only intimate friend), Richard Fox, Richard Empson and Edmund Dudley to do his business. But it seems that he did not fully trust anyone, insisting that he personally should audit the household accounts, through which he channelled most of the royal revenues.

Henry certainly knew how to turn kingship into a profitable business. He minimized expenditure by the avoidance of war and the enforcement of efficient administration, and was able to raise such vast sums from his own resources that he did not need to rely on Parliament. In Henry's reign the royal income from customs duties rose by around one-quarter, and revenues from Crown lands increased more than tenfold. Henry extended the range of offences for which fines were payable, and made sure the fines made their way into his own pockets. He asserted his feudal rights, exacting large sums from land deemed to be held directly from the king, and extracting fines for breaches in feudal obligations: for example, the duke of Buckingham was fined £2,000 (a vast sum in those days) because he had failed to seek royal permission for his widowed mother to remarry.

Henry's close attention to financial affairs meant that when he died in 1509, suffering from rheumatoid arthritis and gout, he left his son and heir, Henry VIII, not only a throne that was secure from dynastic rivals and a country unthreatened by foreign powers, but also such an accumulation of royal wealth that it took even the spendthrift young king some years to dissipate his inheritance. As to his own future in the afterlife, Henry left money so that 10,000 masses might be said for the salvation of his immortal soul.

1499
Henry makes peace with the Scots

(23 November) Execution of Perkin Warbeck, along with the Yorkist claimant Edward, earl of Warwick

1500
(19 June) Death of Henry's third son, Edmund

1501
Henry's eldest son Arthur marries Catherine of Aragon

Edmund de la Pole, earl of Suffolk, a Yorkist claimant, attempts to raise forces in Europe to mount a revolt. He is later (1506) imprisoned in the Tower of London

1502
Henry arranges for the marriage of his daughter Margaret to James IV of Scotland. The marriage takes place in 1503

(2 April) Death of Henry's son Arthur

1503
(11 February) Death of Henry's queen, Elizabeth of York, in childbirth

(23 June) Henry arranges the betrothal of his son Henry to the widowed Catherine of Aragon

1509
(21 April) Death of Henry

Henry VIII
1509-1547

Handsome Renaissance prince, bluff King Hal or monstrous, bloated tyrant? These clichés are often deployed to trace Henry's career from glamorous, athletic youth to ulcerated, ill-tempered old age, and all have an element of truth in them. Henry was a larger-than-life character, a man who exuded and exercised power (although always within the framework of the law), and promoted and insisted on the glory and supreme authority of kingship. But at the same time he was a loose cannon, a reckless unstatesmanlike figure who failed to make the most of his inheritance and opportunities.

Biography

BORN 28 June 1491, at Greenwich Palace

FATHER Henry VII

MOTHER Elizabeth of York

MARRIED (1) Catherine of Aragon, (2) Anne Boleyn, (3) Jane Seymour, (4) Anne of Cleves, (5) Catherine Howard, (6) Catherine Parr

CHILDREN By Catherine of Aragon: Mary (the future Mary I); by Anne: Elizabeth (the future Elizabeth I); by Jane: Edward (the future Edward VI)

SUCCEEDED 21 April 1509

CROWNED 23 June 1509

ROYAL HOUSE Tudor

STYLE Henry the Eighth, by the Grace of God, King of England, France and Ireland, Defender of the Faith and of the Church of England, and also of Ireland, on earth the Supreme Head

DIED 28 January 1547, in London

BURIED St George's Chapel, Windsor Castle

Henry undoubtedly made a huge impact. His efforts to secure the succession by producing a male heir led him to sever the English Church from the authority of Rome; he thus, despite his own doctrinal conservatism, let loose the Protestant Reformation in England. His opportunism in dissolving the monasteries led to the greatest change in land ownership in England since the Norman Conquest, while his extravagance and military adventurism abroad left his kingdom in dire financial straits. And yet this wilful, egotistical, ungenerous, superficially charming creature gave the English people the image they wanted of an English king, an image that ensured his enduring personal popularity with the majority of his subjects through much of his reign.

THE GILDED YOUTH

It says much for the political stability that Henry's father had achieved in England – after decades of civil war – that Henry succeeded, at the vulnerable young age of 17, without a breath of opposition. He also succeeded to a kingdom whose coffers were full, thanks to the widely detested financial exactions his father had made on his subjects. A contemporary, George Cavendish, described the new king as 'natural, young, lusty and courageous ... entering into the flower of pleasant youth'; according to Cavendish, England was on the threshold of a golden world.

The young king ruled in his own right as soon as he came to the throne, and within two days made a gesture that he presumably thought would make him popular: he arrested his father's two most loathed collectors of taxes and fines, Sir

Richard Empson and Edmund Dudley. They were charged – groundlessly – with high treason, thrown into the Tower of London, and executed the following year. Empson and Dudley were not the last of the Crown's most dedicated ministers to suffer such ingratitude from their king.

Henry cultivated a much less austere image than his father, although he was in reality no less cold and ruthless. (Thomas More commented, before he and the king fell out, that 'If my head could win him a castle in France … it should not fail to go.') Henry loosened the royal grip on the purses of the nobility, embarked on military adventures in France, and transformed his court into a place of unsurpassed glamour, in which Henry – handsome, athletic and cultured – made sure he was the most brilliant jewel. 'Avarice is fled the country,' wrote a courtier, Lord Mountjoy, to Erasmus, 'our king is not after gold, or gems, or precious metals, but virtue, glory, immortality …' In 1519 a more disinterested observer, the Venetian diplomat Sebastian Giustiani, reported on the young king to the doge and senate:

> He is very accomplished and a good musician; composes well; is a capital horseman, and a fine jouster; speaks good French, Latin and Spanish; is very religious … He is extremely fond of hunting … He is also fond of tennis, at which game it is the prettiest thing to see him play; his fair skin glowing through a shirt of the finest texture.

Henry liked to dress like a peacock, and there are contemporary descriptions of some of his more extravagant costumes, for example one in the Turkish fashion of white damask, 'all embroidered with roses made of rubies and diamonds'.

Henry VIII by Hans Holbein the Younger (1536). The German-born Holbein painted a number of portraits at the court of Henry VIII, including those of Sir Thomas More and Jane Seymour (see page 135). It was on the basis of a flattering depiction by Holbein of Anne of Cleves (a match with whom had been urged on Henry by his chancellor Thomas Cromwell, with fatal results for the latter), that Henry chose her to be his fourth wife.

The handsomest potentate I ever set eyes upon: above the usual height, with an extremely fine calf to his leg, his complexion very fair and light, with auburn hair … and a round face so very beautiful that it would become a pretty woman, his throat being rather long and thick. A VENETIAN DIPLOMAT DESCRIBES THE YOUNG HENRY IN 1515.

Timeline

1491
(28 June) Birth of Henry

1493
Made constable of Dover Castle and lord warden of the Cinque Ports

1494
Becomes duke of York

1502
(2 April) Death of his elder brother Arthur makes Henry heir apparent

1509
(21 April) Succeeds

(11 June) Marries Catherine of Aragon

(23 June) Crowned

1510
(17 August) Execution of Henry's father's ministers, Empson and Dudley

With all these distractions it is not surprising that the young king had an aversion to work – the business of governing his kingdom does not seem to have interested him greatly. Fortunately, from 1511 Henry benefited from the services of a formidably able administrator, Thomas Wolsey, the son of an Ipswich butcher, who in 1515 became both a cardinal and lord chancellor of England. But Henry always made it clear who held the real power, and made sure, when things went wrong, that it was his ministers who took the blame.

HENRY, FRANCE AND THE HABSBURGS

Unlike his father, whose diplomatic initiatives were largely defensive, Henry was disposed to throw his weight about in Europe. He regarded Francis I of France, another glamorous prince, as both a personal and a strategic rival. Francis in turn was caught up in a struggle for dominance in western Europe (especially Italy) with Charles V, the Habsburg ruler of Austria, Burgundy, the Netherlands, Spain and Naples, and who in 1519 was elected Holy Roman Emperor. A measure of Henry's ambition is that he briefly considered standing for election as emperor himself, and also supported Wolsey's aspiration to become pope. Neither were realistic objectives, but Henry was determined to play a part in the great geopolitical game between the Habsburgs and France that was just beginning, and which would dominate western Europe for centuries.

The Mary Rose *as depicted on the Anthony Roll, a survey of Henry VIII's navy completed in 1546. Originally built in 1509–10, the* Mary Rose *sank in an engagement with the French outside Portsmouth Harbour on 19 July 1545. Lifted from the water in 1982, the wreck and various artefacts found inside it – including cooking utensils, backgammon boards and a shawm (an early form of oboe) – are now displayed in a museum in Portsmouth.*

In 1522, after successes by the emperor's forces over the French in Italy, Henry declared war on France. The war proved costly, and attempts to raise taxes led to resentment at home. After imperial forces captured Francis I at the Battle of Pavia (1525), Henry and Wolsey sought to restore the balance of power by abandoning the emperor and signing a peace treaty with France. But they overestimated their influence, and the English cloth trade with the Netherlands suffered as a result. What was of more immediate concern to Henry was that with Italy – and thus the papacy – under the thumb of the Emperor Charles, his chances of persuading the pope to grant him a divorce from the emperor's aunt were next to zero.

The young Catherine of Aragon in a contemporary copy of a portrait by Michael Sittow (c. 1510).

THE KING'S 'GREAT MATTER'

Catherine of Aragon, daughter of Ferdinand and Isabella of Spain and aunt of the Emperor Charles V, had previously been married to Henry's elder brother, Arthur, prince of Wales. Arthur had died in 1502, aged 15, the year after the wedding. Following her marriage to Henry in 1509, Catherine failed to produce a child that lived beyond infancy until 1516, when she gave birth to a baby girl, Mary. Thereafter she suffered more miscarriages and stillbirths, making Henry increasingly anxious about the absence of a male heir. By 1526 he began to consider divorce, and his infatuation with one of Catherine's ladies-in-waiting, Anne Boleyn, firmed his resolve. After a decade and a half of marriage, Henry conveniently

> Alas, sir! In what have I offended you? What cause Hath my behaviour given to your displeasure, That thus you should proceed to put me off, And take your good grace from me? Heaven witness, I have been to you a good and humble wife, At all times to your will conformable.

WILLIAM SHAKESPEARE, *HENRY VIII* (1613), II.iv. CATHERINE OF ARAGON APPEALS TO HENRY, IN VERY SIMILAR TERMS TO THOSE SHE USED AT HER HEARING BEFORE HENRY AND THE POPE'S REPRESENTATIVES IN 1529.

> I will not allow anyone to have it in his power to govern me, nor will I ever suffer it. HENRY VIII, WORDS RECORDED BY A VENETIAN DIPLOMAT IN 1516.

1511
(1 January) Catherine gives birth to a son, Henry, who dies on 22 February

Thomas Wolsey becomes a member of Henry's Privy Council

(13 November) Henry joins the Holy League against Louis XII of France

1512–1513
English campaigns in France

1513
(August) English and imperial forces defeat French at Battle of the Spurs, in Flanders

(9 September) James IV of Scotland and the flower of the Scottish nobility are annihilated by the English at the Battle of Flodden

1514
(April) Henry declares truce with France

1515
Wolsey becomes lord chancellor

1516
(18 February) Catherine of Aragon gives birth to the future Queen Mary I

1518
(October) Treaty of London: Wolsey arranges peace among the western European powers, who agree to unite against the Turks

1519
(May) Henry puts himself forward as a candidate to become Holy Roman Emperor (a plan thwarted in June, when Charles V is elected emperor)

1520
(May) Henry meets Charles V at Dover and Canterbury

(June) Henry meets Francis I of France at the Field of the Cloth of Gold: Henry's daughter Mary betrothed to Francis's son; French agree to abandon Scottish alliance

1521
Henry publishes Defence of the Seven Sacraments, an anti-Lutheran book, gaining the title Defensor Fidei ('Defender of the Faith') from the pope

(25 September) Treaty of Bruges: Henry forms alliance with the Emperor Charles V against France

1522
Resumption of war with France and Scotland

recalled that the Bible prohibited a man from marrying his brother's wife, citing Leviticus 20:21. Catherine countered by testifying that her first marriage had never been consummated and was therefore void. For her part, Anne withheld her favours until she was sure Henry was going to make her his queen.

Henry's project to divorce Catherine became known as 'the king's great matter', so much did it occupy him. Appeals to the pope in Rome to grant an annulment fell on deaf ears. Diplomats and experts in canon law met and deliberated, to no avail. Frustrated by the lack of progress, Henry made Wolsey his scapegoat. The cardinal died a bitter man on his way to London to face treason charges, ruefully commenting, 'If I had served God as diligently as I have done the king, He would not have given me over in my grey hairs.'

Henry appointed as his new chancellor the humanist scholar

The showpiece meeting between Henry VIII and Francis I of France that took place near English-held Calais in June 1520, as depicted in a painting (1845) by Friedrich Bouterwek (but based on an anonymous earlier work). Planned by Cardinal Wolsey, this was a spectacular diplomatic encounter of rival Renaissance princes: a temporary palace covering an area of nearly 12,000 square yards was erected, and lavish arrangements were made for jousting, dancing and banqueting (2200 sheep were consumed during the course of the meeting). Such was the quantity of expensive gold fabric on display in the tents and costumes that the site of the meeting was named Le Camp de Drap d'Or *('the Field of the Cloth of Gold').*

Thomas More, who tried to persuade the king to take Catherine back. But Henry was determined to have his way, and set about asserting that his position as king made him supreme in his own realm, owing obedience to no earthly institution. In January 1533 Henry married Anne Boleyn; and in the same year Thomas Cranmer, the new Archbishop of Canterbury, declared Henry's marriage to Catherine void.

The Henrician Reformation

The English Church, of which Henry now saw himself as head, thus began its schism with Rome. Henry himself was excommunicated by the pope, hardening his resolve. Henry's motives were not doctrinal – in theological matters (in which he took a keen interest) he was a conservative, and in 1521 had published a book attacking Luther, earning him the title 'Defender of the Faith' from the pope. As far as Henry was concerned, it was a matter of who should be master of the English Church. To this end he employed his able new minister, Thomas Cromwell, to draft Acts of Parliament, notably the 1534 Act of Supremacy, to make clear that it was Henry who was the Church's 'supreme head on earth'.

Although Henry was doctrinally conservative, some key figures around him – including Cromwell, Cranmer and Queen Anne herself – had Lutheran sympathies. Equally, there were others with strongly traditionalist leanings. Thomas More had resigned as lord chancellor in 1532, and in 1535 was found guilty of having treasonously denied the royal supremacy, for which he lost his head. The following year a rebellion against Henry's religious policies known as the Pilgrimage of Grace broke out in the north of England, and, although it was suppressed, it showed up weaknesses in the power of the state. Henry proceeded cautiously: although he commissioned an English translation of the Bible (a key demand of Protestant reformers), the 1539 Act of Six Articles asserted a number of traditional Catholic doctrines, such as transubstantiation and the celibacy of priests.

1523
Henry's proposed tax increases opposed by Parliament

1526
Henry begins to woo Anne Boleyn and to seek a divorce from Catherine

1527
(30 April) Formation of Anglo-French alliance

1528
(22 January) Henry and Francis I of France declare war on the emperor, but in six months a truce is declared

1529
The case for the annulment of Henry's marriage to Catherine is heard before Cardinal Campeggio and Cardinal Wolsey at a legatine court in London, but the matter is referred to Rome, leading to Wolsey's downfall and the appointment of Thomas More as his replacement as lord chancellor

1531
(January) The pope forbids Henry to remarry unless his marriage to Catherine is annulled

1532
More resigns as lord chancellor

> Never prince had wife more loyal in all duty and in all true affection than you have ever found in Ann Bullen ... with which name and place I could willingly have contented myself, if God and your grace's pleasure had so been pleased.

ANNE BOLEYN PLEAS IN VAIN TO HENRY FROM THE TOWER OF LONDON, 6 MAY 1536.

1533

Thomas Cromwell becomes Henry's secretary of state

(25 January) Henry secretly marries Anne Boleyn

(10 April) Henry's marriage to Catherine declared void

(July) Henry excommunicated by the pope

(7 September) Birth of Anne Boleyn's daughter, the future Queen Elizabeth I

1534

Act of Supremacy makes Henry the supreme head of the English Church

1535

(6 July) Execution of Thomas More

1536–1540

Dissolution of the monasteries

1536

Wales and England are formally united

(19 May) Execution of Anne Boleyn

(30 May) Henry marries Jane Seymour

(October) Pilgrimage of Grace begins against Henry's religious policies

1537

(24 October) Jane dies after giving birth (12 October) to the future Edward VI

1539

(April) Act of Six Articles establishes traditional Catholic doctrines for the English Church

One of the immediate provocations of the Pilgrimage of Grace was the beginning of the dissolution of the monasteries, which was to continue until 1540. There was no particular doctrinal issue at stake – Henry, aided by Cromwell, simply saw the riches of the monasteries and helped himself. Most of the extensive monastic lands ended up in the hands of the aristocracy and a rising new class of country gentlemen, and many of the great abbey churches were plundered for building materials, leaving England studded with the 'bare ruined choirs' mourned by Shakespeare.

DECLINING POWERS

Henry was as ungrateful to Cromwell for his devoted services as he had been to Cromwell's one-time master, Cardinal Wolsey. Anne proved no more able to provide Henry with a male heir than Catherine had, and was soon dispensed with, Cromwell doing the dirty work: she faced trumped-up charges of adultery and incest, and suffered the axe. Cromwell dealt similarly with the Poles and Courtenays, two families who were potential dynastic rivals to the Tudors. The Tudor position was strengthened when Henry's third wife, Jane Seymour, produced the longed-for male heir, but the effort killed her.

Cromwell's downfall was to suggest that Henry take as his fourth bride a Flemish/German princess, Anne of Cleves, a marriage that would support Cromwell's effort to build an anti-French and anti-Habsburg alliance with the Protestant German princes. Cromwell had told Henry of Anne's great beauty, but when the king met her he was physically revolted by 'the Flanders Mare', and immediately after marrying her set about having the union annulled. Cromwell's enemies seized the opportunity to conspire against him, and the king was persuaded his minister was both a Protestant extremist and a traitor. Cromwell met his end as so many of his victims had – on the axeman's block.

Henry's marital misfortunes continued when he wed the youthful but unchaste Catherine Howard, whose infidelities caused her to lose her head. Although he found more content with his final wife, Catherine Parr, Henry had by now become fat, peevish, self-pitying and chronically unwell. He found no one of the same calibre as Cromwell to manage the government of the kingdom, and confused his countrymen by wavering between

Jane Seymour, third wife of Henry VIII, portrayed by Hans Holbein the Younger (1536).

reform and reaction in his religious policies.

But Henry still saw himself as a prince among princes, and embarked once more on the great game of kings. He revived his alliance with the emperor against Francis I, who was joined by France's old allies against England, the Scots. Henry attempted to neutralize the threat from the north by suggesting a union of his young son Edward and the infant daughter of James V – the future Mary Queen of Scots. Henry attempted to impose this match by sending his armies over the border, a campaign known as 'the Rough Wooing'. It was a typically misjudged effort: a pro-French party came to dominance in Scotland, the French attacked the south coast of England, and the war was financially disastrous. In desperation, Henry sold off the monastic lands (and so lost a great source of revenue) and debased the coinage, leading to galloping inflation. In 1546 he made peace with France.

By then Henry did not have long to live. It is thought he suffered from gout, dropsy and chronic sinusitis, and may well have had syphilis. A jousting accident in 1536 had resulted in a thigh wound that kept him from his customary athletic pursuits, thus contributing to his ever-increasing girth (he achieved a waist measurement of 54 inches). The wound never properly healed, and the resulting ulceration may have contributed to his death. He was buried alongside Jane Seymour, the only one of his wives whose death he had mourned, and the only one to have provided him with a legitimate male heir – his burning aim through so much of his reign.

1540
(6 January) Henry marries Anne of Cleves

(9 July) Annulment of Henry's marriage to Anne

(28 July) Henry marries Catherine Howard; Cromwell beheaded the same day

1542
(13 February) Catherine Howard beheaded

(24 November) English defeat Scots at Solway Moss

1543
(12 July) Henry marries Catherine Parr

1544
Act of Succession establishes that Henry is to be succeeded by his son Edward; then, if he has no issue, by Mary, his daughter by Catherine of Aragon; and then, if she has no issue, by Elizabeth, his daughter by Anne Boleyn

(July) Henry crosses to Calais to lead a further campaign against France

1546
(7 June) Treaty of Ardres: Henry makes peace with France

1547
(28 January) Death of Henry

❝ He never spared a man in his anger, nor woman in his lust. ❞
SIR ROBERT NAUNTON, *FRAGMENTA REGALIA* (1641).

EDWARD VI
1547-1553

Edward VI, the only male issue from his father's six marriages, was only 9 years old when he succeeded to the throne, and only 15 when he died. Yet his brief reign witnessed a huge cultural shift, as Protestantism was established for the first time as the state religion of England.

Biography

E dward, himself a devout Protestant, was not just a pawn in this religious revolution. A cold, precocious and somewhat haughty boy, he was intensely interested in theological matters. Despite this serious-mindedness, foreign ambassadors found Edward both quick-witted and affable, and commented on his good looks and 'becoming stature'. Although he was probably a little small for his age, and perhaps short-sighted, he was by no means a sickly child; it was only in his last two years that his health gave way.

BORN 12 October 1537, at Hampton Court

FATHER Henry VIII

MOTHER Jane Seymour

MARRIED never married

CHILDREN none

SUCCEEDED 28 January 1547

ROYAL HOUSE Tudor

STYLE Edward the Sixth, by the Grace of God, King of England, France and Ireland, Defender of the Faith and of the Church of England, and also of Ireland, on earth the Supreme Head

DIED 6 July 1553, at Greenwich Palace

BURIED Henry VII's Chapel, Westminster Abbey

EDWARD'S UPBRINGING

Edward's mother, Jane Seymour, died of puerperal fever 12 days after giving birth. Edward had a somewhat lonely childhood, but seems to have been genuinely fond of his Protestant stepmother, Catherine Parr, and spent some time with his half-sister Elizabeth, only four years his senior and also a fellow Protestant. He was more distant with his other half-sister, Mary, who was not only 21 years his senior, but also a Catholic. (When he was king, he tried to get her to abandon the mass, but, as he disappointedly recorded in his journal, 'She answered that her soul was God's and her faith she would not change, nor dissemble her opinion with contrary doings.')

The boy-king Edward VI in a painting by Guillim Stretes (c. 1547–56). Edward's short reign saw the establishment of Protestantism in England for the first time.

THE KINGS AND QUEENS OF ENGLAND

Edward's education, from the age of six, was entrusted to a group of Protestant humanists – Richard Cox, Sir John Cheke and Sir Anthony Cooke. Quite why his father Henry VIII – who, although he rejected the supremacy of the pope, adhered to Catholic doctrine – allowed his heir to be exposed to the opinions of such men, is unclear. Religion apart, Edward achieved a solid educational grounding, mastering Latin, French and Greek. He understood international affairs, was fascinated by fortifications, and showed a keen interest in reforming the currency that his spendthrift father had debased. Edward enjoyed sports and pastimes as much as any boy, but would upbraid himself if he spent too long at these pursuits instead of studying.

PROTECTOR SOMERSET

In his will Henry VIII had arranged for a council of regency, consisting of a number of peers, to rule during his son's minority. But Edward's uncle, Edward Seymour, earl of Hertford, had other plans. As Henry lay dying on 28 January 1547, Seymour brought his nephew to the Tower of London, and when the Council of Regency met there three days later, they agreed that Seymour should be protector. Only once Seymour had grasped supreme power was the news of the old king's death made public: Edward was duly declared king, and Seymour was created duke of Somerset.

Somerset had shown himself an effective soldier in campaigns against the Scots, but proved less able as a politician, alienating many in the council by his tactlessness and autocratic manner. His government introduced a number of moderate measures to establish the Protestant Reformation in England, including, in 1549, a new prayer book. This provoked rebellion among the Catholics of Devon and Cornwall, and was followed by a peasant rising in Norfolk, led by Robert Kett and largely provoked by the enclosure of common land. Somerset's enemies blamed these outbreaks on his lack of ruthlessness and his concern to defend the poor against the depredations of the 'new men' made rich in the previous reign. His former ally, Sir William Paget, wrote to him: 'It is a pity that your too much gentleness should be an occasion of so great an evil as is now chanced in England by these rebels.'

Timeline

1537
(12 October) Birth of Edward

1547
(28 January) Succeeds

(31 January) Edward's uncle, Edward Seymour, earl of Hertford (and later duke of Somerset), becomes protector

Repeal of the Act of Six Articles, which had established Catholic doctrines for the English Church

(10 September) English defeat the Scots at the Battle of Pinkie, east of Edinburgh, putting an end to the English plan to marry Edward to the infant Mary Queen of Scots

1549
(January) Introduction of new prayer book

(20 March) Execution of Somerset's younger brother, Thomas Seymour, for plotting to overthrow him

(June) Outbreak of rebellion against prayer book by Catholics in the West Country

(July) Outbreak of peasant rebellion in Norfolk

(August) Both rebellions crushed

(10 October) Somerset overthrown by John Dudley, earl of Warwick (later duke of Northumberland)

1552

(22 January) Execution of Somerset

Introduction of revised prayer book

Edward contracts measles and smallpox

1553

Archbishop Cranmer drafts Forty-Two Articles as basis of doctrine of English Church

(6 July) Edward dies of tuberculosis

NORTHUMBERLAND SEIZES POWER

Somerset's rival John Dudley, earl of Warwick (and later duke of Northumberland), put down Kett's rebellion, and in October engineered Somerset's overthrow, taking over the reins of government for himself. Somerset, although spared for a time and even restored to the council, was falsely accused of a number of crimes, and met his end in January 1552. The king briefly noted the event in his journal: 'The duke of Somerset had his head cut off upon Tower Hill between eight and nine o'clock in the morning.' The common people had more sympathy for 'the good duke', and at his execution many dipped their handkerchiefs in his blood, as if he were a martyr.

The change of regime in 1549 did not bring about a change in religious direction. In 1552 Thomas Cranmer, the Archbishop of Canterbury, introduced a more fervently anti-Catholic prayer book, and the following year drew up the Forty-Two Articles of Religion, a seminal document on matters of faith in the reformed Church of England. But there was a change in emphasis. Religious toleration and social conscience (albeit moderated by self-interest) under Somerset turned to unalloyed and rapacious ambition under Northumberland, whose reforming policies appear to have been motivated not so much by theology as by a desire to get his hands on the wealth of the Church.

THE END OF EDWARD

Henry VIII had decreed in his 1544 Act of Succession that if Edward died without issue, the succession was to go to his Catholic daughter Mary. Her sex and her religion made this an undesirable outcome in the eyes of many, so various efforts were made to find a suitable dynastic match for young Edward. Henry had attempted to persuade the Scots by force of arms that his son should marry Mary, their infant queen. Somerset, whom Henry had used to implement this pig-headed policy, continued to pursue it after Henry's death, defeating the Scots at Pinkie in September 1547. Not surprisingly, the Scots reacted by arranging a marriage for Mary with the French dauphin.

Various other European princesses were apparently considered, but in 1552 Edward contracted both measles and smallpox, making him less of a catch. Although he appears to have recovered from both of these, early in the next year he developed 'a tough, strong, straining cough', accompanied by 'a weakness and faintness of spirit'. By May, as he coughed up livid, black, stinking sputum, he was fading fast, and on 6 July he died, almost certainly of pulmonary tuberculosis. In his final prayer he is said (in the manner of royal last words) to have pleaded for his people and his faith: 'O Lord God, save Thy chosen people of England. O my Lord God, defend this realm from papistry, and maintain Thy true religion.' As it turned out, the chosen people rejected the Protestant heir he (and Northumberland) had nominated, in favour of Mary Tudor, the zealous upholder of that same papistry which Edward held in such abhorrence.

JANE
1553

Lady Jane Grey – the Nine Days' Queen – is one of the most tragic figures in English history, the innocent victim of her family's unscrupulous ambitions. A young woman of marked beauty and intelligence, she was only 15 when she was proclaimed queen, and only 16 when her enemies put her to death.

Jane, the daughter of Henry Grey, marquis of Dorset and later duke of Suffolk, derived her claim to the throne from her maternal grandmother, Mary Tudor, who was the aunt of the young king, Edward VI, and the sister of Henry VIII.

THE MANOEUVRINGS BEGIN

Jane received a good education from her tutors, and at the age of nine she went to live in the household of Catherine Parr, the sixth wife of Henry VIII, who, after the king's death, married the Lord Admiral, Thomas Seymour, an ambitious man who was brother to Edward VI's mother, the late Jane Seymour, and to Edward Seymour, the Protector Somerset. After Catherine Parr's death in September 1548 Thomas Seymour made Jane his ward, and planned to marry her to the young king, whose Protestant fervour was the equal of Jane's. But Seymour's plans came to naught, when in the following year he was executed for treason.

Since the overthrow of the Protector Somerset in October 1549, the regency had been in the hands of John Dudley, duke of Northumberland, another ambitious Protestant magnate. When Edward VI first fell sick, in 1552, Northumberland feared for his future should the king die, realizing that he would lose power, wealth and very likely his head if the 1544 Act of Succession came into play: this laid down that should Edward die without issue, he would be succeeded by his Catholic half-sister Mary.

THE DUDLEY PLOT

By May 1553 it was clear that Edward was dying. With the connivance of Jane's ambitious father, and against her own wishes, Northumberland arranged for Jane to marry his son, Lord Guildford Dudley. At the same time, Northumberland

Biography

BORN October 1537, at Bradgate Park, her family home in Leicestershire

FATHER Henry Grey, marquis of Dorset, later duke of Suffolk

MOTHER Lady Frances Brandon

MARRIED Lord Guildford Dudley

CHILDREN none

SUCCEEDED 6 July 1553 (proclaimed 10 July)

CROWNED unknown

ROYAL HOUSE Tudor

DEPOSED 19 July 1553

DIED 12 February 1554

BURIED Church of St Peter ad Vincula, within the Tower of London

Timeline

1537
(October) Birth of Jane

1553
(21 May) Jane marries Lord Guildford Dudley

(6 July) Succeeds

(10 July) Proclaimed queen

(19 July) Deposed

(22 August) Execution of duke of Northumberland

1554
(12 February) Execution of Jane and her husband

(23 February) Execution of Jane's father

persuaded the king that the throne should go to his devoutly Protestant cousin rather than to his Catholic half-sister. He had more difficulty with the council, whom he browbeat into accepting that it would be unfit for the crown to pass to a woman. Northumberland, 'in a great rage and fury, trembling for anger', successfully terrorized the reluctant council into agreeing that the succession should go to 'the heirs male' of Lady Jane; he then, at the last moment, changed the wording, so that the succession would go to 'the Lady Jane and her heirs male'.

Edward died on 6 July. On 9 July Jane was brought to the council at Syon House, to the west of London, where she was told that the king was dead and that she was queen. She was shocked, rather than thrilled, muttering a prayer that God would help her govern England. The following day she travelled by barge to the Tower of London, and was publicly proclaimed queen. To the fury of her in-laws, she refused to make her husband king.

A PITIFUL END

The news that Edward had been succeeded by his little-known cousin rather than by his half-sister Mary was not received well by the populace, who still felt sympathy for Mary's mother, so badly treated by Henry VIII. Northumberland had badly miscalculated, and by 12 July Mary was heading for London with an army of 20,000 men. She met with no resistance. What little support Jane had ebbed away over the next few days, and the end came on 19 July when Jane's father, the duke of Suffolk, acknowledged Mary as queen.

Suffolk was rewarded with a pardon, but Northumberland was executed in August. Jane and her husband were also sentenced to death for treason. They were kept in the Tower of London for some months, and Mary was inclined to pardon her hapless rival. But when Suffolk became involved in a rebellion against Mary early the following year, Mary was pressed to agree to Jane's death. A contemporary chronicler has left us the following account of her execution: 'She tied the kercher about her eyes; then feeling for the block said, "What shall I do? Where is it?" One of the standers-by guiding her thereto, she laid her head down upon the block, and stretched forth her body and said: "Lord, into thy hands I commend my spirit!" And so she ended.'

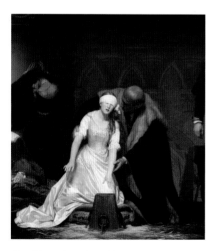

Detail from the painting The Execution of Lady Jane Grey *by Paul Delaroche (1833).*

MARY I
1553-1558

If Mary had succeeded in her aim of extirpating Protestantism from England, it is unlikely that history would have remembered her as 'Bloody Mary'. Although some 300 martyrs to the Protestant cause were burnt at the stake, the Marian persecution was not a unique phenomenon in English history: the reign of her successor and half-sister – whom history remembers as 'Good Queen Bess' – saw the deaths of almost as many Catholic martyrs.

Mary's was a miserable life. She was rejected by her father, and separated from her mother. Her marriage was childless, and her love for her husband unreciprocated. Her health was never good, and she suffered from bouts of lassitude and depression. When she was young, observers thought she would turn out 'a handsome lady', but by the time of her marriage, at the age of 38, a Spanish gentleman present described her as 'not at all beautiful: small, and flabby rather than fat … She is a perfect saint,' he concluded, 'and dresses badly.'

THE REJECTED PRINCESS

Mary, a vivacious if sickly child, was educated by her mother and Margaret Pole, countess of Salisbury (later executed by her father), and grew to be an intelligent and studious girl who loved both music and dancing. When Henry VIII's marriage to Catherine was declared void in 1533, Mary was 17 years of age. Various European princes had been lined up as prospective marriage partners, among them the dauphin of France, his father Francis I, her cousin the Emperor Charles V, and James V of Scotland. But now that she was declared a bastard and excluded from the line of succession, her marital prospects, at least in the dynastic stakes, seemed slim.

For some years Mary was out of her irascible father's favour. She was stripped of the title of princess, and made a lady-in-waiting to her younger half-sister Elizabeth. She was prevented from visiting her dying mother, and barred from attending her funeral. Eventually, in 1536, Mary – against her conscience and to her eternal regret – was persuaded by the Spanish ambassador to acknowledge the

Biography

BORN 18 February 1516, at Greenwich Palace

FATHER Henry VIII

MOTHER Catherine of Aragon

MARRIED Philip of Spain (King Philip II from 1556)

CHILDREN none

SUCCEEDED *de jure* 6 July 1553; *de facto* 19 July 1553

CROWNED 1 October 1553

ROYAL HOUSE Tudor

STYLE Mary the First, by the Grace of God, Queen of England, France and Ireland, Defender of the Faith

DIED 17 November 1558, at St James's Palace, London

BURIED Westminster Abbey

1516
(8 February) Birth of Mary

1533
(10 April) The marriage of Mary's mother, Catherine of Aragon, to her father, Henry VIII, is declared void, and Mary is thus legally illegitimate

1536
(7 January) Death of Mary's mother

(22 June) Mary reluctantly acknowledges Henry VIII as supreme head of the English Church

1541
(27 May) Execution of Mary's old governess, the countess of Salisbury

1544
Act of Succession establishes that Henry VIII is to be succeeded by Mary's half-brother Edward; then, if he has no issue, by Mary herself; and then, if she has no issue, by Mary's half-sister Elizabeth

invalidity of her parents' marriage, her own illegitimacy and Henry's position as supreme head of the Church in England. But her grovelling letter did bring her back into her father's favour, and towards the end of his reign Henry changed his mind about the succession, and decided that if his Protestant son Edward died without issue, the throne would go to Mary.

Throughout Edward's reign, at great personal risk, Mary defied the king and continued to practise as a Catholic. When she was visited by Nicholas Ridley, the Protestant Bishop of London, she dismissed him with the following words:

My Lord, for your gentleness to come and see me, I thank you; but for your offering to preach before me, I thank you never a whit.

As well as lecturing Mary, his elder by 21 years, on matters of religion, Edward – pompously pious beyond his years – also admonished her for her love of dancing.

The small clique of Protestant nobles who tried to defy Henry's wishes and make the young Lady Jane Grey queen on the death of Edward VI badly miscalculated, for even most of the Protestants in England preferred to see Henry's eldest daughter on the throne, despite her Catholicism. When Mary entered London at the head of a loyal army and was proclaimed queen, the people cheered and bells rang out across the kingdom. Lady Jane was confined to the Tower of London.

RIGHT: Mary I by Anthonis Mor van Dashorst (1554). A visiting ambassador described her as being 'of low stature, with a red and white complexion, and very thin. Her eyes are white and large and her hair reddish.'

THE HATED SPANISH MATCH

Unlike her father, Mary was reluctant to sign the death warrants of those who threatened the crown, but the softness of her heart was matched by the stubbornness of her head and the zealousness of her faith.

Mary was determined to restore England to Catholicism, and to this end fixed her heart on a marriage to Philip of Spain, the son of her cousin, the Emperor Charles V. The sympathy that she had gained among her subjects quickly evaporated at the prospect of a Spanish marriage. The House of Commons lodged a protest, boys threw snowballs at the Spanish envoys, and in January 1554 Sir Thomas Wyatt raised a rebellion in Kent and marched on the capital. Mary attempted to rouse the loyalty of her subjects with a speech at the Guildhall:

> I say to you, on the word of a prince, I cannot tell how naturally the mother loveth the child, for I was never the mother of any; but certainly, if a prince and governor may as naturally and earnestly love her subjects as the mother doth love the child, then assure yourselves that I, being your lady and mistress, do as earnestly and tenderly love and favour you. And I, thus loving you, cannot but think that ye as heartily and faithfully love me; and then I doubt not but we shall give these rebels a short and speedy overthrow.

Even though the citizens of London remained uncommitted, Mary's troops remained loyal, and Wyatt and his men were routed in the so-called Battle of Fleet Street. Wyatt was executed, and Mary was at last persuaded to sign Lady Jane's death warrant.

Mary married Philip on 25 July in Winchester Cathedral. She was ten years older than her husband, and by now whatever looks she'd had had faded. 'To speak frankly with you,' wrote one Spanish wedding guest to a friend back home, 'it will take a great God to drink this cup.' Mary's efforts to produce a Catholic heir, so that the Protestant Elizabeth could be prevented from succeeding her, proved in vain. Mary's first pregnancy turned out to be a phantom one, and, after a year, Philip left England for good, apart from a brief visit two years later, when Mary suffered another phantom pregnancy – but this time only she believed it to be genuine. For his part Philip had achieved his objective of

1547
(28 January) Henry VIII succeeded by Mary's half-brother, Edward VI

1553
(6 July) Death of Edward VI

(10 July) The Protestant Lady Jane Grey is proclaimed queen

(19 July) Mary proclaimed queen

(August) Restoration of the Catholic bishops

(1 October) Mary's coronation; she refuses to be crowned sitting on the same chair as her Protestant half-brother Edward had

1554
(7 February) Defeat of Sir Thomas Wyatt's rebellion

(12 February) Execution of Lady Jane Grey

(25 July) Mary marries Philip of Spain

(December) Parliament acknowledges the pope as supreme head of the Church in England

> ❝ In life a Dian chaste;
> In truth Penelope;
> In word and deed steadfast …
> What need I more to say? ❞

JOHN HEYWOOD, 'A DESCRIPTION OF A MOST NOBLE LADY', IN WHICH MARY'S COURT POET OFFERED A FLATTERING BUT NOT ENTIRELY INACCURATE PICTURE OF HIS QUEEN.

1555

(February) Marian persecution begins with the burning of John Rogers, a Protestant preacher, in London

(August) Philip leaves England

(16 October) Bishops Latimer and Ridley burnt at the stake

1556

(March) The Catholic Reginald Pole succeeds the Protestant Thomas Cranmer as Archbishop of Canterbury

(21 March) Cranmer burnt at the stake

1557

(7 June) Mary declares war on France

1558

(7 January) Loss of Calais to the French

(17 November) Death of Mary

The burning in Oxford of Thomas Cranmer, Archbishop of Canterbury, in 1556, in an illustration from John Foxe's Actes and Monuments, *a profoundly influential work of Protestant martyrology first published in 1563 and more commonly known as* Foxe's Book of Martyrs.

obtaining England as an ally in his war against France.

The French war, coming on top of Mary's religious persecutions at home, was hugely unpopular, and led to the loss of Calais, the last, tiny piece of the great French empire once held by the kings of England. Mary took the grief of it to her grave: 'When I am dead and opened,' she declared, 'you shall find "Calais" lying in my heart.' She died of influenza on 17 November 1558, knowing that Elizabeth would be her heir and that her dream of restoring Catholicism to England had failed. 'I felt', her husband coldly noted at her passing, 'a reasonable regret.'

Mary's Counter-Reformation

Mary, lacking the pragmatism of the other Tudor monarchs, but unlike them possessed of a conscience, never grasped the political realities of her time. It has been said that if she had executed fewer heretics and beheaded more traitors, she might have fared better. There was no possibility that she would ever be able to persuade the nobility and gentry to surrender the monastic lands they had purchased from her father, nor to win over to Rome her people's hearts and minds by means of the stake and the gibbet.

Although she persuaded a reluctant Parliament to repeal the religious reforms of her half-brother Edward,

to revive old laws against heresy, and to restore the pope as the supreme head of the English Church, her creation of Protestant martyrs such as Archbishop Cranmer only served to shore up the Reformers' cause. The psychology of martyrdom is summed up in the words of Bishop Hugh Latimer to his fellow bishop Nicholas Ridley, as the flames licked about their feet: 'Be of good comfort, Master Ridley, and play the man. We shall this day light such a candle, by God's grace, in England as I trust shall never be put out.' The Reformation in England had picked up too much momentum to be stopped in its tracks.

ELIZABETH I
1558-1603

Good Queen Bess, Gloriana, the Virgin Queen – Elizabeth now seems to us not so much a figure of flesh and blood as a character in a masque, an icon of Englishness, a symbol of majesty. This was the woman who renounced her womanhood to become the epitome of a prince, a goddess-like figure presiding over a golden age in which England defied the power of Spain and embarked on the adventure of empire.

Such is the myth, and it is a myth to which Elizabeth herself contributed, as a deliberate tool of policy. She had – as her father had had before her – a natural grasp of what her people expected of the man or woman who wore the crown. Elizabeth was above all the consummate politician, prudent and pragmatic where her half-brother Edward and her half-sister Mary had been led by their consciences into unwise zealotry. The uncertainties and dangers of her childhood and youth made her cautious and wary, reluctant to commit herself to any one course of action where indecision or ambiguity could be maintained to her advantage. These were qualities that were to serve her in good stead throughout her 45-year reign, a period so identified with her personally that it is known as the Elizabethan Age.

BIRTH AND EDUCATION

From her birth Elizabeth was a disappointment to her father, Henry VIII, for the simple reason of her sex, which made her – in his eyes – unfit to be his heir. Had he not discarded, at great trouble to himself and his realm, his first wife because she could bear him nothing but a girl-child, Elizabeth's half-sister Mary? At first, Henry was happy that Elizabeth's mother, Anne Boleyn, had at least shown herself fertile, but

Biography

BORN 7 September 1533, at Greenwich

FATHER Henry VIII

MOTHER Anne Boleyn

MARRIED never married

CHILDREN none

SUCCEEDED 17 November 1558

CROWNED 15 January 1559

ROYAL HOUSE Tudor

STYLE Queen of England, France and Ireland, Defender of the Faith and of the Church of England, and also of Ireland, on earth the Supreme Head

DIED 24 March 1603, at Richmond

BURIED Westminster Abbey

> I will never be by violence constrained to do anything. I thank God that I am endued with such qualities that if I were turned out of my realm in my petticoat, I were able to live in any place in Christome. ELIZABETH ADDRESSES PARLIAMENT, 5 NOVEMBER 1566.

The 'Ditchley portrait' of Elizabeth I by Marcus Gheeraerts the Younger (c. 1592), commissioned by Sir Henry Lee to mark Elizabeth's visit to his estate of Ditchley in 1592. The largest surviving portrait of the queen, it shows Elizabeth standing on top of England, with her feet firmly planted in the county of Oxfordshire, where Ditchley is situated. The painting also includes an adulatory sonnet, to the right of the queen's farthingale.

when Anne went on to suffer a miscarriage and a stillbirth, Henry began to look elsewhere, and by 1536 his eye had settled on Jane Seymour. Anne's fate was sealed, and in May of that year she was executed on trumped-up charges of adultery and incest, treasonous acts on the part of a queen consort. Elizabeth was not quite three when her mother lost her head. Henry's marriage to Anne was declared void, and Elizabeth was thus legally illegitimate. When Jane Seymour, who became Henry's third wife, bore him a boy-child in 1537, Elizabeth's chance of succeeding to the throne became increasingly remote. The Act of Succession of 1544 declared that if Edward should die without issue, the crown would pass to Mary, and only if she died childless would the succession pass to Elizabeth.

Elizabeth was largely brought up at Hatfield House in Hertfordshire, although she did attend court on special occasions. She was not entirely excluded from her father's affections, and Henry's sixth wife, Catherine Parr, treated Elizabeth almost like her own daughter. The young princess, by all accounts a serious girl, was provided with a number of excellent tutors, most notably the humanist scholar Roger Ascham, and mastered not only Latin and Greek, but also Italian, French and Spanish. Ascham was impressed with his pupil: 'She hath obtained that excellency of learning, to understand, speak and write, both wittily with head and fair with hand, as scarce one or two rare wits in both the universities have in many years reached unto.' She was also exposed to the principles of English Protestantism, but her lack of enthusiasm for theology was an indication of her future pragmatism as far as religion was concerned. 'There is only one Jesus Christ,' she was once reported as having said, 'and all the rest is a dispute over trifles.'

THE KINGS AND QUEENS OF ENGLAND

PERILS OF A PRINCESS

After her father's death, Elizabeth moved into the household of Catherine Parr and her new husband, Thomas Seymour. Seymour, a man of overweening ambition, apparently made advances to Elizabeth, and, after the death of his wife in childbirth, proposed marriage. Elizabeth wisely prevaricated, as in January 1549 Seymour was charged with treason against Edward VI and for plotting against his own brother, the Protector Somerset. Elizabeth was subjected to intensive and humiliating interrogations, but gave nothing away that might incriminate her. Seymour was condemned to death.

For the rest of Edward VI's short reign Elizabeth, as a fellow Protestant, was in favour, but when Edward defied his father's Act of Succession and named the Protestant Lady Jane Grey as his successor, Elizabeth sided with her Catholic half-sister Mary, and was at Mary's side when she rode into London to claim the throne. This show of loyalty did not prevent the arrest of Elizabeth in January 1554 on suspicion of involvement in Sir Thomas Wyatt's rebellion. Wyatt and many other English Protestants objected to Queen Mary's proposed marriage to the Catholic Philip of Spain, and Elizabeth was the obvious focus of Protestant discontent. She was sent, in tears, to the Tower of London, while the captured rebels were tortured to extract evidence against her. Mary's advisers urged that Elizabeth go to the block, but Elizabeth survived. She spent a year under house arrest at Woodstock, where, on a window pane, she scratched the following motto:

> *Much suspected by [of] me,*
> *Nothing proved can be.*

Throughout the rest of Mary's short reign Elizabeth kept a low profile, outwardly conforming to the re-established Catholic faith, and declaring her undying loyalty to the queen. It was in such circumstances of suspicion and danger, as heads rolled and heretics burnt, that Elizabeth first learnt the necessity of presenting the right image.

ELIZABETH'S ACCESSION

Mary had been desperate for a Catholic heir, but it is likely that her child-bearing years were over by the time she married Philip at the age of 38. Certainly there was no issue from the match, and Mary could not persuade Parliament to alter her father's Act of Succession, which meant that the Protestant Elizabeth would succeed her. In the event, Elizabeth's succession on 17 November 1558 was greeted with great rejoicing: the bells rang out from every church, and bonfires blazed across the land.

The smoothness of Elizabeth's accession has been ascribed to Sir William Cecil (later Lord Burghley), who had been on Edward VI's privy council, and whom Elizabeth made her private secretary and principal secretary of state on becoming queen. He was to prove a tireless and loyal minister to Elizabeth until his death in 1598. 'My lord,' Elizabeth said to him in his gouty old age, 'we make use of you, not for your bad legs, but for your good head.' Elizabeth was also blessed by other wise and experienced advisers, who, if not without their rivalries with each other, were creatures of the queen, not of outside factions, and served her until they died. Her courtiers, on the other hand, came in and out of favour with dazzling rapidity, but she always made sure that she kept court politics firmly separated from the serious business of running the real world.

A painting by an unknown artist (c. 1580) believed to depict Elizabeth I dancing with Robert Dudley, earl of Leicester, to music played on the violin and bass viol. The woman's position suggests that the pair are dancing the volta, a lively Renaissance dance in which the woman at one point springs into the air, and is held up by the hands and free leg of her male partner.

THE MARRIAGE QUESTION

Uppermost in everybody's minds was the question of who the 25-year-old queen should marry, for it was assumed by all that a monarch of the weaker sex would need a king to help her rule. The fact that Elizabeth never did wed has been a conundrum to historians, as it was a bafflement to her contemporaries. At the time there were those who whispered she had some 'secret reasons', perhaps some hidden physical deformity she could not bear to let a husband see. More recently, some have speculated that she was not sexually attracted to men. Regarding this latter suggestion, one has only to think of her public flirtations with her various favourites such as the earl of Leicester and the earl of Essex, and the occasional outbursts of jealousy – she was furious with Sir Walter Ralegh when he began an affair with one of her maids of honour – to have little doubt as to her sexual orientation, and the strength of her feelings.

Her attachment to Robert Dudley, earl of Leicester, was the most durable of her affections. It has been suggested that she would have married him had not the council refused to sanction it, partly because Leicester's father, the duke of Northumberland, had been the power behind the treasonous plot to put Lady Jane Grey on the throne, and partly because Leicester was, in the words of the Spanish ambassador, 'a light and greedy man'. Also hanging over Leicester was the death of his first wife, Amy Robsart, in suspicious circumstances. Romantics like to believe that Elizabeth, unable to marry the man she loved, refused to marry at all.

But there is probably a more statesmanlike reason behind Elizabeth's maintenance of her single state. She had seen the difficulties that a foreign marriage had caused her half-sister Mary, drawing her into foreign wars that were deeply unpopular with her own people. And whereas Mary was by temperament anxious to be guided, indeed dominated, by a strong male hand, Elizabeth showed no such inclination, once telling Leicester, when he had overstepped the mark on some matter, 'God's death, my lord, I will have here but one mistress and no master.' The alternative to a foreign match was to marry one of the leading nobles of the land – such as Leicester – but the obvious danger here was that the queen would thus be seen showing favour to one particular family, thereby creating factionalism and strife among the aristocracy. Not that Elizabeth did not know how to play one faction off against the other – but she was never going to permit any one group to gain the upper hand.

Thus it was not necessarily by default that Elizabeth cultivated the image of the Virgin Queen. Whether she actually remained *virgo intacta* is unknown, but to her people she presented herself as the woman who was wed not to one man, but to her whole realm. And, when the threat of foreign invasion arose, her virginity – always represented as a jewel in Renaissance iconography – became a symbol of the inviolability of England, that 'precious stone set in a silver sea' (as one of her more effective propagandists put it).

Elizabeth's *via media*

'I would not open windows into men's souls,' Elizabeth famously declared, and, broadly speaking, her religious policy aimed to

Timeline

1533
(7 September) Birth of Elizabeth

1536
(19 May) Execution of Elizabeth's mother, Anne Boleyn, after which Elizabeth is declared a bastard

1544
Act of Succession names Elizabeth third in line to the throne, after her half-brother Edward and half-sister Mary

1547
(28 January) Accession of Edward VI on death of Henry VIII

1553
(19 July) Mary I proclaimed queen following death of Edward

1554
(January) Elizabeth sent to the Tower on suspicion of involvement in Sir Thomas Wyatt's rebellion

When she smiled, it was pure sunshine, that everyone did choose to bask in, if they could. But anon came a storm from a sudden gathering of clouds, and the thunder fell in wondrous manner on all alike. SIR JOHN HARINGTON, ELIZABETH'S GODSON, DESCRIBES HER MOODS, SIMILAR IN THEIR EFFECT TO THOSE OF HER FATHER. LIKE EVERYTHING ELSE ABOUT HER, THEY MAY HAVE BEEN AN INSTRUMENT OF POLICY, KEEPING COURTIERS, MINISTERS AND PARLIAMENT NEVER KNOWING WHETHER THEY HAD PLEASED THE QUEEN ENOUGH. 'WE ALL LOVED HER,' WROTE HARINGTON, 'FOR SHE SAID SHE LOVED US.'

Mary Stuart, queen of Scotland, in a portrait by a follower of the 16th-century French miniaturist François Clouet.

1558
(17 November) Elizabeth succeeds on the death of Mary

1559
(15 January) Crowned

Act of Supremacy makes Elizabeth 'supreme governor' of the English Church, while Act of Uniformity restores Protestant practice

1560
Death of the wife of the earl of Leicester, Elizabeth's favourite for some years

(6 July) By the Treaty of Edinburgh, both the French and the English agree to withdraw their forces from Scotland; the French have been supporting the Catholic regent, Mary of Guise, mother of Mary Queen of Scots, while the English have been supporting the Protestant Lords of the Congregation

enforce outward conformity to Protestantism while not enquiring too closely as to her subjects' privately held beliefs. Elizabeth steered a middle way (the famous '*via media*') between the ardent and absolutist Catholicism of Mary and her Habsburg relatives on the one hand, and the levelling theocrats of Calvinism on the other.

It was under Elizabeth that the modern character of the Church of England, still to this day in England the established Church, began to take shape. In 1559, the year after Elizabeth's accession, Parliament passed the Act of Uniformity, which made the use of the Protestant *Book of Common Prayer* compulsory, and the Act of Supremacy, which required all public officials to swear an oath recognizing Elizabeth as 'supreme governor' of the Church in England (a more modest title than that claimed by her father, who had been 'supreme head'). The doctrine of the Church of England was summed up in the Thirty-Nine Articles, finally agreed in 1571, which blend (sometimes ambiguously) both Catholic and Protestant beliefs and practices.

Elizabeth did not share her half-sister's inclination to burn those with whom she disagreed on theological matters, but she had no compunction in sending traitors to their deaths. The 200–300 English martyrs remembered by the Roman Catholic Church from Elizabeth's reign were not so much the victims of religious intolerance (only four men were burnt for heresy under Elizabeth, and they were all Anabaptists), as of European power politics. Their fate was sealed when in 1570 Pope Pius V, a more uncompromising pontiff than his predecessor, issued a bull excommunicating Elizabeth and declaring 'her to be deprived of her pretended title to the aforesaid crown and of all lordship, dignity and privilege whatsoever'. He thus declared open season on the English queen, granting permission to her own Catholic subjects and to the Catholic powers of Europe to seek her overthrow.

THE TROUBLE WITH MARY

In the eyes of the Catholic Church, the rightful queen of England was Mary Queen of Scots, granddaughter of Henry VII, whose daughter Margaret had married James IV of Scotland. Mary's Catholicism was not to the taste of her subjects, but in the end it was the rivalries between the Scottish nobles and not religion that drove Mary from her throne, forcing her to seek the protection of her cousin Elizabeth in England.

It was not long after Mary's arrival in England in 1568 that the plots against Elizabeth began, and there seems little doubt that Mary was involved in most of them, in one way or another. In 1569 there was the rebellion of the northern earls (it was apparently this that encouraged the pope to issue his bull of excommunication against Elizabeth), and in 1571 an international conspiracy, called the Ridolfi Plot, was exposed. Across Europe, the religious divide became more and more polarized following the 1572 St Bartholomew's Day Massacre of Protestants in France and the outbreak of a Protestant revolt against Spanish rule in the Netherlands. The Jesuits were infiltrating clandestine missionaries into England, and to Elizabeth and her council these priests appeared no less than hostile agents of a foreign power.

Although Elizabeth herself gave a convincing display of *sang froid* in the face of danger, the atmosphere of suspicion around her increased. The queen resisted all attempts by her advisers to persuade her to rid herself of the viper in their midst, until in 1586 government spies found conclusive evidence of Mary's involvement in the Babington Plot, another conspiracy against Elizabeth's life. Although Mary was tried and found guilty, Elizabeth prevaricated for three months before signing her cousin's death warrant. After the execution, she gave a display of grief, fury and regret, declaring that she had never intended the sentence to be carried out.

THE THREAT FROM SPAIN

The death of Mary did not put an end to the danger for Protestant England. Elizabeth was as reluctant as her grandfather Henry VII to become involved in foreign wars, partly on grounds of the expense, and had mostly succeeded in playing off the two great European powers, France and Spain, against each other. But in 1585 she had reluctantly agreed to give military support to the Dutch revolt against Spain, and this, combined with the execution of Mary Queen of Scots and the attacks by English privateers on Spanish shipping returning from the New World, provoked Philip II of Spain into a massive retaliatory action, intended to clear England of Protestantism once and for all.

In the summer of 1588 the Armada, a great fleet of some 130 ships under the duke of Medina Sidonia, set out from Lisbon. The plan was to sail up the English Channel, pick up a Spanish army from Flanders under the duke of Parma, and then cross to England. But as the Spanish fleet made its way up the Channel, it was

1562
Elizabeth offers aid to the French Huguenots (Protestants), and sends troops to occupy Le Havre

1563
(27 July) English troops expelled from Le Havre

1564
(23 April) Birth of William Shakespeare

1568
(16 May) Mary Queen of Scots flees to England and seeks Elizabeth's protection

1569
(November–December) Rebellion by the Catholic earls of Northumberland and Westmorland in the north of England

1571
Thirty-Nine Articles lay down doctrine and practice of the Church of England

Exposure of the Ridolfi Plot to place Mary Queen of Scots on the throne in place of Elizabeth

1572
(2 June) Execution of Thomas Howard, duke of Norfolk, for his part in the Ridolfi Plot

1575
(14 November) Elizabeth refuses the crown of the Netherlands, offered by the Dutch rebels

1580

Beginning of covert Jesuit mission to England

(November) Defeat in County Kerry, Ireland, of Spanish and Italian troops sent to aid Irish rebels

1583

Exposure of Throckmorton's Plot against Elizabeth

1586

Evidence uncovered associating Mary Queen of Scots with the Babington Plot against Elizabeth's life

1587

(8 February) Execution of Mary Queen of Scots

(19 April) Sir Francis Drake sacks the Spanish naval port of Cadiz, delaying the embarkation of the Armada until the following year

1588

(July–August) Defeat and dispersal of the Spanish Armada

(4 September) Death of the earl of Leicester

1589

Failure of Sir Francis Drake's expedition to take Lisbon

1591

English forces under the earl of Essex sent to support the Protestant Henry IV of France

1592

Elizabeth recalls Essex from France

harried by the faster and more manoeuvrable ships of the English navy. Eventually the Spanish fleet anchored off Calais, only to be dispersed during the night by English fireships. Driven out to sea, the Spanish suffered much loss of life in an engagement off Gravelines.

Meanwhile, England prepared for invasion. When the Spanish fleet was first sighted off Cornwall, beacon fires were lit on hilltops across the kingdom. Elizabeth herself rode out to address her troops at Tilbury, where she gave a speech that rings down through the centuries:

> I know I have the body of a weak and feeble woman, but I have the heart and stomach of a king, and a king of England too, and think foul scorn that Parma or Spain or any prince of Europe should dare to invade the borders of my realm …

As it turned out, as the southerly winds gained strength, the cumbersome Spanish ships found it impossible to make headway back towards Calais. Pursued by the English fleet, the Spaniards were forced to sail north in worsening conditions. When they eventually limped home they had lost dozens of ships on the rocky coasts of Scotland and Ireland, and thousands of men had perished. In the end it was the weather that proved decisive, but the failure of the Armada enormously enhanced the prestige of England and its queen.

THE FINAL YEARS

By now the myth of Elizabeth the Magnificent was securely established, carefully cultivated by the queen herself. She turned her public appearances into living theatre, and showed herself across the land in lavish royal progresses (largely paid for by her wealthy hosts), demanding and receiving the love of her people. The poet Edmund Spenser made her the central figure in his allegorical epic, *The Faerie Queene*; Sir Walter Ralegh described her (at the age of 58) as 'riding like Alexander, hunting like Diana, walking like Venus'; while the official royal portraits displayed a richly dressed and fabulously bejewelled creature, staring out through an inscrutable white mask.

But the reality of Elizabeth's last years did not match the myth. Poor economic conditions and bad harvests led to considerable suffering, and Parliament proved increasingly reluctant to do the queen's bidding. The Tudor project to settle Ireland and end the hegemony of the Catholic Gaels, begun under Mary and continued under Elizabeth, led to a succession of rebellions, with some support from the Catholic powers of Europe. The last of these rebellions in Elizabeth's reign, headed by Hugh O'Neill, earl of Tyrone, led to the downfall of Elizabeth's last favourite, Robert Devereux, earl of Essex. A strutting turkey-cock with more courage than sense, Essex vowed to defeat Tyrone, but instead, after experiencing some minor reversals, made a private truce with the rebel earl in September 1599. Elizabeth was furious, and even more so when, against her orders, Essex returned to England. Continuing with his folly, he attempted to raise an armed rebellion in London, but it was a forlorn hope, and the queen refused even to interrupt her dinner when she heard the news. He was found guilty of treason, and executed in February 1601.

Apparently undaunted by her favourite's treachery, and despite deteriorating health, Elizabeth continued to assert herself as queen of England. When Robert Cecil, who had taken over the position of most trusted adviser from his father, Lord Burghley, had told the poorly queen she must go to bed, she responded: 'Must? Is must a word to be used to princes? Little man, little man, thy father, if he had been alive, durst not have used that word.'

Just as earlier in her reign Elizabeth had proved coy about her marital intentions, so in her later years she avoided the question of her successor. This may have been calculated, as a nominated successor would encourage the growth of factions and create an alternative centre of power. It may have been simple vanity, a reluctance to allow for the possibility that any other ruler of England could match her in her people's affections. At the end of November 1601, with little more than a year still to live, she gave Parliament the benefit of one of her finest pieces of oratory, the so-called Golden Speech:

> *Although God hath raised me high, yet this I count the glory of my crown, that I have reigned with your loves … And though you have had, and may have, many mightier and wiser princes sitting in this seat, yet you have never had, nor shall have, any that will love you better.*

It was brilliant touches such as this that made the English, in the more uncertain times of her Stuart successors, recall with fondness what became known as 'Good Queen Bess's golden times'. Earlier English monarchs had regarded England as their possession and their plaything; for Elizabeth, or so it appeared to her people, her sense of obligation to her country was at the core of her being.

1594
Beginning of the Nine Years' War against English rule in Ireland, led by the earls of Tyrone and Tyrconnell

1596
English expedition against Cadiz and other Spanish ports, led by Essex and Lord Howard of Effingham

1598
(4 August) Death of William Cecil, Lord Burghley. His son Robert takes over as Elizabeth's chief adviser

1599
Essex sent to Ireland to crush rebellion, makes peace with Tyrone and returns to England against Elizabeth's orders

1601
(25 February) Execution of Essex, following his abortive rebellion in January

(30 November) Elizabeth makes her 'Golden Speech' to Parliament

1603
(24 March) Death of Elizabeth

JAMES I
1603-1625

The accession of James VI of Scotland – great-grandson of Margaret Tudor and great-great-grandson of Henry VII – to the throne of England in 1603 ended centuries of intermittent warfare between the two countries. Known in his own time as 'the wisest fool in Christendom', James was a timid, scholarly man whose learning bordered on pedantry. His lofty conception of kingship, embodied in the doctrine of 'the divine right of kings', blinded him to the political realities of his day, and sowed the seeds of the civil war that was to divide England in the reign of his son Charles.

Biography

BORN 19 June 1566, at Edinburgh Castle

FATHER Henry Stewart, Lord Darnley

MOTHER Mary Queen of Scots

MARRIED Anne of Denmark

CHILDREN three sons and four daughters, of whom the following survived into adulthood: Henry (prince of Wales, died 1612), Elizabeth (married Frederick of the Palatinate, later king of Bohemia), Charles (the future Charles I)

SUCCEEDED 24 March 1603 (he had been crowned king of Scotland on 29 July 1567)

CROWNED 25 July 1603

ROYAL HOUSE Stuart

STYLE King of England, Scotland, France and Ireland, Defender of the Faith and of the Church of England, and also of Ireland, on earth the Supreme Head

DIED 27 March 1625, at Theobalds House, Hertfordshire

BURIED Westminster Abbey

Physically, James was unprepossessing. One contemporary, Sir Anthony Weldon, left a malicious but not inaccurate description: 'His eyes large, ever rolling after any stranger came in his presence … His beard was very thin, his tongue too large for his mouth, which ever made him speak full in the mouth, and made him drink very uncomely …' James's physician, Sir Theodore Mayerne, also left an account of his master's physical characteristics: 'King James's legs were slender, scarcely strong enough to carry his body … he was very clumsy in his riding and his hunting, and frequently met with accidents.' Mayerne adds that James was 'very promiscuous in his use of wines', but apparently rarely actually inebriated. Other sources attest to the king's garrulity and delight in obscenity ('I give not a turd for your preaching,' he told one Scottish minister). The picture we are left with is thus of a corpulent, coarse, clumsy, slobbering buffoon – but then James never was very popular with his English subjects.

THE BOY KING

James did not have an ideal upbringing. He was the only son of Mary Queen of Scots and her second husband, Lord Darnley. When James was only eight months old his father was blown up while staying in a house in Edinburgh. It was widely believed, with considerable justification, that he had been murdered by James Hepburn, earl of Bothwell, probably

James I in a painting attributed to John de Critz (c. 1605).

at the bidding of Mary herself, who shocked her countrymen by marrying Bothwell – after he had abducted and raped her. The Scottish lords rose in revolt, deposed Mary, and on 24 July 1567 made the one-year-old James king of Scotland. After a brief attempt to regain power the following year, Mary was forced to flee to England. James never saw his mother again. He does not seem to have grieved over much when, after 19 years of plotting against Queen Elizabeth, the mother he had barely known was put to death.

Brought up a Protestant, James was given a rigorous education, and among his tutors was the distinguished Scottish humanist George Buchanan. A succession of regents ruled during his minority, and the king became a pawn in the interminable internecine squabbles of the Scottish nobility. The 'timorous disposition' that Sir Anthony Weldon so despised in the older king is hardly surprising, and more than once the young James was seized by rival magnates, and made to fear for his life.

THE SCOTS ARE COMING

After James took power himself in 1585 he managed to impose his rule over the various rival factions, and restored a degree of stability to his realm. In 1586 he concluded a treaty of alliance with Elizabeth, and lodged only a formal protest when his mother was executed the following year. With Mary's death, James became the heir presumptive to the English throne, although Henry VIII's will had excluded from the succession the descendants of his sister, Margaret Tudor.

Timeline

1566
(19 June) Birth of James

1567
(9/10 February) Murder of James's father, Lord Darnley

(24 July) James declared king of Scotland on the overthrow of his mother, Mary Queen of Scots. James Stewart, earl of Moray, becomes regent

(29 July) James crowned king of Scotland, as James VI

1570
(23 January) Assassination of Regent Moray by supporters of the exiled Mary. Matthew Stewart, earl of Lennox, becomes regent

1571
Assassination of Lennox. John Erskine, earl of Mar, becomes regent

1572
(29 October) Death of Mar, possibly by poison. James Douglas, earl of Morton, becomes regent, having held effective power since 1570

1579
Esmé Stewart arrives in Scotland from France, and becomes James's favourite

1581
(2 June) Morton, having been overthrown, is executed for the murder of James's father. James makes Esmé Stewart duke of Lennox

1582

Ruthven Raid: James abducted by William Ruthven, earl of Gowrie, held captive for ten months, and forced to dismiss Lennox

1585

James assumes power in Scotland

1586

Makes treaty of alliance with England, and is granted a pension by Elizabeth

1600

Gowrie Conspiracy: James claims he has been attacked while visiting their house by John Ruthven, earl of Gowrie, and his brother Alexander; both his alleged assailants are killed by the king's attendants

1603

(24 March) James succeeds to throne of England as James I

(25 July) Crowned king of England

1604

Parliament rejects James's proposal of a union with Scotland; end of war with Spain

1605

(5 November) Discovery of Gunpowder Plot to blow up king and Parliament

1606

(31 January) Execution of the Gunpowder Plot conspirators by hanging, drawing and quartering

To the intense frustration of her ministers, Elizabeth never made it clear who was her preferred choice of successor, although the treaty of 1586 acknowledged James's right to the English throne. Some time before Elizabeth's death her chief adviser, Robert Cecil, entered into a secret correspondence with James, in an effort to ensure a smooth transition.

Elizabeth died on 24 March 1603. In a remarkable display of stamina, the messenger bearing the news rode the 400 miles north from London to Edinburgh in just three days. Just over a week later James set off on the journey south, glad to leave his poor kingdom for such a rich one. By the time he had reached York he had run out of money, and was obliged to write to the Privy Council in London to request more funds.

KING AND PARLIAMENT

James was initially welcomed by his English subjects, who were relieved, after half a century of female rule, to have a king on the throne again – and what's more a Protestant king with male heirs in tow. But it was not long before James's popularity began to wane. After the carefully cultivated majesty of Elizabeth, James cut a homely and undignified figure. Ironically, while Elizabeth projected the image of absolute power but never asserted it, it was the other way round with her uncharismatic successor.

James had been used to bulldozing the Scottish Parliament into doing his bidding, and he failed to recognize the growing sense of independence and power in the Parliament of England. Elizabeth had been irritated with some of the advice Parliament had thought fit to offer her, and its reluctance to grant her all the tax revenues she requested, but she never pushed the constitutional issues at stake to the test. James, on the other hand,

God's wounds! I will pull down my breeches and they shall also see my arse! JAMES I, WHEN TOLD THAT HIS ENGLISH SUBJECTS WISHED TO SEE HIS FACE.

I will govern according to the common weal, but not according to the common will. JAMES I, IN DECEMBER 1621.

George Villiers, 1st duke of Buckingham, by Peter Paul Rubens (c. 1625). The son of a minor nobleman, Villiers rose to high office under the patronage of James I.

had worked it all out intellectually. 'Kings are justly called gods,' he told the English Parliament, 'for that they exercise a manner or resemblance of divine power upon earth.' He continued:

> *For if you will consider the attributes of God, you shall see how they agree in the person of a king. God hath power to create or destroy; make or unmake at his pleasure; to give life or send death; to judge all and to be judged nor accountable to none; to raise low things and to make high things low at his pleasure. And the like power have kings.*

Needless to say, this sort of thing did not go down well, and in response Parliament asserted its 'liberties and privileges', particularly its sole right to grant new taxes. Increasingly, James attempted to rule without summoning Parliament, raising money for his unaffordable extravagances through a variety of unpopular stratagems, such as the sale of monopolies and the imposition of custom duties via the courts. He also sold peerages, and created the new rank of baronet primarily as a means of raising revenue.

The favourites

In his formative years, with his father dead and his mother absent, James was kept from the company of women. As a result, he developed strong emotional attachments to a succession of good-looking male favourites, whom he in turn raised to positions of power. When James first came south, his patronage of his Scottish courtiers, such as his former pageboy, Robert Carr, caused resentment, and throughout his reign James made politics a very personal affair, restricting his favours to a small court circle while ignoring the aspirations of a wider section of his subjects.

After the death of his capable chief minister, Robert Cecil, in 1612, James chose Carr – still only 25 – as his replacement. It was a poor choice, Carr turning out to be both corrupt and

1607
(4 July) James prorogues Parliament after it again rejects James's proposal of a union with Scotland

(14 September) The Flight of the Earls: the former Irish rebel leaders, the earls of Tyrone and Tyrconnell, flee from Ulster, which is subsequently opened up to settlement ('plantation') by Scottish Protestants

1610
Failure of the so-called Great Contract, by which James was to receive a regular income from Parliament in exchange for surrendering his feudal rights

1611
(25 March) James makes Robert Carr, his favourite, Viscount Rochester

James creates the rank of baronet as a way of raising funds

1612
(24 May) Death of Robert Cecil, James's chief minister; his place as secretary of state is taken by Robert Carr

(6 November) Death of Henry, prince of Wales, from typhoid

1613
(14 February) Marriage of James's daughter Elizabeth to the Protestant Frederick V, elector palatine of the Rhine

(3 November) James makes Carr earl of Somerset

The Gunpowder Plotters in a contemporary engraving. Robert Catesby and Guy Fawkes, respectively mastermind and explosives expert of the Catholic conspiracy against James I, are the second and third figures from the right.

1614

(7 June) James dissolves the 'Addled Parliament', so called because it passes no legislation, owing to the deadlock between it and the king

1615

Carr disgraced after he and his wife are found guilty of the murder of Sir Thomas Overbury

1616

(23 April) Death of William Shakespeare

James begins to sell peerages

1617

(January) James makes his favourite, George Villiers, earl of Buckingham

(June) James imposes the Five Articles of Perth on the Scottish Church, enforcing Anglican practices

1618

(7 January) Francis Bacon becomes lord chancellor

(29 October) Execution of Sir Walter Ralegh (at the behest of the Spanish king) on a charge of treason dating back to 1603

1619

James refuses assistance to his son-in-law, Frederick V, as the Thirty Years' War gets underway in Europe

ineffective. His successor was another handsome young man, George Villiers – 'sweet Steenie' – whom James made duke of Buckingham. Buckingham was more competent than Carr, but he was a haughty opportunist, and proved no more popular with Parliament or people.

James undoubtedly had strong homosexual leanings, at least at the emotional level. He addressed Buckingham as his 'sweet child and wife', and had no reservations about kissing his favourites in public, in a fashion that contemporaries variously described as 'lascivious' and 'slabbering'. But James was not entirely immune to female physical charms, and did more than his marital duty by his queen, Anne of Denmark, fathering three sons and four daughters. However, he found that Anne's interest in little other than clothes and jewellery only confirmed his prejudice against women as shallow, stupid creatures.

RELIGION AND FOREIGN POLICY

James was suspicious of the Presbyterianism of his fellow Scots, and insisted on his right to appoint bishops as a means of controlling the Church – 'No bishop, no king' was his motto. In England, he steered a middle ground between Catholics and Puritans, and was tolerant of both, insisting merely on loyalty. Despite this toleration, and the end of the war with Catholic Spain, in 1605 a group of Catholic conspirators led by Robert Catesby planned to blow up the king during the state opening of Parliament. But on 5 November one of the plotters, Guy Fawkes, was found with barrels of gunpowder in the vaults of the House of

James the author

James – sarcastically known as the British Solomon – was one of the most literary kings of England, writing poems, translations, and works on politics and theology, albeit none of them of any great merit. Among his better known works are: *Daemonologie* (1597), reflecting James's interest in witchcraft; *Basilikon Doron* (1599), a treatise on the art of kingship in the form of a letter to his son; and *A Counterblaste to Tobacco* (1604), in which James attacks the novel fad of tobacco smoking. James's finest contribution to literature, however, was the Authorised or King James Version of the Bible, which he commissioned from a committee of Anglican divines.

Lords, and the so-called Gunpowder Plot was foiled. To this day in Britain, fireworks are let off every 5 November, and effigies of Guy Fawkes burnt.

James's foreign policy reflected his pacific approach to religion at home. Seeking for even-handedness in his dynastic arrangements (and also vainly imagining he could heal the religious wounds of Europe), he married his daughter Elizabeth to the leading German Protestant prince, Frederick of the Palatinate, and entered into lengthy negotiations to marry his eldest surviving son Charles to the daughter of the Catholic king of Spain. This last proposed match was deeply unpopular with James's Protestant subjects, especially as the Spaniards had successfully demanded the execution of Sir Walter Ralegh, whose activities in the New World had been an irritant to Spain. When in 1621 Parliament criticized the proposed match, James furiously tore out the relevant page from the journal of the House of Commons.

In his last few years James, although only in his fifties, was slipping into premature senility and suffering from chronic inflammation of the kidneys. Power effectively passed to his son Charles, himself infatuated with (and thus controlled by) Buckingham, and the two travelled together to Madrid to pursue the Spanish marriage. But they were rejected, and in their humiliation joined in the popular clamour for war with Spain. On 27 March 1625, having suffered a stroke, James died peacefully in his bed. The quietness of his passing says something for his abilities as a ruler, given that so many of his Stuart predecessors had suffered violent and untimely deaths. Such a violent end was also to be the lot of James's unwise son, Charles.

1621
Francis Bacon impeached for corruption, but pardoned by James

The House of Commons objects to James's plan to marry his son Charles to a Spanish princess, calls for war on Spain, and denies the king has a right to imprison members of Parliament who criticize his foreign policy. In response, James arrests the MPs Sir Edward Coke and John Pym

1622
(8 February) James dissolves Parliament

1623
(May) James makes George Villiers duke of Buckingham

(30 August) Buckingham and Prince Charles leave Madrid, after the Spanish finally reject Charles's marriage proposal

1624
(February) Parliament meets, declares monopolies illegal and votes to help Frederick V recover the Palatinate

(10 March) Declaration of war on Spain

(December) Marriage treaty with France, by which Charles is to marry Henrietta Maria, daughter of Henry IV

1625
(27 March) Death of James

CHARLES I
1625-1649

A proud, pious and ultimately rather pathetic figure, Charles absorbed his father's delusions about the 'divine right of kings', with disastrous consequences. His stubbornness in religious matters, and his attempts to turn himself into an absolute monarch and rule without Parliament, eventually pitched the country into civil war, culminating in his trial and execution for treason. England was divided against itself as it had never been before, and to his countrymen the dead king was either a blameless martyr, or a bloody tyrant who had met with his just deserts.

Biography

C harles, though a small man (only 5 ft 4 in), cut a more dignified figure than his father, James I. He took greater care of his person, and although somewhat shy and prone to a stammer, set great store by courtesy, refinement and good taste. His court was notably less debauched than that of James I: 'King Charles was temperate, chaste and serious,' wrote Lucy Hutchinson, the wife of one of the men who signed Charles's death warrant in 1649, 'so that the fools and bawds, mimics and catamites of the former court grew out of fashion. Men of learning and ingenuity in all arts were in esteem and received encouragement from the king, who was a most excellent judge and a great lover of paintings . . .'

Among the artists patronized by Charles were van Dyck and Rubens, two of the finest painters of the period. But the concomitant of Charles's aestheticism was an aloofness from the ordinary people, with whom he never mixed and to whom he was quite indifferent. He possessed neither the common touch nor the charisma of the Tudors – or indeed of his son, Charles II – and treated kingship, not as a pleasure or a privilege, but as a gloomy duty.

THE PRINCE AND HIS MARRIAGE

Charles was a studious, lonely and rather unhappy boy, always addressed by his father as 'baby Charles'. He was very fond of his elder brother Henry and elder sister Elizabeth, and was devastated when Henry died in 1612 and bereft when his sister left England to marry a German prince in 1613.

With Charles now the heir apparent, the question of his own marriage became of prime importance. James intended that he should marry the infanta of Spain, a bastion of Catholicism in Europe. The proposed marriage was widely

BORN 19 November 1600, at Dunfermline Palace, Fife

FATHER James I

MOTHER Anne of Denmark

MARRIED Henrietta Maria, daughter of Henry IV of France

CHILDREN Four sons and five daughters, including: Charles (the future Charles II), Mary (princess royal, later married to the son of the prince of Orange), James (the future James II), Henry (duke of Gloucester), Henrietta Anne, Elizabeth

SUCCEEDED 27 March 1625

CROWNED 2 February 1626

ROYAL HOUSE Stuart

STYLE King of England, Scotland, France and Ireland, Defender of the Faith and of the Church of England, and also of Ireland, on earth the Supreme Head

DIED 30 January 1649 (beheaded), in Whitehall, London

BURIED St George's Chapel, Windsor Castle

opposed in Protestant England, but pursued in a spirit of romantic gallantry by Charles, who, accompanied by James's favourite, the duke of Buckingham, made an incognito journey to Spain. 'My sweet boys and venturous knights,' simpered the feeble old king as he waved them on their way, 'worthy to be put in a new romanzo.' Arriving in Madrid unannounced, Charles found that his hosts, once they had got over their surprise, insisted that the marriage could only go ahead if Charles converted to Roman Catholicism. Furthermore, he was refused access to the infanta without a chaperone, and when he attempted to get round this by jumping over a garden wall, the startled princess fled.

Humiliated, Charles returned to England calling for war with Spain. As his father grew more and more incapable, the prince and Buckingham set about negotiating a marriage with Henrietta Maria, daughter of Henry IV of France, Spain's bitter enemy.

James died in March 1625, and Charles married Henrietta Maria soon after he succeeded. Their first meeting was not auspicious: the French princess, only 16 years old and rather young for her age, with bulging eyes and sticking-out teeth, burst into tears at the sight of her husband-to-be. For some years their relations were rather cool, but they grew to be fond of each other, and in 1630 she bore him an heir. However, the queen's fancy French fashions and her openly practised Catholicism never made her popular with the more stolid of Charles's Protestant subjects.

Henrietta Maria, queen consort of Charles I, by Sir Anthony van Dyck (c. 1633). The new American colony of Maryland, founded in 1632, was named in her honour.

Timeline

1600
(19 November) Birth of Charles

1604
(July) Travels down to London to rejoin his father

1612
(6 November) Death of Charles's elder brother Henry from typhoid

1623
Charles travels to Spain to seek the hand of the Spanish infanta, but is rejected

1625
(27 March) Succeeds to the throne

(1 May) Marries (by proxy) Henrietta Maria of France (marries in person on 13 June, at Canterbury)

(May) Charles calls his first Parliament

EARLY STRUGGLES WITH PARLIAMENT

When Charles called his first Parliament, in May 1625, the House of Commons was dominated by Puritans – the name given to those of a more extreme Protestant or 'Low Church' bent who favoured simplicity, preaching and improvised prayer, and who were vitriolically opposed to all things 'popish'. The Puritans were strongly critical of Charles's marriage, and opposed to the king's own 'High Church' religious practices, which placed more emphasis on ritual and the use of the Prayer Book.

Parliament also deeply mistrusted the mercurial Buckingham, whom Charles had kept on as chief minister, and was critical of

Triple portrait of Charles I, an anonymous copy (c. 1750) of a painting by Sir Anthony van Dyck (1599–1641).

1626

(2 February) Crowned

(June) Charles dissolves Parliament after it threatens to impeach Charles's chief minister, the duke of Buckingham

1628

Parliament issues the Petition of Right

(23 August) Assassination of Buckingham

1629

Charles dissolves Parliament, which does not meet again until 1640

1630

(29 May) Birth of Charles's heir, the future Charles II

1633

(14 October) Birth of Charles's second son, the future James II

1638

National Covenant in Scotland against Charles's attempt to impose Anglican practices

1639

(May) Thomas Wentworth, later earl of Strafford, becomes Charles's chief adviser

(24 May) Beginning of First Bishops' War between Charles and the Scots

the conduct of the war with Spain. Furthermore, it proved reluctant to grant the king the money he demanded unless its own powers were increased. Charles took all this as a personal slight and a slur on his honour – an attitude he was to maintain throughout his reign whenever Parliament offered criticism or asserted its rights. When the next Parliament threatened to impeach Buckingham for his poor handling of the war, Charles dissolved it (June 1626). He then sought to bypass Parliament by raising funds via a 'forced loan', and arresting those who refused to pay.

All this further alienated Parliament. When it met again in 1628 it drew up the Petition of Right, declaring that taxes unauthorized by Parliament, arbitrary imprisonment, forced billeting of troops on the populace and the imposition of martial law on civilians were all illegal. In order to obtain funds, Charles reluctantly gave his assent to the Petition, so making it law. The assassination of Buckingham – who had in the meantime involved England in a war in support of the French Protestants – removed one difficulty, but Charles's fourth Parliament, meeting in 1629, kept up the offensive, abhorring High Church practices as 'popish' and again condemning the levying of taxes without their consent. Charles reacted by attempting to dissolve Parliament, a move that was initially thwarted when a number of members held the speaker down in his chair, while three resolutions condemning the king's actions were read out loud to the chamber.

THE 'ELEVEN YEARS' TYRANNY'

After this, Charles determined to do without Parliament altogether, and thus began the period known by his detractors as the Eleven Years' Tyranny. Technically, Charles may have been acting within the law, but he was seriously out of temper with the times. Unable to raise money via Parliament, Charles sought to make economies, beginning by bringing the wars with Spain and France to an end. He also imposed 'ship money', a tax unsanctioned by Parliament, to pay for the upkeep of the navy.

In 1633 Charles courted further unpopularity with his appointment of William Laud, his principal adviser, to the see of Canterbury. Archbishop Laud, like Charles a proponent of the anti-Calvinist movement known by its enemies as Arminianism, brought in more and more High Church ceremonial and liturgy – to the utter horror of the Puritans, whom Laud in turn described as 'a wolf held by the ears'.

It was Charles's inflexibility in religious matters that was to prove his undoing. Bishops – the king's appointees – were never popular with the Presbyterian Scots, and when Charles attempted to impose the English Prayer Book on the Scottish Church, thousands of them signed the National Covenant rejecting both bishops and Prayer Book. Charles determined to impose his will by force, and thus began the so-called Bishops' Wars.

THE ROAD TO CONFLICT

Charles badly needed funds to fight the rebellious Scots, and his two closest advisers, Laud and Thomas Wentworth, earl of Strafford, urged him to summon Parliament. The so-called Short Parliament met in April 1640, and insisted on airing its pent-up grievances before discussing the funding of a war to which it was opposed. Charles would have none of it, and dissolved Parliament the following month. In August the Scots crossed the Border, and Charles was again persuaded of the necessity of summoning a Parliament.

The Long Parliament began to sit in November 1640. Charles for once swallowed his pride, accepting the abolition of ship money and similar 'illegal' taxes, and agreeing that Parliament should be summoned at least every three years, and should not be dissolved without its consent. He also gave up Strafford to his enemies, having previously sworn to protect him, and on 12 May 1641 the hated 'Black Tom' went to the block. Parliament was by no means done. In November it issued the Grand Remonstrance, listing all the abuses of power of the king's government since Charles's accession.

When Parliament demanded control of the army, fearing that Charles would use it

1640
(13 April–5 May) Short Parliament

(20 August) Beginning of Second Bishops' War; Scots invade northern England

(3 November) Beginning of Long Parliament

(25 November) Strafford is sent to the Tower

(December) The House of Commons declares ship money illegal, calls for the abolition of episcopacy and impeaches Archbishop Laud

1641
(12 May) Execution of Strafford

(23 November) Parliament votes in favour of the Grand Remonstrance

1642
(4 January) Charles goes to Parliament to arrest the 'Five Members'

(4 July) Parliament forms a committee of public safety, to prepare for war

(22 August) Charles raises his standard against Parliament

(25 October) Indecisive battle at Edgehill

1644

(2 July) Decisive Parliamentary victory at Marston Moor

(14 July) Henrietta Maria leaves England for France, and will never see her husband again

(22 October) Parliament's Scottish allies take Newcastle

1645

(10 January) Execution of Archbishop Laud

(14 June) Parliamentarian victory at Naseby

(13 September) The Royalist commander in Scotland, the marquis of Montrose, is defeated at Philiphaugh

1646

(6 May) Charles surrenders to the Scots

(25 June) Fall of Oxford to the Parliamentarians, ending First Civil War

(23 December) Scots hand over Charles to Parliament

against them, the king's advisers judged that public opinion might regard this as a step too far. Urged on by his more decisive wife (whom Parliament was threatening to impeach), Charles attempted to reassert his authority, accusing five of his leading opponents in the Commons, among them John Pym and John Hampden, of treason. On 4 January 1642 the king went to the House of Commons himself, at the head of 400 armed men. But by the time Charles had entered the chamber, his enemies had absented themselves, and his attempted coup against Parliament had failed.

THE CIVIL WAR

Both sides – Royalists and Parliamentarians – now mobilized for war. The king and queen left London, a hotbed of anti-Royalism, and in February the queen went to the Low Countries to raise money by pawning the crown jewels. On 22 August 1642 Charles raised his standard at Nottingham, calling for the aid of all his subjects in suppressing 'the rebellion of the earl of Essex [the Parliamentary commander] in raising forces against him'. At the beginning of hostilities, the Royalists broadly controlled the north and west of England (the court was based at Oxford), while the Parliamentarians controlled the south and east.

After a few skirmishes, the real fighting began at the Battle of Edgehill in October. Charles himself commanded forces in the field during the ensuing war, but control of strategy was in the hands of his cousin, prince Rupert of the Rhine. For the next two years battles were fought all over England, with neither side gaining a major advantage, until the Royalist defeat at Marston Moor, near York, after which the king lost control of the north. Following the Parliamentary victory at Naseby in June 1645, Charles, who did not have adequate resources for such a long war, realized his position was hopeless, and in May 1646 he surrendered to a Scottish Presbyterian army, in the hope of negotiating his way out of his difficulties.

The Scots handed Charles to Parliament in 1647, but the king was then forcibly seized by the army, which was increasingly at odds with Parliament. Charles managed to escape to the Isle of Wight, where the Parliamentary governor kept him in Carisbrooke Castle. From here, Charles continued to negotiate separately with the Scots Presbyterians, Parliament and the army, all of whom believed that Charles had an essential part to play in any constitutional settlement. Charles eventually came to an understanding with the Scots, whereby he would introduce Presbyterianism into England in return for military support. In July 1648 Royalist risings broke out in

THE KINGS AND QUEENS OF ENGLAND

The beheading of Charles I in an etching by Jan Luyken (1649–1712). After his execution Charles's body was placed in the vault of the tomb of Henry VIII in St George's Chapel, Windsor. In 1813 workmen accidentally broke into the vault, and the contents of his coffin were examined by the prince regent in the presence of a royal physician.

various places, and a Scots army crossed the border into England. But Charles's hopes evaporated as the risings were put down and the Scots were decisively defeated at Preston on 17 August.

TRIAL AND EXECUTION

Charles had backed the wrong horse. While he was brought to Windsor, the army purged the Long Parliament (which had sat since 1640) of those suspected of Royalist sympathies. The remaining 'Rump Parliament' passed an act establishing a court to try Charles, 'that man of blood', for high treason and 'other offences against the kingdom'. The trial began in London on 2 January 1649. Charles refused to plead, claiming that monarchs only answer to God. When told that he was before a court of justice, the king replied, 'I find I am before a power.' His refusal to plead was taken as an admission of guilt, and he was sentenced to death. Charles himself was convinced that his death would make him a martyr to the Royalist cause, and ensure the succession of his son. He told his young daughter that he was dying 'for the laws and liberties of this land, and for maintaining the true Protestant religion'.

On the day of his execution, 30 January 1649, Charles wore a double shirt, in case he should shiver in the cold and the watching crowd think he trembled with fear. 'I would have no such imputation,' he said. 'Death is not terrible to me; I bless my God I am prepared.' On the scaffold, specially erected for the occasion outside the Banqueting House in Whitehall, Charles then uttered his final words, his stutter quite gone: 'I go from a corruptible to an incorruptible crown, where no disturbance can be, no disturbance in the world.' Then in a flash of the headsman's axe he was gone.

1647
(18 May) House of Commons votes to disband the army

(4 June) Army forcibly takes Charles from Parliamentary custody

(2 August) Charles rejects the army's proposals for constitutional reform

(7 August) Oliver Cromwell leads the army into London, where it takes control of Parliament

(November) Charles escapes to the Isle of Wight, but is imprisoned there

(December) Charles reaches agreement with the Scots, who will restore him in return for the imposition of Presbyterianism

1648
(1 May) Second Civil War breaks out in England

(17 August) The Scots army that has invaded England in support of Charles is defeated by Cromwell at Preston

1649
(30 January) Charles beheaded

INTERREGNUM
1649-1660

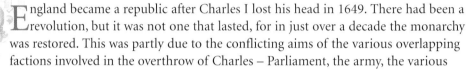

England has only ever had one period without a ruling monarch. The so-called Interregnum ('between reigns') comprised two phases: the Commonwealth (1649–53), when power was in the hands of Parliament; and the Protectorate (1653–9), when Oliver Cromwell and then his son Richard held power as lords protector.

E ngland became a republic after Charles I lost his head in 1649. There had been a revolution, but it was not one that lasted, for in just over a decade the monarchy was restored. This was partly due to the conflicting aims of the various overlapping factions involved in the overthrow of Charles – Parliament, the army, the various Puritan sects, and more radical groups such as the Diggers and the Levellers. With the backing of the army, Cromwell emerged as the strongman, but he never achieved a broadly based popularity, and the Protectorate did not long survive his death.

That the country was still wedded to the idea of a king is shown by the fact that Cromwell himself was offered the crown in 1657. A restored monarchy seemed to offer the only way out of the constitutional impasse, and it was with some relief that many in England welcomed back Charles II in 1660.

Sir Peter Lely's portrait of Cromwell. It was while sitting for this portrait that Cromwell famously told the painter, 'Mr Lely, I desire you would use all your skill to paint my picture truly like me, and not flatter me at all, but remark all these roughnesses, pimples, warts and everything as you see me. Otherwise I never will pay a farthing for it.' It was this instruction that gave rise to the expression 'warts and all'.

THE RISE OF CROMWELL

Cromwell was a Puritan by religion, a country gentleman by birth and a soldier by vocation. He entered Parliament in 1628 as MP for Huntingdon. Although a strong critic of Charles I in the Long Parliament (which began to sit in 1640), he was not at this stage amongst the most prominent of the leaders of the opposition to the king. Following the outbreak of the Civil War he raised a troop of horse for Parliament, and ignored conventional opinion by promoting promising soldiers whatever their class or religious affiliation: 'I would rather have a plain russet-coated captain that knows what he fights for … than that which you call "a gentleman",' he wrote to one critic. His military abilities brought him to prominence among the Parliamentarian commanders, and his cavalry played a key role in the decisive victory at Marston Moor in 1644.

Cromwell recognized the weakness that resulted from politicians and peers directing the military effort against the king, and as second-in-command to Lord Fairfax established the centrally controlled New Model Army. He led this professional new army to victory at Naseby in 1645, bringing the first phase of the Civil War to an end.

At this stage Parliament attempted to reassert its control over the army. Many soldiers were disgruntled by arrears in their pay, and alienated by Parliament's plan to impose Presbyterianism – at odds with the independent, more radical religious and political beliefs widespread among the troops. Cromwell emerged as the mouthpiece of this discontent, and became the effective leader of the army in its political rupture with Parliament. Cromwell was behind the army purge that resulted in the Rump Parliament, and it was the army above all who called for the king to be tried for treason.

The Commonwealth

After the execution of Charles I (a 'cruel necessity' according to Cromwell), England needed a new constitution. The monarchy was abolished by act of Parliament in March 1649, as 'unnecessary, burdensome and dangerous to the liberty, safety and public interests of the people'. In May another act declared that the people of England constituted a 'Commonwealth and Free State', governed by 'the supreme authority of this nation, the representatives of the people in Parliament'. The latter comprised the House of Commons, the Lords having been abolished. Executive power was held by a council of state, elected by and responsible to the Commons.

Over the next two years Cromwell was distracted by military campaigns in Ireland and Scotland, both of which he succeeded in bringing into the Commonwealth. The Irish Catholics had been in rebellion since 1641, and aligned themselves with Royalist resistance. Cromwell proceeded ruthlessly, and his massacres at Drogheda and Wexford in 1649 made his name a byword for barbarity in Ireland. The Scots meanwhile had proclaimed the exiled Charles II as king of Scotland, in return for his acceptance of Presbyterianism. Cromwell marched an army north, and, before doing battle, wrote to the General Assembly of the Church of Scotland to try to persuade them to change their minds, famously imploring, 'I beseech you in the bowels of Christ, think it possible you are mistaken.'

Timeline

1649
(30 January) Execution of Charles I

(17 March) Parliament abolishes the monarchy

(19 March) Parliament abolishes the House of Lords

(19 May) England becomes a Commonwealth

(11 September) Cromwell's troops put the garrisons of Drogheda and (11 October) Wexford to the sword

1650
(3 September) Cromwell defeats the Scots at Dunbar

1651
(1 January) Charles II crowned king of Scotland

(3 September) Cromwell defeats Charles at Worcester

(27 October) Surrender of Limerick ends resistance in Ireland

1652
(May) Sea battle off Dover marks the beginning of the First Dutch War

1653

(18–20 February) Three Days' Battle off Portland against the Dutch

(20 April) Cromwell forcibly expels the Rump Parliament

(July–December) Barebones Parliament

(16 December) Cromwell becomes lord protector

1654

(April) End of First Dutch War

1655

(22 January) Cromwell dissolves Parliament (which has sat since 3 September 1654) when it tries to increase its powers

(March) Suppression of small-scale Royalist rebellion (Penruddock's Rising)

1656

(February) Beginning of war with Spain

1657

(31 March) Parliament offers Cromwell the crown

1658

(3 September) Death of Cromwell; succeeded as lord protector by his son Richard

The Scots proved implacable, and were roundly defeated by Cromwell at Dunbar in September 1650. However, they recovered sufficiently to crown Charles at Scone, near Perth, in January 1651 and to march with him into England. This last Royalist cast of the dice came to a predictable end at Worcester, where in September Cromwell led a vastly superior Commonwealth force to victory, and Charles was once again forced into exile.

THE END OF THE RUMP PARLIAMENT

The Rump Parliament that held power under the Commonwealth proved too conservative for many elements in the army, who desired more radical change. Commercial interests led to a war over trade with the Dutch Republic, to the dismay of Cromwell and others in the army who saw the Dutch not as trade rivals but as fellow Protestants, and therefore as natural allies against papistry.

On 20 April 1653 Cromwell mounted a coup against Parliament, marching two files of musketeers into the House of Commons. Brandishing the mace, the symbol of Parliament in session, he declared, 'What shall we do with this bauble? Here, take it away.' He then turned furiously on the members: 'You have sat here too long for any good you have been doing. Depart, I say, and let us have done with you. In the name of God, go.'

THE PROTECTORATE

Initially, Cromwell and the army council replaced the Rump Parliament with a nominated assembly, known as the Barebones Parliament (it took its name from the MP for London, a preacher with the typically Puritan name Praise-God Barebone). Confrontation between the moderate majority and the radical minority led the former to dissolve the assembly in December 1653. The next constitutional innovation was the Instrument of Government issued by the army. This retained a single-chamber Parliament, but gave most of the power to Cromwell, who became lord protector.

Cromwell – mockingly known by his enemies as Crum-Hell or Old Noll – pleased his followers by ending the Dutch war and embarking on a war with Catholic Spain. He was broadly tolerant in religious matters, once episcopacy was abolished, and readmitted the Jews to England. As Cromwell became established in power his government lost some of its reforming zeal, but he successfully kept the various competing factions in check and worked towards reconciliation.

The protector had an uneasy relationship with his Parliaments. The first one refused to ratify the Instrument of Government and was dissolved in 1655. After an abortive Royalist rising, Cromwell instituted a form of martial law, dividing England into 12 military districts, each one under the control of a major-general. The humble social origins and Puritan fanaticism of the major-generals was widely resented, and the Parliament called in January 1657 brought their rule to an end.

The new Parliament was dominated by conservatives. It proposed a new constitution, the Humble Petition and Advice, by which Cromwell was offered the crown. He refused this, knowing the army would be vehemently opposed, and insisted on keeping his title of lord protector. However, he agreed that he should now be able to nominate his successor. Cromwell was thus King Oliver in all but name. This impression was reinforced when, on his death in 1658, his son Richard succeeded him as protector. 'King Dick', although inexperienced, was not incompetent, but a worsening financial situation and the opposition of the old army radicals and republicans drained power away from him, and his rule lasted only a few months. The political vacuum left created conditions ripe for the restoration of the Stuarts.

1659
(7 May) Restoration of Rump Parliament

(25 May) Richard Cromwell resigns as lord protector; Rump Parliament re-establishes Commonwealth

(12 October) Rump Parliament expelled by the army

(16 December) Resumption of the Long Parliament (which first sat in 1640)

1660
(16 March) Dissolution of Long Parliament

(25 April) New Convention Parliament proclaims Charles II king of England

The forcible dissolution of the Long Parliament by Cromwell's soldiers, 20 April 1653, as depicted in a contemporary Dutch engraving. Originally called by Charles I in 1640, the Long Parliament was purged in December 1648 of those members opposed to the king's trial for treason. It was the 'Rump' of remaining members of the Long Parliament who arranged Charles's trial and execution, and who then established the Commonwealth.

CHARLES II
1660–1685

After the dour period of the Commonwealth and the Protectorate – when the theatres were closed, dancing and other forms of revelry frowned upon, and even holidays such as Christmas cancelled – the return of a glittering Stuart court headed by the Merry Monarch himself was to many English people a welcome change. Charles's conciliatory approach helped to heal the wounds of decades of conflict, but his artful management of men and affairs also deferred any resolution of the constitutional issues that had torn England apart.

Biography

Charles had neither the delusions of his father regarding the divine right of kings, nor his father's melancholic disposition. He was an amiable, tolerant, and at times quite amoral man, with a twinkle in his eye and a succession of mistresses in his bed. Old Rowley (as he was nicknamed, after a prize stallion in the royal stud) presided over an age in which classical decorum was spiced with ribaldry and wit. This was the age of Dryden, Farquhar, Vanbrugh and Congreve, the age of Wren's new London and Newton's orderly universe, the age in which reason and science entered the ascendancy, and the Enlightenment was born. But under this shimmering surface darker currents flowed, as doctrinal disputation, zealotry and blind unreason continued to draw blood.

BORN 29 May 1630, at St James's Palace, London

FATHER Charles I

MOTHER Henrietta Maria

MARRIED Catherine of Braganza

CHILDREN no legitimate issue; illegitimate children included James, duke of Monmouth

SUCCEEDED 30 January 1649 *de jure*, but 29 May 1660 *de facto*

CROWNED 1 January 1651 (as king of Scotland); 23 April 1661 (as king of England)

ROYAL HOUSE Stuart

STYLE King of England, Scotland, France and Ireland, Defender of the Faith and of the Church of England, and also of Ireland, on earth the Supreme Head

DIED 6 February 1685, at Whitehall, London

BURIED Westminster Abbey

Sir Christopher Wren's plan for the rebuilding of the City of London after the Great Fire of September 1666. Work on the new St Paul's Cathedral began in June 1675, and was completed on 20 October 1708, Wren's 76th birthday.

Timeline

1630
(29 May) Birth of Charles

1649
(30 January) Succeeds *de jure* on his father's death

1651
(1 January) Crowned king of Scotland

(3 September) Defeated at Worcester

1660
(4 April) Issues Declaration of Breda, offering political amnesty and religious toleration

(29 May) Succeeds *de facto*

(October) Parliament withdraws toleration of Non-Conformists

1661
(23 April) Charles crowned king of England

1662
Scottish Parliament establishes episcopacy in Scotland

(19 May) Act of Uniformity expels Presbyterians from Church of England

(21 May) Charles marries Catherine of Braganza

(22 October) Sells Dunkirk to Louis XIV

THE RESTORATION

In the eyes of Royalists, Charles succeeded to the throne as soon as his father's head parted from his body that cold winter's day in 1649. Parliament took a contrary view, and in a matter of weeks had abolished the monarchy by statute. Though in penurious exile in the Netherlands, Charles did not abandon the struggle. He was nothing if not a survivor, finding friends wherever he could, and as readily abandoning them.

In 1650 he persuaded his most loyal Scottish ally, the marquis of Montrose, to raise a desperate Highland revolt against the Covenanters (Presbyterians) who held power in Scotland. But after Montrose's defeat and capture, Charles left the marquis to his fate and began negotiations with the victors, accepting the Covenant in return for their support. Charles had no particular

A romanticized depiction – in an engraving dated 1754 – of the fugitive Charles II lying beneath the 'Royal Oak' in the grounds of Boscobel House, Shropshire, following his defeat at the Battle of Worcester, September 1651. Aided by a Catholic family called Pendrell, Charles spent a day hiding in the tree's branches to evade his Parliamentarian pursuers. Standing next to the recumbent Charles is his fellow fugitive Colonel William Carlis, who hid with him.

intention of keeping his word, but was content to be crowned king of Scotland on 1 January 1651. He marched south with the Scots against the forces of the English Parliament, but the last phase of the Civil War came to an end with his defeat at Worcester in September. Charles himself was obliged to hide for a day in an oak tree before he could make good his escape to France.

With little in the way of resources, and without powerful foreign support, Charles made no more serious attempts to retake his kingdom. But by the end of the 1650s divisions among the various factions in England created a power vacuum, and the return of the king was negotiated by the capable but apolitical general, George Monck. Charles entered London as king on 29 May 1660.

The previous month Charles had issued the Declaration of Breda, promising a political amnesty and religious toleration, and this had eased the path for his return. After he was restored to power, there was indeed surprisingly little vengefulness, even against the regicides (those who had signed Charles I's death warrant in 1649): of the 41 who were still alive, only 9 were executed. A particularly macabre fate was served upon the embalmed corpse of Oliver Cromwell, which was dug up from its resting place in Westminster Abbey, and the head struck off. The headless remains were suspended from a gibbet at Tyburn, while the head itself was stuck on a pole and displayed on top of Westminster Hall, where it remained for some twenty years.

MINISTERS AND PARLIAMENTS

George Savile, marquis of Halifax, who served Charles through a number of ministries, wrote that the king 'lived with his ministers as he did with his mistresses; he used them, but he was not in love with them'. Although averse to concerted application, and thus happy to leave the hard work to his ministers, Charles was disinclined ever to rely on any one man, nor to give anyone his unflagging loyalty.

In exile Charles had inherited one of his father's more astute advisers, Edward Hyde, and at the Restoration he made Hyde lord chancellor and earl of Clarendon. Clarendon encouraged Charles to uphold constitutional government, but Clarendon's popularity was weakened by the expensive failure in 1667 of the Second Dutch War, and Charles turned his back on him. Threatened with impeachment, Clarendon fled to France. Other ministries followed, such as the Cabal (so called after the initials of the ministers: Clifford, Arlington, Buckingham, Ashley and

> Here lies our sovereign lord the king
> Whose word no man relies on,
> Who never said a foolish thing,
> Nor ever did a wise one.

THE PREMATURE EPITAPH PENNED FOR CHARLES BY ONE OF HIS COURTIERS, JOHN WILMOT, EARL OF ROCHESTER. THE KING FAMOUSLY RESPONDED: 'THIS IS VERY TRUE: FOR MY WORDS ARE MY OWN AND MY ACTIONS ARE MY MINISTERS'.'

Lauderdale), and that of the earl of Danby, who, though an expert political fixer, ended up in the Tower in 1679, another scapegoat for the king.

Like his father, Charles found he could not manage without Parliament, although he would have liked to have done so. Parliament was to him a necessary evil, a means of raising money. Parliament in turn suspected (with some justification) that Charles shared the Stuart taste for absolutism, and (again with some justification) that Charles was a closet Catholic in league with foreign powers.

RELIGIOUS DISPUTES

Charles's first Parliament was determinedly Anglican, and in October 1660 rejected the toleration of Non-Conformists (i.e. non-Anglican Protestants) enshrined in the Declaration of Breda. Further acts through the 1660s sought to impose conformity and uniformity in the Church of England.

Parliament would have been horrified if it had been aware of Charles's secret Treaty of Dover with the French in 1670. In return for substantial subsidies from Louis XIV, Charles agreed to support the French king's campaigns against the Dutch, and to convert to Catholicism. As it turned out, Charles waited until he was on his deathbed before going over to Rome, but he prepared the ground in 1672 with his Declaration of Indulgence, once more extending toleration to Catholics and Non-Conformists. Parliament was outraged, and forced Charles to withdraw the Declaration the following year. Charles was also obliged to give his assent to the Test Act, barring Catholics from holding public office.

1664
(5 April) Triennial Act requires Parliament to be held at least every three years

1665
(22 February) Start of Second Dutch War

(September) Outbreak of plague in London (continues until the following September)

1666
(2–6 September) Great Fire of London

(23 November) Rising of Scottish Covenanters ends in defeat at Rullion Green

1667
(June) Dutch fleet sails up the Medway and destroys nine ships of the Royal Navy

(30 August) Dismissal of Clarendon

1670
(May) Treaty of Dover with France, by which Charles secretly agrees to convert to Catholicism

1672
(15 March) Charles issues Declaration of Indulgence, offering religious toleration to Catholics and Non-Conformists

1673
(8 March) Charles withdraws Declaration of Indulgence

(29 March) Gives royal assent to Test Act barring Catholics from public office

1678

(6 September) Titus Oates, an Anglican clergyman, reveals the details of the non-existent Popish Plot against Charles

(30 November) Catholics barred from sitting in Parliament

1679

(24 January) Charles dismisses Parliament, fearing it will exclude his Catholic brother James from the succession

(26 May) Charles suspends (and later dissolves) the next Parliament after it introduces an Exclusion Bill against James

(1 June) Scottish Covenanters defeat government force at Drumclog

(22 June) Covenanters defeated at Bothwell Bridge, ending the anti-government rising in south-west Scotland

(7 October) Charles suspends another Parliament over the Exclusion Bill

1680

(15 November) The House of Lords rejects the Exclusion Bill

1681

(28 March) Another Parliament dissolved after it reintroduces the Exclusion Bill

1683

Exposure of Rye House Plot to kill Charles and his brother, in which Charles's illegitimate Protestant son, the duke of Monmouth, is implicated

1685

(6 February) Death of Charles

The Killing Time

Like his father and grandfather, Charles disliked Presbyterianism, the dominant denomination in Scotland, which rejected the Anglican Prayer Book and episcopacy. Charles took the view that Presbyterianism was 'not a religion for gentlemen', and, like his Stuart predecessors, saw bishops as a means of imposing royal control over the Church. When in need of Scots support in 1650, Charles had accepted the Covenant, the oath by which the Scots swore to defend their religion. But after the Restoration he abandoned his earlier commitment, and determined to impose bishops and his own authority on the Scottish Church. Dissenting ministers were forced out of their parishes, and many congregations followed them, holding secret conventicles in remote parts of the country. While government dragoons sought them out, the more extreme of the Covenanters called for the establishment of a Calvinist theocracy. There were uprisings in 1666 and 1679, both put down mercilessly, and the 1680s witnessed a period of brutal government repression remembered for many years after as the Killing Time.

In this atmosphere of feverish anti-Catholicism, the Popish Plot of 1678 – a hoax conspiracy by which Jesuit agents supposedly planned to murder Charles and replace him with his openly Catholic brother James – fell on fertile soil. Charles himself must have had his doubts, for he told his brother, 'I am sure no man in England will take away my life to make you king.' Nevertheless, in the hysteria 35 suspects were executed, Catholics were barred from Parliament by another Test Act, and Parliament moved to exclude James from the succession – a move that Charles successfully resisted, although he temporarily sent his brother into exile. Another secret treaty with France brought him, in return for a promise not to intervene in Europe, more subsidies from Louis XIV, enabling him to rule without Parliament for the rest of his reign.

THE KING'S MARRIAGE AND THE KING'S MISTRESSES
In later life, Bishop Gilbert Burnet recalled a conversation with Charles: 'He said once to myself, he was no atheist, but he could not think God would make a man miserable only for taking a little pleasure out of the way.' Charles took more than just a little pleasure out of the way, and had already fathered a number of bastards before his marriage in 1662 to a Portuguese princess, Catherine of Braganza. She brought him Bombay and Tangier, but failed to provide him with an heir.

Her barrenness and her Catholicism led to suggestions that Charles should divorce her, but this he would not countenance. However, he maintained a number of mistresses, including Barbara Villiers (who became duchess of Cleveland), Louise de Kéroualle (duchess of Portsmouth) and the actress Nell Gwyn. The duchess of Portsmouth was deeply unpopular with the king's subjects, being haughty, Catholic and French, and when during the anti-papist fever of 1681 a mob took Nell Gwyn's carriage for that of the foreign mistress, the actress leant out of the window and protested, 'Good people, let me pass. I am the Protestant whore.' Bishop Burnet recalled that Charles 'never treated her [Nell Gwyn] with the decencies of a mistress, but rather with the lewdness of a prostitute – as she had been, indeed, to a great many. And therefore,' Burnet continued, 'she called the king her Charles the Third, since she had been formerly kept by two of that name.' Charles may not have dignified Nell Gwyn with a title, but otherwise he was more than generous, and on his deathbed begged his brother, 'Let not poor Nelly starve.'

Nell Gwyn – former orange-girl, celebrated Restoration actress, and long-term mistress of Charles II – in a portrait from the studio of Sir Peter Lely, c. 1675. The diarist Samuel Pepys described her as 'pretty, witty Nell'. Having previously been the mistress of Charles Hart and Charles Sackville, she dubbed the king her 'Charles the Third'.

Charles's amorous exploits took their toll, and it is likely that his end was hastened by mercurial poisoning – mercury then being used as a specific against syphilis. His last years were relatively tranquil, with the country restored to stability after the Popish Plot and the Exclusion Crisis, the royal finances on a good footing, and the king's own popularity on a par with the first years of his reign.

In February 1685 Charles suffered a stroke while shaving. His death was a drawn-out affair, and he told those around him that he had been 'an unconscionable time dying; but he hoped they would excuse it'. Up the back stairs to his chamber, so often used by the king's female visitors, one of his gentlemen ushered Father John Hudleston, who had assisted Charles in his escape after Worcester, and who now received the king into the Church of Rome. Early the next morning, kept awake by pain, Charles asked the time, and then said, 'Open the curtains, that I may once more see day.' In a while he lapsed into unconsciousness, and around noon passed away in peace.

JAMES II
1685-1689

James has been painted by posterity as a Catholic despot on the European model, whose overthrow was essential for the establishment of constitutional monarchy in Britain. This was certainly the view of the Whig politicians who had a near-monopoly of power throughout the century that followed James's fall. They dubbed the largely bloodless regime change that sent James packing off to France the 'Glorious Revolution'.

A contemporary politician, the earl of Lauderdale, commented that James had 'all the weakness of his father without his strength'. These common weaknesses included inflexibility, a belief that all opposition was malicious, and an inability or unwillingness to grasp political realities. Lauderdale went on to say that James was 'as very a papist as the pope himself', which he asserted would be his ruin. However, James's religiosity was seamed with hypocrisy, for he was as much a libertine as his brother Charles II, fathering several illegitimate children by two different mistresses. But James lacked his brother's intelligence, and had none of his qualities of charm and humour. Instead, averse to any public display of emotion, he affected a somewhat stiff and formal manner. The Scots had an apt nickname for him: 'Dismal Jimmy'.

JAMES, DUKE OF YORK

James, who bore the title duke of York from infancy, was no more than a boy during the Civil War, and escaped to France to join his mother in 1648. In exile James served with the French army, and then, after his brother changed alliances, fought for the Spanish, proving himself a brave (if not brilliant) soldier. After the Restoration he became lord high admiral, in which capacity he served with reasonable distinction in the Second and Third Dutch Wars.

In September 1660 James married Anne Hyde, the daughter of Charles II's chief minister, Edward Hyde, earl of Clarendon. She converted to Catholicism before her husband did – the diarist Samuel Pepys remarked that 'the duke of York, in all things but in his codpiece, is led by the nose by his wife'. Charles

King James II by an unknown artist, c.1689. Whatever the ultimate motives behind James's moves towards toleration of Catholicism, such measures as the Declaration of Indulgence were interpreted by many as steps towards Catholic domination, and raised the political temperature to dangerous levels.

insisted that their two daughters, Mary and Anne, be brought up as Protestants.

Both James and his wife had converted in secret, but following the 1673 Test Act, which required all holders of public offices to swear an anti-Catholic oath and take Anglican communion, James was obliged to declare his religion, and to resign as lord high admiral. The same year, Anne Hyde having died in 1671, James married an Italian Catholic princess, Mary of Modena ('a very great bigot' according to James's daughter Anne). James's Catholicism became more and more of a political issue. By the end of the decade the country had been whipped up into anti-Catholic hysteria by the fabricated 'Popish Plot'. This was followed by the Exclusion Crisis (1679–81), during which the anti-Catholic faction in Parliament known as the Whigs attempted, unsuccessfully, to bar James from the succession. Their opponents (staunch Anglicans rather than Catholics) were known as Tories.

A BRIEF REIGN

Tory support ensured that James succeeded without significant opposition in February 1685. James himself was somewhat surprised, having expected hostility in Parliament and even armed rebellion. His suspicions were confirmed a few months later when in June his brother's illegitimate, Protestant son, the duke of Monmouth, mounted an insurrection in the West Country and proclaimed himself king. But Monmouth attracted little support, and his ragtag band of followers were defeated at Sedgemoor. Many of the rebels, including Monmouth himself, were put to death; others were transported. Monmouth's revolt

Timeline

1633
(14 October) Birth of James

1646
Captured by Parliamentarian forces on the fall of Oxford

1648
Escapes to the Continent

1660
(3 September) Marries Anne Hyde

1665
(3 June) Leads the Royal Navy to victory over the Dutch at Lowestoft

1671
(31 March) Death of Anne Hyde

c. 1672
(or possibly earlier) Converts to Roman Catholicism

(28 May) Defeated by Dutch fleet in Sole (Southwold) Bay

1673

(29 March) After Charles gives royal assent to the Test Act, James resigns as lord high admiral

(30 September) Marries Mary of Modena, by proxy

1678

Fabricated Popish Plot alleges Catholic conspiracy to assassinate Charles II and replace him with James

1679–1681

Parliament attempts to exclude James from the succession

1685

(6 February) James succeeds

(23 April) Crowned

(6 July) Monmouth's rebellion defeated at Sedgemoor

1686

(June) James begins to bring Catholic officers into the army

1687

(4 April) James issues Declaration of Indulgence

coincided with a similarly doomed rising in Scotland by another Protestant champion, the earl of Argyll.

Despite the lack of support for these rebellions, they confirmed James in his fear of his subjects, and also in his conviction that to make any concessions at all to his opponents would be a fatal error. He thus proceeded to strengthen the army, controversially commissioning many Catholic officers, and had a court confirm his power to excuse individuals from the provisions of the anti-Catholic Test Acts. Whether James simply wished for religious toleration or whether in the long term he intended to re-impose Catholicism and assert absolute monarchical power is not clear, but his subjects became increasingly convinced that the latter was the case. In 1687 James issued a Declaration of Indulgence, establishing freedom of worship for both Catholics and Non-Conformists (non-Anglican Protestants), and made moves to increase the numbers of Catholics in local government and the universities.

James's opponents were at this stage largely content to sit back and wait. Mary of Modena had failed to produce a male Catholic heir (the five girls she had given birth to had all died in infancy), and thus the crown would pass on James's death to a Protestant heir, James's daughter Mary, safely married to a Dutch Protestant prince, William of Orange. But in November 1687 Mary of Modena announced that she was pregnant. Buoyed up with the prospect of a Catholic son (who would have precedence over his female children), James went on the offensive. He prosecuted seven bishops, including the Archbishop of Canterbury, for refusing to read the Declaration of Indulgence from the pulpit, and in Ireland set about replacing Protestants with Catholics in government, the army and the professions. In England, in anticipation of parliamentary elections, he embarked on a large-scale purge in an effort to ensure a Parliament that would be compliant with his wishes.

THE CRISIS POINT

For their part, James's opponents spread rumours that the queen's pregnancy (her first in five years) was a fiction; and when the birth of a baby boy – James Francis Edward – was announced on 10 June 1688 it was said that the child in question was a waif who had been smuggled into the queen's chamber in a warming pan. On 30 June the dissident bishops were acquitted, and the same day a group of nobles – known as the 'Immortal Seven' – wrote to James's son-in-law, William of Orange, to ask him to come to England, ostensibly to investigate the circumstances of the royal birth and James's manipulation of the electorate, but in effect to ask him to assume the throne.

William bided his time while his agents tested the water in England. The Immortal Seven had written 'there are nineteen parts of twenty of the people throughout the kingdom who are desirous of a change'. This was very far from the truth: the movers of the 'Glorious Revolution' comprised a small section of the nobility, a powerful political class that had lost positions and privileges under James's catholicizing policies.

THE GLORIOUS REVOLUTION

William landed with 12,000 men at Torbay, Devon, on 5 November 1688, under a banner proclaiming 'The Liberties of England and the Protestant religion I will maintain.' He did not directly claim the throne (which might well have provoked a patriotic reaction by the many in England – especially in the army – who were as yet uncommitted), but declared that he had come in response to an invitation to ensure a free Parliament and freedom of religion, and to inquire into the legitimacy of young Prince James.

William advanced only very slowly towards London, leaving it to James's army to decide whether it would strike the first blow, and thus be responsible for initiating civil war. Gradually James's support fell away, and he himself was plunged into despair. On 11 December James's nerve broke, and he fled. In January 1689 the Convention Parliament meeting in London declared that by his flight James had abdicated. The next day it offered the crown jointly to James's daughter Mary and to her husband, who now became William III.

But it was not all over for James, or for his supporters, the so-called Jacobites (after *Jacobus*, the Latin version of his name). In 1689 the Highlanders rose in Scotland, and in the same year James landed in Ireland with forces provided by Louis XIV of France. In July 1690 James was defeated at the Boyne, where his courage failed him and he fled the field – earning the contempt of both sides, and the Irish nickname *Séamus an Chaca* ('James the Shite'). He returned to France, his tail between his legs, and became a pensioner of the French king, spending his declining years in private devotions and public pomposity. His hosts found him an intolerable bore.

1688
(10 June) Birth of a son, James Francis Edward, to James and Mary of Modena

(30 June) A group of Whig grandees invites William of Orange to come to England

(5 November) William lands in England

(23 December) James escapes to France

1689
(January) Convention Parliament offers English crown jointly to William and Mary

(March) James lands in Ireland

(27 July) Highland Jacobites defeat Williamite forces at Killiecrankie

(28 July) Williamite forces relieve Jacobite siege of Londonderry

(21 August) Highland Jacobites defeated at Dunkeld

1690
(1 July) James defeated at the Boyne

1691
(12 July) Final defeat of Irish Jacobites at Aughrim

1701
(6 September) Death of James

WILLIAM III & MARY II

1689-1702

Although William III of England (II of Scotland) was a Dutchman, he had a fair share of Stuart blood, being a grandson of Charles I. William ruled jointly with his Stuart wife (and first cousin) Mary, the Protestant daughter of the deposed James II, until her premature death from smallpox at the age of 32. She was a popular figure, but after her death 'Dutch Billy' had to deal with increasing hostility from his subjects. There was more than a dash of ingratitude in this, as William had fought tirelessly to preserve their liberties and their Protestant religion, and to prevent Louis XIV of France from dominating Europe.

Biography

BORN 4 November 1650, at The Hague (William); 30 April 1662, at St James's Palace, London (Mary)

FATHER William II, prince of Orange (William); James II (Mary)

MOTHER Mary, daughter of Charles I (William); Anne Hyde (Mary)

CHILDREN none

SUCCEEDED 12 February 1689

CROWNED 21 April 1689

ROYAL HOUSE Orange (William); Stuart (Mary)

STYLE King and Queen of England, Scotland, France and Ireland, Defender of the Faith and of the Church of England, and also of Ireland, on earth the Supreme Head

DIED 8 March 1702 (William); 28 December 1694 (Mary)

BURIED Westminster Abbey

William's father, the prince of Orange, died within a few days of his birth. It was a time of political turmoil in the United Provinces of the Netherlands, and the dominant republicans sought to exclude the princes of Orange from holding power. Nevertheless, William was brought up to rule, and developed qualities of charm and political astuteness. When in 1672 the Dutch became convinced that Louis XIV, in alliance with England, was about to launch an attack against the United Provinces, there was a popular clamour for William to be made captain general.

William was a tenacious if not a brilliant soldier: his desperate resistance to French attacks increased his popularity, and he was made stadholder (chief magistrate). The young prince went on to build a European alliance against Louis XIV's territorial aggression, and one of his principal motivations in accepting the English crown in 1689 was to ensure that a vacillating England came down firmly on his side in the great European war.

A LOYAL IF LOVELESS MARRIAGE

In 1677 William travelled to England to marry his first cousin Mary, the 15-year-old daughter of James, duke of York, brother of Charles II. Although James had converted to Catholicism, Mary was brought up a Protestant, at Charles's insistence. Charles himself had no legitimate children, so Mary was second in line to the throne after her father. The question of Mary's marriage thus had great political consequence, and had been subject to discussion since she was eight years old. Charles initially favoured the French

Timeline

1650
(4 November) Birth of William; eight days later he succeeds his father as prince of Orange

1662
(30 April) Birth of Mary

1672
William becomes captain general of the United Provinces, and subsequently stadholder

1673
William forces French out of United Provinces

1677
(4 November) Marriage of William and Mary

1688
(30 June) William invited to come to England

(5 November) William lands in England with 12,000 troops

(11 December) James II flees

dauphin, the son of Louis XIV, but the English Protestants pressed for a Dutch alliance, and Charles and James agreed. Mary was informed of the result of these discussions, married William on 4 November 1677, and returned with the prince to the United Provinces. It was not a happy marriage, and Mary's three pregnancies ended either in miscarriage or stillbirth. William – who in public was reserved to the point of chilliness – appeared unresponsive to Mary's undoubted charm and beauty. He discreetly preferred one of her ladies-in-waiting, Elizabeth Villiers.

Nevertheless, Mary remained loyal to William, and to the Protestant cause, and after her father came to the throne she showed her support of those of her fellow countrymen who suffered under James's catholicizing policies. When William was

(January) Convention Parliament declares that James has abdicated, and offers English crown jointly to William and Mary

(12 February) Declaration of Rights; William and Mary proclaimed joint sovereigns of England

(March) James lands in Ireland

(April) Convention of Estates offers Scottish crown to William and Mary

(21 April) Coronation of William and Mary in London

(May) French forces arrive in Ireland; Britain and United Provinces join European alliance against France; Toleration Act extends toleration to Non-Conformists in England

(27 July) Highland Jacobites defeat Williamite forces at Killiecrankie

(28 July) Williamite forces relieve Irish Jacobite siege of Londonderry

(31 July) Williamite forces defeat Irish Jacobites at Newtown Butler

(21 August) Highland Jacobites defeated at Dunkeld

1690

(30 June) French fleet defeats Royal Navy off Beachy Head

(1 July) William defeats James at the Boyne

invited to England to replace James on the throne, she travelled to The Hague to see him off, and when a faction in the English Convention Parliament offered her the throne as queen regnant (i.e. as sole ruler), she declined, writing 'that she was the prince's wife, and never meant to be other than in subjection to him, and that she did not thank anyone for setting up for her an interest divided from that of her husband'. In the end, Parliament established William and Mary as joint sovereigns, although she happily allowed her husband sole executive power, apart from those times when he was out of the country, when she acted as regent. For his part, William came to appreciate his wife's many qualities, and was devastated by her untimely death. As she lay dying he confided in Bishop Gilbert Burnet 'that from being the happiest he was now going to be the miserablest creature on earth'.

THE ESTABLISHMENT OF CONSTITUTIONAL MONARCHY

William and Mary became joint sovereigns on the terms set out by the Convention Parliament in England and its Scottish equivalent, the Convention of Estates. These innovative constitution-making bodies, called by William, established Britain as the constitutional monarchy that it is today. The English body accused James of having broken 'the Original Contract between king and people', while the Scots declared that James had 'invaded the fundamental

Mary II, joint sovereign of England, Ireland and Scotland with her cousin and husband William III. After her death from smallpox in 1694 ('full of spots', according to the diarist John Evelyn), William was inconsolable, but he refused to consider remarriage to secure the Protestant succession.

The Massacre of Glencoe

After the suppression of the Jacobite revolt in the Highlands in 1689, the government obliged the clan chiefs to take an oath of allegiance to William and Mary. When the chief of the Macdonalds of Glencoe missed the deadline for taking his oath, the authorities decided to make an example of Macdonald and his refractory clansmen. Early on the morning of 13 February 1692 government troops billeted with the Macdonalds set about massacring their hosts, burning their homes and forcing the survivors out onto the mountains in the bleak winter weather. There was a sense of outrage throughout Scotland, not least because of the treacherous breach of hospitality. The Scottish Parliament held Sir John Dalrymple, secretary of state, responsible. William dismissed Dalrymple, but granted him immunity from prosecution, so implicating himself in the whole sordid business.

1691
(12 July) Final defeat of Irish Jacobites at Aughrim

(October) Surrender of Limerick ends Jacobite resistance in Ireland

1692
(13 February) Massacre of Glencoe

(February) Establishment of National Debt

(May) Royal Navy decisively beats French at La Hogue, ending invasion threat

(3 August) William defeated by French at Steinkirke, in the Spanish Netherlands

1693
William vetoes bills to exclude 'placemen' (paid servants of the crown) from Parliament; another act calls for elections every three years

1694
Establishment of the Bank of England

(May) William dismisses Tory ministers, replacing them with a Whig 'Junto'

(28 December) Death of Mary

1695
Scottish Parliament demands public investigation of Massacre of Glencoe

(1 September) William takes Namur from the French

constitution of the kingdom, and altered it from a legal limited monarchy to an arbitrary despotic power'.

The English Convention offered William and Mary the crown in February 1689 only on condition that they accept the Declaration of Rights (converted to the Bill of Rights in December of that year; the Scottish Convention issued an even more radical document, the Claim of Right). The Declaration detailed the rights and liberties of the subject, limited the power of the crown, and settled the succession on the children of Mary, or if Mary died without issue, on her Protestant sister Anne and her heirs. Catholics were barred from the succession, as were those who married Catholics (a condition that pertains to this day in Britain).

The Declaration itself did not mention a contract between ruler and people, but this was now the dominant constitutional idea, and was famously articulated by the philosopher John Locke in his *Two Treatises of Government*, published in 1690. Locke justified the Glorious Revolution (as the overthrow of James II was known) by asserting that kings rule not by divine right but by popular consent, as embodied in a 'social contract'. By this contract, individuals give up certain 'natural' rights for 'civil' rights, and if a government fails to protect these civil rights, it may be justly overthrown.

THE WARS OF SUCCESSION

Such constitutional theorizing was all very well, but the new dispensation could not be defended by pieces of paper alone. James and his supporters, the Jacobites,

1697

(September) Treaty of Ryswick brings temporary peace with France, which recognizes William's right to the throne

1701

(February) Beginning of War of the Spanish Succession in which Britain, the United Provinces and the Holy Roman Empire form an alliance against France

(12 June) Act of Settlement confirms terms of Bill of Rights denying the succession to Catholics (especially the heirs of James II): following the death in 1700 of William, the last surviving child of Mary's sister Anne, the succession is settled on the nearest Protestant claimant, the Electress Sophia of Hanover, a granddaughter of James I

(6 September) Following the death of James II, Louis XIV recognizes his son as James III

1702

(8 March) Death of William

sought to reverse the Glorious Revolution by military means. In the Highlands of Scotland, John Graham of Claverhouse, Viscount Dundee – who had persecuted the Covenanters on behalf of Charles and James – roused the clansmen to rebellion and led them to victory over a government force at Killiecrankie on 27 July 1689. But the fortunes of the Highlanders were reversed at Dunkeld on 21 August, and the last vestiges of the Highland rebellion were extinguished the following year.

A more serious threat arose in Ireland, where James himself landed in March 1689. Louis XIV determined to use the campaign in Ireland to distract William from the war on the Continent and lent James his support, putting troops ashore at Bantry Bay on 1 May. For the Irish Catholics, it was an opportunity to reverse the incursions of Protestant settlers, who had been taking land from the native Irish for the previous century and a half, a process that had accelerated after Cromwell's campaign in 1649–50. The Jacobites took control of the whole island, apart from the Protestant enclaves of Londonderry and Enniskillen. William's forces relieved the sieges of both towns, and achieved decisive victories at the Boyne (after which James fled to France, never to return) and Aughrim. Jacobite resistance ended when Limerick surrendered in October 1691. For centuries the more feverishly anti-Catholic Protestants of Northern Ireland have celebrated William's victory at the Battle of the Boyne, idolizing 'King Billy' as the 'Great Deliverer'. Few are aware that William's victory was as enthusiastically celebrated in ardently Catholic Spain and Austria as a blow against the common enemy, Louis XIV.

Although James was now a spent force, Louis was not, and fighting continued through the 1690s. In 1690 itself, a French fleet inflicted a serious defeat on the English off Beachy Head, causing an invasion scare in London. But over the following years the Royal Navy asserted its pre-eminence in the Channel, and William took the war to Flanders. By 1697 both sides were exhausted, and the Treaty of Ryswick brought a temporary end to the fighting. In addition, Louis recognized William as king – although he was to go back on his word in September 1701, when, on the death of James II, he recognized James's son, James Francis Edward, as James III of England and VIII of Scotland.

William was not long to survive this reverse. His health had been in decline, and the following March he died from complications after a fall from his horse, which had stumbled on a molehill. Thereafter the Jacobites would raise their glass not only to 'the king over the water', but to 'the little gentleman in black velvet'.

ANNE
1702–1714

With Anne the line of Stuart monarchs, who had ruled England since 1603 and Scotland since 1371, came to an end. Fittingly, perhaps, it was during Anne's reign that the two countries were formally united, as Great Britain. Unlike some of her Stuart forebears, Anne was largely content to rule as a constitutional monarch, but was not averse to exercising such powers as she possessed.

Anne's health was never good. Her many pregnancies resulted in only one child who survived infancy – and he died while still a boy. Nor did her limited intellect fit her well for the role of queen – her one-time friend Sarah Churchill wrote, 'she certainly … meant well and was not a fool; but nobody can maintain that she was wise, nor entertaining in conversation. She was … ignorant in everything but what the parsons had taught her as a child.' This was perhaps over-generous: the distinguished historian J.P. Kenyon asserts in his book on the Stuarts that 'Queen Anne was the quintessence of ordinariness; she also had more than her fair share of small-mindedness, vulgarity and downright meanness.'

Needless to say, this was not how Anne saw herself. At her accession she tried to create an image of a new Elizabeth, declaring, 'I know my own heart to be entirely English.' All those who heard her knew that she thus asserted her fitness for the throne over the late William III, a Dutchman, and her French-reared half-brother, the would-be James III. She continued her address thus: 'I can very sincerely assure you there is not anything you can expect or desire from me, which I shall not be ready to do for the happiness and prosperity of England.'

A PROTESTANT PRINCESS

Although both Anne's parents – James, duke of York (later James II) and his first wife Anne Hyde – converted to Catholicism, Anne's uncle, Charles II, insisted that she and her elder sister Mary be brought up as Protestants. In 1683, at the age of 18, Anne married the amiable, handsome and not very bright Danish prince, Jørgen or George, a son of King

Biography

BORN 6 February 1665, at St James's Palace

FATHER James II

MOTHER Anne Hyde

MARRIED Prince George of Denmark

CHILDREN most of her 17 or more pregnancies ended in miscarriage or stillbirth; only 5 resulted in live births, and of these only William, duke of Gloucester, survived infancy, dying at the age of 11 in 1700

SUCCEEDED 8 March 1702

CROWNED 23 April 1702

ROYAL HOUSE Stuart

STYLE (following the 1707 Union with Scotland) Queen of Great Britain, France and Ireland, Defender of the Faith and of the Church of England, and also of Ireland, on earth the Supreme Head

DIED 1 August 1714, at Kensington

BURIED Westminster Abbey

The future Queen Anne, with her son William, duke of Gloucester. William was the only one of her children to survive infancy, but he too was dead before she became queen.

Timeline

1665
(6 February) Birth of Anne

1683
(28 July) Marries Prince George of Denmark

1688
(23 November) During Glorious Revolution deserts her father James II

1692
Final quarrel between Anne and her sister Mary; they never see each other again

1700
(29 July) Death of William, Anne's only surviving child

1701
(12 June) The Act of Settlement establishes that after Anne's death the succession will go to the nearest Protestant claimant, the Electress Sophia of Hanover, and her heirs

1702
(8 March) Anne succeeds to the throne

(23 April) Crowned

1704
(18 May) The Tory Robert Harley, later earl of Oxford, becomes secretary of state

(2 August) Marlborough defeats French at Blenheim

1706
(12 May) Marlborough defeats French at Ramillies

Frederick III and a fellow-Protestant, whose frequent exclamations of surprise earned him the nickname *'Est-il possible?'* ('Is it possible?'). Despite his shortcomings, George proved a devoted husband, although emotionally Anne came increasingly to rely on her old friend Sarah Churchill (née Jennings), wife of John Churchill, the great general and future duke of Marlborough. Anne addressed Sarah as 'Mrs Freeman', while Sarah addressed Anne, even when queen, as 'Mrs Morley'. Despite the suggestions of some historians, there is no compelling evidence that there was a sexual component in their relationship.

It was Sarah, a convinced Whig, who persuaded Anne to abandon her father during the Glorious Revolution, and side with William and Mary. Her betrayal of her father was something that was later to cause Anne considerable anguish, and it was not long after her sister and brother-in-law came to power that Anne began to fall out with them, she and Sarah referring to William as 'Mr Caliban'. One of the main bones of contention was William's suspicion that Marlborough was a covert Jacobite, and that he and his wife were trying to drive a wedge between Anne and her sister. The quarrel came to a head in 1692 when Mary tried to insist that Anne dismiss Sarah, which she refused to do. The two sisters never saw each other again. When Anne eventually came to the throne one of her first actions was to appoint Sarah to the important positions of mistress of the robes and keeper of the privy purse. At the same time, Sarah's husband was made captain general of the armed forces.

ANNE AND THE POLITICIANS

The new queen took her duties conscientiously, attending cabinet meetings once or twice a week, but attempting to stay aloof from party and faction. Her early ministries contained both Whigs and Tories, and were headed by two old friends, Sidney Godolphin and the duke of Marlborough, both of whom were more political managers than politicians.

In the early years of her reign, Marlborough's generalship brought Anne a string of spectacular victories over the French in mainland Europe. The policy of pursuing a land war on the Continent was opposed by the Tories, but supported by the Whigs – and Marlborough himself. Anne came to resent Sarah's lobbying in favour of the Whigs, and relations between the two steadily deteriorated – in a letter to Sarah's husband Anne accused her of 'teasing and tormenting' her. Sarah was eventually replaced in Anne's affections by Abigail Masham, her bed-chamber woman and a tool of the Tory politician Robert Harley.

Political manoeuvrings continued, but eventually war-weariness set in, and both the country and Anne herself veered in favour of the Tories. The queen dismissed Sarah in 1710 after a fierce row (Jonathan Swift wrote that 'five furies reigned' in the duchess's breast), and the duke was disgraced after opposing peace proposals in Parliament the following year.

The Tories under Harley (later earl of Oxford) came to power, but there were divisions within the ministry over the succession to the ailing and childless queen. Oxford supported the 1701 Act of Settlement, by which Catholics were excluded from the succession, and thus after Anne's death the throne would pass to the nearest Protestant claimant, the Electress Sophia of Hanover (granddaughter of James I) or her heirs. However, Oxford's Tory colleague, Henry St John, Viscount Bolingbroke, would not rule out a return of Anne's half-brother, the Catholic James Francis Edward Stuart.

On 27 July 1714 Anne dismissed Oxford, but the possibility of a Jacobite faction taking power was forestalled when Anne suddenly suffered what was probably a cerebral haemorrhage. Fatally ill, she passed the lord treasurer's staff not to Bolingbroke, but to Charles Talbot, duke of Shrewsbury, a moderate Whig who ensured that George of Hanover succeeded peacefully to the throne of Great Britain. Anne herself died on 1 August. Her physician, Dr Arbuthnot, wrote to Jonathan Swift, 'I believe sleep was never more welcome to a weary traveller than death was to her.'

1707
(1 May) Act of Union unites England and Scotland; the latter loses its own Parliament, but sends members to Westminster

1708
(13 February) Dismissal of Harley

(23 March) The Jacobite 'Old Pretender', James Francis Edward Stuart, lands briefly in Scotland, but soon returns to France after the French fleet sent to support him is defeated

(30 June) Marlborough defeats French at Oudenarde

1709
(31 August) Marlborough defeats French at Malplaquet

1710
Anne finally dismisses her one-time favourite, Sarah Churchill, wife of the duke of Marlborough

(8 August) Whig ministry falls; replaced by Harley and another Tory, Henry St John (later Viscount Bolingbroke)

1711
(31 December) Dismissal of Marlborough

1713
(March) Treaty of Utrecht ends War of the Spanish Succession (known as Queen Anne's War in North America): France cedes territories to Britain, and recognizes the Protestant succession

1714
(27 July) Anne dismisses Harley

(1 August) Death of Anne

GEORGE I
1714-1727

No king could better have suited the age in which power slipped away from the monarchy and into the hands of an aristocratic oligarchy than the dull, unglamorous Georg Ludwig, elector of Hanover and duke of Brunswick-Lüneburg. George (as he was known in England) preferred the quiet life of his German homeland to the bustle of Great Britain. Lady Mary Wortley Montagu, his contemporary, said that 'he would have been so well contented to have remained in his little town of Hanover that if the ambition of those about him had not been greater than his own, we should never have seen him in England'.

Biography

BORN 28 May 1660, at Osnabrück, Hanover

FATHER Ernest Augustus, duke of Brunswick-Lüneburg and elector of Hanover

MOTHER Princess Sophia of the Palatinate, electress of Hanover, daughter of Elizabeth, queen of Bohemia, the eldest daughter of James I

MARRIED Sophia Dorothea, daughter of the duke of Lüneburg-Celle

CHILDREN George (the future George II) and Sophia Dorothea (who married Frederick William I of Prussia, and became the mother of Frederick the Great)

SUCCEEDED 1 August 1714

CROWNED 20 October 1714

ROYAL HOUSE Hanover

STYLE King of Great Britain, France, Ireland, Duke of Brunswick-Lüneburg, Elector of Hanover, Defender of the Faith

DIED 11 June 1727, at Osnabrück, Hanover

BURIED Hanover

George was the great-grandson of James I via the latter's eldest daughter Elizabeth, and would have been fiftieth in line to the throne of Great Britain had not the 1701 Act of Settlement barred Catholics from the succession. Despite having had over a decade to prepare for his accession, George made no effort to familiarize himself with the language of his future subjects, and once he became king he spent as much time as he could in his native Hanover. For their part, his British subjects knew him as the 'Turnip-Hoer', after he announced his ambition to close the elegant royal park of St James's in London to the public so that he could turn it over to the cultivation of root vegetables.

An equestrian portrait of George I, by Sir Godfrey Kneller (1717).

George's parents

It was only by a whisker that Britain did not have a Queen Sophia. The old Electress Sophia, George's mother, named as Anne's heir in the Act of Settlement, died on 8 June 1714, just a few weeks before Anne herself. A patron and friend of the great mathematician and philosopher Leibniz, Sophia was in her own right a lively, cultured and intelligent woman, with a better command of languages than her son.

In contrast, Sophia's husband, Duke Ernest Augustus, was something of a dullard, with few interests apart from his dukedom. George, whom Lady Mary Wortley Montagu described as 'an honest blockhead', took after his father. He had none of his mother's cultural interests, and his only enjoyments seem to have been horses, women and the consumption of large quantities of food. (An idea of his priorities can be gleaned from the fact that when he first arrived in London in 1714 he brought with him 18 cooks – but only one washerwoman.)

Sophia Dorothea of Celle, cousin and wife of George I, as portrayed by William Faithorne after a mezzotint by Johann Kerseboom (c. 1683–1725). Sophia's marriage to George was an exceptionally unhappy one. Familiarity between the pair rapidly turned to contempt, and when Sophia unwisely began a liaison with a Swedish count, George not only divorced her, but incarcerated her in his castle at Ahlden in Lower Saxony, where she remained in captivity until her death in 1726.

His wife, her lover and the *maîtresse en titre*

George made his first visit to England in 1680, as a prospective husband of the future Queen Anne. However, there was no attraction felt on either side, and George returned to Hanover, where, two years later, at the age of 22, he married his 16-year-old cousin, the lively but naïve Sophia Dorothea of Celle. It was not a happy match – in fact before long antipathy had turned to mutual loathing, and at some point in the early 1690s she began an indiscreet affair with a handsome Swedish soldier, Count Philip Königsmark. In 1694 the count disappeared, never to be seen again, and George divorced Sophia Dorothea, imprisoning her for the 32 remaining years of her life at the castle of Ahlden. She was forbidden ever to see her children or, indeed, to receive any visitors.

The scandal and the mystery of the count's fate kept Europe entertained for years, and Sophia Dorothea's infidelity was later to give the Jacobites the opportunity of suggesting that the future George II was not the king's son, but another man's bastard. George himself was sometimes mockingly represented as a turnip, the symbol of a cuckold – in 1718 William Stratford, a rural clergyman, recalled how on George's coronation day some rustics celebrated with a pyrotechnical display in the form of a huge turnip with three candles stuck in its top.

Before, during and after his marriage, George consoled himself with a number of mistresses. His official mistress, with the title *maîtresse en titre*, was Melusine von der Schulenburg, later duchess of Kendal. When she joined King George in England she was met with a certain hostility, and accused (with justification) of rapaciousness.

1660
(28 May) Birth of George

1680
Makes first visit to England, but declines to marry Princess Anne

1682
(21 November) Marries Sophia Dorothea of Celle

1694
(28 December) Divorces Sophia Dorothea

1714
(8 June) Death of George's mother, the Electress Sophia

(1 August) George succeeds to throne of Great Britain

(18 September) Arrives in London

(20 October) Crowned

1715
(27 March) The Tory politician Viscount Bolingbroke flees to France

(9 July) Another Tory politician, Robert Harley, earl of Oxford, is imprisoned by the Whigs

(6 September) Jacobite rising begins in Scotland

(12–14 November) Jacobites defeated at Preston

(13 November) Inconclusive battle at Sheriffmuir

(22 December) The Old Pretender lands in Scotland

'Good people,' protested the duchess, 'why do you plague us so? We have come for your own goods.' To which the mob replied, 'Aye, and for our chattels too.' The novelist Horace Walpole remembered being introduced as a boy to the king and the duchess, and recalled the latter as 'a very tall, lean, ill-favoured old Lady'. Walpole's father, the politician Robert Walpole, declared that 'she was in effect as much a queen of England as ever any was'.

Another German lady shared George's life in England. This was Sophia von Kielmansegge, a lively, friendly soul who became the countess of Darlington. She appeared to have had as much influence over George as 'La Schulenburg', and was as heartily disliked by the English. Everybody assumed she was also George's mistress, but in fact she may have been his half-sister – her mother, the countess von Platen, had been *maîtresse en titre* to Ernest Augustus, George's father – but he was far from being the only man who had enjoyed her favours, so whether she was related to George is open to question. Horace Walpole remembered La Kielmansegge being 'as corpulent and ample as the Duchess was long and emaciated'; in particular he noted 'an ocean of neck that overflowed and was not distinguished from the lower parts of her body'.

THE HANOVERIAN SUCCESSION

The framers of the 1701 Act of Settlement must have been content with their decision to settle the succession on the House of Hanover, for George proved a useful ally against the French in the War of the Spanish Succession (1701–14), in which he fought with some distinction. The French king, Louis XIV, had recognized James II's son, the Catholic James Francis Edward Stuart, as King James III of England. The Old Pretender's claim to the throne was supported by many Tories, the party in power through much of the reign of Queen Anne. The Whigs, in contrast, supported the Hanoverian succession, and came to power just before Anne's death, so allowing for a smooth transition from one ruling dynasty to another.

George was in no rush to leave the certainties of Hanover for a faraway realm of which he knew little. Anne died on 1 August, but it was not until 18 September that George landed at Greenwich – in thick fog.

Among the English politicians, George naturally favoured the Whigs. Not only did the Tories have Jacobite sympathies, they had made peace with the French, so, in George's eyes, betraying the

Grand Alliance against Louis XIV. The hegemony of the Whigs in British politics was to last half a century. The Tories were totally eclipsed.

GEORGE AS KING

Shy and reserved – he preferred the company of old German friends and his two Turkish servants, Mustapha and Mahomet, to big public occasions – George was not a popular figure in Britain. He was already 54 by the time he became king, and thus had nothing of the promise of youth, but his experience of government and lack of imagination did, by and large, help him to avoid making any particularly foolish blunders. Hanover had been a well-ordered despotism, in which parliamentary government was unknown, and dissent unthought of. Britain was an altogether larger, messier, less compliant place, and George found that he could not necessarily get his way with his ministers (with whom he conversed in French). Indeed, he could not, by the terms of the Act of Settlement, even leave the country without the permission of Parliament, until this clause was repealed in 1715 – after which he returned to Hanover as often as he could.

George's perceived preference for Hanover led to the first schism in the Whig government. James, Earl Stanhope and the earl of Sunderland accompanied George on his visit to his

1716
(10 February) The Old Pretender returns to France

(26 April) Septennial Act establishes parliamentary elections at least every seven years

1717
(January) Britain, France and the Netherlands form Triple Alliance against Spain

(February) After the French agree with Britain to oppose the Jacobite cause, the Old Pretender moves to Rome

(April) The Whig politicians Robert Walpole and Viscount Townshend go into opposition, rallying around the prince of Wales after he quarrels with his father

(1 July) Harley acquitted of aiding the Jacobites

1718
(August) Austria joins Triple Alliance to form Quadruple Alliance

1719
(10 June) Scottish-Spanish Jacobite force defeated at Glenshiel

An Emblematical Print on the South Sea Scene by William Hogarth (1721). Hogarth's satirical etching shows a crowd consumed by political speculation at the time of the stock market crash of 1720. The 'South Sea Bubble' was set in motion by the South Sea Company, which tempted large numbers of middle-class investors to make quick money through rash financial speculations. George I was implicated in the scandal, which did little to enhance his already scant popularity.

1720
Walpole and Townshend return to power; South Sea Bubble bursts

1721
(April) Walpole becomes first lord of the treasury (effectively prime minister) and chancellor of the exchequer

1722
(October) Discovery of a Jacobite plot organized by Bishop Atterbury of Rochester

1723
(June) Bolingbroke pardoned and returns from exile

1727
(11 June) Death of George

homeland in 1716, while Robert Walpole and Viscount Townshend fiercely attacked Stanhope for making British interests subservient to those of Hanover. Walpole and Townshend went into opposition, allying themselves with George's son, the prince of Wales (the future George II), who detested his father as much as his father loathed him.

There was a reconciliation between father and son in 1720, and Townshend and Walpole returned to government. Their period in opposition meant that they were untainted by the scandal known as the South Sea Bubble. The South Sea Company had been set up some years previously, and in 1718 George became its governor. There was an unsustainable boom in South Sea stocks, followed by the inevitable collapse, and George, his ministers and his two German lady friends were all tainted with accusations of sleaze and dodgy dealings. Walpole skilfully managed to extract the king from the mess, and thus strengthened his own grip on power. Over the next twenty years he headed a succession of ministries, and is regarded as Britain's first prime minister. George became increasingly content to give his ministers a free hand, and to spend more time in Hanover, where, on a visit in 1727, he died, largely unmourned, of a stroke.

The Old Pretender

James Francis Edward Stuart – known as the Old Pretender to distinguish him from his son, Charles Edward, the Young Pretender – was too lacklustre a figure ever to present a convincing threat to the Hanoverian succession. Spiritless, gloomy and devoutly religious, he had been brought up in exile in France, surrounded by second-rate sycophants and dominated by his mother, Mary of Modena, a Catholic bigot.

It was not that the Jacobite cause lacked supporters in Britain. Many resented the advent of a German monarch – there was widespread rioting at George's accession – and believed that James, the son of the last Stuart king, was the rightful heir. But James did nothing to cultivate support, failing to guarantee religious toleration in Britain, and refusing to consider converting to Protestantism himself – which would have made him a much more acceptable prospect to many of his would-be subjects. His most effective supporter was Viscount Bolingbroke, a Tory politician who had held power under Queen Anne, and who, after her death, joined James in exile. But Bolingbroke was among those who had begged James to convert, and the two soon fell out.

Bolingbroke despaired of this prince who 'dwelt in a maze of unrealities', writing that 'he was a man who expected every moment to set sail for England or Scotland, but who did not very well know for which'. He had in fact sailed up the Firth of Forth in 1708, but the French fleet sent to support him was sent packing by the Royal Navy. In 1715 there was a large-scale Jacobite rising in Scotland, led by the earl of Mar. But Mar was a poor general, and the effort fizzled out after an inconclusive battle at Sheriffmuir. By the time James landed at Peterhead, in the north-east of the country, the rebellion was pretty much over, and he was obliged to turn on his heel and scuttle back to France.

James – whom the Scots dubbed 'Old Mister Melancholy' – never set foot on British soil again. In 1719 there was a smaller-scale rising in the western Highlands, supported by some Spanish troops, but this was efficiently dealt with by Hanoverian forces at Glenshiel. It was not until 1745 that the Jacobites rose again, this time led by the Young Pretender. It was to prove yet another fiasco, and a bloody disaster for the Highlanders. James himself lingered on for another twenty years: he died in Rome in 1766, long after hopes of a Stuart restoration had been confined to the dustbin of history.

GEORGE II
1727-1760

George II was as stolid a figure as his father, and – apart from a liking for music – shared his father's lack of interest in the arts. George preferred soldiering, and his active career stretched from Oudenarde in 1708 to Dettingen in 1743, the last occasion on which a British monarch led his troops in battle. George also shared his father's political common sense, realizing he could only rule through ministers approved by the House of Commons – but he made it clear that his ministers could not rule without royal support.

George was born and brought up a German, and the suspicion that he favoured his Hanoverian homeland over his adopted country gave ammunition to his political opponents. In particular, George's concerns in mainland Europe were seen to be at odds with Britain's expanding colonial and mercantile interests, which by the end of George's long reign saw Britain the dominant power in both India and North America.

GEORGE AND HIS WOMEN

George – christened Georg August – was his father's only son. His must have been a lonely childhood: his only sister was four years his junior, and when he was ten his father confined his mother to house arrest in the castle of Ahlden, following her adultery with a Swedish adventurer. George never saw his mother again, although he always carried a portrait miniature of her wherever he went. The trauma of separation no doubt contributed to his later inability to form intimate relationships, and to his general reserve. The only emotion he displayed in public was ill temper, particularly apparent when his piles were playing up.

George was lucky in his choice of wife, whom he married in 1705. Caroline of Ansbach was both beautiful and intelligent, and often guided her husband's hand in politics. Lord Hervey, one of her husband's courtiers, wrote, 'Her predominant passion was pride, and the darling pleasure of

Biography

BORN 30 October 1683, at Herrenhausen Palace, Hanover

FATHER George I

MOTHER Sophia Dorothea of Celle

MARRIED Caroline of Ansbach (Wilhelmina Charlotte Caroline, daughter of the Margrave of Brandenburg-Ansbach)

CHILDREN Frederick (prince of Wales), Anne (married William IV of Orange-Nassau), Amelia Sophia Eleanor, Caroline Elizabeth, William Augustus (duke of Cumberland), Mary (married Frederick II of Hesse-Cassel), Louisa (married Frederick V of Denmark)

SUCCEEDED 11 June 1727

CROWNED 4 October 1727

ROYAL HOUSE Hanover

STYLE King of Great Britain, France, Ireland, Duke of Brunswick-Lüneburg, Elector of Hanover, Defender of the Faith

DIED 25 October 1760, in the Palace of Westminster, London

BURIED Westminster Abbey

Timeline

1683
(30 October) Birth of George

1694
George's mother imprisoned by his father for adultery

1705
(22 August) George marries Caroline of Ansbach

1707
(6 January) Birth of Frederick, later prince of Wales

1708
(July) George fights with distinction against the French at Oudenarde

1717
Sets up alternative court at Leicester House, after a quarrel with his father

1721
(15 April) Birth of William Augustus, later duke of Cumberland

1727
(11 June) Succeeds

(4 October) Crowned

1728
(December) Frederick arrives in England

1729
North and South Carolina become British colonies

1730
(15 May) Resignation of Viscount Townshend from Robert Walpole's ministry

George II in a portrait by Isaac Whood (1738).

her soul was power.' Caroline tolerated George's many mistresses, who included her own lady of the bedchamber, Mrs Howard. Despite his roving eye, George was grief-stricken when Caroline died in 1737, following a uterine rupture. As she lay on her deathbed she urged him to marry again. 'No,' he replied, 'I shall have mistresses.' 'That's no obstacle,' she said. George did not marry again, but a German woman, Lady Yarmouth, saw to his not inconsiderable sexual needs.

RELATIONS WITH THE OLD KING

Given his father's treatment of his mother, it is perhaps not surprising that Prince George loathed the old king. The feeling was mutual. It is possible that the only person that George *père* felt any affection for was his daughter Sophia Dorothea. He certainly felt none for his son, and relations were exacerbated by the fact that both were, to put it bluntly, pig-headed dullards. George *père* also took against Caroline of Ansbach (as he did against any intelligent woman), calling her '*cette diablesse Madame la Princesse*' ('this she-devil, Madame the Princess').

Once they were in England, the antipathy between father and son was further complicated by politics. There were a number of clashes, such as that arising from the refusal of George *père* to make his son regent when he visited Hanover. This was followed in 1717 with a row concerning the christening of the prince and princess of Wales's second son: the prince asked his father to be godfather, but the latter insisted on the British tradition, whereby this role was taken by the lord chamberlain, the duke of Newcastle. George *fils* was furious, and appeared to threaten the duke with violence. In response, the king threatened to arrest his son and daughter-in-law. Although he did not go this far, he banished them from St James's Palace, and forbade them to take their children with them, allowing them only one visit a week. The old king's vindictiveness recalled his malicious treatment of his former wife, whom he still held imprisoned at Ahlden.

The banished couple set up home at Leicester House, and this became an alternative court, attracting opposition politicians such as Viscount Townshend and Robert Walpole. The latter had a particularly close relationship with Caroline, and they continued to be political allies and friends (even lovers, it was said) until her death. When Walpole rejoined his father's ministry in 1720, the prince of Wales took umbrage, but when he succeeded to the throne seven years later his wife, who recognized Walpole's many merits, persuaded her husband to keep him on as his chief minister.

PEACE AND WAR

Walpole acquired control of the new king's powers of political patronage, and proved an effective manager of Parliament on the king's behalf. He also reconciled many former Jacobites to the Hanoverian succession – so that when in 1745 the Young Pretender brought his Highland army south into England, he found only negligible support for his obsolete cause. In foreign affairs Walpole kept England at peace, with which even George,

1732
(June) Establishment of colony in Georgia

1737
(September) Frederick breaks with his parents

(20 November) Death of Caroline of Ansbach

1738
(4 June) Birth of a son, the future George III, to Frederick, prince of Wales

1739
(October) Beginning of war with Spain

(November) British capture Porto Bello (in modern Panama) from the Spanish

1740
Beginning of the War of the Austrian Succession

1742
(11 January) Resignation of Robert Walpole

1743
(16 June) George leads his troops into battle at Dettingen

(August) Henry Pelham becomes first lord of the treasury

The fighting at Dettingen, 27 June 1743, in an engraving by Elias Baeck. The Battle of Dettingen, in which a 'Pragmatic Army' of British, Hanoverian and Hessian troops defeated a larger French force under the duc de Noailles, was the last time that a British monarch (George II in this case) personally led his troops into battle.

the soldier-king, seems to have been content, as long as he still held power over appointments in the armed forces.

George's soldierly bent led him to favour his second son and 'martial boy', William Augustus, duke of Cumberland, over his oldest son, Frederick, prince of Wales. The mutual loathing between George and his father was repeated between George and Frederick, and the latter became the focus for opposition politicians, as his father had in the previous reign, until his premature death in 1751 (brought on after he was struck by a cricket ball). Walpole eventually fell from power in 1742, having in 1739 reluctantly conceded to popular clamour for war with Spain.

The conflict escalated into the War of the Austrian Succession (1740–8), in which Britain found itself fighting not only Spain but also France and Prussia. George himself took command of the 'Pragmatic Army' of Britain and its allies,

The Young Pretender

Charles Edward Stuart – Bonnie Prince Charlie – would have been King Charles III had his harebrained 1745 campaign succeeded – an unlikely outcome – and had his father, the Old Pretender, gone through with his promise to resign his claim to the throne in favour of his son.

Charles was born in Rome, and brought up speaking French, like his father. Also like his father, Charles suffered from the delusions and vanities that so often go with living in an exiled court. With all the fizz and innocence of youth, Charles took upon himself the heroic destiny of restoring the Stuart line. When the promised French aid failed to materialize, he mounted a private expedition, landing with a few companions on the west coast of Scotland on 25 July 1745, and summoning the Highland clans to rally to his support. Many recognized his claim, but few were enthusiastic, judging the rebellion a lost cause without assistance from France.

And yet the charisma of the 'Young Chevalier' and the loyalty of the Highland chiefs to the House of Stuart stirred many into action. One of those who reluctantly responded to the call was the experienced soldier, Lord George Murray, who became Charles's field commander.

Unfortunately, Charles suffered from the common Stuart failing of taking robust advice as personal attack, and so failed to heed the outspoken Murray's counsel at various crucial junctures in the campaign.

At first things went well. Edinburgh surrendered, and its womenfolk swooned at the prince's feet. An inexperienced Hanoverian force was defeated at Prestonpans, to the east of the city, and the decision was made to press south into England. By 6 December the poorly equipped Highland army – dismissed as 'a pack of tatterdemalions' by one observer – had reached Derby, only a hundred miles from London. And yet the English Jacobites, if there were any, stayed resolutely indoors.

With no visible support in England, the decision was made to turn around and head back north. Murray managed the retreat with considerable skill, but could not dissuade the prince from seeking battle with a strong and experienced government force at Culloden, near Inverness. Here, on 16 April 1746, the Highlanders were cut to pieces. The Hanoverian commander, the duke of Cumberland (second son of the king) earned his nickname 'Butcher' by the ruthlessness and brutality with which his men dealt with the defeated remnants of the Pretender's army.

Charles himself became a fugitive, making his way with a few loyal companions westward across the wilder parts of the Highlands, and then island-hopping around the Hebrides, keeping one step ahead of the pursuing redcoats. Despite a price of £30,000 on his head, no one betrayed him, and on 20 September 1746 he managed to slip away on a French frigate. It had been a year of high excitement and adventure. The four remaining decades of the prince's life formed a sad anticlimax, as the prince sought to sustain his spirits from the bottle while dreaming of what might have been. By the time of his death his right to the throne of Great Britain was unrecognized by any European power.

Charles had no legitimate issue, so on his death the claim passed to his brother, Cardinal Henry Benedict Stuart, known to his few loyal followers as Henry IX. But history had moved on. When in 1796 Henry's palace in Italy was sacked by French Revolutionary troops, the British government aided his escape, and George III even awarded him a pension. By then it was Jacobins, not Jacobites, who were the most feared enemies of the House of Hanover. When Henry died in 1807, and was buried in St Peter's, Rome, it was the future George IV who paid for the monument.

The Battle of Culloden, 1746, in an engraving by Laurie and Whittle (1797).

and led it to victory over the French at Dettingen in 1743. At one point George's horse bolted, taking the king with it, but George managed to dismount, and spent the rest of the battle directing operations on foot. It was Britain's first victory in Europe since the great days of Marlborough, and was widely celebrated – although as the war progressed, there were the inevitable grumblings that it was being conducted more in the interests of Hanover than of Great Britain.

'I hate all Boets and Bainters': George and the arts

In 1745 George was shown Hogarth's painting *The Road to Finchley*, which depicts the king's soldiers attempting to leave London to take on the Jacobite rebels, while dallying with all the temptations that city life affords (especially whores and hard liquor). The king was outraged, and the following dialogue ensued:

> *'Pray, who is this Hogarth?' 'A painter, my liege'. 'I hate bainting and boetry too! neither the one nor the other ever did any good! Does the fellow mean to laugh at my guards?' 'The picture, may it please your Majesty, must undoubtedly be considered a burlesque.' – 'What, a bainter burlesque a soldier? He deserves to be picketed for his insolence! Take this trumpery out of my sight.'*

Although hating all 'Boets and Bainters' (as his father had before him), George did have a soft spot for music, and in particular for the work of his fellow German, George Frideric Handel, who wrote four anthems for George's coronation, including *Zadok the Priest* (performed at every British coronation since). Other royal commissions included the oratorio *Judas Maccabaeus* (1746), to celebrate the victory over the Jacobites at Culloden, and *Music for the Royal Fireworks* (1749), to celebrate the Peace of Aix-la-Chapelle.

1744
(21 February) British fleet defeated off Toulon

(December) Pelham and his brother, the duke of Newcastle, form a ministry

1745
(30 April) British and Dutch defeated by French at Fontenoy

(25 July) Young Pretender lands in Scotland

(August) George makes peace with Prussia

(21 September) Jacobite victory at Prestonpans

(6 December) Jacobites reach Derby, then retreat northwards

1746
(17 January) Jacobite victory at Falkirk

(16 April) Jacobites routed at Culloden, the last pitched battle on British soil

(20 September) Young Pretender escapes to France

1748
(October) Treaty of Aix-la-Chapelle ends War of the Austrian Succession

1751
(20 March) Death of Frederick, prince of Wales

1752
(September) Britain and its colonies adopt the Gregorian calendar

1754

(March) Newcastle becomes prime minister following the death of his brother

(3 July) British colonial force under George Washington defeated by French in Ohio valley

1756

(May) British declaration of war against France marks formal beginning of Seven Years' War

1757

(June) Robert Clive's victory at Plassey secures British dominance in Bengal

(July) Newcastle forms ministry with William Pitt the Elder

1758

(June) British capture Louisbourg, Cape Breton Island, from the French

(July) British fail to take Fort Ticonderoga from the French

1759

'Year of Victories' for Britain over France: capture of Guadeloupe (May), victory at Minden (August), capture of Quebec (September), victory at Quiberon Bay (November)

1760

(January) Sir Eyre Coote defeats French at Wandewash, India

(25 October) Death of George

An engraving showing the fireworks display arranged by the duke of Richmond in London, 15 May 1749. Handel wrote his celebrated Fireworks Music *for the event, held to celebrate the end of the War of the Austrian Succession.*

A number of ministries followed that of Walpole, the most notable being that headed by the duke of Newcastle and William Pitt the Elder, which saw Britain achieve great victories in the Seven Years' War (1756–63; known as the French and Indian War in North America). By the time hostilities commenced George was 73 – far too old for active service – but he continued to take an interest in the progress of the war, even though its strategic conduct was in the capable hands of Pitt, whom he disliked. War gave George an occasion for one of his few attempts at humour: when Newcastle complained that General Wolfe – whose victory over the French was to deliver Canada into British hands – was a madman, the king grumbled, 'Mad is he? Then I hope he will bite some of my other generals.'

George did not survive to see the successful outcome of the war, although he lived through 1759, the 'Year of Victories'. He died suddenly on 25 October 1760 of a ruptured aortic aneurysm while sitting on the water-closet. It was said that his aorta – the major artery from the heart – exploded with such *éclat* that his German valet-de-chambre thought he had broken wind.

THE KINGS AND QUEENS OF ENGLAND

GEORGE III
1760-1820

George was conscious that he was the first British-born king since James II, and the first of the Hanoverian monarchs to speak English as a native. 'Born and educated in this country, I glory in the name of Briton,' he declared to the House of Lords on his accession. George saw himself as a patriot-king, his duty to guide the country along the paths of virtue. In contrast, his opponents portrayed him as a tyrant out to subvert the constitution, and then, as his role in politics diminished, as a symbol of unthinking reaction. By the time of his death he was, in Shelley's words, 'An old, mad, blind, despised and dying king.'

George was a stubborn and not very intelligent man, with lofty, if narrow, ideals that could get in the way of the pragmatism and common sense necessary in politics. He has been blamed for the loss of the American colonies, but the folly of Britain's policy in that matter was not his alone. He has also been condemned for preventing Catholic emancipation – a kick in the teeth to his subjects in Ireland. As for subverting the constitution, historians have generally concluded that for the most part George ruled within constitutional limits as they were then understood.

UPBRINGING AND MARRIAGE

George's view of politics was in his youth guided by two key influences: his father, Frederick, prince of Wales; and his tutor, John Stuart, earl of Bute. Frederick loathed his father, George II, and despised the circle of Whig politicians around him. Bute, too, portrayed the dominant Whigs as nothing but corrupt self-servers, and imbued his charge with the naive belief that, with the prompting of the king, Britain could be ruled by virtue alone, without the messy compromises necessary in the management of men and affairs. Not that Bute actually suggested the king could do

Biography

BORN 4 June 1738, in London

FATHER Frederick, prince of Wales

MOTHER Princess Augusta of Saxe-Gotha

MARRIED Charlotte Sophia of Mecklenburg-Strelitz

CHILDREN nine sons and six daughters: George (the future George IV), Frederick (duke of York; predeceased his elder brother), William (the future William IV), Charlotte (married King Frederick of Württemberg), Edward Augustus (father of Queen Victoria), Augusta Sophia, Elizabeth, Ernest Augustus (became king of Hanover), Augustus Frederick, Adolphus, Mary, Sophia, Octavius, Alfred, Amelia

SUCCEEDED 25 October 1760

CROWNED 25 September 1761

ROYAL HOUSE Hanover

STYLE By the Grace of God, of the United Kingdom of Great Britain and Ireland, King, Defender of the Faith (after the Union of Great Britain and Ireland, 1 January 1801)

DIED 29 January 1820, at Windsor Castle

BURIED St George's Chapel, Windsor

George III with General Robert Ramsden, in a painting by David Morier (c. 1705–1770).

Timeline

1738
(4 June) Birth of George

1751
(20 March) Death of George's father, Frederick, prince of Wales

1755
John Stuart, earl of Bute, becomes George's tutor

1760
(25 October) George succeeds

1761
(8 September) Marries Charlotte Sophia of Mecklenburg-Strelitz

(25 September) Crowned

1762
(May) Bute becomes prime minister

(12 August) Birth of the future George IV

1763
(February) Treaty of Paris ends Seven Years' War

(April) Bute resigns as prime minister; succeeded by George Grenville

1765
First sign of George's 'madness'

(22 March) Stamp Act infuriates American colonists

(16 July) Grenville replaced as premier by the marquis of Rockingham

without Parliament – he upheld the constitutional monarchy that had been established by the Glorious Revolution in 1689. It was more a matter of emphasis.

George was only 12 when his father died, and no doubt when Bute became his tutor (and possibly his mother's lover) four years later he represented something of a father figure, the source of all wisdom. Politics apart, Bute encouraged his charge to value refinement and culture, in contrast to the perceived coarseness of his grandfather. In turn, George entrusted Bute with the task of finding him a wife among the German Protestant princesses (George may have gloried in the name of Briton, but marrying one beneath his own rank seems not to have been an option).

Bute accordingly came up with Charlotte Sophia of Mecklenburg-Strelitz, who arrived in London on 8 September 1761 and married George on the same day – never having met him before. A contemporary diarist cautiously commented of the new queen, 'she has every requisite to adorn an amiable mind'. Against the odds, it turned out to be a successful, 57-year marriage. Charlotte was a strong character, and she gave George not only 15 children but great support and devotion. George in turn was never happier than when in the close circle of his family, and such was his enduring love for Charlotte that he broke with tradition and did without the usual clutch of royal mistresses.

A DECADE OF INSTABILITY

By the time he married Princess Charlotte, George had been on the throne nearly a year. Since 1756 Britain had been fighting a successful European and colonial war against France, under the skilful guidance of the duke of Newcastle and William Pitt the Elder. But Bute had poisoned George against these capable Whig ministers, and in the new climate of distrust Pitt resigned in 1761

> ‘ Caesar had his Brutus … Charles the First his Cromwell, and George the Third … [‘Treason,’ cried the Speaker] … may profit by their example. ’

PATRICK HENRY, SPEECH IN THE VIRGINIA CONVENTION, 1765.

and Newcastle the following year. The king appointed Bute to replace Newcastle as first lord of the treasury, and it was Bute's ministry that negotiated the 1763 Treaty of Paris that ended the Seven Years' War.

The treaty caused popular and patriotic outrage for the concessions it made to the French. Bute himself resigned – he had turned out a man of straw – and for the rest of the decade a series of ministries attempted to deal with the fallout of the war, particularly the financial consequences. It was in this climate that the decision was made to make the American colonists – whose security had hitherto been underwritten by the British taxpayer – stump up for their own defence. It was a decision that both the king and the House of Commons were agreed upon.

LOSING THE COLONIES

During the 1760s various ministries had attempted to levy taxes on the American colonists – the Stamp Act had been passed, then repealed in the face of American protest, and the same had happened to the 'Townshend duties' on imports into the colonies. Political stability was achieved in Britain in 1770 with the advent of Lord North to the premiership (he was to remain in power for 12 years), but under his administration the two sides became further polarized, especially following the so-called 'Intolerable Acts' of 1773.

King George backed his ministers in all this, and thus, after fighting broke out in 1775, he became in the eyes of American patriots the embodiment of tyranny. The 1776 Declaration of Independence laid the blame firmly – if not entirely fairly – at the door of the king:

> The history of the present king of Great Britain is a history of repeated injuries and usurpations, all having in direct object the establishment of an absolute tyranny over these states.

The document goes on to list a string of crimes attributable to the king, from squashing the democratic institutions of the

1766
Repeal of Stamp Act (February) followed by Declaratory Act (March), asserting Parliament's right to make laws for the colonies

(July) Earl of Chatham (William Pitt the Elder) replaces Rockingham as premier

1767
(9 June) Parliament passes Townshend Revenue Act

(December) Chatham succeeded by duke of Grafton

1768
(September) British send troops to Massachusetts after protests

1770
(10 February) Lord North becomes prime minister

(5 March) British troops fire on protesters in Boston

(12 April) Repeal of Townshend Revenue Act

1773
(16 December) Boston Tea Party

1774
Intolerable Acts; British close Boston harbour; First Continental Congress joins colonies together in protest against British policy

1775
(18 April) Skirmishes at Lexington and Concord mark beginning of American Revolution

(17 June) Battle of Bunker Hill

1776
(4 July) American Declaration of Independence

1777
(October) British defeated at Saratoga

1781
(19 October) British surrender at Yorktown

1782
(March) Lord North resigns; succeeded as prime minister by Rockingham

(1 July) Rockingham dies; succeeded by earl of Shelburne

1783
(April) Fox–North coalition comes to power

(3 September) British recognize American independence

(December) George brings about fall of Fox–North coalition; Pitt the Younger becomes prime minister

1788–1789
George temporarily incapacitated by his illness; regency crisis

1793
(13 February) Britain forms coalition against Revolutionary France following execution of Louis XVI

The marquis de Lafayette and General George Washington order the final storming of Yorktown, 17 October 1781, as depicted by Auguste Couder (1836). George III took defeat in the American War of Independence badly: 'I cannot conclude without mentioning how sensibly I feel the dismemberment of America from this empire,' he grumbled to prime minister Shelburne.

colonies and blocking their freedom to trade, to waging war against them and plundering their seas, ravaging their coasts, burning their towns and destroying the lives of the people.

As the war proceeded George proved slower than his ministers to recognize the futility of prolonging the fight, even after the disaster at Yorktown in 1781. He actually considered abdicating over the issue, but eventually became reconciled to the political and military realities. In 1785 he was able to greet John Adams, the first US ambassador to London, with the following words:

> I was the last to consent to the separation, but the separation having been made … I say now that I would be the first to meet the friendship of the United States as an independent power.

REVOLUTION IN THE AIR

Lord North's ministry fell in March 1782 over the loss of the colonies, and a further period of political instability ensued. There were attempts to reduce the king's power – in 1780 the House of Commons had passed a motion that 'The influence of the crown has increased, is increasing and ought to be diminished', and in 1782 Parliament put through some measures to achieve this. After two short-lived ministries, in April 1783 Lord North returned in coalition with the radical Whig, Charles James Fox, a man so loathed by George that he once more considered abdicating. But instead the king brought about the defeat of the coalition by informing the

Farmer George

This disparaging nickname was awarded to George III by his political enemies. It refers to George's keen interest in agricultural improvement, and George himself, under the pseudonym Ralph Robinson, contributed articles on farming to Arthur Young's *Annals of Agriculture*.

House of Lords that he would consider any peer voting for the government's India Bill to be his enemy. It was the most blatantly unconstitutional move by any British monarch in the 18th century – and yet it met with the approval of the electorate, who in 1784 backed William Pitt the Younger, the king's choice as prime minister.

Meanwhile, the prince of Wales showed his defiance of his father by associating with Fox and his dissolute friends – which caused distress to the king on both political and moral grounds. When George suffered a mental breakdown in 1788, there was a political battle between Pitt and the opposition, led by Fox, over the powers the prince of Wales should have as regent, but the crisis passed when the king recovered.

A greater crisis for the monarchy came with the French Revolution of 1789, and more particularly with the execution of Louis XVI on 21 January 1793. Within a week Britain was at war with France. The conflict continued, with only one brief period of peace, over the next two decades, at first against the various Revolutionary regimes, and then against the Emperor Napoleon. In the new atmosphere, Pitt put aside the ideas for parliamentary reform he had advocated during the 1780s and turned to extreme and oppressive reaction against radicals in Britain. Now any talk of reform was regarded as an assault on the constitution, and an incitement to revolution and regicide.

Union with Ireland and Catholic emancipation

Through the 1790s George was content to leave the government of the country to Pitt, and adopt a more symbolic role, as a bulwark of tradition and order against the revolutionary tide. But he had not finished with politics. Revolution did not come to Britain, but it did to Ireland, where in 1798, aided by the French, the United Irishmen mounted an insurrection, drawing support from both Catholics and Presbyterians.

The rising was crushed with the brutality typical of Britain's dealings in Ireland over the centuries, but Pitt believed something should be done to alleviate the discontent in that unhappy country. He therefore proposed to abolish the separate Irish Parliament and unite the country with Great Britain, with the Irish sending MPs to Westminster. At the same time he proposed to free Catholics (the vast majority of the Irish population) from

1795
(October) Pitt introduces repressive domestic measures

1798
United Irishmen's revolt

1801
(1 January) Union of Great Britain and Ireland

(14 March) Pitt resigns after George refuses to agree to Catholic emancipation; succeeded by Henry Addington (later Viscount Sidmouth). Crisis followed by another episode of George's illness

1802
(27 March) Treaty of Amiens temporarily halts hostilities with France

1803
(16 May) War with France resumes

1804
George temporarily incapacitated again

(May) Pitt replaces Addington as prime minister

1805
(21 October) Admiral Nelson defeats Franco-Spanish fleet off Trafalgar

1806
(23 January) Death of Pitt; replaced by 'Ministry of All the Talents'

1807
(24 March) Ministry falls after George again refuses to agree to Catholic emancipation; duke of Portland becomes prime minister

1809
(4 October) Portland succeeded as prime minister by Spencer Percieval

1810
(October) Beginning of George's final illness

1811
(5 February) Prince of Wales becomes prince regent

1812
(11 May) Percieval assassinated; succeeded by Lord Liverpool

1812–1814
War with USA

1815
(18 June) Battle of Waterloo marks final defeat of Napoleon

1817
(March) More repressive measures in Britain, including suspension of habeas corpus

1819
(16 August) Peterloo Massacre: troops attack peaceful political meeting in Manchester, killing 11 and wounding 400

1820
(29 January) Death of George

the curtailments on their liberties that had been in force since the 17th century. Chief among these had been a ban on Catholics sitting in Parliament.

The union came about in 1801, but the king – who was now officially king of the 'United Kingdom of Britain and Ireland' – asserted that if he gave the royal assent to any bill offering Catholic emancipation he would be in violation of his coronation oath, in which he had sworn to uphold the Protestant religion. To his credit, Pitt felt so strongly on the issue that he resigned.

THE MADNESS OF KING GEORGE

Further fruitless attempts to bring up the subject of Catholic emancipation were made by ministers over the next decade, but George was adamant. By now his powers were failing, and he inevitably played a lesser and lesser role in politics. He was not only ageing and going blind and deaf, but the mental collapse he had suffered in 1788–9 recurred in the wake of the political crisis of 1801. He recovered, but the illness returned for a spell in 1804, and then in 1810 it came to stay, perhaps brought on by grief at the death of his favourite daughter, Amelia. Apart from a few lucid intervals, George remained violently insane for the rest of his life. The queen was given custody of her husband, and in 1811 the prince of Wales was made prince regent.

Modern medical opinion holds that George's mental instability was probably due to an inherited metabolic disease known as porphyria, which affects the nervous system and causes excruciating pain, fits, psychosis and a range of other symptoms. In 2004 high levels of arsenic were found in a few surviving strands of George's hair, and arsenic is known to precipitate attacks of porphyria. By a bitter irony, the arsenic almost certainly came from the antimony used in the medicine that his physicians administered to George in an attempt to control his symptoms.

The mad old king was held at Windsor Castle until his death, sometimes restrained by a straitjacket, sometimes chained to a chair, sometimes purged, sometimes bled. He grew a wild white beard, and talked endlessly to himself, or, as he supposed, to angels. On one occasion he took an oak tree for the king of Prussia. At Christmas 1819 he gabbled nonsensically for 58 hours non-stop, before falling, exhausted, into a coma. He never recovered consciousness, and on 29 January 1820 he died.

GEORGE IV

1820-1830

George has always been a figure of ridicule, whether as youthful prince of Wales, middle-aged prince regent, or elderly king. Byron called him Fum the Fourth, while to others he was Prinny or, because of his girth, the Prince of Whales. He may have been warm-hearted and generally well-intentioned, but he behaved all his life like a spoilt adolescent, and brought the British monarchy to a new low in the public esteem. To many of his subjects he was nothing but a fat, feckless fornicator, and even *The Times*, the mouthpiece of the British establishment, wrote in its obituary of him that 'there never was an individual less regretted by his fellow creatures'.

By his flatterers, George was dubbed 'the First Gentleman in Europe', and was hailed as an arbiter of taste and patron of the arts – the greatest such royal patron since Charles I. But as with Charles, George's aestheticism was accompanied by a disregard for the wants of his people, and his extravagance was widely resented as Britain suffered economic distress in the wake of the Napoleonic Wars.

THE PRINCE AND HIS BROTHERS

Like other playboy princes of Wales before and since, George reacted against the rigid, pious atmosphere of his parental home. In this rejection of stifling virtue and onerous duty, George was exuberantly joined by his younger brothers, especially Frederick, duke of York. Throughout their lives these generally straightforward, hot-blooded princes were mired in scandal, debt and the company of unsavoury associates. In 1819, as the old king neared his end, the poet Shelley damned the lot of them:

> Princes, the dregs of their dull race, who flow
> Through the public scorn – mud from a muddy spring –
> Rulers who neither see nor feel nor know
> But leech-like to their fainting country cling.

Similarly, George and his brothers were endlessly, scurrilously and sometimes obscenely caricatured in popular, mass-produced prints by the likes of Gillray and Rowlandson. No prince's dignity could survive such assaults.

Biography

FULL NAME George Augustus Frederick

BORN 12 August 1762, at St James's Palace, London

FATHER George III

MOTHER Charlotte Sophia of Mecklenburg-Strelitz

MARRIED (1) Maria Fitzherbert (marriage not recognized under English law), (2) Caroline of Brunswick

CHILDREN Charlotte (by Caroline)

SUCCEEDED 29 January 1820

CROWNED 19 July 1821

ROYAL HOUSE Hanover

STYLE By the Grace of God, of the United Kingdom of Great Britain and Ireland, King, Defender of the Faith

DIED 26 June 1830, at Windsor

BURIED St George's Chapel, Windsor

The future George IV in a portrait by Sir Thomas Lawrence (1769–1830). The Times gave him an unusually harsh obituary: 'If he ever had a friend – a devoted friend in any rank of life – we protest that the name of him or her never reached us.'

From the age of 18 George had agitated to have his own separate establishment. His father – who loved the prince as his son but despaired of him as a future king – resisted until George was 21. Thus in 1783 George set up his household at Carlton House, London, which soon became the centre of an alternative court and a focus for opposition politicians – recalling the role that Leicester House had played for George's grandfather and great-grandfather in their quarrels with their respective fathers.

George was not a political animal, and it was personal attraction that drew him to Charles James Fox, the radical leader of the Whigs, a brilliant, vivacious, impulsive, larger-than-life character, who in a few short years managed to dissipate a vast fortune on drink and gambling. Both his politics and his morals made him repugnant to George's father, which can only have increased the attraction for the young prince. When in power, briefly, in 1783, Fox tried to secure George an allowance of £100,000 a year – but was successfully outmanoeuvred by the king, who secured the fall of Fox's ministry soon afterwards. A few years later, when George III suffered his first bout of mental incapacity, Fox agitated in Parliament for the prince to acquire full regal powers as regent. When George recovered, and discovered how Fox and his son had, as he saw it, conspired against him, he swore never to have a Whig as a minister ever again.

PRINNY RAMPANT

> *Georgie Porgie, pudding and pie,*
> *Kissed the girls and made them cry;*
> *When the boys came out to play*
> *Georgie Porgie ran away.*

Like many nursery rhymes, this one began as satire – George was a notoriously shameless womanizer, and it was said that he requested a lock of hair from every woman he slept with, which he placed inside an envelope with her name on it. Rumour has it that by the time of his death he had accumulated a collection of 7,000 such envelopes.

Not all these encounters were without feeling. George could be as sentimental as any callow youth, and fell hopelessly in love with Mary Robinson, an actress four years his senior. He called her Perdita, after the character in Shakespeare's

THE KINGS AND QUEENS OF ENGLAND

Winter's Tale, and himself Florizel, Perdita's lover in the play. But his passion was short-lived, and, after he had deserted her, she threatened to publish their correspondence. The king was obliged to hand over £5,000 for the letters.

George had dropped his Perdita when he became obsessed with the twice-widowed Maria Fitzherbert, a Roman Catholic six years his senior. This time it was more than infatuation, but she would not become his mistress, so on 15 December 1785 they secretly underwent a form of marriage ceremony. The marriage was not, however, legally valid: the 1772 Royal Marriage Act declared null and void any union entered into by a member of the royal family under the age of 25 without the permission of the monarch; furthermore, if George married a Catholic, he would be barred from the succession by the 1701 Act of Settlement.

George had not only broken the law; he was deeply in debt – to the tune of £200,000 or more. The king, appalled at his son's behaviour, refused to help. In a gesture of showy petulance, the prince abandoned Carlton House and took a cab to Brighton, accompanied by Mrs Fitzherbert. Eventually, in 1787, Parliament came to the prince's financial aid. The following year, King George suffered his first bout of madness. When the prince was sent for, his father tried to strangle him.

A FARCICAL MARRIAGE

George went on accruing massive debts, and was aware that if he contracted a dynastic marriage that met with his father's approval, the king would pay off his creditors. By 1795 he had been living with Mrs Fitzherbert for a decade, and, as far as he was concerned, the spark had gone out of their relationship. He was ready for marriage – or, at least, for the increase in income that marriage would entail. The trouble was the woman he chose to marry, the German princess, Caroline of Brunswick.

Princess Caroline was a coarse, fleshy, uninhibited, colourful woman, with hot blood in her veins and an energetically foul mouth. She also stank. Prince George had no notion of these aspects of his fiancée's character, and when they first met at St James's Palace on 5 April 1795 the prince turned to one of his courtiers to mumble, 'Harris, I am not well; pray get me a glass of brandy.' The princess, not to be outdone in tact, loudly

Timeline

1762
(12 August) Birth of George

1779
Begins short affair with Mary 'Perdita' Robinson

1783
George establishes his own household at Carlton House

1785
(15 December) Marries (illegally) Mrs Fitzherbert

1788–1789
George's father, George III, temporarily incapacitated by his illness; regency crisis

1793–1802
War with Revolutionary France

1795
(8 April) Marries Caroline of Brunswick

1796
(7 January) Birth of Princess Charlotte

1803–1815
Napoleonic Wars

1811
(5 February) George becomes prince regent

1812
(11 May) Prime minister Spencer Perceval assassinated; succeeded by Lord Liverpool

1812–1814
War with USA

1815
(18 June) Battle of Waterloo marks final defeat of Napoleon

The wedding of the prince of Wales (the future George IV) to Caroline of Brunswick, 8 April 1795, as depicted by John Graham (1755–1817). Bride and groom would live together for only a few weeks – just long enough for Caroline to conceive a daughter, Charlotte Augusta (1796–1817).

1817
(March) Repressive measures in Britain, including suspension of habeas corpus

(6 November) Death of George's daughter, Princess Charlotte

1819
(16 August) Peterloo Massacre: troops attack peaceful political meeting in Manchester, killing 11 and wounding 400

1820
(29 January) George succeeds

(10 November) Collapse of bill to annul George's marriage to Caroline

1821
(19 July) George crowned

1827
(February) Lord Liverpool resigns as prime minister; succeeded briefly by George Canning and then Lord Goderich

1828
(25 January) Duke of Wellington becomes prime minister

1829
(10 April) George reluctantly agrees to Catholic emancipation

1830
(26 June) Death of George

announced how surprised she was to find her fiancé so fat and unattractive. The two were married three days later, but only after the prince's friends had got him so drunk he couldn't run away. The drink did the trick, for nine months after their wedding night Princess Caroline gave birth to a girl, Charlotte. After this the couple separated, the prince acquiring custody of his daughter.

George promptly sought solace in the arms of Lady Jersey, but before long had successfully persuaded Mrs Fitzherbert to return to his bed. The public's sympathy was all with the abandoned princess, who capitalized on the prince's unpopularity by making extravagant public appearances in London, especially at venues where George and Mrs Fitzherbert were likely to be present. Over the next decade there were constant rumours that Caroline's sex life was unthwarted by the desertion of the prince. In the end this prompted a 'Delicate Investigation' by the Privy Council, which in December 1805 cleared her of the charge of bearing another man's son, but nevertheless found her behaviour to be indiscreet.

From 1814 Caroline lived abroad, mostly in Italy, indulging her tastes for vulgar ostentation, mad extravagance and – allegedly – foreign lovers. But when George became king in 1820 she turned down an offer of £50,000 per year to stay abroad, and waddled back to Britain to claim her place as queen. The crowds in London greeted her return rapturously – principally as a means of getting back at a repressive government and an uncaring monarch during a period of severe economic depression.

George was horrified by Caroline's reappearance, and his ministers introduced a bill to annul the marriage on the grounds of adultery. The hearing in the House of Lords went on for months, and day after day the country was transfixed with the colourful testimony of a string of Italian servants, until in November 1820 the proceedings collapsed. The following July Caroline attempted to attend George's coronation, but was physically prevented from entering Westminster Abbey. It proved to be a fatal humiliation. Shortly afterwards she fell ill, and within three weeks was dead.

REGENT AND KING

George's coronation was a redefining moment for the British monarchy, the moment when pomp and ceremonial overtook political significance. The splendour and spectacle of George's coronation did something to reconcile his subjects to their king, and George went on to make popular public appearances in Dublin and Edinburgh – he was the first reigning monarch to visit Ireland since the 1690s and the first in Scotland since the 1630s. In 1822, in celebrations organized by Sir Walter Scott, the king paraded round Edinburgh to tumultuous cheers, having squeezed himself for the occasion into a kilt and flesh-coloured tights. George's flair for showmanship and ostentation had at last found a useful outlet.

George had suffered from the same problems as other princes of Wales, whose fathers or mothers have enjoyed lengthy reigns: what on earth to do with himself. When war broke out with France in 1793, he begged his father for a command in the army, but was refused, while George's younger brother, the duke of York, was allowed to go on active (albeit inglorious) service in the Low Countries. George tried again during the Napoleonic Wars, but was once more turned down by his father.

George's chance to make a difference might have arrived when he became prince regent in 1811 during his father's final incapacity, but he was content to keep the existing Tory ministry in power, having abandoned the Whigs after his old friend Charles James Fox died in 1806. The Tories were to remain in power right through the regency and George's reign as king, first under Lord Liverpool, and then under the duke of Wellington.

A contemporary cartoon satirizing the pressure brought to bear by the duke of Wellington on George IV over Catholic emancipation. The duke is shown disciplining the king, who is being supported on the back of his mistress Lady Conyngham. Wellington obtained the strongly anti-Catholic George's consent to the introduction of a Catholic Relief Bill in 1829 only with great difficulty.

George does not appear to have suffered from any strong political principles, although he was at heart a died-in-the-wool reactionary. He lacked the political skill to exert control over his ministers, but by and large he was content with what they did. An exception was Catholic emancipation, which he opposed as fervently as his father had done. But unlike his father, he eventually – in a show of tears and tantrums – allowed himself to be persuaded to sign the bill into law on 10 April 1829.

By now George was a gouty old man, his vast bulk proving too great a burden for his ankles, his liver bloated by years of alcoholic excess. He was physically unable to sustain the public shows with which he had begun his reign, and led a generally quiet life at Windsor with his pious last mistress, Lady Conyngham. When his body at last gave up the remorseless struggle against a lifetime of abuse, the sentiments of many of his subjects were summed up in an epigram by Walter Savage Landor:

> *George the First was always reckoned*
> *Vile, but viler George the Second;*
> *And what mortal ever heard*
> *Any good of George the Third?*
> *When from earth the Fourth descended*
> *God be praised, the Georges ended.*

George the builder

George loved all the fine things of life, and nowhere has his taste left a more visible legacy than in his patronage of architecture. He undertook much rebuilding at Buckingham Palace and Windsor Castle, but it was his favourite architect, John Nash, who created the buildings most associated with the period: in London, Regent Street and the terraces around Regent's Park; and in Brighton (which George turned into the fashionable place to be beside the sea) the remarkable Brighton Pavilion, an oriental fantasy that embodies all of George's tireless extravagance and wilful detachment from reality.

THE KINGS AND QUEENS OF ENGLAND

WILLIAM IV

1830-1837

William – known as the 'Sailor King' from his long naval career – was not a remarkable man in himself, being a less brilliant (if also less selfish and more liberal) figure than his elder brother, George IV. But his reign was remarkable for one of the most significant lurches towards modern democracy in British history, the Great Reform Act of 1832. It was a move that William personally opposed, but he had enough of a grasp of his constitutional position to smooth its passage into law.

George IV's only legitimate child, Princess Charlotte, had died in 1817, leaving George's oldest surviving brother, Frederick, the duke of York, as his heir to the throne. But Frederick died in 1827, before George, so William, then duke of Clarence, was next in line. It was not a position that he might have expected to find himself in, and he was 64 years old at the time of his accession – the oldest person to succeed to the throne in British history.

A NAVAL PRINCE

William's father, George III, sent him off to join the navy at the age of 13, with the following instruction: 'I desire he may be received without the smallest marks of parade … The young man goes as a sailor, and, as such, I add again, no marks of distinction are to be shown unto him.' William saw active service in the American Revolution, during which George Washington approved an abortive plan to kidnap the young prince. Also at this time William met and made friends with the future Admiral Nelson, who wrote of him:

> *In his professional line, he is superior to two-thirds, I am sure, of the list [i.e. the officers in the Royal Navy]; and in attention to orders, and respect to his superior officer, I hardly know his equal.*

This sounds like damning with faint praise, and certainly once he acquired his own command, William proved unpopular with his fellow officers, and, on account of his harsh discipline, also with his men.

William's career at sea ended in 1790, but he continued to rise up the ranks: by the end of the decade he was a full admiral, and by 1811 admiral of the fleet. Finally, in 1827,

Biography

FULL NAME: William Henry

BORN 21 August 1765, at Buckingham Palace, London

FATHER George III

MOTHER Charlotte Sophia of Mecklenburg-Strelitz

MARRIED Adelaide, daughter of the duke of Saxe-Meiningen

CHILDREN by Adelaide he had two daughters, Charlotte and Elizabeth, who both died in infancy. He had previously fathered ten illegitimate children by his mistress, Dorothea Jordan

SUCCEEDED 26 June 1830

CROWNED 9 September 1831

ROYAL HOUSE Hanover

STYLE By the Grace of God, of the United Kingdom of Great Britain and Ireland, King, Defender of the Faith

DIED 20 June 1837, at Windsor

BURIED St George's Chapel, Windsor

1765
(21 August) Birth of William

1778
Joins Royal Navy as a
midshipman

1789
Made duke of Clarence

1790
Retires from active service

1791
Begins affair with Mrs Jordan, by
whom he fathers ten illegitimate
children

1811
Ends his affair with Mrs Jordan

1818
(11 July) Marries Princess
Adelaide of Saxe-Meiningen

1819
(21 March) Birth of his daughter
Charlotte, who dies the same day

1820
(10 December) Birth of his
daughter Elizabeth

Silly Billy

William, like most of the House of Hanover, was
not renowned for his brains. It was said that during
a royal visit to the Bedlam hospital for lunatics, one
of the inmates had pointed to the duke of Clarence,
as he then was, and shouted, 'Silly Billy! Silly Billy!'
To William's embarrassment the nickname stuck. He
got his own back, however. When he became king
and held his first meeting of the privy council, he
gleefully demanded of the assembled company,
'Who's the Silly Billy now?'

William was given the largely ceremonial rank of lord high
admiral, and in this role he achieved some reforms (such as the
abolition of flogging except for mutiny). However, he also
managed, by his unpredictability, to irritate his colleagues at the
Admiralty beyond distraction – so much so that the government
threatened to resign unless he retired, which he duly did after 15
months in the job.

CLARENCE, MRS JORDAN AND THE FITZCLARENCES

As William's active nautical career was coming to its end, the
prince, looking to his future prospects, badgered his father for a
dukedom and the parliamentary grant that would come with it.
After all, his elder brother Frederick was duke of York. But
George refused, until William threatened to stand for a seat in
the House of Commons. Appalled at the prospect of his son
numbering himself among the commoners of his realm, the king
conceded, and William was made duke of Clarence in 1789.

With an endearing disregard for what the world thought of
his domestic arrangements, William, soon after he returned from
sea, openly set up house in Bushy Park with an Irish actress, Mrs
Jordan (the stage name of Dorothea Bland; she had not actually
been married, but it was marginally more respectable for an
actress to be a Mrs than a Miss). She was a notable beauty, with
considerable charms, as described by William Hazlitt: 'She was
the child of nature whose voice was a cordial to the heart …
whose singing was like the twang of Cupid's bow.'

Over the next twenty years Mrs Jordan bore William ten
children, who were surnamed Fitzclarence ('Fitz' in a surname
originally indicated illegitimacy). Despite his parliamentary
grant, William often found himself financially
embarrassed, and so Mrs Jordan – in between her
many confinements – gamely continued her stage
career. The affair ended in 1811, and Mrs Jordan
died in 1816, near Paris, in poverty.

William, like his brother George, knew that if he
married his income would be increased. He did not
actually succeed in this aim until 1818, when his
proposal (the latest of many that had ricocheted
around the courts of Europe) was accepted by a
German Protestant princess, Adelaide of Saxe-

1821
(4 March) Death of Elizabeth

1827
William appointed lord high admiral

1828
Resigns as lord high admiral

1830
(26 June) Succeeds

(August) Duke of Wellington's Tories defeated in general election; Whigs under Lord Grey come to power

1831
(9 September) William crowned

(October) House of Lords rejects Great Reform Bill

1832
(4 June) Lords passes Great Reform Bill after William promises to create more peers to ensure its passage

1833
(29 August) Factory Act restricts the employment of children

Meiningen. By this time, with the death of his brother George's daughter Charlotte in 1817, there was a certain urgency for him to make a royal match and produce a legitimate heir. Although he himself was now enamoured of an English heiress called Miss Wyckham, he put his own desires aside and did his dynastic duty.

Princess Adelaide bore William two daughters, but both died in infancy. His continuing attachment to his children by Mrs Jordan gave him some consolation – and Adelaide too showed them great kindness. When he became king he gave all the Fitzclarences titles, the oldest boy, George Augustus, becoming earl of Munster. George Augustus was deeply embittered when his cousin Victoria became queen in 1837 – for was not he the son of a king? The injustice of it gnawed away at him, and in 1842 he shot himself.

An informal king

The reputation of the British monarchy had reached a nadir with George IV. In his earlier years George had incurred the loathing of his people by the careless extravagance of his lifestyle, while by the end of his reign he had earned their indifference by secluding himself at Windsor. William, an affable, garrulous, somewhat eccentric and quite unselfconscious soul, lacked his brother's reserve. As king he acted, after a fashion, on the advice he had received from the marquis of Anglesey, a veteran of Waterloo, in 1830:

> Your Royal Highness must bear this in mind – you must keep a brilliant court . . . without making yourself too common, you must nevertheless frequently show yourself amongst your subjects.

Sometimes he could take familiarity too far – at least in the eyes of some. Mrs Arbuthnot, whose husband moved in high Tory circles, complained:

> The king is somewhat wild and talks and shows himself too much. He walked up St James's Street the other day quite alone, the mob following him, and one of the common women threw her arms round him and kissed him.

The coronation of William IV and his queen consort, Adelaide of Saxe-Meiningen, in Westminster Abbey in September 1831, as depicted in an aquatint by W. Read (fl.1818–37). Adelaide gave her name to the capital city of South Australia, which was named in her honour in 1834.

Here we have in a nutshell the dilemma that faces the monarchy to this day: to maintain mystique by keeping a distance from one's subjects, but so risk accusations of aloofness; or to court popularity and risk making a fool of oneself. Happily for William, he lost no sleep pondering this question; he was quite content just to be himself.

The Great Reform Act

In politics William was more flexible than his elder brother, in that he was prepared to tolerate Whigs as well as Tories in his ministries, although favoured the latter. The Tories were voted out of office in the general election of August 1830 – shortly after William succeeded – and a Whig government under Lord Grey came to power. The Whigs, who won a further election the following year, were committed to parliamentary reform, and introduced a bill that sought to correct some of the abuses in the electoral system. Among these was the unrepresentative nature of seats in the House of Commons – some members sat for so-called 'rotten boroughs', villages with only a handful of inhabitants, while some of the big new industrial cities had no members of Parliament. There were also 'pocket boroughs', where the decision as to who should be elected was in the hands of the local landowner. The bill introduced standard rules as to who should have the vote, and extended the franchise more evenly among middle-class men. It was a long way from proposing universal franchise, but it was bitterly opposed by the Tories and by the House of Lords, partly on the grounds that such reforms would infringe the property rights of landowners – these rights were taken to include the right to control the local MP – and partly because any concession to reform, no matter how small, would, it was feared, open the floodgates, and herald the destruction of the established order.

William himself, who by instinct aligned himself with the landowning classes, opposed the bill, which had passed the Commons but was likely to be defeated in the Lords. In May 1832 Grey asked the king to create 50 new peers, which William refused to do. Grey resigned, but his Tory opponent, the duke of Wellington, could not assemble enough support to form a ministry, so William was reluctantly obliged to promise Grey that he would create sufficient peers to pass the bill. The Lords got the message, and allowed the bill to become law.

William once said, 'I have my view of things, and I tell them to my ministers. If they do not adopt them, I cannot help it. I have done my duty.' Although generally speaking he grasped the limits of royal power in a constitutional monarchy, he overstepped the mark in November 1834 when, contrary to the will of Parliament, he dismissed the Whig ministry and asked the Tories to form an administration. However, after the necessary election, the Tories found they were without a majority, and the king was obliged to ask the Whigs, under Lord Melbourne (whom he heartily disliked), to return to government.

Towards the end of his reign, William was anxious that he should survive long enough for his niece and heir, Victoria, to reach the age of majority before he died. William loathed his sister-in-law, Victoria's mother, the widowed duchess of Kent, and hated the idea that she might become regent. William succeeded in his aim, living for a month after Victoria celebrated her 18th birthday. During his final illness his doctors told an anxious public that the king was suffering from hay fever. In fact, like his brother, his system had been weakened by alcoholic cirrhosis and circulatory problems, and in the end he was carried off by pneumonia. His last words were said to have been, 'The Church, the Church.'

1834
(6 March) Six agricultural labourers – the 'Tolpuddle Martyrs' – are sentenced to transportation for forming a trade union

(1 August) Slavery abolished throughout the British Empire, following the Emancipation Act of 1833

(14 August) New Poor Law establishes workhouses for the able-bodied poor

(November) William dismisses Lord Melbourne's Whig ministry and asks Robert Peel to form a Tory government

1835
(18 April) Peel resigns after Tories fail to gain majority in general election; Melbourne returns to power

1837
(20 June) Death of William

VICTORIA

1837-1901

William IV was the last British monarch to defy the wishes of Parliament. In the course of the long reign of his niece, Queen Victoria – the longest reign in British history – the monarchy became an almost entirely ceremonial institution. The queen was consulted by her ministers, and she expressed her views, but there was no question of her will overriding theirs or that of Parliament, however much she desired to hang on to real power.

Biography

FULL NAME: Alexandrina Victoria

BORN 24 May 1819, at Kensington Palace, London

FATHER Edward Augustus, duke of Kent

MOTHER Victoria of Saxe-Coburg-Saafeld

MARRIED Albert of Saxe-Coburg-Gotha

CHILDREN Victoria (princess royal), Albert Edward (the future Edward VII), Alice, Alfred, Helena, Louise, Arthur, Leopold, Beatrice

SUCCEEDED 20 June 1837

CROWNED 28 June 1838

ROYAL HOUSE Hanover

STYLE By the Grace of God, of the United Kingdom of Great Britain and Ireland, Queen, Defender of the Faith, Empress of India (this last title was added 1 May 1876)

DIED 22 January 1901, at Osborne House, Isle of Wight

BURIED The royal mausoleum at Frogmore House, near Windsor Castle

Victoria's reign saw not only a diminution of royal power, but the transformation of Britain. In 1837 the country had a largely agrarian economy, and was ruled by an aristocratic oligarchy. By the time of Victoria's death in 1901, Britain had become a bourgeois, industrial democracy ruling the biggest empire the world has ever seen.

Victoria herself – egotistical, stubborn and perennially unamused – was not an enormously sympathetic character. Although she was besotted with her husband, she did not particularly like her children, and was inclined to favour those politicians who flattered her most. She upheld rigorous standards of duty and personal morality – against which her eldest son reacted energetically – yet showed little interest in her people, so many of whom lived in abject poverty.

Although the monarchy survived her reign in good heart, there were times, especially after she withdrew to Windsor following her husband's death, when her subjects wondered quite what she was for. She herself never seems to have felt the need to tell them, but by the end of the 19th century Britain had become the world's greatest power, and Victoria unwittingly embodied her people's imperial aspirations. In retrospect the Victorian age – although an age of science, progress and reform – has also become a byword for stifling social convention, ruthless economic self-interest and rampant moral hypocrisy; and Victoria also stands as an icon of these.

FROM PRINCESS TO QUEEN

Victoria was the daughter of Edward Augustus, duke of Kent, the fourth son of George III, and the German princess,

Victoria of Saxe-Coburg-Saafeld, the widow of Prince Karl of Leiningen. George's oldest son, George IV, died without a direct heir, as did his brother, William IV, leaving William's niece Victoria as next in line to the throne, her own father having died when she was just eight months old.

Victoria was christened Alexandrina Victoria, and as a child was known as 'Drina'. She was brought up in some isolation at Kensington Palace with her mother, her half-sister Féodore or Feodora, who was 12 years her senior, a German governess called Louise Lehzen, and her collection of 132 dolls. Her Uncle Leopold, who lived in Surrey until he became king of the Belgians in 1831, acted as a surrogate father, as her letters to him reveal, while his letters to her are full of advice on her future role as queen.

Victoria's domineering mother was on bad terms with her brothers-in-law, George IV and William IV. She boycotted the latter's coronation, and kept her daughter firmly away from the 'wicked uncles'. Victoria led a sheltered life, even sleeping in her mother's bedroom, until, in the early hours of 20 June 1837 she was woken to be informed that she was now queen of Great Britain and Ireland. (Victoria did not succeed to the throne of Hanover, however, as by the Salic law pertaining there, no woman could be monarch. Instead, another uncle, Ernest Augustus, became king of Hanover.)

The 18-year-old Queen Victoria in her coronation robes, in a painting by George Hayter (1838).

The British prime minister at the time, Lord Melbourne, an amiable and avuncular Whig of the old school, took the young queen under his wing; his only child was mentally retarded, and Victoria perhaps provided him with a surrogate daughter. The more scurrilously minded referred to the young queen as 'Mrs Melbourne', and a contemporary, Charles Greville, astutely observed, 'Melbourne is everything to her … her feelings are sexual, though she does not know it.' For the teenage queen, it was a thrilling, romantic friendship with a worldly older man.

DEAR ALBERT

Melbourne was eclipsed in Victoria's affections by her cousin, a minor German princeling called Albert of Saxe-Coburg-Gotha. It wasn't exactly love at first sight – she had met him when they were both 17, and when in July 1839 there was talk of Prince Albert coming to England as a possible husband she confided to her journal that she had no great wish to see him:

> *'Certainly better wait for a year or two,' said Lord M[elbourne], 'it's a very serious question.'*
> *I said I wished if possible never to marry. 'I don't know about that,' he replied.*

Timeline

1819
(24 May) Birth of Victoria

1820
(23 January) Death of Victoria's father, the duke of Kent

1837
(20 June) Succeeds

1838
(28 June) Crowned

(18 September) Foundation of Anti-Corn Law League, to agitate against protectionist laws keeping cost of wheat high

1838–1842
First British intervention in Afghanistan ends in disaster

1839
Bedchamber Crisis

1839–1842
First Opium War with China

1840
(10 February) Victoria marries Prince Albert

(21 November) Birth of Victoria's first child, also called Victoria

1841
(23 August) Sir Robert Peel (Tory) succeeds Lord Melbourne (Whig) as prime minister

(9 November) Birth of Victoria's second child, the future Edward VII

1842
Mines Act bans women and young children working underground

But when Albert arrived in October, Victoria was instantly smitten:

> *Albert really is quite charming, and so excessively handsome, such beautiful blue eyes, an exquisite nose, and such a pretty mouth with delicate moustachios and slight but very slight whiskers; a beautiful figure, broad in the shoulders and a fine waist.*

Within a matter of days Victoria had proposed to Albert (it was not done for a man to propose if he was of inferior rank). They were married in February 1840, and Victoria recorded of her wedding night that 'We did not sleep much.' In fact she and Albert enjoyed a remarkably vigorous love life, given the sexual repression we associate with the Victorian era.

The downside of all this energetic concupiscence, as far as Victoria was concerned, was the 'nasty objects' that appeared as a result. Although she had nine of them, Victoria did not like babies, and was not particularly enthusiastic about children ('only very occasionally do I find the rather intimate intercourse with them either agreeable or easy'). She preferred Albert. The public image of the perfect royal family, happily and soberly gathered around the Christmas tree – an innovation that Albert introduced to Britain from Germany – did, however, appeal to the expanding, morally minded bourgeoisie, which had pulled up its collective skirts in

> ❝ Victoria is said to be incredibly stubborn and her extreme obstinacy to be constantly at war with her good nature. ❞ PRINCE ALBERT ANXIOUSLY RECORDS WHAT IS SAID ABOUT HIS FUTURE WIFE, BEFORE HIS VISIT TO ENGLAND IN 1839.

horror at the carryings-on of Victoria's uncles, the six-bottle men with their vast debts and their unspeakable mistresses.

Albert himself was more than just a Prince Charming. He was a well-educated, cultured, hard-working and serious-minded young man. Although adored by his wife, he was, initially at least, treated with great suspicion by his adopted countrymen: he was too impecunious, too low-ranking, too intellectual – and too German. Parliament cut his proposed allowance, squabbled about his position in the hierarchy of precedence, and would not award him the title of prince consort until 1857. Although he gave his wife and her ministers advice, he was largely kept out of the business of politics, and instead devoted his considerable energies to encouraging science, technology and the arts. It was Albert who was the moving force behind the complex of museums in South Kensington (nicknamed 'Albertopolis'), and for the Great Exhibition of 1851, which showcased British inventions and manufactures to the world.

Although a devoted father, Albert's relations with his eldest son, Albert Edward, were strained: Bertie (as he was known) did not rise to his father's high academic or ethical expectations. Worries about his son, combined with a tendency to overwork, took its toll on Albert's health, and he became increasingly unwell. His death, of typhoid, on 14 December 1861, left Victoria utterly bereft.

Mrs Brown

Victoria was only 42 when Albert died, but she behaved as if her life were over. For her four remaining decades she dressed in black; and for several years after Albert's death – suffering, in her own words, 'paroxysms of despair' – she eschewed public appearances except when she had unavoidable official duties. She became the 'Widow of Windsor', secluding herself at Windsor Castle – where every night Albert's clothes were still laid out on the bed – or hiding away in either of the two private mansions Albert had designed for her – Osborne House in the Isle of Wight, or Balmoral Castle in the Scottish Highlands.

It was at the latter that she developed a dependence on a Scottish servant, John Brown, whom she greatly admired, not least because of his plain-spoken, forthright manner. Inevitably her fondness for Brown caused jealousies, and the jealousies generated rumours that the two were sexually involved,

The Great Exhibition of 1851. Queen Victoria visited the Exhibition on 7 and 24 June, and saw for herself the implications of the machine age: 'Went to the machinery part, where we remained 2 hours, and which is excessively interesting and instructive. What used to be done by hand and used to take months doing is now accomplished in a few instants by the most beautiful machinery.'

1846–1851
Irish famine

1846
(28 June) Repeal of Corn Laws

(30 June) Whigs come to power under Lord John Russell

1847
Law limiting working hours of 13–18-year-olds to no more than ten hours a day

1848–1849
Unsuccessful revolutions against absolute monarchies and empires throughout Europe

1848
(April) Last great demonstration by the Chartists (advocates of radical political and social reform) – Victoria dismisses them as 'worthless and wanton men'

1851
Great Exhibition

1852
(20 December) Lord Aberdeen (Peelite) succeeds the Tory Lord Derby as prime minister

1853–1856
Crimean War against Russia; queen institutes Victoria Cross medal for gallantry

1855
(5 February) Lord Palmerston (Liberal) becomes prime minister

1856–1860
Second Opium War with China

The exterior of Balmoral Castle, Deeside. The present building was completed in 1856.

or even secretly married – hence 'Mrs Brown' became the butt of many a ribald joke. Although it is unlikely that there was any substance in the tittle-tattle, Victoria was prostrated by Brown's death in 1883, and at her own death she requested that she be buried with not only a memento of Albert (a dressing gown) but also with a lock of her former servant's hair.

Victoria's withdrawal from her subjects following Albert's death eroded the popularity of the monarchy, and even brought about a short-lived upsurge in republican sentiment. In 1871 the radical member of Parliament, Sir Charles Dilke, gave voice to the thoughts of many when he declared,

If you can show me a fair chance that a republic here will be free from the political corruption which hangs about the monarchy, I say, for my part – and I believe that the middle classes in general will say – let it come.

But such republican views did not take firm root in Britain, partly because the politicians in power had uses for the institution of monarchy.

LAMB, PEEL, PAM, DIZZY, AND THE GRAND OLD MAN
No British monarch has seen more prime ministers come and go than Victoria (her score of ten has only been equalled by the present queen). Before the emergence of broad-based two-party politics, she had some power as a coalition-maker among the various factions of Whigs and Tories. But by the 1850s the Whigs had evolved into the Liberal Party, and the Tories into the Conservative Party, while two Reform Acts, in 1867 and 1884,

THE KINGS AND QUEENS OF ENGLAND

extended the franchise much further than the Great Reform Act of 1832 had done. These measures gave the vote to the majority of adult males – but not to a single woman, an exclusion of which Victoria heartily approved. She herself deprecated 'the stream of destructive democracy' and declared that she would not be 'a sovereign of a democratic monarchy'. Nevertheless, that was what she was.

With the encouragement of Albert, Victoria eventually learnt to practise neutrality (up to a point) in party politics – although she had strong personal preferences among the personalities involved. Before the arrival of Albert and his moderating influence, Victoria had reacted against the Tory sympathies of her uncles and strongly favoured the Whigs, particularly as embodied in her dear 'Lord M' – William Lamb, Viscount Melbourne. When Sir Robert Peel, a Tory, attempted to form a ministry in 1839, he suggested to the queen that it would be appropriate is she were to dismiss those ladies of the bedchamber who were married to Whigs – he would take this as a sign of her confidence in him. But the queen flatly refused, declaring 'The Queen of England will not submit to such trickery,' and Peel was unable to form a government. When the Whigs fell in 1841 and Peel once more came to power, Albert quietly ensured that the Whig ladies of the bedchamber handed in their resignations. Victoria herself came to regret her behaviour in the 'Bedchamber Crisis' of 1839: 'Perhaps I should act differently if it was all to be done again,' she reflected.

Victoria came to change her view of Peel. In 1839 he had been, in her opinion, 'such a cold, odd man'; but by 1842 he was 'a great statesman, a man who thinks little of party and never of himself'. However, she neither liked nor trusted Lord Palmerston, the popular and robust foreign secretary, and later prime minister. The British public might call their womanizing hero 'Pam', but to Victoria he was the dreaded 'Pilgerstein', and she strongly

1857
Indian Mutiny

1858–1859
Derby's second ministry

1859–1865
Palmerston's second ministry

1861
(16 March) Death of Victoria's mother

(14 December) Death of Prince Albert

1865
(18 October) Russell again prime minister following death of Palmerston

1866
Derby's third ministry

1867
(15 August) Second Reform Act

1868
Disraeli's first ministry (Conservative)

1868–1874
Gladstone's first ministry (Liberal)

1870
Education Act encourages spread of elementary schools

1874–1880
Disraeli's second ministry

' The Queen is most anxious to enlist everyone who can speak or write or join in checking this mad, wicked folly of "Woman's Rights" with all its attendant horrors, on which her poor feeble sex is bent, forgetting every sense of womanly feeling and propriety. ' VICTORIA GIVES HER JUDGEMENT ON WOMEN'S SUFFRAGE IN A LETTER TO THEODORE MARTIN, IN 1870.

1876
(1 May) Victoria becomes empress of India

1877
Victoria demands war against Russia, but is restrained

1878–1881
Second Afghan War

1879
Foundation of Irish Land League to agitate for land reform

Zulu War in South Africa

1880–1881
First Boer War

1880–1885
Gladstone's second ministry

1884
Third Reform Act

1885–1886
Lord Salisbury's first ministry (Conservative)

1886
Gladstone's third ministry; defeat of first bill to give home rule to Ireland

1886–1892
Salisbury's second ministry

1887
Victoria's Golden Jubilee celebrations

1892–1894
Gladstone's fourth and final ministry

Four generations of royalty in an undated photograph showing Queen Victoria and three future kings: her son Edward VII, her grandson George V, and her great-grandson Edward VIII.

disapproved of his policy of encouraging nationalist movements within the Austrian empire. Her personal preferences were even more sharply contrasted in relation to the two great colossi of Victorian politics, Benjamin Disraeli, the Conservative leader, and William Ewart Gladstone, his Liberal rival.

Disraeli – 'Dizzy' – utterly charmed the queen when he became prime minister in 1868. Victoria wrote to her eldest daughter in something of a swoon:

> *Mr Disraeli … has always behaved extremely well to me, and has all the right feelings for a minister towards the sovereign … He is full of poetry, romance and chivalry. When he knelt down to kiss my hand, which he took in both of his, he said 'in loving loyalty and faith'.*

Disraeli – also a successful novelist – certainly knew how to tickle the queen's vanity: when she published her journal of her life in the Highlands, he murmured, to her delight, 'We authors, ma'am …'; and Victoria was thrilled when he suggested, in 1876, that she adopt the title 'Empress of India' (in return she made him earl of Beaconsfield). Disraeli himself explained his approach to the

sovereign: 'I never deny; I never contradict; I sometimes forget.' He might have added that he also supplied her with plenty of gossip, which she thoroughly enjoyed.

In contrast, Victoria felt a deep antipathy for Gladstone, the 'Grand Old Man' of the Liberal Party, four times prime minister, a committed if stern reformer, and a mighty orator: 'He speaks to me as if I were a public meeting,' she complained. After the fall of Gladstone's first ministry in 1874 she wrote of him thus to her eldest daughter:

> *So vy arrogant, tyrannical and obstinate with no knowledge of the World or human nature [and] a fanatic in religion. All this and much want of égard towards my feelings … make him a very dangerous & unsatisfactory Premier.*

Gladstone may have been too concerned with the welfare of the ordinary people and the troubles of Ireland for Victoria's taste (she regarded his proposals for Irish home rule as deeply disloyal), but he is generally regarded as one of the greatest statesmen of the 19th century. Gladstone himself believed that Albert had prejudiced the queen in favour of the Conservatives, noting as early as 1846 that 'through him she has become so attached to Conservative ideas that she could hardly endure the idea of the opposite Party as her ministers'.

Victoria Imperatrix

From 1876 the British empire had an empress, and in the last quarter of the 19th century Britain transformed from a colonial into an imperial power, its mission no longer just to trade and settle, but to educate, civilize and rule its vast domains in North America, the Caribbean, Africa, Asia and the Antipodes, and to set an example to the rest of the world. It was the 'empire on which the sun never sets' (partly, according to one wag, because God doesn't trust an Englishman in the dark).

Victoria was the symbol at the pinnacle of a vast hierarchy of power straddling the world, and her restoration to public adulation was completed by the celebrations attending her Golden Jubilee in 1887, followed a decade later by her Diamond Jubilee. 'The cheering was quite deafening,' Victoria wrote on the latter occasion, 'I was much moved and gratified.'

The old queen had by now become the 'Grandmother of Europe'. Her sons and daughters had married into royal houses across the continent – one grandson became Kaiser Wilhelm II of Germany, a granddaughter married Tsar Nicholas II of Russia, and other granddaughters became queens of Greece, Norway, Romania, Spain and Sweden. As she and they grew older, she became fonder of her children, and was a devoted and regular correspondent both with them and with her many grandchildren. Indeed she lived to see the birth of four of her successors: her son, Edward VII; her grandson, George V; and two great-grandsons, Edward VIII and George VI. But as the old century closed and she peacefully neared her end, it is unlikely that Victoria had the remotest inkling of the cataclysms that were shortly to overwhelm Europe, hurling so many of her far-flung brood from their thrones. She had, as the world entered the 'century of the common man', outlived her era.

1893
(13 January) Foundation of Britain's first socialist party, the Independent Labour Party

(8 September) Defeat of second home rule bill

1894–1895
Lord Rosebery heads Liberal government

1895–1902
Salisbury's third ministry

1897
Victoria's Diamond Jubilee celebrations

1899
Start of second Boer War

1900
(27 February) Foundation of Labour Representation Committee

1901
(22 January) Death of Victoria

Edward VII
1901-1910

Chubby-cheeked, convivial, hugely popular, and without a moral fibre in his not insubstantial body, Edward VII presided over a brief, colourful coda to the Victorian age, an Indian summer in which the *anciens régimes* of Europe spiralled unwittingly towards annihilation, while, almost unnoticed, the industrial proletariat began to organize. The fact that the British monarchy survived the catastrophe of the First World War is due in part to Edward's cultivation of a new mystique for the ancient institution, manifested in lavish displays of pomp and circumstance. Edward understood the most important thing about the monarchy in the age of democracy: *to be seen.*

Biography

FULL NAME: Albert Edward

BORN 9 November 1841, at Buckingham Palace, London

FATHER Prince Albert of Saxe-Coburg-Gotha

MOTHER Victoria

MARRIED Alexandra, daughter of Christian IX of Denmark

CHILDREN Albert Victor ('Eddy'; died in 1892), George (the future George V), Louise, Victoria, Maud, Alexander John (died within a day of his birth)

SUCCEEDED 22 January 1901

CROWNED 9 August 1902

ROYAL HOUSE Saxe-Coburg-Gotha

STYLE By the Grace of God, of the United Kingdom of Great Britain and Ireland and the British Dominions beyond the Seas, King, Defender of the Faith, Emperor of India

DIED 6 May 1910, at Buckingham Palace

BURIED St George's Chapel, Windsor

Where his parents were devoted to duty, Edward was devoted to pleasure – not only to good cigars, fine wines and rich food (hence one of his nicknames, 'Tum-Tum'), but also to the sporting life: gaming, race horses, yachting, shooting, and other men's wives. He was the despair of his father, and his mother blamed him for hastening the death of her dear Albert: 'It quite irritates me to see him in the room,' she confided to Lord Clarendon. Victoria kept him away from the business of state, and, with nothing else to do during his sixty years as heir to the throne, it is not surprising that he should have become mired in self-indulgence and scandal.

Prince of Wales

Christened Albert Edward and known to friends and family as 'Bertie', the young prince of Wales did not inherit his father's intelligence, nor his appetite for hard work. Both his temper and his attention span were short, but he loved company, was a natural diplomat, and was possessed of considerable charms. His father had designed a rigorous educational scheme intended to produce not only a

> That boy ... I never can or shall look at him without a shudder. QUEEN VICTORIA DID NOT HAVE THE HIGHEST OPINION OF HER ELDEST SON.

conscientious constitutional monarch, but also 'a perfect man'. Edward did not find the effort of attending to this exhausting syllabus at all congenial. Frivolity was more his line.

The young prince spent a period as an undergraduate at Cambridge University, where he failed to take a degree. He would have preferred to pursue a career in the army, but was only allowed to serve briefly, in 1861, with the Grenadier Guards. It was during this time that he became involved with an actress, and the whisper of scandal caused his father deep concern. Albert's health had never been good, and was exacerbated by hard work, but when he succumbed to typhoid on 14 December 1861 Victoria blamed her eldest son – and never forgave him. To her, he was no more than a worthless and irresponsible playboy, bringing the monarchy into disrepute. This reputation was reinforced when he was cited in a divorce case, and, on another occasion, implicated in a scandal relating to cheating at cards. It was not until 1892 that the queen allowed him to see the minutes of cabinet meetings.

Marriage and mistresses

No doubt Victoria thought that if he married Edward might settle down into domestic contentment and fatherly responsibility. A dynastic match was arranged with Alexandra, daughter of Prince Christian of Denmark (later King Christian IX). She was beautiful, elegant and quietly dignified, and gave Edward six children, five of whom survived into adulthood. The career of the oldest, Albert Victor (known as 'Eddy'), was, like that of his father, attended by scandal, but when he died in 1892, Alexandra was devastated, keeping the room where he expired as a shrine.

Despite his mother's pious hopes, one woman was never going to be enough for 'Edward the Caresser' (as he came to be known). While Alexandra confined herself to family duties in Marlborough House in London and Sandringham House in Norfolk, Edward gadded about like a tomcat. Among his many conquests were the actresses Lillie Langtry and Sarah Bernhardt, together with various aristocratic ladies, such as Jennie Jerome (American wife of Lord Randolph Churchill and mother of Winston) and the countess of Warwick. Discreet adultery was almost de rigueur among the British aristocracy at this period, and Alexandra was indulgent of her husband's peccadilloes. She

King Edward VII and his wife Queen Alexandra aboard the royal yacht at Cowes in 1909, a year before his death. Edward treated his marriage with indifference, and kept a string of mistresses throughout his life.

Timeline

1841
(9 November) Birth of Edward

1861
Serves briefly in the army

(14 December) Death of his father, Prince Albert

1863
(10 March) Marries Princess Alexandra of Denmark

1864
(8 January) Birth of Edward's eldest son, Albert Victor ('Eddy')

1865
(3 June) Birth of another son, the future George V

1892
(14 January) Death of Eddy

1901
(22 January) Edward succeeds

1902
(31 May) Treaty of Vereeniging ends Second Boer War

(11 July) A.J. Balfour becomes Conservative prime minister

(9 August) Edward crowned

1903
(May) Edward's visit to France paves way for Entente Cordiale

(3 October) Foundation of Women's Social and Political Union – the suffragettes

1904
(8 April) Conclusion of Entente Cordiale with France

1905
Abortive revolution in Russia

(4 December) Liberals under Sir Henry Campbell-Bannerman form government

1906
(12 January) Liberals win general election, and newly formed Labour Party wins 29 seats

(10 February) Launch of HMS *Dreadnought* initiates naval arms race with Germany

1907
Entente Cordiale expands to Triple Entente with Russia

Whatever happened to Albert?

Although christened Albert Edward and known to friends and family as 'Bertie', when he succeeded the new king announced that he would be known as Edward, the name of so many of his forebears. He tactfully explained that this was no slight to his father (with whom he had not been on good terms), but that no other Albert could match his father's unique qualities.

even permitted his last mistress, Alice Keppel, to attend Edward's deathbed. (By an intriguing coincidence, Alice Keppel's great-granddaughter, Camilla Parker Bowles, also became a royal mistress – to the present prince of Wales, many years before they married.)

THE EDWARDIAN ERA

Given that Edward's reign lasted such a short time, it is remarkable how large the 'Edwardian era' looms in the British view of the past. It is perhaps because it drew to a close a hundred-year period in which Britain had been involved in no major European war; and before the curtain came bloodily down the rich and titled abandoned themselves to one last wild round of house parties. This is the nostalgic view, but in reality British society was undergoing considerable upheavals. The suffragettes were agitating violently for the vote, the trade unions were flexing their industrial muscles, and in the 1906 general election the newly formed Labour Party made significant gains. 'We are all socialists now,' Edward is said to have remarked. The king, of course, was nothing of the sort, and when

Lillie Langtry, born Emilie Charlotte Le Breton, only daughter of the Dean of Jersey, and thus known as the Jersey Lily. She was the mistress of a number of well-connected and famous men, including Edward when he was prince of Wales.

in 1909 the radical Liberal government introduced a budget laying the foundations of the modern welfare state, he refused to create the hundreds of new Liberal peers that would aid its passage through the House of Lords.

The international scene was also changing, as Europe formed itself into armed camps, and Britain abandoned its long-held position of 'splendid isolation'.

Edward VII's Coronation Durbar passes through the centre of Delhi, 1 January 1903. Edward had become Emperor of India on ascending the British throne in 1901.

Edward is credited with paving the way for the 1904 Entente Cordiale – an alliance with France, England's ancient enemy – by his state visit to Paris the previous year, in which his easy manner and willingness to speak French endeared him to his hosts. This was a new role for a British monarch – as ambassador for his country – and one that was to play an increasingly important part in the duties of the royal family in the 20th century.

Edward had less success on the diplomatic front with his nephew, Kaiser Wilhelm II, who believed that Britain had now joined an imagined conspiracy by France and Russia (already France's ally) to encircle and annihilate the German empire. 'I believe the emperor of Germany hates me,' Edward despondently remarked.

Edward had backed the modernizing reforms of the army initiated by Haldane, the secretary for war, and had also backed the expansion of British naval power under Admiral Fisher, which did not make Anglo-German relations any easier. Even though Edward was the 'Uncle of Europe', with relatives amongst nearly every royal house, war was no longer as unthinkable as it once had been. Edward himself wrote to his prime minister, H.H. Asquith, expressing the view that a European war was 'possible', but, he hoped, 'improbable'.

Edward had always been fond of cigarettes and cigars (after his mother's death he deliberately lit up in places where she had forbidden smoking), and his addiction directly led to his death from bronchitis on 6 May 1910. He attended to official business until near the end, and was cheered by the news that his horse had just won at Kempton Park. Edward's funeral was as lavish and spectacular as his coronation, his state openings of Parliament, and such grand imperial occasions as the Delhi Durbar of 1903. Behind the gun carriage on which the old king's body lay there marched no fewer than nine crowned heads, a sight not seen before or since. It was the swansong of an older Europe that was soon to be lost for ever.

1908
(summer) Edward visits Tsar of Russia

(8 April) H.H. Asquith succeeds Campbell-Bannerman as Liberal prime minister

1909
Edward makes a state visit to Berlin

(December) Refuses to make new Liberal peers to enable the passage of David Lloyd George's radical 'People's Budget' through the House of Lords

1910
(5 February) Liberals win general election

(6 May) Death of Edward

GEORGE V
1910-1936

As Victoria had reacted against her 'wicked uncles', and Edward VII had reacted in turn against her strait-laced ways, so George V rejected his father's extravagant playboy lifestyle in favour of quiet domesticity and dull devotion to duty. George, sensitive about his German ancestry, put himself forward as a patriot-king: when H.G. Wells criticized his 'alien and uninspiring court', he declared, 'I may be uninspiring, but I'll be damned if I'm an alien.'

Biography

FULL NAME: George Frederick Ernest Albert

BORN 3 June 1865, at Marlborough House, London

FATHER Edward VII

MOTHER Alexandra of Denmark

MARRIED Mary of Teck

CHILDREN Edward (later Edward VIII, then duke of Windsor), Albert (duke of York, later George VI), Mary (married the earl of Harewood), Henry (duke of Gloucester), George (duke of Kent), John (died young)

SUCCEEDED 6 May 1910

CROWNED 22 June 1911

ROYAL HOUSE Saxe-Coburg-Gotha until 1917, when renamed Windsor

STYLE By the Grace of God, of Great Britain, Ireland, and of the British Dominions beyond the Seas, King, Defender of the Faith, Emperor of India (from 12 May 1927)

DIED 20 January 1936, at Sandringham House, Norfolk

BURIED St George's Chapel, Windsor

George was the very opposite of a *flâneur*, the part which his father had played so charmingly. His older brother, the scandalous Eddy (Albert Victor), had taken on this role, while George, not expecting to be king, pursued a career in the navy, where he acquired a lifetime's attachment to punctuality, good order and discipline. In retrospect, George felt that the navy had not provided the best training for kingship: like William IV before him – another naval man who had not expected to succeed to the throne – he found that the straight talking and direct manner required of the sailor ill fits a man for dealing with politicians. Nevertheless, George acquitted himself well in the various political and constitutional crises he had to deal with.

DUKE OF YORK AND PRINCE OF WALES

George served in the Royal Navy until his elder brother's death in 1892. He had sailed to many parts of the empire and the Far East, but whether these voyages broadened his rather limited mind is a moot point. He very much preferred England, and, in particular, his parents' home at Sandringham in Norfolk. Possibly the best bit about 'Abroad' was the stamps: George's main passion in life – apart from shooting large numbers of game birds – was his extensive stamp collection.

On return to dry land the young prince was created duke of York, and, as next in line to the throne after his father, he had now to think how he was going to fit himself to his future role as king. He was 26 years old, and, at least according to his cousin, Kaiser Wilhelm II of Germany, a 'merry and genial' fellow. He began – reluctantly, and with difficulty – to study German, the common language of so many of his relatives, scattered about the royal houses of Europe. He was also persuaded to abandon his attachment to his cousin Marie –

Timeline

1865
(3 June) Birth of George

1879
Joins the Royal Navy, after serving as a naval cadet for two years

1892
(14 January) Death of George's elder brother Eddy; George subsequently leaves the navy and is created duke of York

1893
(6 July) Marries Mary of Teck

1894
(23 June) Birth of the future Edward VIII

1895
(14 December) Birth of Albert, the future George VI

1897
(25 April) Birth of Mary

1900
(31 March) Birth of Henry

1902
(20 December) Birth of George

1905
(12 July) Birth of John

the future Marie of Romania – for a dynastic match with a more distant cousin, Princess Mary of Teck, who had been engaged to his late brother. Together the royal couple had six children, whom they brought up with some severity, unable, or unwilling, to show much in the way of affection. Prior to George's accession, they led a simple and secluded life, largely at York Cottage, a relatively modest house in the grounds at Sandringham.

On the death of his grandmother, Queen Victoria, George became prince of Wales. His father – whom Victoria had kept away from official political business until he was fifty – made sure George had a better preparation for kingship than he himself had had, and shared official papers with his son. He also dispatched him on tours of Europe and the empire. George was not altogether at ease in this ambassadorial role, and when a courtier delicately suggested he adopt a less gruff demeanour he was told, 'We sailors never smile when on duty.'

THE PEERS, THE PEOPLE'S BUDGET AND THE PARLIAMENT ACT

In his diary, George noted his father's death with a conventional but no doubt heartfelt formula: 'I have lost my best friend and the best of fathers.' Edward VII

> ❝ My father was frightened of his mother; I was frightened of my father, and I am damned well going to see to it that my children are frightened of me. ❞
>
> THIS REMARK, POSSIBLY APOCRYPHAL YET VERY MUCH TO THE POINT, WAS ATTRIBUTED TO GEORGE V BY RANDOLPH S. CHURCHILL IN HIS 1959 BIOGRAPHY OF LORD DERBY.

1909

(30 November) House of Lords rejects Liberal government's 'People's Budget'

1910

(15 February) Liberals under Asquith win general election; subsequently George promises to create new peers to allow passage of the budget

(6 May) George succeeds to the throne

(12 December) Liberals win general election

1911

(22 June) George's coronation

(10 August) Parliament Act restricts power of House of Lords

(December) Introduction of national insurance scheme

1912

(11 April) Asquith introduces Irish home rule bill; bitterly opposed by Ulster Protestants and Conservatives

1913

(January) House of Lords rejects home rule bill; Ulster Protestants begin to arm themselves

(4 June) The suffragette Emily Davison is killed when she throws herself in front of the king's horse at the Derby

(25 November) Pro-home rule Irish Volunteers formed in southern Ireland

had died during a period of acute political turmoil. The success of the newly formed Labour Party in the 1906 general election had pushed the Liberal government to the left, and in 1909 David Lloyd George, the chancellor of the exchequer, introduced the so-called 'People's Budget', which contained such pioneering welfare provisions as old-age pensions, while increasing taxes on the very rich. Edward VII had refused the request of the prime minister, H.H. Asquith, to create sufficient numbers of new Liberal peers to get the budget through the House of Lords – which predominantly consisted of wealthy Conservative landowners, none of whom were elected.

The Liberals went to the country on the issue, and in the election of 28 January 1910 won a reduced but still workable majority in the House of Commons. The old king died in May, and George, realizing the days when the monarch and the aristocracy could defy the elected representatives of the people were over, gave Asquith an undertaking that he would create the required number of peers. This turned out not to be necessary, but the Liberal government proposed to bring in legislation to restrict the powers of the Lords. George agreed to another election in December 1910 to see whether the voters would give the government a mandate on this important constitutional issue. They did, and in 1911 the Commons passed the Parliament Act, which prevented the Lords from rejecting any money bill coming from the lower house, and restricted its ability to veto other legislation.

THE GREAT WAR

George was faced with a subsequent political crisis over Irish home rule, which the Liberal government was determined to grant – it had been rejected by the Lords on two occasions in the previous century. Home rule was bitterly opposed by the Ulster Protestants, who, backed by many in the Conservative Party, promised to take up arms to oppose it, fearing that any

Ireland-wide devolved assembly would be dominated by Catholics. George attempted to conciliate the various sides, summoning them to a meeting in July 1914. But by that time Europe was hurtling towards total war, and the issue was shelved for the duration of the hostilities.

At a shooting party the year before, the prince of Wales recorded the day's sport:

> My left arm ached from lifting my gun, my shoulder from the recoil, and I was deaf and stunned from the banging … When in the late afternoon the carnage stopped almost 4000 pheasants had been killed. The bright limp carcasses were laid out in rows of 100; the whole place was littered with feathers and spent cartridges.

Although himself an enthusiastic shooter, even the king thought that they had 'perhaps gone too far'. It was a portent of things to come.

During the war the king and queen played the parts expected of them, visiting the troops, keeping up morale and never questioning the rightness of their country's cause. There was an upsurge in anti-German feeling, even in the canine realm: dachshunds (unless wearing patriotic colours) were attacked in the streets, and German shepherds quietly became Alsatians. The king did his bit to placate the jingoists, changing his family name from the very Germanic Saxe-Coburg-Gotha to the more acceptable Windsor.

When it was all over, a generation of young men had all but disappeared, leaving their elders in a state of shock and bemusement. George laid the blame for all the slaughter not on his belligerent subjects nor on his intransigent ministers nor on his

A meeting of Allied war commanders and statesmen at the time of the offensive on the Somme, summer 1916: from left to right, French commander Joseph Joffre, French president Raymond Poincaré, King George V of Britain, French commander Ferdinand Foch and British general Douglas Haig.

1914
(28 June) Assassination of the Austrian archduke Franz Ferdinand in Sarajevo sets in train the events that lead to the outbreak of the First World War

(July) House of Lords passes home rule bill, but excludes Ulster from its provisions

(4 August) Britain declares war on Germany

1915
(26 May) Asquith forms coalition government

1916
(24 April) Easter Rising in Dublin against British rule

(1 July) On the first day of the Battle of the Somme, 20,000 British soldiers are killed

(4 December) Fall of Asquith's government; new coalition government led by David Lloyd George

1917
(19 June) George changes family name from Saxe-Coburg-Gotha to Windsor

(6 November) Beginning of Bolshevik Revolution in Russia

1918
(11 November) Armistice brings First World War to an end

(14 December) General election results in Conservative-dominated coalition led by Lloyd George; vote extended to all women over 30 and all men over 21

1919

(18 January) Death of Prince John

(21 January) Sinn Féin members elected to Westminster Parliament in 1918 proclaim independent Irish republic; beginning of Anglo-Irish War

(28 June) Treaty of Versailles imposes punitive terms on Germany

1921

(July) Unemployment in Britain reaches 2.5 million

(6 December) Anglo-Irish Treaty ends Anglo-Irish War: southern Ireland becomes an independent dominion within the British Commonwealth, with the British monarch remaining as head of state; Northern Ireland stays as part of the UK

1922

(19 October) Collapse of Lloyd George's coalition; Conservatives under Andrew Bonar Law come to power

(31 October) Fascists under Mussolini take power in Italy

1923

(20 May) Bonar Law resigns due to ill health; succeeded as prime minister by Stanley Baldwin

1924

(22 January) Britain's first Labour government comes to power, under Ramsay MacDonald

(29 October) Conservatives return to power under Baldwin

obstinate, unimaginative generals, but on his cousin, Kaiser Wilhelm. 'I look upon him,' he noted in his diary just after the end of the war, 'as the greatest criminal known for having plunged the world into this ghastly war.'

Aftermath

It was a changed world. The three great European empires had been wiped from the map: the rump states of Germany and Austria were now republics, and the Russian empire had convulsed into the Union of Soviet Socialist Republics. That the British monarchy survived the Great War owes much to George's meticulous adherence to political neutrality, and his sympathy with the plight of the soldiers who returned from the war to find themselves thrown on the scrapheap. In 1921 he wrote privately to his ministers:

> It is impossible to expect people to subsist upon the unemployment benefit … The King appeals to the government to meet this grave … difficulty with the same liberality as they displayed in dealing with the enormous daily cost of the war.

In 1924 George did his constitutional duty and summoned Ramsay MacDonald to form Britain's first socialist administration, noting in his diary, 'Today, 23 years ago dear Grandmama died. I wonder what she would have thought of a Labour government.' The Labour government did not survive for long, and in 1926 the country experienced its first and last general strike, as the trade unions came out in support of the miners, who were facing wage cuts. George feared revolution, and was all too well aware of the fate of his cousins, the tsar and tsarina, shot in a cellar by the Bolsheviks and their bodies thrown down a well. (George himself had barred their coming to Britain after the revolution, not wishing to associate himself too closely with so unpopular a regime.)

Last years

George had ruined his health with smoking, and his later years were dogged by anxieties about his son and heir Edward, who was taking after his grandfather both as playboy prince and as seducer of married women. 'After I am dead, the boy will ruin himself in twelve months,' he grumbled, with uncanny prescience.

George's Silver Jubilee in 1935 saw the expression of much popular affection for the old king. But George barely survived his

George, prince of Wales (later George V) and his family at Abergeldie Castle, 1906. The one-year-old Prince John, George's epileptic youngest son, is in the arms of his mother, the princess of Wales (later Queen Mary).

jubilee year. When his physician, Lord Dawson of Penn, told him he would soon be recuperating in the Sussex seaside resort of Bognor Regis, he is said to have retorted, 'Bugger Bognor!' These were apparently his last words as he lay dying in his beloved Sandringham. It is thought that the king's end may have been hastened by a lethal injection of opiates, so that news of his death could be released in time to make the next morning's edition of *The Times*, the voice of the establishment. It would have been unseemly for such sombre news to be released through the more downmarket evening papers.

After his death, the future poet laureate, John Betjeman, wrote an affectionate and only slightly ironic tribute:

> *Spirits of well-shot woodcock, partridge, snipe*
> *Flutter and bear him up the Norfolk sky.*

It was a fitting apotheosis for the dull, quiet, conscientious man who enjoyed nothing better than a day's shooting in the English countryside.

1926
(3–12 May) General Strike

1928
(2 July) Franchise extended to all women over 21; Britain achieves universal adult suffrage

1929
(30 May) Labour forms minority government under Ramsay MacDonald

(4 October) Wall Street Crash

1931
(24 August) Labour government resigns; George invites Ramsay MacDonald to form coalition National Government

(18 September) Japanese invade Chinese Manchuria

(December) Canada, South Africa, the Irish Free State, Australia and New Zealand achieve self-government, but with the British monarch remaining as head of state

1933
(30 January) Hitler becomes Chancellor of Germany

1935
George celebrates his Silver Jubilee

(3 October) Italy invades Abyssinia (Ethiopia)

(14 November) Baldwin's Conservatives win general election

1936
(20 January) Death of George

Edward VIII
1936

Edward was the only British monarch ever to surrender the crown voluntarily. To some he was a romantic figure who gave up everything for love, while to others he was a selfish playboy who neglected his duties to his country and flirted with Nazism. Certainly his own family never forgave him.

Biography

Edward – known by family and friends as David, his last Christian name – suffered from a severe upbringing at the hands of his priggish parents, and from a rather inadequate education. He was a naval cadet from 1907 to 1911, and during the First World War he was allowed to serve in the army, although not on active service. On visits to the Western Front, he showed that he had something of the common touch of his grandfather, Edward VII, and was a popular figure with the troops.

FULL NAME Edward Albert Christian George Andrew Patrick David

BORN 23 June 1894, at the White Lodge, Richmond Park

FATHER George V

MOTHER Mary of Teck

MARRIED Wallis Simpson

CHILDREN none

SUCCEEDED 20 January 1936

CROWNED never crowned

ROYAL HOUSE Windsor

STYLE By the Grace of God, of Great Britain, Ireland, and of the British Dominions beyond the Seas, King, Defender of the Faith, Emperor of India

DIED 28 May 1972, in Paris

BURIED Frogmore, near Windsor

THE PLAYBOY PRINCE

After the war, Edward was sent on tours of the British empire, the USA and South America. He also visited many parts of Great Britain as the Depression bit deeper, and showed himself as something of a populist. He had already annoyed the Conservatives when he made a contribution to the miners' welfare fund in the wake of the 1926 General Strike; ten years later – after he had become king – he again irritated the Conservative government, when, on a visit to an area of South Wales badly hit by unemployment he declared that 'Something should be done.'

Away from his official duties, Edward preferred the company of a close circle of friends drawn from fashionable Anglo-American high society rather the usual landed aristocracy. In 1928 his father gave him his own residence, Fort Belvedere, near Sunningdale in Berkshire, and here he entertained a succession of mistresses, mostly wealthy married women. It was one of these women, Lady Furness,

> Hark the herald angels sing
> Mrs Simpson pinched our king.

VERSION OF THE CHRISTMAS CAROL POPULAR WITH SCHOOLCHILDREN FOLLOWING EDWARD'S ABDICATION.

The duke and duchess of Windsor standing by a swimming pool at their home in Lisbon, Portugal, summer 1940.

Timeline

1894
(23 June) Birth of Edward

1907–1911
Trains as naval cadet

1914
(6 August) Joins Grenadier Guards, serving through the First World War

1919
Tours Canada and the USA

1920
Tours Australia and New Zealand

1921–1922
Tours India and the Far East

1925
Tours South America

1930
Begins affair with Mrs Simpson

1931
Tours South America again

1932
Tours areas of high unemployment in Britain

who in 1930 introduced him to Mrs Wallis Simpson, an American socialite of no great beauty but some wit. She had divorced her first husband in 1927, and married a second in 1928. Edward was smitten, and the two soon became lovers. His somewhat cloying letters to her suggest a boyish emotional dependence, and a surprising immaturity for a man approaching his forties.

THE ABDICATION CRISIS

On 20 January 1936 Edward's father died, and he became king. The British public was totally unaware of Edward's affair with Mrs Simpson, as the British press – then much more submissive than now – bowed under government pressure to keep the matter quiet. This was not the case in either America or Europe, where the newspapers had a field day. In October Mrs Simpson obtained a preliminary decree of divorce from her second husband, Ernest Simpson.

The king confided to the Conservative prime minister, Stanley Baldwin, his intention of marrying his mistress. Baldwin

1936

(20 January) Succeeds

(17 July) Beginning of Spanish Civil War

(27 October) Mrs Simpson obtains a divorce

(11 December) Abdicates

(12 December) Created duke of Windsor

1937

(3 June) Marries Mrs Simpson in France

(October) Visits Nazi Germany

1940

(June) On fall of France, moves to Spain, then Portugal, where he consorts with Nazi sympathizers

(August) Taken by the Royal Navy to the Bahamas, where serves as governor until the end of the Second World War

1945

Returns to live in France

1951

Publishes his memoirs, *A King's Story*

1952

Attends funeral of his brother, George VI

1953

Attends funeral of his mother, Queen Mary

1972

(28 May) Death of Edward

1986

(24 April) Death of the duchess of Windsor

was appalled: she was a commoner, she was American, she was a double-divorcée. The Church of England, of which Edward was titular head, was similarly aghast. The leader of the Labour opposition and the prime ministers of the Commonwealth dominions were also consulted, and agreed with Baldwin that Edward's proposal of a morganatic marriage – one in which his wife would not receive the title of queen – was unacceptable.

The whole affair became public knowledge on 3 December, when it was discussed both in the newspapers and in Parliament. On 10 December the king decided to abdicate, and the following day he announced his decision in a radio broadcast:

> At long last I am able to say a few words of my own … you must believe me when I tell you that I have found it impossible to carry the heavy burden of responsibility and to discharge my duties as king as I would wish to do without the help and support of the woman I love.

He left for the Continent that night, and on 3 June 1937 he and Mrs Simpson were married at the Château de Candé, France.

His family never forgave him. Immediately after the abdication his mother, Queen Mary, exclaimed, 'All *this* thrown away for *that*.' Two years later she wrote to him:

> I do not think you have ever realized the shock which the attitude you took up caused your family and the whole nation. It seemed inconceivable to those who made such sacrifices during the war that you, as their king, refused a lesser sacrifice.

DUKE OF WINDSOR

After the abdication the new king, George VI, made his elder brother duke of Windsor; although his wife became the duchess, she was denied the title 'royal highness'. They lived largely in France, from where, in October 1937, they visited Germany, meeting Hitler and other Nazis. During the Second World War the government, suspecting that the Nazis might use Edward as a puppet king should they proceed with an invasion of Britain, dispatched the duke to the Bahamas out of harm's way.

After the war the duke and duchess returned to France, where, at Neuilly near Paris, they led the life of the idle rich, and became friends with their neighbours Oswald Mosley, the former leader of the British fascists, and his wife Diana. The duke and duchess rarely visited Britain, although they were present at the funerals of George VI and Queen Mary. They were buried in the royal mausoleum at Frogmore, near Windsor.

GEORGE VI
1936-1952

A shy and retiring man, who struggled through much of his life with a stutter, George VI might have been Britain's least known monarch of the 20th century had not his reign coincided with the Second World War. Although somewhat eclipsed by his charismatic wartime prime minister, Winston Churchill, King George, with his wife Queen Elizabeth, played an important role as symbols of national unity in Britain's struggle against Nazi Germany.

George was born on the anniversary of the death of his great-grandfather Prince Albert, and, largely to mollify his great-grandmother, Queen Victoria, was christened Albert Frederick Arthur George – 'Bertie' for short. A rather sickly boy, he was starved of affection by his over-strict parents, and was put in the shade by his more outgoing, glamorous elder brother David, the future Edward VIII.

PRINCE ALBERT, DUKE OF YORK

As an adolescent George trained as a naval cadet at Dartmouth Naval College, showing himself as a conscientious if not a sparkling pupil. He began to serve in the navy proper in 1913, and was present in 1916 at the Battle of Jutland, the largest naval engagement of the First World War. His chronic gastric troubles resulted in a duodenal ulcer in 1917, and for a time he was seriously ill.

After the war George spent a year as an undergraduate at Cambridge University, and in 1920 was made duke of York, the traditional title given to the sovereign's second son. As he was not expected to succeed to the throne, he was not required to marry into royalty (and with the collapse of the German, Austrian and Russian empires, there were far fewer ruling royals to choose from). His fancy lighted upon Lady Elizabeth Bowes-Lyon, the vivacious daughter of the earl of Strathmore, a Scottish aristocrat. She initially rejected his proposals of marriage, but the two eventually wed in Westminster Abbey in April 1923. The BBC had wanted to broadcast the ceremony, but the Archbishop of Canterbury turned down the request on the grounds that 'men in public houses may listen to the ceremony with their hats on'.

Biography

FULL NAME Albert Frederick Arthur George

BORN 14 December 1895, at Sandringham, Norfolk

FATHER George V

MOTHER Mary of Teck

MARRIED Lady Elizabeth Bowes-Lyon

CHILDREN Elizabeth (the future Elizabeth II), and Margaret (later countess of Snowdon)

SUCCEEDED 11 December 1936

CROWNED 12 May 1937

ROYAL HOUSE Windsor

STYLE By the Grace of God, of Great Britain, Ireland, and of the British Dominions beyond the Seas, King, Defender of the Faith, Emperor of India. (This last title was dropped on Indian independence in 1947, and the title 'King of Ireland' in 1949, when Ireland became a republic and left the Commonwealth.)

DIED 6 February 1952, at Sandringham

BURIED St George's Chapel, Windsor

Timeline

1895
(14 December) Birth of George

1909–1913
Trains as naval cadet

1913–1917
Serves in Royal Navy

1917–1919
Serves in Royal Naval Air Service and then RAF

1919–1920
Studies at Cambridge University

1923
(26 April) Marries Lady Elizabeth Bowes·Lyon

1926
(21 April) Birth of the future Elizabeth II

1930
(21 August) Birth of Princess Margaret

1936
(11 December) George succeeds on his brother's abdication

1937
(12 May) Crowned

(28 May) Neville Chamberlain becomes prime minister

(7 July) Japanese launch war against China

1938
(13 March) Germany annexes Austria

(29 September) At Munich, Britain and France allow Hitler to occupy the Czech Sudetenland

(George himself was not quite so hide-bound, having in 1921 established the annual Duke of York's Camp, at which boys from public – i.e. fee-paying – schools mixed with boys from less privileged backgrounds.)

It was a successful marriage. Elizabeth's own upbringing, in marked contrast to her husband's, had been characterized, in her own words, by fun and kindness. She brought him the love and security he craved, and also two daughters, Elizabeth and Margaret, and together they formed a close and happy family, living quietly at 145 Piccadilly in London.

A young Prince Charles talks to his grandfather, King George VI.

THE RELUCTANT MONARCH

George never expected to be king, and, although he had undertaken public duties, such as tours of the empire, his shyness meant that he shunned the limelight, and his stammer made public speaking an ordeal (although he did eventually receive help from a speech therapist). Following the abdication of his brother Edward VIII on 11 December 1936, he confessed in his diary that he 'broke down and sobbed like a child'. But his sense of duty gave him no choice, and he duly took up the burden of kingship. Like his grandfather Edward VII, he eschewed the name Albert on ascending the throne, and became George VI.

Until the outbreak of the Second World War, George supported his prime minister, Neville Chamberlain, in his policy of appeasement towards Nazi Germany and Fascist Italy. After Chamberlain's resignation in May 1940 George would have preferred as his successor Lord Halifax, the appeasing foreign secretary, but he accepted Winston Churchill, with whom, after initial mistrust, he worked well through the war. He was as determined as Churchill to fight on alone after the fall of France, confiding to his mother on 27 June 1940, 'Personally I feel happier now that we have no allies to be polite to and to pamper.'

George and the queen insisted on staying in London throughout the years of air raids. There was talk of sending the two girls to safety in Canada, but instead they were evacuated to Windsor. The queen explained their decision: 'The princesses would never leave without me and I couldn't leave without the king, and the king will never leave.' It was the East End of the city that took the brunt of the Blitz, but when Buckingham Palace took a hit in September 1940 the queen told a policeman, 'I'm glad we've been bombed. It makes me feel I can look the East End in the face.'

TWILIGHT OF EMPIRE

The 'white' dominions had already achieved virtual independence by the 1931 Statute of Westminster, and after the Second World War the conversion of the British empire into the Commonwealth of Nations accelerated. In 1947 George reluctantly gave up his title 'emperor of India' when the subcontinent achieved independence. Two years later, George lost another title, 'king of Ireland', when Eire left the Commonwealth and became a republic. In the same year the remaining Commonwealth nations recognized George as head of the Commonwealth.

By this time, George, a heavy smoker, was suffering from rapidly deteriorating health, not helped by the strains of the war years. In March 1949 he underwent an operation to remove a blood clot from his leg, and in September 1951 surgeons removed his left lung, in an attempt to halt the spread of cancer. They were unsuccessful, and George died five months later, aged only 56. It was said that his wife never forgave her brother-in-law Edward for passing on the burden of kingship to a man whose health and confidence had never been strong. To the poet Edith Sitwell she wrote, 'How small and selfish is sorrow. But it bangs one about until one is senseless.' She was to outlive her beloved Bertie for half a century.

1939
(15 March) Germany occupies the rest of Czechoslovakia

(3 September) Britain declares war on Germany

1940
(7 May) Winston Churchill becomes head of a coalition government

(13 September) Buckingham Palace hit by a German bomb

1945
(7 May) Germany surrenders unconditionally

(26 July) Labour under Clement Attlee wins landslide election victory; proceeds to establish welfare state and to nationalize key industries

(10 August) Japanese seek peace terms

1947
(15 August) India and Pakistan become independent republics within the Commonwealth

1949
(18 April) Ireland leaves the Commonwealth

(27 April) George becomes head of the Commonwealth of Nations

1951
(23 September) Surgeons remove George's left lung

(26 October) Conservatives under Churchill win general election

1952
(6 February) Death of George

ELIZABETH II
1952-PRESENT

Elizabeth II celebrated her Golden Jubilee in 2002. By then she was already one of the longest-reigning monarchs in British history, and had seen as many prime ministers come and go as Queen Victoria. Her half century and more as queen has seen momentous changes both at home and abroad: in the UK, the end of social deference, the erosion of the established Church, the virtual abolition of the political power of the hereditary peers, and the establishment of Britain as a more tolerant, multicultural society; globally, the final withdrawal from empire, the end of the Cold War, and the integration of Britain into the European Union.

Biography

FULL NAME Elizabeth Alexandra Mary

BORN 21 April 1926, at 17 Bruton Street, London W1

FATHER George VI

MOTHER Elizabeth, née Bowes-Lyon

MARRIED Philip Mountbatten

CHILDREN Charles (prince of Wales), Anne (princess royal), Andrew (duke of York), Edward (earl of Wessex)

SUCCEEDED 6 February 1952

CROWNED 2 June 1953

ROYAL HOUSE Windsor

STYLE By the Grace of God, of the United Kingdom of Great Britain and Northern Ireland and of Her Other Realms and Territories Queen, Head of the Commonwealth, Defender of the Faith

Through all this, Elizabeth has discreetly and properly played her constitutional role – at least as far as we are aware, for certain state papers will remain undisclosed for several more decades. It is a role Elizabeth was not born to, but from the age of 10, when her uncle Edward VIII abdicated, she knew that she would succeed her father to the throne. She appears to have contemplated this prospect with the same gravity and dedication to duty as George V, her 'Grandpa England'.

FROM LILIBET TO ROYAL BRIDE

As a small child Elizabeth was called 'Lilibet' by her tight-knit family. She and her younger sister Margaret were educated at home by a succession of governesses, notably 'Crawfie' – Marion Crawford – who remained in royal service until Elizabeth's marriage. In 1950 Crawfie published her account of her experiences in a book called *The Little Princesses*, having been assured by the American publisher that they would obtain clearance from the Palace. Elizabeth's mother was furious at what she regarded as a breach of confidence, even though the book did much to popularize the royal family. Crawfie was

Queen Elizabeth II and Prince Philip with their children, Charles and Anne, at Balmoral, 28 September 1952.

completely shunned, and never allowed to see her former charges again. The equivocal attitude of the royal family to publicity has continued ever since: they want and need coverage in the press – but only on their own terms.

As an older girl, Elizabeth received more specialist instruction, especially in modern languages and history, but her education was disrupted by the outbreak of the Second World War. Like hundreds of thousands of other city children, Elizabeth, then 13, and her younger sister were evacuated to the countryside, where they would be safe from enemy bombing. They spent the war years at Windsor, or at Balmoral Castle in Scotland, while their parents remained in London.

In the last year of the war Elizabeth persuaded her father to allow her to serve in the ATS, the Women's Auxiliary Territorial Service, where, as a subaltern, she trained as a driver, and also learnt vehicle maintenance. After the war Elizabeth became attached to her dashing although not always diplomatic cousin, Lieutenant Philip Mountbatten RN, formerly Prince Philip of Greece and Denmark, who had seen active service on a number of ships during the war. They were married in November 1947, and Philip was made duke of Edinburgh. Their first child, Charles, was born the following year.

A NEW ELIZABETHAN AGE?

Through 1951 the health of Elizabeth's father grew worse, and the rather serious young princess undertook a number of ceremonial duties on his behalf. It was the year of the Festival of Britain, an optimistic exhibition of national pride, modern design and technological progress, and to many it celebrated the end of the austerity of the post-war years. Journalists began to talk of a 'New Elizabethan Age', although this was more wishful thinking than measured historical judgement, for economic recovery was slow, and accompanied by a gradual diminishment of Britain's role in the world.

Elizabeth was staying at the Treetops Hotel – a safari hotel literally built in the tops of trees – in a game park in Kenya on the night her father died. When she heard the news on 6 February 1952 she immediately flew home. Her coronation took place on 2 June 1953; it was the first such event to be televised, and was seen by millions of people around the world. On the

Timeline

1926
(21 April) Birth of Elizabeth

1939
Evacuated from London on outbreak of war

1945
Serves in the ATS

1947
Tours South Africa with her parents

(20 November) Marries Prince Philip

1948
(14 November) Birth of Prince Charles

1950
(19 February) Birth of Princess Anne

1952
(6 February) Elizabeth succeeds

1953
(2 June) Crowned

1953–1954
Makes six-month tour of the Commonwealth

1955
(5 April) Winston Churchill, Conservative prime minister, resigns and is succeeded by Anthony Eden

1956
(June–December) Suez Crisis

1957

(9 January) Eden resigns and is replaced by Harold Macmillan as prime minister

(6 February) Ghana (formerly Gold Coast) becomes the first of Britain's African colonies to gain independence

1960

(19 February) Birth of Prince Andrew

(6 May) Princess Margaret, the queen's sister, marries Anthony Armstrong-Jones

1963

(18 October) Macmillan resigns and is succeeded by Alec Douglas-Home

1964

(10 March) Birth of Prince Edward

(16 October) Labour Party wins general election; Harold Wilson becomes prime minister

1969

(25 April) British troops deployed in Northern Ireland

(1 July) Investiture of Prince Charles as prince of Wales at Caernarfon Castle

1970

(19 June) Conservatives under Edward Heath win general election

same day news came from the Himalaya that a British-led expedition had put two men – New Zealander Edmund Hillary and Sherpa Tenzing Norgay – on the summit of Mount Everest.

The family firm

It was Elizabeth's father, George VI, who first coined the phrase 'the family firm' for the royal family, and its job. Elizabeth has always taken her duties very seriously (somewhat priggishly and humourlessly in the view of some, although those who have met her invariably deploy the adjective 'gracious' in respect of her manner). She and her husband Philip sought to inculcate these notions of duty and hard work into their four children.

For the three boys, their training began with attendance at Gordonstoun School, a public (fee-paying) school in the Scottish Highlands with an ethos involving strict discipline and energetic outdoor pursuits. Philip had himself been at the school, but his eldest son apparently did not enjoy the experience. None of the children were particularly academic, but Charles and Edward managed to scrape through Cambridge University, the former at Trinity College and the latter at Jesus College ('We have a friend in Jesus,' his father was heard to quip). All three served in the armed forces: Charles and Andrew were in the Royal Navy for some years, but Edward abandoned his training in the Royal Marines to pursue theatrical interests.

The job of 'the family firm' is largely ambassadorial – attending functions, unveiling plaques, acting as patrons of charities, making tours abroad. Prince Edward formed his own TV production company, but was criticized for using his royal position for business ends, and in 2002 abandoned his commercial interests to concentrate on public duties.

The Palace and the press

The reserve – or subservience – displayed by the newspapers at the time of the 1936 abdication crisis is long gone. The private lives of the royals now comprise one of the main feeding grounds of the tabloid press, and the royal family has found that its cautious move into the media limelight with the carefully controlled 1966 documentary *Royal Family* has reaped the whirlwind.

Monarchs from the time of Elizabeth I have realized the importance of maintaining a high profile in the public eye (a lesson forgotten at their peril, as

Victoria found when she withdrew into seclusion after Albert's death), but in desiring to put themselves in the media spotlight the royal family have found it difficult to control what the media choose to publish. Photographs of Prince Andrew's estranged wife having her toes sucked by her financial adviser, or a taped telephone conversation in which Prince Charles expresses his desire to be reincarnated as his mistress's tampon, are not the kind of things the Palace press office would like to see in print.

FOUR DIVORCES AND A FUNERAL

Nothing has given the press more column inches than the tangled love lives of the younger royals. It started in the 1950s, when the queen's sister, Princess Margaret, expressed her intention of marrying Group Captain Peter Townsend. But as he was a divorcé, it was made clear to her that he was not a suitable match, and she was obliged to give him up. Her subsequent marriage to the fashionable photographer Anthony Armstrong-Jones (later earl of Snowdon) ended in divorce, as did the first marriages of three of the queen's children.

In 1973 Anne – known in her youth as 'Princess Sourpuss' because of her grumpy manner – married an army officer, Captain Mark Phillips, a fellow member of Britain's Olympic equestrian team. She divorced him in 1992, and later that year married a naval officer, Timothy Laurence. Her younger brother Andrew wed the ebullient Sarah Ferguson ('Fergie') in 1986, the couple becoming the duke and duchess of York (cruelly, the Rubenesque Sarah, who is now an ambassador for Weight Watchers, was dubbed 'the duchess of Pork' by the press). They

1973
(1 January) Britain joins European Community (later the European Union)

(14 November) Anne marries Mark Phillips

1974
(28 February) Labour returns to power under Harold Wilson

1976
(16 March) Wilson resigns; succeeded by James Callaghan

1977
Elizabeth celebrates her Silver Jubilee

1979
(3 May) Conservatives under Margaret Thatcher win general election

1981
(29 July) Charles marries Lady Diana Spencer

1982
(April–June) Falklands War

1983
(9 June) Conservatives under Margaret Thatcher win general election

1984–1985
Miners' strike against pit closures

1986
(23 July) Andrew marries Sarah Ferguson

1987
(11 June) Conservatives under Margaret Thatcher win general election

1989
(10 November) Fall of Berlin Wall symbolizes end of Cold War

1990
(28 November) John Major becomes new prime minister

1992
(9 April) Conservatives under John Major win general election

(28 April) Anne and Mark divorce

(12 December) Anne marries Timothy Laurence

1996
(30 May) Andrew and Sarah divorce

(28 August) Charles and Diana divorce

1997
(1 May) Tony Blair's 'New Labour' party wins general election

(31 August) Death of Diana

divorced in 1996, although reportedly keep on good terms. Prince Edward, who some believed would remain a bachelor, married Sophie Rhys-Jones, a public relations consultant, in 1999, and the two became the earl and countess of Wessex, reviving a title last used by Harold Godwineson, the king whose death at Hastings marked the end of Anglo-Saxon England.

It has been above all the love life of the heir to the throne that has made the headlines. As a young man Charles lost his heart to Camilla Shand, an outgoing, horsy type, whom he first met at a polo match in 1970. She is the great-granddaughter of Alice Keppel, Edward VII's last *amour*, and apparently introduced herself with the words, 'My great-grandmother was the mistress of your great-grandfather. How about it?' The two became lovers, but Charles's great-uncle, Lord Mountbatten, insisted that for a future king the principle 'bedded can't be wedded' must be observed. Camilla married Andrew Parker Bowles, an army officer, in 1973, and helped Charles cast around for a suitable mate. What was required for the wife of the prince of Wales was an aristocratic woman young enough to be without a 'history'. Eventually a suitable girl was identified, and in 1981 Charles, then aged 32, married Lady Diana Spencer, a shy 20-year-old with little experience of the world. For her and a gullible public it was a fairytale wedding, but, as Diana later ruefully commented, 'There were three of us in the marriage – it was rather crowded.' She was referring to Charles's affair with Camilla, which continued throughout the marriage. Charles apparently had no intention of ditching his mistress, although he did his dynastic duty in Diana's bed by fathering two boys, William and Harry, the requisite 'heir and a spare'. Starved of his affection, and apparently unsupported by his family, Diana herself took lovers, and the couple divorced in 1996.

Through all these ups and downs, Diana remained a very popular figure in Britain. She saw herself as the 'queen of people's hearts', and her 'touchy-feeliness' was in marked contrast to the traditional reserve of the Windsors. When she was killed in a car accident in Paris in 1997 there was a most extraordinary outbreak of hysteria across the country. Millions of people who had never met her were

Elizabeth II in the state coach during the Golden Jubilee procession from Buckingham Palace to St Paul's Cathedral, June 2002. The coach, built for George III in 1762, was also used for the queen's coronation and Silver Jubilee.

THE KINGS AND QUEENS OF ENGLAND

plunged into inexplicable outpourings of grief. There was popular anger that the royal family was neither visibly distressed nor showing sufficient deference to the dead princess, whom many felt they had used so badly. On the eve of Diana's state funeral the queen was persuaded to broadcast a tribute to her former daughter-in-law: 'I for one,' said the queen, 'believe there are lessons to be drawn from her life and from the extraordinary and moving reaction to her death.'

THE FUTURE OF THE MONARCHY

The monarchy reached a low point in public popularity at the time of Diana's death, but has since recovered. Charles was for a time painted as the villain of the piece, and there were even suggestions that the succession should skip a generation, and be settled on his oldest son, Prince William. After a decent interval, on 9 April 2005 Charles married Camilla, one tabloid wearily headlining the announcement of their engagement, 'Boring Old Gits To Wed'.

The queen herself is rarely if ever criticized, or her role questioned, and discussions of a republican alternative to the monarchy are rarely heard in the media. This may change after her death – she has given no indication that she wishes to abdicate.

Those of republican bent point out that the royal family is above all a symbol of inherited privilege, and that its members identify themselves firmly with the moneyed upper class, in terms of their activities, social life and preference for private education. What is needed, argue the republicans, is a written constitution and an elected president. This would also save the taxpayer a large amount of money. Those who prefer the status quo point out that the role of head of state in the UK is purely ceremonial, so why not maintain a thousand or more years of tradition and keep the job in the royal family? The whole veil of mystery surrounding them (albeit increasingly frayed) makes them, according to their advocates, effective ambassadors abroad for UK exports, and attracts large numbers of tourists to Britain.

For the moment the British seem to be content to bumble along with the way things are, but whether the long-running pageant of folly, vanity, greed and brutality (or wisdom, elegance, selfless service and splendour, depending on your point of view) will survive long into its third millennium is impossible to say.

1998
(10 April) Good Friday Agreement brings peace to Northern Ireland

1999
(6 May) Elections held for new Scottish Parliament and Welsh Assembly

(10 June) Edward marries Sophie Rhys-Jones

(11 November) Number of hereditary peers in House of Lords reduced to 92, so ending the House's traditional Conservative majority

2001
(7 June) Labour Party returned to power under Blair

2002
Elizabeth celebrates Golden Jubilee

(9 February) Death of Princess Margaret

(30 March) Death of Queen Elizabeth, the queen mother

2003
(20 March) British forces join Americans in invasion of Iraq

2005
(9 April) Charles marries Camilla Parker Bowles

(5 May) Labour under Blair wins general election

2006
Extended celebrations of Elizabeth's 80th birthday

Dynastic Family Trees

The Anglo-Saxon Kings

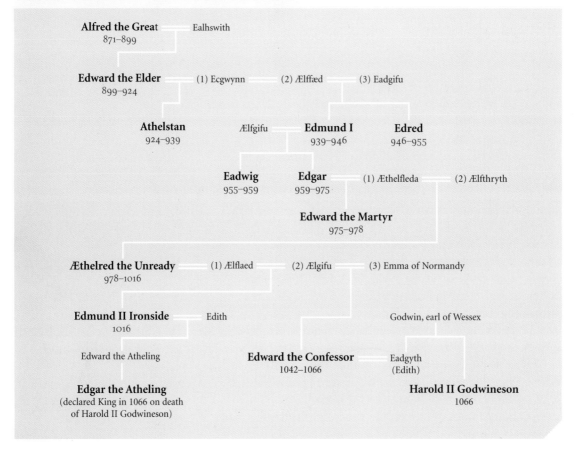

Alfred the Great — Ealhswith
871–899

Edward the Elder — (1) Ecgwynn — (2) Ælffæd — (3) Eadgifu
899–924

Athelstan — Ælfgifu — **Edmund I** — **Edred**
924–939 — 939–946 — 946–955

Eadwig — **Edgar** — (1) Æthelfleda — (2) Ælfthryth
955–959 — 959–975

Edward the Martyr
975–978

Æthelred the Unready — (1) Ælflaed — (2) Ælgifu — (3) Emma of Normandy
978–1016

Edmund II Ironside — Edith — Godwin, earl of Wessex
1016

Edward the Atheling — **Edward the Confessor** — Eadgyth (Edith)
1042–1066

Edgar the Atheling — **Harold II Godwineson**
(declared King in 1066 on death of Harold II Godwineson) — 1066

THE NORSE KINGS

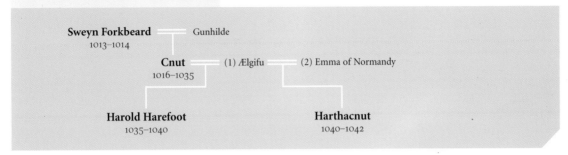

Sweyn Forkbeard ═══ Gunhilde
1013–1014

           Cnut ═══ (1) Ælgifu   ═══   (2) Emma of Normandy
         1016–1035

Harold Harefoot   **Harthacnut**
1035–1040   1040–1042

THE NORMANS AND EARLY PLANTAGENETS

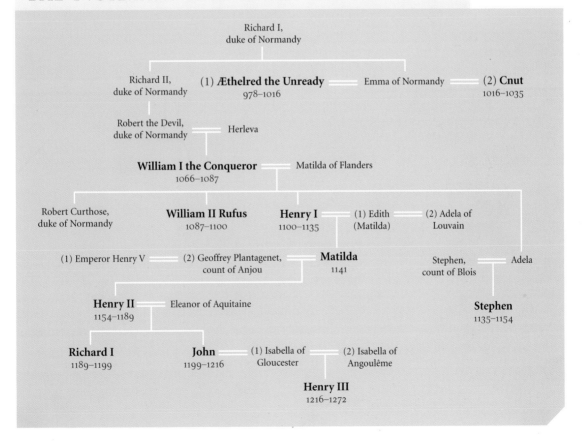

Richard I,
duke of Normandy

Richard II,   (1) **Æthelred the Unready**   Emma of Normandy ═══ (2) **Cnut**
duke of Normandy   978–1016   1016–1035

Robert the Devil,   ═══   Herleva
duke of Normandy

William I the Conqueror ═══ Matilda of Flanders
1066–1087

Robert Curthose,   **William II Rufus**   **Henry I** ═══ (1) Edith   ═══   (2) Adela of
duke of Normandy   1087–1100   1100–1135   (Matilda)   Louvain

(1) Emperor Henry V ═══ (2) Geoffrey Plantagenet, ═══ **Matilda**   Stephen,   ═══   Adela
                  count of Anjou   1141   count of Blois

Henry II ═══ Eleanor of Aquitaine   **Stephen**
1154–1189   1135–1154

Richard I   **John** ═══ (1) Isabella of   ═══   (2) Isabella of
1189–1199   1199–1216   Gloucester   Angoulême

Henry III
1216–1272

THE LATER PLANTAGENETS

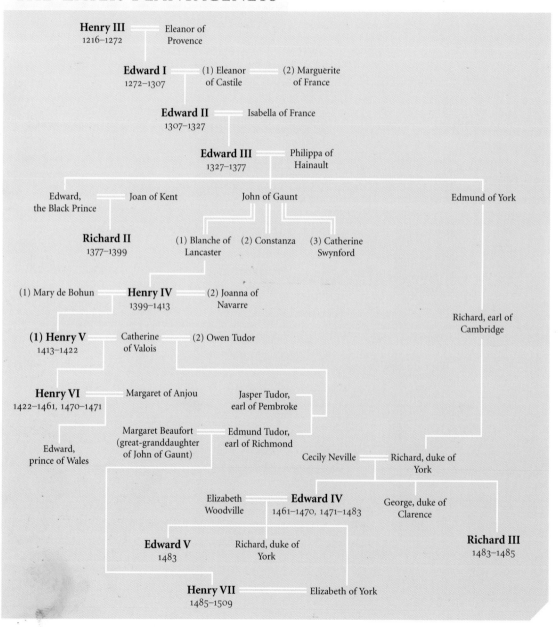

Henry III 1216–1272 — Eleanor of Provence

Edward I 1272–1307 — (1) Eleanor of Castile — (2) Marguerite of France

Edward II 1307–1327 — Isabella of France

Edward III 1327–1377 — Philippa of Hainault

Edward, the Black Prince — Joan of Kent   John of Gaunt   Edmund of York

Richard II 1377–1399   (1) Blanche of Lancaster   (2) Constanza   (3) Catherine Swynford

(1) Mary de Bohun — Henry IV 1399–1413 — (2) Joanna of Navarre

Richard, earl of Cambridge

(1) Henry V 1413–1422 — Catherine of Valois — (2) Owen Tudor

Henry VI 1422–1461, 1470–1471 — Margaret of Anjou   Jasper Tudor, earl of Pembroke

Margaret Beaufort (great-granddaughter of John of Gaunt) — Edmund Tudor, earl of Richmond

Cecily Neville — Richard, duke of York

Edward, prince of Wales

Elizabeth Woodville — Edward IV 1461–1470, 1471–1483   George, duke of Clarence

Edward V 1483   Richard, duke of York

Richard III 1483–1485

Henry VII 1485–1509 — Elizabeth of York

THE TUDORS AND STUARTS

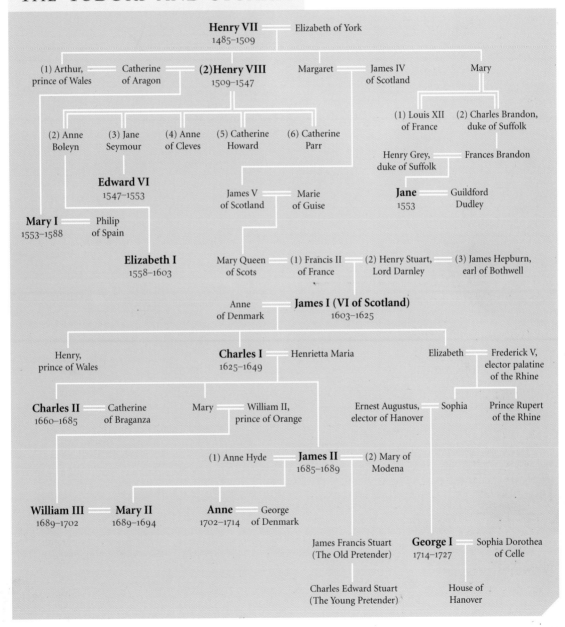

Henry VII ══ Elizabeth of York
1485–1509

(1) Arthur, ══ Catherine ══ **(2)Henry VIII**   Margaret ══ James IV   Mary
prince of Wales   of Aragon   1509–1547   of Scotland

(1) Louis XII ══ (2) Charles Brandon,
of France   duke of Suffolk

(2) Anne   (3) Jane   (4) Anne   (5) Catherine   (6) Catherine
Boleyn   Seymour   of Cleves   Howard   Parr

Henry Grey, ══ Frances Brandon
duke of Suffolk

Edward VI
1547–1553

James V ══ Marie   **Jane** ══ Guildford
of Scotland   of Guise   1553   Dudley

Mary I ══ Philip
1553–1588   of Spain

Elizabeth I
1558–1603

Mary Queen ══ (1) Francis II ══ (2) Henry Stuart, ══ (3) James Hepburn,
of Scots   of France   Lord Darnley   earl of Bothwell

Anne ══ **James I (VI of Scotland)**
of Denmark   1603–1625

Henry,   **Charles I** ══ Henrietta Maria   Elizabeth ══ Frederick V,
prince of Wales   1625–1649   elector palatine
                                                   of the Rhine

Charles II ══ Catherine   Mary ══ William II,   Ernest Augustus, ══ Sophia   Prince Rupert
1660–1685   of Braganza   prince of Orange   elector of Hanover   of the Rhine

(1) Anne Hyde ══ **James II** ══ (2) Mary of
               1685–1689   Modena

William III ══ **Mary II**   **Anne** ══ George
1689–1702   1689–1694   1702–1714   of Denmark

James Francis Stuart   **George I** ══ Sophia Dorothea
(The Old Pretender)   1714–1727   of Celle

Charles Edward Stuart   House of
(The Young Pretender)   Hanover

THE HOUSE OF HANOVER & HOUSE OF WINDSOR

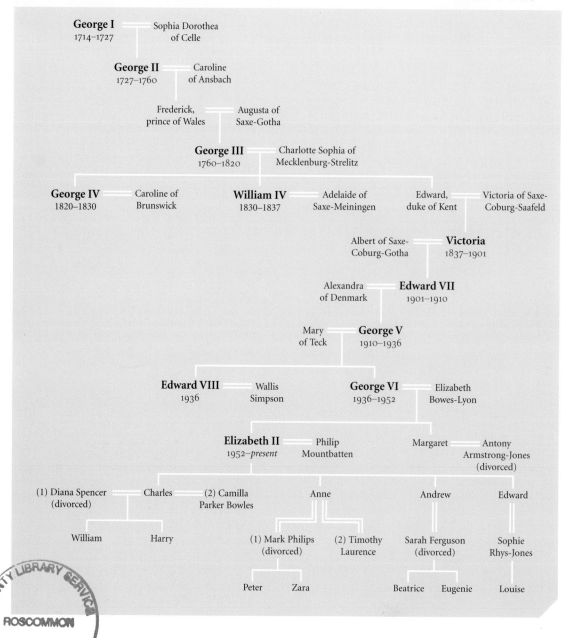

George I
1714–1727 — Sophia Dorothea of Celle

George II
1727–1760 — Caroline of Ansbach

Frederick, prince of Wales — Augusta of Saxe-Gotha

George III
1760–1820 — Charlotte Sophia of Mecklenburg-Strelitz

George IV
1820–1830 — Caroline of Brunswick

William IV
1830–1837 — Adelaide of Saxe-Meiningen

Edward, duke of Kent — Victoria of Saxe-Coburg-Saafeld

Albert of Saxe-Coburg-Gotha — **Victoria**
1837–1901

Alexandra of Denmark — **Edward VII**
1901–1910

Mary of Teck — **George V**
1910–1936

Edward VIII
1936 — Wallis Simpson

George VI
1936–1952 — Elizabeth Bowes-Lyon

Elizabeth II
1952–*present* — Philip Mountbatten

Margaret — Antony Armstrong-Jones (divorced)

(1) Diana Spencer (divorced) — Charles — (2) Camilla Parker Bowles

Anne

Andrew

Edward

William   Harry

(1) Mark Philips (divorced)   (2) Timothy Laurence

Sarah Ferguson (divorced)

Sophie Rhys-Jones

Peter   Zara

Beatrice   Eugenie

Louise

DYNASTIC FAMILY TREES

INDEX

Page numbers in **bold** refer to main entries. Page numbers in *italics* refer to picture captions.

Abdication Crisis 233–4

Acre, siege of 69, *71*, 80–1

Adams, John 200

Addington, Henry, Viscount Sidmouth 201

'Addled Parliament' 156

Adela of Blois 40, 56

Adela of Louvain 52, 55

Adelaide of Saxe-Meiningen 209, 210, 211

Ælffæd (wife of Æthelred the Unready) 24

Ælffæd (wife of Edward the Elder) 14

Ælfgifu (wife of Æthelred the Unready) 24, 27

Ælfgifu (wife of Eadwig) 20

Ælfgifu of Northampton 28, 29, 30, 31, 32

Ælfred *see* Alfred the Great

Ælfric, Ealdorman 25

Ælfthryth 21, 23, 24

Æthelbald, king of Wessex 8

Æthelbert, king of Wessex 8

Æthelfleda (wife of Edgar) 21, 23

Æthelfleda (wife of Edmund I) 18

Æthelfleda, queen of Mercia 8, 14, 15, 16

Æthelred, ealdorman of Mercia 14

Æthelred, king of Wessex 9, 10

Æthelred the Unready 21, 23, *24*, **24–25**, 26, 27, 28, 33, 34, 44

Æthelwold, Bishop of Worcester 22

Æthelwold (cousin of Edward the Elder) 14

Æthelwulf, king of Wessex 8

Agincourt, Battle of 105, *105*, 106

Ahlden Castle 187, 191, 193

Aix-la-Chapelle, Treaty of 195

Albert of Saxe-Coburg-Gotha (Prince Albert) 214–223, *216*, 235

Albert Victor, duke of Clarence 222, 223, 226

Alexander II, king of Scotland 77

Alexander III, king of Scotland 84

Alexander III, pope 37, 65

Alexandra of Denmark 222, 223, 226

Alfred the Atheling 33, 34, 35

Alfred the Great **8–13**, *9*, *10*, 14, 25, 31, 34, 42, 46

Alice of France 69

Alnwick, Battle of 67

American Revolution 199, 200, 209

'Anarchy, the' 55

Andrew, duke of York 238, 240, 241

Angevins 61, 62, 68, 73

Anglo-Saxon Chronicle 11, 13, 18, 21, 23, 51, 58

Anglo-Saxons 9, 31, 34, 39, 45

Annals of Agriculture 200

Anne 174, 181, **183–5**, *184*, 186, 187, 188, 190

Anne, princess royal *238*, 241

Anne of Bohemia 94

Anne of Cleves 126, 131

Anne of Denmark 152, 156, 158

Anselm, Archbishop of Canterbury 49, 53

Aquitaine 92

Archibald, earl of Douglas 100

Arminianism 161

Armstrong-Jones, Anthony, earl of Snowdon 241

Arsuf, Battle of 69

Arthur, prince of Wales 120, 124, 129

Arthur of Brittany 70, 72, 73

Arundel, Thomas, Archbishop of Canterbury 102

Ascham, Roger 144

Ashdown, Battle of 9

Asquith, Herbert Henry 225, 228

Assandune, Battle of 27, 29

Asser 8, 12

Athelney, Isle of 11, 12

Athelstan 14, **16–18**, *17*, 18, 46

Aughrim, Battle of 182

Augusta of Saxe-Gotha 197

Austrian Succession, War of the 194, 195

Babington Plot 149

Bacon, Francis 123, 156

Baldwin, count of Flanders 41

Baldwin, Stanley 233–4

Balliol, Edward 91

Balliol, John 84, 85, 91

Balmoral Castle 218, *218*, 239

Bannockburn, Battle of 85, 88, 91, *91*

Barebones Parliament 167

Barnet, Battle of 110, 113, 117

Baron's War, First 75, 76, 77

Baron's War, Second 78

Basilikon Doron 157

Basing, Battle of 9

Battle of Maldon, The 25

Bayeux Tapestry 39, *43*, 44, 46

Beaufort, Cardinal Henry 103, 107, 108

Beaufort, Edmund, duke of Somerset 108, 109

Beaufort, Margaret 120

Beaufort, Thomas 103

Becket, Thomas 62, *64*, 64, 65

'Bedchamber Crisis' 219

Bedford, duke of *see* John, duke of Bedford

Benfleet, Battle of 11

Berengaria of Navarre 68, 69

Berkeley Castle 89, 91

Bernhardt, Sarah 223

Berwick, duke of *see* FitzJames, James, duke of Berwick

Bishops' Wars 161

Black Death 92, 94

Black Prince *see* Edward, the Black Prince

Blacman, John 108

Blanche of Lancaster 98

Blondel 70

Boleyn, Anne 126, 129, 130, 131, 143, 144

Bolingbroke, Henry *see* Henry IV

Bolingbroke, Viscount *see* St John, Henry, Viscount Bolingbroke

Bonnie Prince Charlie *see* Stuart, Charles Edward

Boroughbridge, Battle of 88

Bosworth Field, Battle of 119, 120, 122, 123

Bothwell, earl of *see* Hepburn, James, earl of Bothwell

Bouvines, Battle of 74

Bowes-Lyon, Elizabeth *see* Elizabeth, Queen of England

Boyne, Battle of the 177, 182

Bramham Moor, Battle of 100

Brandon, Lady Frances 137

Breda, Declaration of 170, 171

Brétigny, Treaty of 93

Brighton Pavilion 208, *208*

Brown, John 217–18

Brunanburh, Battle of 16, 17, 18

Buchanan, George 153

Buckingham, Henry Stafford, duke of *see* Stafford, Henry, duke of Buckingham

Buckingham, George Villiers, duke of *see* Villiers, George, duke of Buckingham

Buckingham Palace 208, 222, 235, 237

Bunting, Basil 19

Burgh, Hubert de 73, 77

Burghley, Lord *see* Cecil, Sir William

burhs 12, 15

Burnell, Robert 83

Burnet, Bishop Gilbert 172, 179

Bute, earl of *see* Stuart, John, earl of Bute

Butler, Lady Eleanor 115

Buttington, Battle of 11

Byrhtnoth, ealdorman of Essex 24

Cabal, the 170

Cabot, Giovanni 124

Cade, Jack 109

Caernarfon Castle 83, *83*

Canterbury Tales 65

Canute *see* Cnut

Carisbrooke Castle 163

Carlton House 204, 205

Caroline of Ansbach 191, 192, 193

Caroline of Brunswick 203, 206, 207

Carr, Robert 155, 156

Castleford, Battle of 19

Catesby, Robert 156, *156*

Catherine of Aragon 125, 126, 129, *129*, 130, 131, 139

Catherine of Braganza 168, 172

Catherine of Valois 102, 106, 107, 120

Cavendish, George 126

Cecil, Robert 154, 155

Cecil, Sir William (Lord Burghley) 145, 151

Chamberlain, Neville 236

Charlemagne 8, 13, 17

Charles I 152, 157, **158–63**, *160*, *163*, 164, 168, 174, 178

Charles II 158, 164, 165, **168–73**, *169*, *170*, 174, 184

Charles IV, king of France 92

Charles VI, king of France 104, 106, 107

Charles VII, king of France 104, 105, 106, 108

Charles VIII, king of France 123

Charles V, Holy Roman Emperor 128, 129, 141

Charles, prince of Wales *236*, 238, 240, 241, 242, 243

Charles the Bald 8

Charles the Simple 14, 42

Charlotte (daughter of George IV) 203, 205, 210

Charlotte Sophia of Mecklenburg-Strelitz 198, 203, 209

Charter of Liberties 53

Chatham, earl of *see* Pitt the Elder, William

Chaucer, Geoffrey 46, 66, 94

Cheke, Sir John 134

Christian IX, king of Denmark 223

Chronicle of the Life of Henry V 104

Church of England 131, 136, 141, 147, 148, 171, 234

Churchill, Arabella 174

Churchill, John, duke of Marlborough 184, 186

Churchill, Sarah 183, 184, 185

Churchill, Winston 237

Civil War 162, 164, 170, 174

Clare, Gilbert de 78, 79

Clare, Richard de (Strongbow) 66

Clarence, Albert Victor, duke of *see* Albert Victor, duke of Clarence

Clarence, duke of *see* George, duke of Clarence

Clarendon, Assize of 63

Clarendon, earl of *see* Hyde, Edward, earl of Clarendon

Cleveland, duchess of *see* Villiers, Barbara, duchess of Cleveland

Clifford's Tower 70

Cnut 25, 26, 28, **28–31**, *28*, *29*, *31*, 32, 34, 46

Commonwealth (1649–53) 164, 165, 166, 168

Commonwealth of Nations 237, 240

Conrad, duke of Burgundy 17

Conrad II, Holy Roman Emperor 31

Constantine II, king of Scotland 16, 17

Conyngham, Lady Elizabeth 208

Cooke, Sir Anthony 134

Counterblaste to Tobacco, A 157

Covenanters 169, 172, 181

Cox, Richard 134

Cranmer, Thomas 131, 136, 142, *142*

Crawford, Marion 238

Crécy, Battle of 92, 93

Cromwell, Oliver 163, **164–7**, *164*, *170*

Cromwell, Richard 164, 167

Cromwell, Thomas 130, 131, 132

Croyland chronicler 111

Crusades 49, 53, 69, 70, 81, 98

Culloden, Battle of 194, *194*, *194*

Cumberland, duke of *see* William Augustus, duke of Cumberland

Cumbria 15, 16

Cynwit, Battle of 11

Daemonologie 157

Dalrymple, Sir John 181

Danegeld 12, 25, 29

Danelaw 11

Danes 8–13, 14, 21, 25, 26, 27

Dante Alighieri 79

Darnley, Lord *see* Stewart, Henry, Lord Darnley

Dauphin *see* Charles VII, king of France

David II, king of Scotland 91

de: for names beginning with 'de', 'de la', etc., *see* under the main part of the name, e.g. 'Burgh, Hubert de'

Despenser, Hugh le 88
Dettingen, Battle of 191, 193, 195
Devereux, Robert, earl of Essex 146, 150
Diana, princess of Wales 242, 243
Diggers 164
Dilke, Sir Charles 218
Disraeli, Benjamin 220
Dissolution of the monasteries 131
Divine Comedy, The 79
Domesday Book 46
Dorset, marquis of see Grey, Henry, marquis
    of Dorset and duke of Suffolk
Dover, Treaty of 171
Drake, Sir Francis 150
Drogheda, massacre of 165
Dudley, Edmund 125, 127
Dudley, John, earl of Warwick and duke of
    Northumberland 136, 137, 138, 146
Dudley, Lord Guildford 137, 138
Dudley, Robert, earl of Leicester 146, 146,
    147
Dunbar, Battle of (1296) 85
Dunbar, Battle of (1650) 166
Dundas, Henry 202
Dundee, Viscount see Graham, John,
    Viscount Dundee
Dunkeld, Battle of 177, 181
Dunstan, St 18, 19, 20, 21, 22, 24
Durbar, Delhi (1903) 225, 225
Dutch Wars 167, 170, 174

Eadgifu 14, 18, 19
Eadgyth (Edith) 34, 35
Eadwig 18, 19, 20, 21
Ealdgyth 38
Ealhswith of Mercia 8, 14
East Anglia 10, 14
Ecgwynn 14, 16
Edgar 18, 20, 21–2, 21, 23, 24
Edgar the Atheling 27, 44, 52, 55, 56
Edgecote Hill, Battle of 113
Edgehill, Battle of 162
Edinburgh, Treaty of 148
Edith (wife of Edmund II Ironside) 27
Edith (wife of Edward the Confessor) see
    Eadgyth
Edmund I 14, 18, 20, 21

Edmund II Ironside 24, 27, 28, 36
Edmund, duke of York 90
Edmund, earl of Kent 80
Edmund Crouchback 76, 78
Edred 14, 18, 19
Edward I 76, 78, 79, 79, 80–5, 81, 84, 86, 90,
    92
Edward II 80, 83, 86–9, 87, 88, 90
Edward III 86, 87, 90–3, 91, 92, 93, 94, 98,
    104, 109, 111
Edward IV 109, 110, 111–14, 111, 112, 114,
    115, 117, 118, 121
Edward V 111, 114, 115, 118, 121
Edward VI 126, 132, 134–6, 134, 137, 138,
    140, 142, 144, 145
Edward VII 214, 217, 221, 222–5, 223, 226,
    228, 232, 236, 242
Edward VIII 221, 226, 230, 231, 232–4, 233,
    236, 238
Edward, earl of Warwick 124
Edward, earl of Wessex 238, 240, 242
Edward, prince of Wales (son of Henry VI)
    107, 108, 109, 110, 112, 113, 117, 121
Edward, the Black Prince 90, 93, 93, 94, 109
Edward Atheling 36, 37
Edward Augustus, duke of Kent 197, 214,
    215
Edward the Confessor 33, 33, 34–7, 35, 37,
    38, 40, 43, 46, 79, 95
Edward the Elder 14–15, 15, 16, 18, 19
Edward the Martyr 21, 23, 24, 95
Eleanor (daughter of King John) 72, 78
Eleanor of Aquitaine 62, 63, 66, 67, 68, 72
Eleanor of Aragon 80
Eleanor of Castile 80, 81, 83, 86
Eleanor of Provence 76, 77, 80
Eleven Years' Tyranny 160–1
Elgiva (wife of Edmund I) 18, 20, 21
Elizabeth I 126, 134, 137, 140, 143–51, 145,
    146, 153, 154
Elizabeth II 235, 236, 238–43, 238, 241, 242
Elizabeth, Queen of England (wife of
    George VI and queen mother) 235, 236,
    238
Elizabeth of Bohemia 152, 157, 186
Elizabeth of York 111, 120, 121, 122, 122,
    126

Elmham, Thomas 102
Elton, Geoffrey Rudolph 136
Emma of Normandy 24, 25, 28, 29, 32, 33,
    33, 34
Empson, Richard 125, 126–7
Enlightenment 168
Entente Cordiale (1904) 225
Erik Bloodaxe, king of Norway 19
Ernest Augustus, elector of Hanover 186,
    187, 188, 197, 215
Erskine, John, earl of Mar 190
Essex, earl of see Devereux, Robert, earl of
    Essex
Ethandun, Battle of 11
Ethelweard 14
Eton College 107, 108
Eustace (son of King Stephen) 56, 59
Evesham, Battle of 79, 79, 80
Exclusion Crisis (1679–81) 171, 173, 175

Faerie Queene, The 150
Fairfax, Lord 165
Fair Maid of Kent see Joan, the Fair Maid of
    Kent
Falaise Castle 41, 73
Falstaff 103
Farnham, Battle of 11
Fawkes, Guy 156, 156
Ferguson, Sarah 241
Festival of Britain 239
Field of the Cloth of Gold 130, 130
Fisher, John, Admiral Lord 225
Fitzclarence, George Augustus, earl of
    Munster 211
Fitzherbert, Maria 203, 205, 206
FitzJames, James, duke of Berwick 174
Flambard, Ranulf 53–4
Fleet Street, Battle of 141
Flight of the Earls 155
Forty-Two Articles of Religion 136
Fox, Charles James 202, 204, 207
Fox, Richard 125
Francis I, king of France 129, 133
Franz Ferdinand, archduke of Austria 228
Frederick III, king of Denmark 184
Frederick, duke of York 197, 203, 207, 209,
    210

Frederick, prince of Wales 191, 194, 197

Frederick, elector palatine of the Rhine 157

French Revolution 201

Froissart, Jean 94, 98–9

Fulk of Neuilly 70, 71

fyrds 10, 12

Gaimar, Geoffrey 31, 33

Gaveston, Piers 86, 87

General Strike (1926) 230, 232

Geoffrey, Archbishop of York 62

Geoffrey, duke of Brittany 62, 66, 67, 70, 72, 73

Geoffrey of Anjou 56, 57, 60, 61, 62

George I 185, **186–90**, *186*, 191, 192

George II 186, 190, **191–6**, *192*

George III 194, **197–202**, *198*, 203, 204, 209

George IV 197, **203–8**, *204*, *206*, *207*, 210, 212, 214, 215

George V 221, 222, **226–31**, *227*, *229*, *231*, 232, 238

George VI 221, 226, 234, **235–7**, *236*, 238, 240

George, duke of Clarence 112, *112*, 113, 114, 117, 118, 121

George, duke of Kent 226

George of Denmark 183, 184

Gesta Stephani 61

Gillray, James 203

Giustiani, Sebastian 127

Gladstone, William Ewart 220, 221

Glencoe massacre 181

Glendower, Owen 99–100, 102

Glenshiel, Battle of 190

Glorious Revolution 174, 177, 181, 184, 198

Gloucester, duke of *see* Humphrey, duke of Gloucester

Godolphin, Sidney 185

Godwine, earl of Wessex 32, 33, 34, 35, 36, 38

'Golden Speech' 151

'Good Parliament' 93, 94

Gourdon, Bertram de 71

Gowrie Conspiracy 154

Graham, John, Viscount Dundee 181

Grand Alliance 189

Grand Remonstrance 161

Great Chronicle of London 112, 118, 119

Great Contract, the 155

Great Exhibition (1851) 217, *217*

Great Rebellion (1173–4) 63, 66, 67

Great Reform Act (1832) 209, 212, 213

Greville, Charles 215

Grey, Henry, marquis of Dorset and duke of Suffolk 137, 138

Grey, Lady Jane *see* Jane

Grey, Lord Charles 212, 213

Grim, Edward 65

Gruffudd, Llywelyn ap 79, 82

Gunhild (wife of Harold Bluetooth) 26

Gunhilde (wife of Sweyn Forkbeard) 26, 27

Gunnhild (wife of Pallig) 26

Gunpowder Plot 156, *156*

Guthrum, Danish king of East Anglia 10, 11

Guy of Burgundy 41

Gwyn, Nell 173, *173*

Gytha Thorkelsdættir 38, *39*

Haakon, king of Norway 17

Haesten of Denmark 10

Haldane, Richard, Viscount 225

Halfdan of Denmark 9

Halidon Hill, Battle of 91

Halifax, Edward Wood, earl of 237

Halifax, marquis of *see* Savile, George, marquis of Halifax

Hampden, John 162

Handel, George Frideric 195

Hanoverian dynasty, commencement of 186

Harfleur, capture of 105

Harley, Robert 185, 188

Harold II Godwineson 36, **38–9**, *39*, *43*, 43, 44, 45, 242

Harold, king of Denmark 26, 30

Harold Bluetooth 26

Harold Hardrada, king of Norway 36, 38, 39

Harold Harefoot 28, **32–3**, 34

Harrying of the North 45

Harthacnut 28, 30, **32–3**, *33*, 34, 36

Hastings, Battle of 39, 42, 43

Hatfield House 144

Hazlitt, William 210

Henrietta Maria 158, 159, *159*, 168, 174

Henry I 37, 40, 48, 51, **52–5**, *53*, *54*, 56, 60

Henry II 59, 60, 61, **62–7**, *63*, *64*, 68, 70, 72

Henry III 72, 75, **76–9**, *77*, 80, 82

Henry IV 96, 97, **98–101**, 102, 103, 109, 120

Henry IV, king of France 158, 159

Henry V 98, 101, **102–6**, *103*, *105*, *106*, 107, 121

Henry VI 102, **107–10**, *107*, 111, 112, 113, 117, 120

Henry VII 110, 111, 115, 119, **120–5**, *121*, 126, 152

Henry VIII 120, 125, **126–33**, *127*, *130*, 134, 136, 137, 139, 143, 144, 153

Henry V, Holy Roman Emperor 56, 60

Henry VI, Holy Roman Emperor 70

Henry 'the Young King' 62, 65, 66, 67

Henry (Prince Harry) 242

Henry, prince of Wales (son of James I) 152, 159

Henry of Blois, Bishop of Winchester 57, 58, 59

Henry of Cornwall 79

Henry of Huntingdon 23, 52

Henry V (Shakespeare's play) 106

Hepburn, James, earl of Bothwell 152

heregeld 29

Hereward the Wake 45

Herleva 40

Higden, Ranulf 89

Hillary, Sir Edmund 240

History of the English 31, 33

Hitler, Adolf 234

Hogarth, William 195

Holinshed, Raphael 101

Holme, Battle of 14

Holy River, Battle of the 30

Home rule for Ireland 229

Homildon Hill, Battle of 100

Hotspur, Harry *see* Percy, Henry

Howard, Catherine 126, 132

Howard, Thomas, duke of Norfolk 149

Hudleston, Father John 173

Hugh the Great 17

Humble Petition and Advice (1657) 167

Humphrey, duke of Gloucester 107, 108, 109

Hundred Years' War 90, 93, 108

Hutchinson, Lucy 158

Hyde, Anne 174, 175, 178, 183, 184

Hyde, Edward, earl of Clarendon 170, 174
Hywel, king of Wales 22

'Immortal Seven' 176
Independence, Declaration of (American)
    200
Indulgence (1672), Declaration of 171
Indulgence (1687), Declaration of 176
Interregnum **164–7**
'Intolerable Acts' (1773) 199
Isabella of Angoulême 72, 74, 76
Isabella of France 86, 87, 89, 90, 91, 92
Isabella of Gloucester 72, 73
Isabelle of France 94
Ivar the Boneless 8–9, 10

Jacobeans 155
Jacobites 177, 181, 185, 188, 190, 193, 194,
    195
James I (VI of Scotland) 151, **152–7**, *152*,
    158, 159, 186
James II (VII of Scotland) 158, 171, **174–7**,
    175, 178, 179, 183, 184
James IV, king of Scotland 123, 148
James, duke of Monmouth *see* Monmouth,
    James Scott, duke of
Jane **137–8**, *138*, 140, 141, 145, 146
Jerome, Jennie 223
Joan of Arc 108
Joan, the Fair Maid of Kent 94
Joanna of Navarre 98, *101*
John 62, 66, 67, 70, **72–5**, *73*, 76, 77
John, duke of Bedford 107, 108
John, Prince (son of George V) 226
John of Gaunt 90, 93, 94, 95, 98, 99, 103,
    108, 109, 112, 120
John the Fearless 105–6
Jordan, Dorothea 209, 210
Judas Maccabaeus 195
Jutland, Battle of 235

Karl, prince of Leiningen 215
Kent, Edward Augustus, duke of *see*
    Edward Augustus, duke of Kent
Kent, George, duke of *see* George, duke of
    Kent
Keppel, Alice 224, 242

Kéroualle, Louise de, duchess of Portsmouth
    173
Kett, Robert 136
Kielmansegge, Sophia von 188
Killiecrankie, Battle of 177, 181
Killing Time, the 172
King James Bible 155
King's College, Cambridge 107, *108*
Kings Langley 97, 104
Kingston, Treaty of 77
Königsmark, Count Philip 187

Labour Party 224, 228
Lancaster, Thomas, earl of *see* Thomas, earl
    of Lancaster
Lancastrian dynasty, commencement of 98
Landor, Walter Savage 208
Lanfranc, Archbishop of Canterbury 42, 48,
    49
Langton, Stephen, Archbishop of
    Canterbury 74, 76
Langtry, Lillie 223, 224
Latimer, Bishop Hugh 142
Laud, William, Archbishop of Canterbury
    161
Laurence, Timothy 241
Lehzen, Louise 215
Leicester, earl of *see* Dudley, Robert
Leicester House 192, 204
Leo IX, pope 42
Leofa 18
Leofric, earl of Mercia 32, 34
Leopold I, king of the Belgians 215
Leopold, duke of Austria 70
Levellers 164
Lewes, Battle of 78, 80
Liberal Party 218
Lincoln, Battle of 58, 61
Lionel of Antwerp 98
Lionel, duke of Clarence 90, 109, 112
Little Princesses, The 238
Liverpool, Charles Jenkinson, earl of 207
Lloyd George, David 228
Locke, John 181
Lollards 103–4
Longespee, William de, earl of Salisbury 62
Long Parliament 161, 163, 165

Longchamp, William 69
Lords Appellant 95, 96, 98
Louis IV, king of France 17
Louis VIII, king of France 74, 76, 77
Louis XIV, king of France 178, 182, 188
Louis XVI, king of France 201
Lovell, Lord 123
Lusignan, Hugh de 73

MacDonald, Ramsay 230
MacMurrough, Dermot, king of Leinster 66
Magna Carta 72, 74, *75*, 76, 77, 79
Magnus, king of Norway 32–3
Malcolm I, king of Scotland 18
Malcolm III, king of Scotland 49, 55
Maldon, Battle of 24
Mar, earl of *see* Erskine, John, earl of Mar
March, earl of *see* Mortimer, Edmund, earl
    of March
March to Finchley, The 195
Marcher lords 46, 82
Margam Annals 73
Margaret, countess of Snowdon 235, 236,
    241
Margaret, Maid of Norway 84
Margaret of Anjou 107, 108, 110, *110*, 113
Margaret of Burgundy 113, 123
Margaret of Scotland, St 55, 56
Margaret Tudor 120, 124, 148, 152, 153
Marguerite of France 80, 84
Marie of Romania 227
Marlborough, Statute of 79
Marston Moor, Battle of 162, 164
Mary I 126, 129, 134, 136, 137, 138, **139–42**,
    140, 144, 145, 147
Mary II 174, 176, **178–82**, *180*, 184
Mary de Bohun 98, 102
Mary of Modena 174, 175, 176, 190
Mary of Orange 158
Mary of Teck 226, 227, 232, 234
Mary Queen of Scots 133, 148, *148*, 149,
    152, 153
Mary Rose 128
Mary Tudor, queen consort of France 120,
    137
Masham, Abigail 185
Matilda 52, 55, 56, 57, 58, 59, **60–1**, *60*, 62

Matilda, duchess of Saxony 62
Matilda (Edith) of Scotland 52, 55, 60
Matilda of Boulogne 56, 59
Matilda of Flanders 41–2, 42, *44*, 48, 52
Maud *see* Matilda
Mayerne, Sir Theodore 152
Medina Sidonia, duke of 149
Melbourne, William Lamb, Viscount 213, 219
Mercia 9, 12, 15, 16, 20, 21
'Merciless Parliament' 95
Meretun, Battle of 9
Messiah 195
Methven, Battle of 9
Milford Haven 119, 122
Monck, George 175
Monmouth, James Scott, duke of 168, 175
Montagu, Lady Mary Wortley 186, 187
Montfort, Guy de 79
Montfort, Simon de (I) 76, 78, 79, 80
Mora 44
More, Thomas 117, 127, 131
Mortimer, Edmund, earl of March 98, 100, 103, 108
Mortimer, Roger 89, 90, 91
Mortimer's Cross, Battle of 112, 114, 121
Morton, John 125
Mosley, Oswald 234
Mountbatten, Lord Louis 242
Mountbatten, Philip (Prince Philip) *see* Philip, duke of Edinburgh
Mowbray, Thomas, duke of Norfolk 98, 100
Murray, Lord George 194
Music for the Royal Fireworks 195

Napoleon Bonaparte 201, 202, 206
Napoleonic Wars 203, 207
Naseby, Battle of 162
Nash, John 208
Nelson, Admiral Horatio 201, 209
Neot, St 11
Neville, Anne 116, 117
Neville, Cecily 111, 116
Neville, George 113
Neville, Richard, earl of Warwick ('Kingmaker') 110, 112, 113, 117
Neville's Cross, Battle of 91

Newcastle, duke of *see* Pelham-Holles, Thomas, duke of Newcastle
New Model Army 165
Nicholas II, tsar of Russia 221
Nine Years' War 150
Norfolk, Thomas Howard, duke of *see* Howard, Thomas, duke of Norfolk
Norfolk, Thomas Mowbray, duke of *see* Mowbray, Thomas, duke of Norfolk
Norfolk, Thomas, earl of *see* Thomas, earl of Norfolk
Norman dynasty, commencement of 50
Normandy 34, 48
Normans 42
North Briton, The 199
North, Lord Frederick 199
Northampton, Battle of 109, 112
Northampton, Treaty of 90
Northern Earls, Rebellion of the 148
Northumbria 9, 14, 18, 19, 20, 21, 27, 39, 45
Northumberland, duke of *see* Dudley, John, earl of Warwick and duke of Northumberland
Northumberland, earl of *see* Percy, Henry, earl of Northumberland

Oates, Titus 172, 173
Olaf Guthfrithsson, Norse king of Dublin 16, 18
Olaf Haroldson, king of Norway 30
Old Pretender *see* Stuart, James Francis Edward
Oldcastle, Sir John 103
Olivier, Sir Laurence 106, *106*
O'Neill, Hugh, earl of Tyrone 150
Ordinances, the 87, 89
Osborne House 218
Osburh 8
Oswald, Archbishop of York 22
Otto the Great 14, 17
Oudenarde, Battle of 191, 192
Overbury, Sir Thomas 156
Owain of Strathclyde 17

Paget, Sir William 135
Pallig 26

Palmerston, Henry John Temple, Viscount 219
Paris, Treaty of (1763) 199
Parker Bowles, Camilla 223, 242
Parliament Act (1911) 228
Parr, Catherine 126, 132, 134, 137, 144, 145
Pavia, Battle of 129
Peasants' Revolt 94, 95
Peel, Sir Robert 213, 219
Pelham-Holles, Thomas, duke of Newcastle 199
Penruddock's Rising 167
'People's Budget' 228
Pepys, Samuel 176
Percy, Henry (Harry Hotspur) 100, 102
Percy, Henry, earl of Northumberland 100
Perrers, Alice 93
Petition of Right 160
Philip, duke of Edinburgh 238, *238*, 239, *241*, *242*
Philip II, king of France 67, 69, 70, *71*, 74
Philip VI, king of France 91, 92
Philip II, king of Spain 139, 141, 145, 149
Philip the Good 106
Philippa of Hainault 90, 93
Phillips, Captain Mark 241
Pilgrimage of Grace 131
Pinkie, Battle of 136
Pitt the Elder, William 196, 199
Pitt the Younger, William 201
Pius V, pope 148
Plantagenets 60, 61, 62, 119
Poitiers, Battle of 93
Pole, John de la, earl of Lincoln 123
Pole, Margaret, countess of Salisbury 139
Pole, Michael de la 95
Pole, William de la, duke of Suffolk 108
Ponsonby, Sir Frederick 225
Pontefract Castle 96
Popish Plot (1678) 171, 172, 173, 175
Presbyterianism 163, 165, 172
Preston, Battle of 163
Prestonpans, Battle of 194
Princes in the Tower 115, 118, 123, 124
Protectorate (1653–9) 164, 168
Provisions of Oxford 77, 79
Provisions of Westminster 77, 78

Pucklechurch, Gloucestershire 18
Puritans 159, 161, 164, 167
Pusey Horn, The 31
Pym, John 162

Queen Anne's War *see* Spanish Succession,
    War of the

Ralegh, Sir Walter 150, 157
Reading, Battle of 9
Reform Acts (1867 and 1884) 218, 219
Reformation 135, 142
Regularis Concordia 22
Restoration 169, 170
Rey Cross 19
Rhuddlan, Statute of 83
Rhys-Jones, Sophie 242
Richard I Lionheart 62, 66, **68–71**, *69*, *71*, 72
Richard II **94–7**, *95*, *97*, 98, 99, 103, 104, 109
Richard III 110, 113, 114, 115, **116–19**, *116*,
    121, 122
Richard II, duke of Normandy 34
Richard, 3rd duke of York 108, 109, 110,
    111, 112, 116, 117
Richard, 5th duke of York 111, 115
Richard, earl of Cambridge 104
Richard (son of King John) 72, 78
Ridley, Nicholas 140, 142
Ridolfi Plot 149
Rights, Declaration of (1689) 180
Robert Curthose, duke of Normandy 40, 47,
    48, 49, 52–3, 54–5
Robert of Gloucester 57, *59*, 59, 61
Robert the Bruce 85, 87, 88
Robert the Magnificent, duke of Normandy
    40
Robinson, Mary 204, 205
Robsart, Amy 146, 147
Roger of Wendover 78
Roger, Bishop of Salisbury 54, 57, 58
Rogers, John 142
Roses, Wars of the 107, 109, 121
'Rough Wooing, the' 132
Rowlandson, Thomas 203
Royal Family 240–1
Royal Marriage Act (1772) 205
Rump Parliament 163, 165, 166, 167

Runnymede 75
Rupert of the Rhine 162
Russian Revolution 230
Ruthven Raid 154
Rye House Plot 173
Ryswick, Treaty of 182

St Albans, Battles of 109
St Bartholomew's Day Massacre 148
St Brice's Day Massacre 25, 26
St Gervais, convent of 47
St John, Henry, Viscount Bolingbroke 185,
    188, 190
St Stephen, abbey of *47*
Salisbury, countess of *see* Pole, Margaret,
    countess of Salisbury
Sandwich, Battle of 77
Savile, George, marquis of Halifax 170
Saxe-Coburg-Gotha dynasty,
    commencement of 222
Schulenburg, Melusine von der, duchess of
    Kendal 187
Scott, James, duke of Monmouth *see*
    Monmouth, James Scott, duke of
Scott, Sir Walter 109, 207
Scrope, Lord Henry 103
Scrope, Richard, Archbishop of York 100
Sedgemoor, Battle of 175
Sedley, Catherine 174
Seine, Battle of the 105
Senlac Hill 39, 43
Settlement, Act of (1701) 182, 185, 186, 188,
    189, 205
Seven Years' War 196, 199
Seymour, Edward, duke of Somerset 135,
    136, 137, 145
Seymour, Jane 126, 131, 133, 134, 137, 143,
    144
Seymour, Thomas 137, 145
Shaftesbury 12, 23
Shakespeare, William 149, 156
'Shameful Peace, the' 91
Sheriffmuir, Battle of 190
Shrewsbury, duke of *see* Talbot, Charles,
    duke of Shrewsbury
Short Parliament 161
Shrewsbury, Battle of 100, 102, 103

Sidmouth, Viscount *see* Addington, Henry
Sigismund, Emperor 105
Sihtric, Norse king of York 16
Simnel, Lambert 123
Simpson, Wallis 232, 233, *233*, 234
Siward, earl of Northumbria 35, 36
Six Articles (1539), Act of 131
Snowdon, Lord *see* Armstrong-Jones,
    Anthony
Somerset, Edmund Beaufort, duke of *see*
    Beaufort, Edmund
Somerset, Protector *see* Seymour, Edward,
    duke of Somerset
Sophia Dorothea of Celle 187, *187*, 191
Sophia Dorothea of Prussia 187, 192
Sophia, electress of Hanover 185, 187
South Sea Bubble 190
Spanish Succession, War of the 182, 185,
    188
Spencer, Lady Diana *see* Diana, princess of
    Wales
Spenser, Edmund 150
Stafford, Henry, duke of Buckingham 115,
    119, 122
Stamford Bridge, Battle of 39, 43
Stamp Act (1765) 199
Stanhope, James, Earl 190
Stephen 55, **56–9**, *57*, *59*, 60, 63
Stephen, count of Blois 56
Stewart, Henry, Lord Darnley 152, 153
Stirling Bridge, Battle of 85
Stoke, Battle of 123
Strafford, earl of *see* Wentworth, Thomas,
    earl of Strafford
Stratford, William 187
Strathclyde 14, 18
Strecche, John 104
Stuart, Cardinal Henry Benedict 194
Stuart, Charles Edward (the Young
    Pretender) 190, 193, 194
Stuart, James Francis Edward (the Old
    Pretender) 174, 177, 182, 183, 185, 188,
    190, 194
Stuart, John, earl of Bute 197, 198, 199
Stuart dynasty, commencement of 152
Succession, Act of (1544) 133, 136, 137, 141,
    144, 145

Suffolk, duke of *see* Grey, Henry, marquis of
    Dorset and duke of Suffolk
suffragettes 224, 228, 231
Supremacy, Act of (1534) 131
Supremacy, Act of (1559) 148
Sweyn Forkbeard 25, **26**, 27, 28
Sweyn, king of Norway 28, 30, 31
Swift, Jonathan 185
Swynford, Catherine 120
Symonds, Richard 123

Talbot, Charles, duke of Shrewsbury 185
Tenzing Norgay, Sherpa 240
Test Acts 172, 175, 176
Tewkesbury, Battle of 110, 113, 117, 121
Theobald, Archbishop of Canterbury 59,
    64
Thirty Years' War 156
Thirty-Nine Articles 148
Thomas, earl of Lancaster 87, 89
Thomas, earl of Norfolk 80
Thomas of Woodstock 90
Tilbury 150
Tirel, Walter 51
Tolpuddle Martyrs 213
Tories 188, 189, 210, 213, 218
Tostig, earl of Northumbria 36, 38, 39
'Tournament of Lincoln' 76
Tower of London 109, 110, 113, 115, 117,
    118, 123, 124, 127, 135, 138, 140, 145
Townsend, Group Captain Peter 241
Townshend, Charles, Viscount 190, 193
'Townshend duties' 199
Towton, Battle of 109, 113
Trafalgar, Battle of 201
Troyes, Treaty of 106, 107
True Lawe of Free Monarchies, The 157
Tryggvason, Olaf 24, 26
Tudor, Edmund, earl of Richmond 120
Tudor, Jasper, earl of Pembroke 121
Tudor, Owen 120
Tudor dynasty, commencement of 120
Two Treatises of Government 181

Ulf, Jarl of Denmark 30
Uniformity (1559), Act of 95
Union of Great Britain and Ireland 201, 202

Union, Act of (1707) 186
Utrecht, Treaty of 185

Valence, Aymer de 88
Vere, Robert de, earl of Oxford 95
Vergil, Polydore 107, 120
Victoria 213, **214–21**, *215, 217, 220*, 222,
    223, 226, 227, 235
Victoria of Saxe-Coburg-Saalfeld 213, 214,
    215
Vikings 8–9, 10, 11, 15, 19, 24, 25, 26, 29, 42
Villiers, Barbara, duchess of Cleveland 173
Villiers, George, duke of Buckingham *155*,
    156, 157, 159, 160
Vitalis, Orderic 50

Wakefield, Battle of 109, 112
Wales, conquest of 82
Wales, first English prince of 82, 86
Wallace, William 84, 85, *85*
Walpole, Horace 188
Walpole, Robert 188, 190, 193, 196
Walsingham, Thomas 103
Walter, Hubert, Archbishop of Canterbury
    70
Warbeck, Perkin 123, 124
Warwick, John Dudley, earl of *see* Dudley,
    John, earl of Warwick and duke
    of Northumberland
Warwick, Richard Neville, earl of *see* Neville,
    Richard, earl of Warwick
Washington, George 197, 209
Waterloo, Battle of 202, 206
Weldon, Sir Anthony 152, 153
Wellington, Arthur Wellesley, duke of 207,
    213
Wentworth, Thomas, earl of Strafford 161
Wessex 8–13, 14, 16, 21, 22, 27, 55, 242
Westminster Abbey 36, 37, 44, 46, 76, 79, *125*
Wexford, massacre of 165
Whigs 188, 189, 190, 208, 212, 213, 218
White Ship, wreck of the 52, *54, 55*
Wilhelm II, Kaiser of Germany 225, 226, 230
Wilkes, John 199
William I the Conqueror 25, 34, 35, 36, 38,
    39, **40–7**, 41, *43, 44, 47*, 48, 52, 56, 62
William II Rufus 40, 47, **48–51**, *49, 51*, 52, 53

William III (William of Orange) 176, 177,
    178–82, *179*, 183
William IV 197, **209–13**, *211*, 215, 226
William II, prince of Orange 178
William, duke of Gloucester 183
William, prince of Wales (Prince William)
    242, 243
William (son of Henry I) 52, 54, 55
William Augustus, duke of Cumberland 191,
    194
William of Guiseborough 86
William of Malmesbury 22, 23, 49, 50, 52,
    55
William of Poitiers 38, 43, 44
William the Lion, king of Scotland 66
William the Marshal 76, 77
Wilton, Battle of 9, 10
Winchester 9, 10, 33, 34
Winchester, Treaty of 59, 64
Windsor Castle 218, 239
Windsor dynasty, commencement of 229
Wolf tax 22
Wolsey, Cardinal Thomas 128, 129, 131
Wood, Edward, earl of Halifax *see* Halifax,
    Edward Wood, earl of
Woodstock Palace 145
Woodville, Elizabeth 111, 112, 115
Worcester, Battle of 166, 169
World War I 222, 228, 229, 230, 232, 235
World War II 235, 237, 239
Wulfstan I, Archbishop of York 30
Wulfstan II, Archbishop of York 22
Wulfthryth 22
Wyatt, Sir Thomas 141, 145

'Year of Victories' 196
York 15, 16, 18, 39
York, Richard, 3rd duke of *see* Richard, 3rd
    duke of York
York, Richard, 5th duke of *see* Richard, 5th
    duke of York
York dynasty, commencement of 111
Yorktown, Battle of *199*, 200
Young Pretender *see* Stuart, Charles Edward
Young, Arthur 200

Zadok the Priest 195